Western Ceramic Traditions

NUMBER 135 • 2022

Western Ceramic Traditions

Prehistoric and Historic Native American Ceramics of the Western U.S.

Edited by Suzanne Griset

THE UNIVERSITY OF UTAH ANTHROPOLOGICAL PAPERS
THE UNIVERSITY OF UTAH PRESS
Salt Lake City

The Defiance House Man colophon is a registered trademark of The University of Utah Press. It is based on a four-foot-tall Ancient Puebloan pictograph (late PIII) near Glen Canyon, Utah.

LIBRARY OF CONGRESS CATALOGING-IN-PUBLICATION DATA

Names: Griset, Suzanne, editor.
Title: Western ceramic traditions : prehistoric and historic Native American ceramics of the Western U.S. / edited by Suzanne Griset.
Other titles: University of Utah anthropological papers ; no. 135.
Description: Salt Lake City : The University of Utah Press, [2021] | Series: University of Utah anthropological papers ; no. 135 | Includes bibliographical references.
Identifiers: LCCN 2021023920 (print) | LCCN 2021023921 (ebook) | ISBN 9781647690427 (paperback) | ISBN 9781647690434 (ebook)
Subjects: LCSH: Indian pottery—West (U.S.) | Indians of North America—West (U.S.)—Antiquities. | West (U.S.)—Antiquities.
Classification: LCC E78.W5 W45 2021 (print) | LCC E78.W5 (ebook) | DDC 978.004/97—dc23
LC record available at https://lccn.loc.gov/2021023920
LC ebook record available at https://lccn.loc.gov/2021023921

Errata and further information on this and other titles available online at UofUpress.com

Printed and bound in the United States of America.

Contents

Figures

Tables

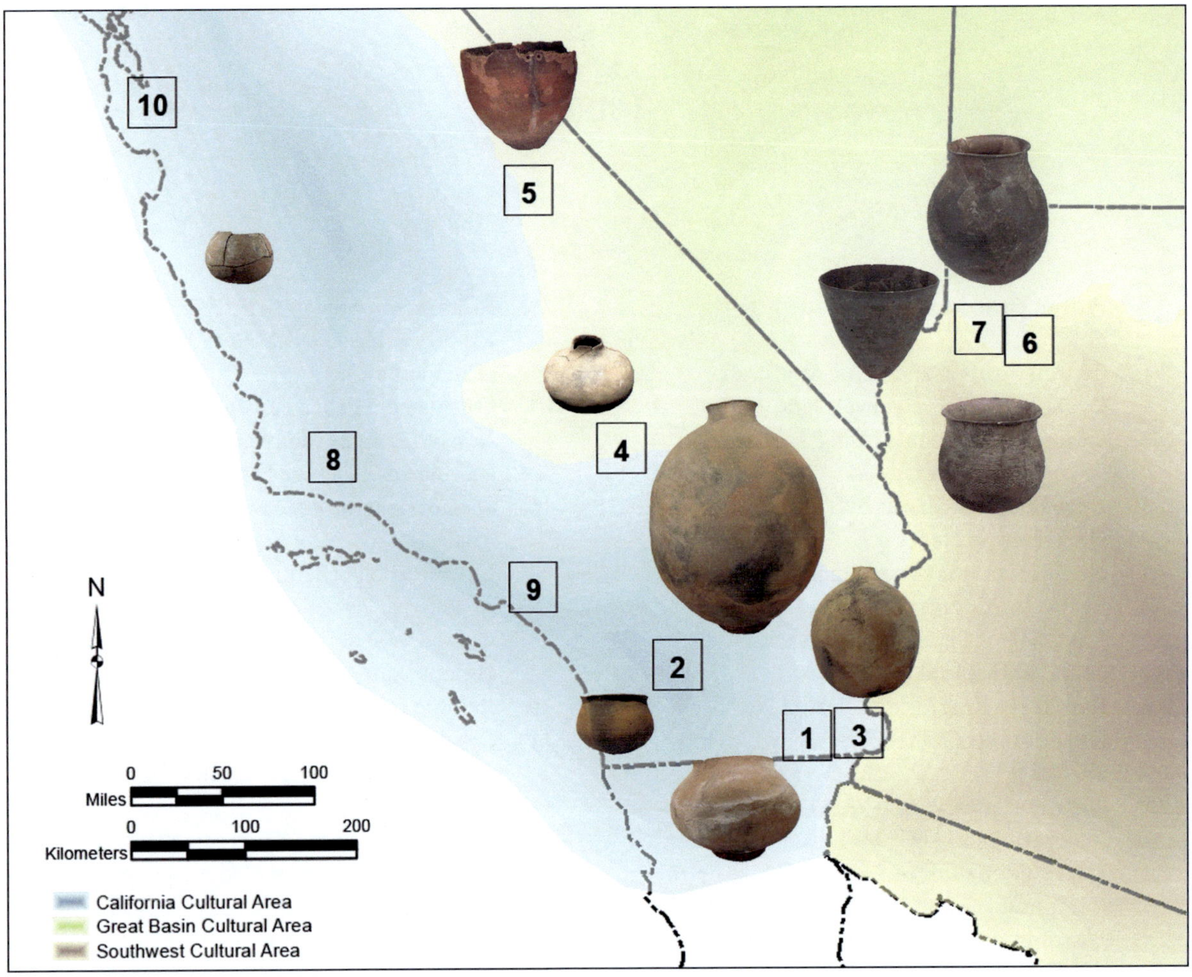

FIGURE 0.1. Map showing the general locations reported by each of the chapters in this volume, and the generalized cultural areas as shown in the *Handbook of North American Indians*, William C. Sturtevant, general editor: California, Volume 8 (1978); Southwest, Volume 10 (1983); and Great Basin, Volume 11 (1986). (Map by Lara Mitchell, SWCA).

Preface

Western Ceramic Traditions

Suzanne Griset

More than 35 years ago, the University of Utah published a similar compilation of plainware ceramic investigations from the Great Basin and adjacent areas (Griset 1986). Fortunately, many new investigative techniques are now available to help date and source the materials used to make these utilitarian, mostly undecorated vessels. Contextual analyses have also contributed to the interpretation of undecorated or plainwares.

Like the earlier volume, the studies presented here include areas throughout California and southern Nevada and deal with prehistoric, protohistoric, and the historic ceramic traditions that derived from the earlier traditions when faced with new foods, cooking techniques, and new ways to manufacture ceramics. Figure 0.1 shows the locations of the ceramics discussed in each chapter in this volume, and an example of the ceramics; Table 0.1 provides the provenience and dimensions of each depicted vessel.

Prehistoric Ceramics

We begin with prehistoric ceramics of southern California's Colorado Desert. Jerry Schaefer asks *When is a Pot Drop Not*, and makes a convincing argument that these features are, in fact, purposeful deposits of portions of vessels along trails across the desert. Just to the west of Schaefer's location, I examine the whole vessel collection from Anza Borrego Desert State Park, looking for patterns in vessel form and manufacture, co-location of different ceramic types, and correlations with landforms. Schaefer's second contribution is an examination of the occurrences of Hohokam ceramics in southern California and what those can tell us about Patayan/Hohokam interactions.

Moving northward into the west central Mojave Desert, Helen Wells reports on the variety of prehistoric ceramics found on the Naval Air Weapons Station, China Lake. Although sparse, the ceramics include a wide variety including coil-and-scrape brown wares from the Owens Valley and/or Great Basin; Boulder, Moapa, and Tusayan gray wares from southern Nevada, a Sosi Black-on-white from the Hopi region, and paddle-and-anvil sherds from the Colorado River area to the south.

Jelmer Eerkens, Jeffrey Ferguson, and Carl Lipo use Neutron Activation Analysis (NAA) and optically stimulated luminescence (OSL) to examine geochemical variation in Owens Valley prehistoric pottery manufacture over time. They hypothesize that potters refined their knowledge about pottery manufacture to best suit the requirements of their local environments and as ceramics become more plentiful, additional clay sources were used and paste recipes were modified to accommodate them.

Karen Harry and Sachiko Sakai examine the dating of Intermountain Brown Ware ceramics found on Virgin Branch Puebloan sites in the eastern Mojave of southern Nevada to test whether they represent the hypothesized Numic expansion into the area. They use OSL to date sherds, with surprising results and implications.

Brenna Wilkerson, Karen Harry, and Spenser Steinberg employ gas chromatography-mass spectrometry (GC-MS) to examine food residues to explore Virgin Branch Puebloan diet and subsistence strategies at sites

Table 0.1. Provenience data for vessels depicted in Figure 0.1

	1, 2 & 3 (Schaefer & Griset)					
	Near #2		East of #2		4 (Wells)	5 (Eerkens et al.)
Pottery Type	Southern California Brown Ware, Hakum Brown Type	Southern California Brown Ware, Hakum Brown Type	Lower Colorado Buff Ware, Colorado Buff Type	Lower Colorado Buff Ware, Salton Buff Type	Great Basin Brown Ware	Owens Valley Brown Ware
Vessel Form	Jar, extra large	Bowl, medium	Jar, large	Jar, large	Jar	Conical Pot (with mending holes)
Vessel Function	Storage	Cooking Storage	Water storage	Storage	Storage	Cooking/Mixing
Provenience	Olla Wash	Ridge above Pinyon Wash	Base of Fish Creek Mountains	Fish Creek Wash	Cronese Lake (Kawaiisu territory)	Olancha Dune Fields
Curated	Anza Borrego Desert State Park, Begole Archaeological Research Center	Anza Borrego Desert State Park, Begole Archaeological Research Center	Anza Borrego Desert State Park, Begole Archaeological Research Center	Anza Borrego Desert State Park, Begole Archaeological Research Center	San Bernardino County Museum (www.sbcounty.gov/museum)	Eastern California Museum
Specimen/ Catalog Number	622-1-98	622-25-1b	622-13-1b	625-12-1	A1900-2213	None at the time it was photographed
Dimensions	58 cm high × 47 cm maximum body diameter	17 cm high × 23 cm maximum body diameter	27 cm high × 38.5 cm maximum body diameter	36 cm hi × 30 cm maximum body diameter	19 cm high × 21 cm max width	27 cm high × 30 cm max diameter at mouth
Photographer	Suzanne Griset	Suzanne Griset	Suzanne Griset	Suzanne Griset	Tamara Serrao-Leiva, Museum Curator	Jelmer W. Eerkens
Image #	No number	No number	No number	No number	No number	No number

located in the lowland and upland regions. They provide a good discussion of the techniques and two methods used to analyze the results and conclude there were no differences in upland/lowland use of the vessels.

Mission Period Ceramics

The next three contributions examine Mission period ceramics from three areas of California where there were no prehistoric ceramic traditions. Catherine Bailey's contribution is a synthesis of her master's thesis and looks at ceramics from the central coast near the missions of Santa Barbara, Santa Inez, and La Purisima and at native villages inland. I characterize two samples of ceramics excavated from Mission San Gabriel in Los Angeles County. Sarah Peelo, Christina Spellman, Chester Liwosz, Linda Hylkema, and Stella D'Oro use a variety of techniques (re-firing, binocular sorting, petrographic analysis, and electron microprobe analysis) to identify the clay used to manufacture ceramics at Mission Santa Clara de Asis, and the implications of the shared community of practice.

As we compiled the images for Figure 0.1, whole mission-made vessels are exceedingly rare, yet the examples for both the central coast and Bay area (see Figure 0.1) proved to be very similar in shape and size—what Peelo and colleagues identify as a "ration bowl" and likely made by the neophytes. Mission San Gabriel's wheel-thrown and hand-modeled ceramics are very fragmentary.

Table 0.1. (cont'd.) Provenience data for vessels depicted in Figure 0.1

6 & 7 (Harry & Sakai, Wilkerson et al.)			8 (Bailey)	9 (Griset)	10 (Peelo et al.)
Tusayan Ware, Virgin series	Shivwits Ware	Paiute (or Inter-mountain Brown Ware)	Unnamed ware from Santa Barbara Mission and Presidio	[No whole mission vessels]	Santa Clara Mission Ware
Jar, corrugated	Jar	Conical Jar	Bowl, small		Bowl, small
Cooking	Cooking	Cooking	Serving Storing		Serving
Lost City (26CK007)	Lost City (26 CK007), House 1	Lost City (26 CK007)	*Saspilil* (CA-SBA-60), Goleta		CA-SCL-30H Feature 99
National Museum of the American Indian, Smithsonian Institution	National Museum of the American Indian, Smithsonian Institution	National Museum of the American Indian, Smithsonian Institution	Department of Anthropology, University of California, Santa Barbara		Santa Clara University, Archaeological Research Lab
147205	139692	146758	1-179		SCU 28-197
23 cm high × 24 cm maximum body diameter	32.4 cm high × 29 cm maximum body diameter	27.3 cm high × 29 cm diameter at mouth	12.1 cm high × 16.3 cm maximum body diameter	×	16 cm high × 19.25 cm maximum body diameter
NMAI Photo Services	NMAI Photo Services	NMAI Photo Services	Kaitlin Brown	Suzanne Griset	Corri MacEwen, SCU
10.2.578	20.2.489	10.7.372	Photo courtesy of Kaitlin Brown		No number

Ceramic Analysis

The last contribution by Don Laylander is a commentary on the current approaches to ceramic analysis and particularly the attachment to ceramic typologies. He advocates attribute-based analyses shared by all analysts via an internet-based ceramic databank. Such an approach is currently being tested by the Lower Colorado Buffware Workshop.

1

When a Pot Drop Is Not

Archaeological and Cultural Contexts of Ceramic Scatters in the Colorado Desert, California

Jerry Schaefer

When Malcolm Rogers conducted his pioneering fieldwork in southeastern California and Western Arizona during the 1920s and '30s, he recorded many "pot drops" or ceramic scatters along prehistoric trails and travel routes. As "pot drops," this term implies accidental or inadvertent breakage, particularly when they occur along trails or routes of travel. Yet Rogers appreciated that the profusion of ceramics, among the most common archaeological features in the Colorado Desert, might signal deliberate behavior and not accidents. Systematic survey and excavation of these phenomena since his time have more precisely documented their ceramic attributes and landscape contexts in greater numbers. This paper will address the alternative interpretation of deliberate agency in the manifestation of these scatters in southeastern Imperial County, California. They were documented, and some recovered, in response to impacts from the All-American Canal (AAC) lining project (Schaefer et al. 2016:29–64).

Background and Research Strategy

As early as the 1920s and '30s, renowned Colorado Desert archaeology pioneer, Malcolm Rogers expressed in his unpublished fieldnotes at the San Diego Museum of Us (formerly Museum of Man) that "pot drops" may represent a more profound phenomenon than simple accidental breakage along major trails in southwestern Arizona and southeastern California. He later wrote about the plethora of ceramic scatters along trails, dispersed every 3 m (10 ft) in places (Rogers 1945a:181). His primary purpose was to relatively date Lower Colorado Buff Ware ceramic types through the technique of "horizontal trail stratigraphy" (Rogers 1945a:181; Waters 1982b:276). This method was based on the premise that the use of certain trail segments changed over time as desert erosion cut off certain routes of travel, while others were abandoned and replaced by alternate routes for cultural or historical reasons. During Rogers' long-term field program, he noticed that some ceramic scatters occurred in spatial clusters of possible symbolic significance, occasionally in proximity to rock cairns and other places for no readily apparent reason (Schaefer et al. 2013; Underwood 2004; Waters 1982b).

Subsequent survey work in the Colorado Desert has documented spatial patterning with greater contextual information and precision. For example, ceramic scatters have been found to be nonrandomly distributed along trails approaching water sources at McCoy Springs on the western side of the McCoy Mountains, Riverside County, California (McCarthy 1993) and on the major trail leading to the White Tanks water source in the Tank Mountains, southwestern Arizona (Schaefer 1993). Ceramic vessels are certainly an item expected to be used at water sources, but these clusters are not found anywhere in proximity to the water or at a location where accidental breakage is more likely to occur.

In another example, survey work was conducted along portions of a major 9.6 km trail along Vinegra Wash (CA-IMP-398) that connects the culturally important *Xam Kwatsan* ceremonial trail to the Colorado River. Along a 3 km stretch, 39 ceramic scatters were documented in close proximity to each other (Apple 2005; Cleland and Apple 2003). One scatter was associated with a trail shrine, and at only a few scatters were lithics or

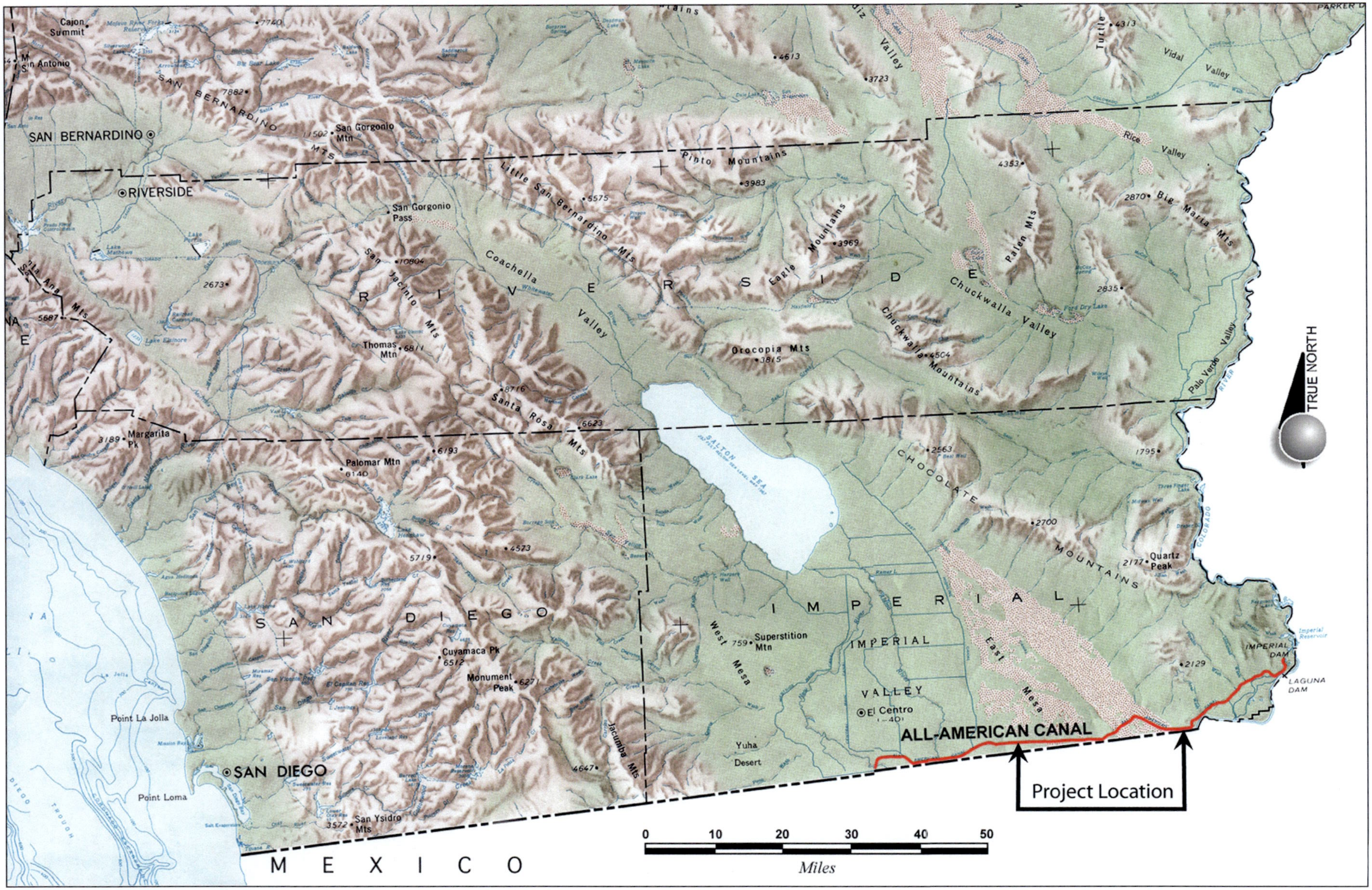

FIGURE 1.1. Project study area on the All-American Canal.

any other artifact types found. Finally, in a more explicit example of ceremonial deposition of ceramics, a large number of sherds from an estimated 70–100 different vessels or parts of vessels were recovered by Malcolm Rogers from a trail shrine (SDM C-1) at the top of Indian Pass, eastern Imperial County, California (Waters 1982d).

These examples all suggest ceramics were intentionally left at specific locations along trails as offerings of an unknown type. Various cultural patterns may be posited to explain this behavior. Yuman ethnographic sources are not generous in discussing spiritual beliefs associated with trails and travel, but there are some hints. In general, fear of the spirits of the dead was widely held among all Yuman groups and has been used to explain certain archaeological patterns (Devereux 1961; Laylander 2014). Tassin wrote in 1877 that if a Mohave person died along a trail, branches were placed over the route and another trail was taken to avoid encounters with the deceased's spirit (Schaefer and Laylander 2014:67–68). Generally, malevolent spirits were to be avoided while either dreaming or awake (e.g., Forde 1931). Archaeologists have inferred such reasons for the presence of shrines, rock alignments, or other barriers along trails. Thwarting bad spirits have also been posited in the cases of course alterations from straight alignments for no apparent reason. Offerings at trail shrines were meant to propitiate such spirits and ensure safe travel. Could intentionally deposited ceramics along trails serve the same purpose? More generally, long-distance travel was inherently risky due to accidents, unpredictable water and food availability, encounters with hostile neighbors, etc., and ceremonial acts might have been undertaken to ensure a safe trip. With regard to ceramic scatters on approaches to tanks and springs, some ethnographic sources indicate that they were associated with malevolent spirits whose encounter might result in dangerous or deadly consequences (Beck 2008; Halpern 1980; Schaefer 1993).

Few ceramic scatters have been collected with the stated purpose of exploring specific cultural functions. In the following discussion, excavation and detailed analysis of eight pot drops provide the empirical data with which to test the hypothesis that ceramic scatters along trails and routes of travel, in many cases, are intentional ceremonial/symbolic expressions. Alternatively, are other explanations, such as random accidental breakage, use as trail markers, ceremonial property disposal, cremation burial, or other aspects of mortuary ritual, supported by the data?

First, we must consider whether the AAC project area follows the same route as a hypothetical trail that figured in east-west transportation and trade between the Colorado River, the Imperial Valley, and the base of the Peninsular Ranges; a total distance of 161 km (100 mi). This would have been the shortest route between Pilot Knob near Yuma, Arizona, and the western side of Imperial Valley, one of several routes used by Yuman-speaking peoples through the desert to the eastern escarpment of the Peninsular Ranges in California (Figure 1.1). The Imperial Sand Dunes form a barrier to the route, but several interdune gaps would have made it more conducive to foot traffic. That is also why the historic Plank Road, Interstate-8, and the AAC itself follow the same general alignment. The AAC route lay along the more northerly and less widely used branch of what is variously referred to as the San Diego Trail or the San Diego-Yuma Trail in the historic period (Russell et al. 2002:85). During infilling of Lake Cahuilla, it would have afforded access to the eastern shoreline from the Colorado River, a distance of 48 km (30 mi). A desert Cahuilla consultant to Clyde Woods identified this route as part of the *Isil-pai-ichi-veh* ("Coyote Trail"). On the western end, it began at Rabbit Peak in the Santa Rosa Mountains and proceeded south to the Coyote Mountains and then east, crossing the Imperial Sand Dunes at the International Border (Russell et al. 2002:85). No specific Yuman name or identification of the trail across the Imperial Sand Dunes exists in the ethnographic literature, and the principal physical evidence is the string of ceramic scatters on the east-west route through the dunes and East Mesa. Shifting sands and loose surface sediments preclude finding actual physical traces of a trail as one might find on desert pavements or other hardened desert surfaces.

Archaeological evidence of the trans-dune travel route is manifested by dispersed ceramic scatters between Pilot Knob and Buttercup Pass in the Imperial Sand Dunes (Underwood 2004). Additional scatters occur on the western edge of the dunes (Schaefer 2002). Some circular reasoning cannot be avoided, however, since the array of scatters is the principal evidence of a prehistoric route of travel. An alternative east-west travel route was also used around the southern edge of the Imperial Sand Dunes. That was the one shown to the Anza Expedition by Native American Sebastian Tarabal in 1774 (Bolton 1930, 1948).

A total of 31 ceramic scatters were recorded along the AAC lining project route (Figure 1.2, Table 1.1). A ceramic scatter was defined as containing only ceramics with few or no other associated artifact types such as lithics, milling equipment, or ecofacts such as animal bone. No human remains were found in association with any of the ceramic scatters. These sites contained as few as four sherds and as many as over 700 based on surface

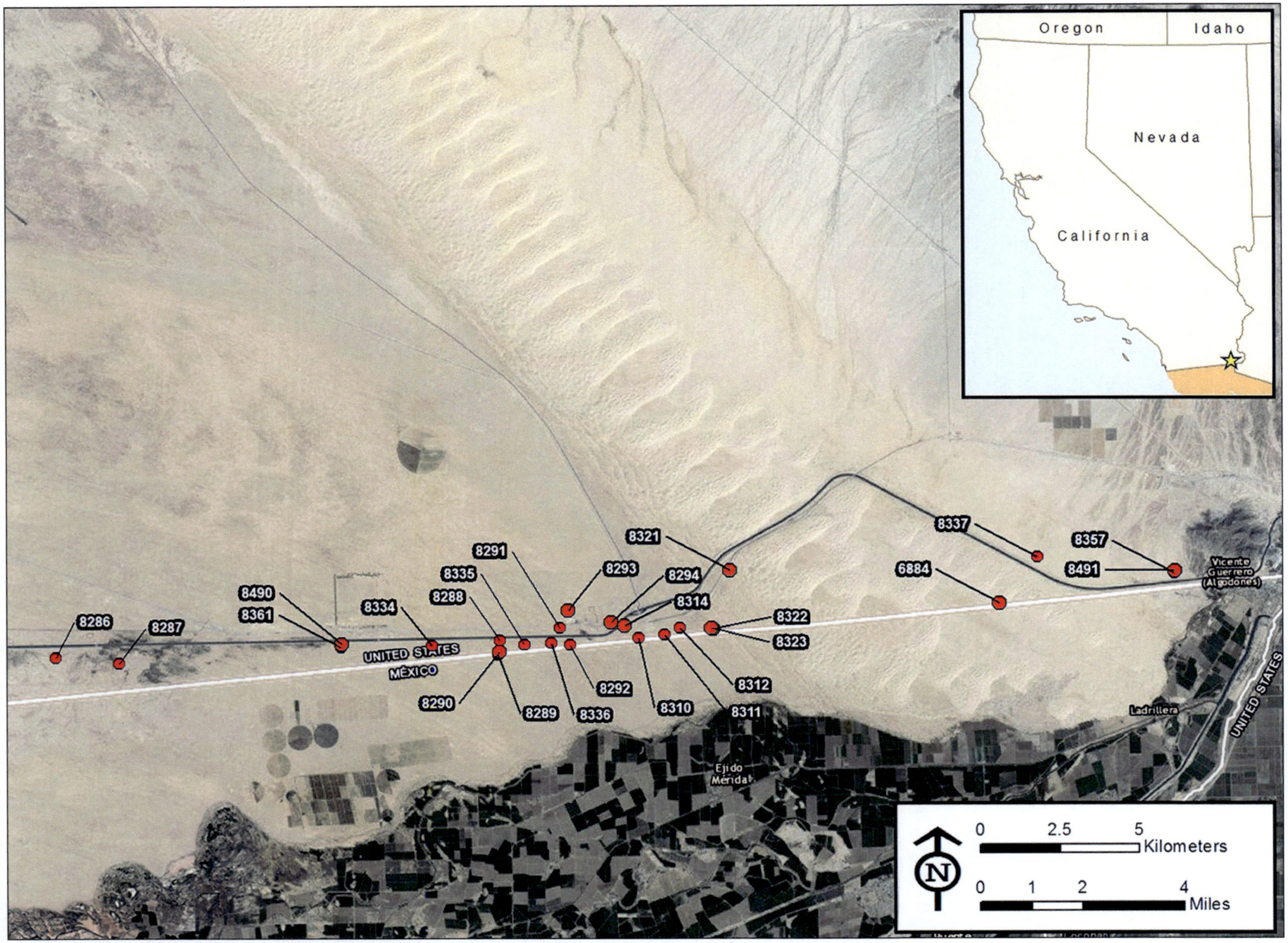

FIGURE 1.2. Recently documented ceramic scatters along the All-American Canal right-of-way.

Table 1.1. Ceramic Scatters in the AAC APE—Survey Level Data

Trinomial (CA-IMP-)	Ceramic Type	Surface Sherd Count	Site Size (m²)	STP Count	Test Results	Treatment
6884H	Colorado Beige, Salton Buff	34	450.00	0	—	Recovered
8286	Salton Buff	5	4.00	1	Negative	Preserved
8287	Black Mesa Buff	46	64	1	Negative	Preserved
8288	Salton Buff	6	4	1	Negative	Preserved
8289	Black Mesa Buff	5	0.25	1	Negative	Preserved
8290	Black Mesa Buff	10	0.5	1	Negative	Recovered
8291	Tumco Buff	105	375	1	Negative	Preserved
8292	Tumco Buff	5	1	0	—	Preserved
8293	Sacaton Red-on-Buff	27	15	1	Negative	Recovered
8294	Parker Buff	91	600	1	Negative	Recovered
8310	Tumco Buff	6	4	2	Positive	Preserved
8311	Tumco Buff	13	24	1	Positive	Preserved
8312	Parker Buff	8	30	1	Negative	Recovered
8314	Colorado Beige, Black Mesa Buff, Tumco Buff	>700 in 16 scatters	940	6	Positive	Recovered 3 loci, Preserved 13 loci
8321	Tumco Buff	13	50	1	Negative	Recovered
8322	Black Mesa Buff	34	12	1	Negative	Recovered
8323	Black Mesa Buff	3	0.25	0	—	Recovered
8334	Tumco Buff	61	12	0	—	Preserved
8335	Tumco Buff	20	24	0	—	Preserved
8336	Tumco Buff	21	7.5	0	—	Preserved
8337	Black Mesa Buff	15	1.5	0	—	Preserved
8357	Tumco Buff	35	27	0	—	Recovered
8361	Black Mesa Buff	4	9	0	—	Preserved
8490	Black Mesa Buff	22	6	0	—	Recovered
8491	Parker Buff	11	8	0	—	Recovered

survey artifact counts. The average surface sherd count was 53 with a standard deviation of ±130. It should also be noted that 17 sherd isolates also were recorded, defined as from one to three sherds in a delimited area. The smallest ceramic scatters covered a surface area ranging between <1 m² to as much as 150 m². Twenty-nine of these scatters appear to represent a single vessel each; two sites contained two and four vessels, respectively. One unusual large ceramic scatter site, IMP-8314, contained at least 16 loci or discrete ceramic scatters within an area of 600 × 340 m.

An additional 52 ceramic scatters were previously recorded within or adjacent to the AAC project route, but many of these could not be relocated in the shifting dune or alluvial sands and silts, and others had been destroyed by historic and modern activities. Among the previously recorded scatters were a series of at least 15 scatters within an interdune area in the Imperial Sand Dunes, branded by the discoverers on the site record as "Pot Drop Valley" (CA-IMP-3058/H, -3059, and -3061). These sites have been entirely destroyed by off-road vehicular activity, but their prior existence supports the idea of a transit corridor through the otherwise uninhabitable sand dunes. Figure 1.2 gives the impression of a narrow transit corridor, but it should be recognized that a much wider route of travel may be defined through additional inventory in Imperial County and Mexico.

Field Methods

Sixteen of the 31 newly recorded ceramic scatters were initially examined with shovel test pits (STPs) prior to data recovery (Schaefer and Andrews 2005). All the scatters were hypothesized to be largely surface manifestations. The testing program was designed to address this assumption for purposes of National Register of Historic Properties (NRHP) eligibility determination and, importantly, to address Native American concerns that some of the scatters might mark the location of cremation burials. No burnt or calcined bone was found on the surface at any of the tested sites.

From one to six STPs were excavated at each site to a minimum depth of 60 cm or whenever the loose sandy substrata collapsed on the pit. STPs at 11 scatters were negative; those at five additional scatters were positive.

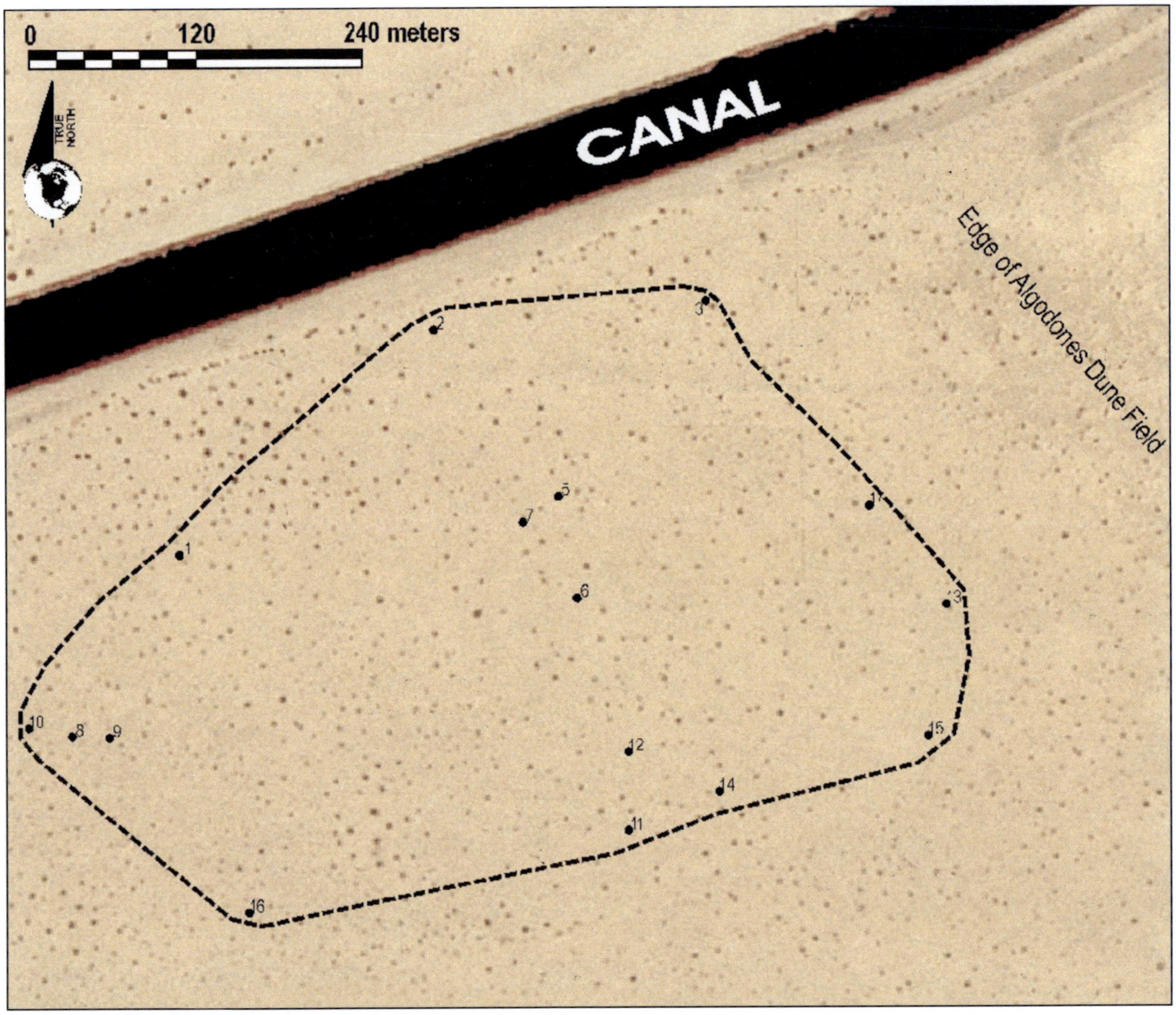

FIGURE 1.3. Detail of CA-IMP-8490, view north.

At all of the positive tests, additional sherds of the same ceramic type as were observed on the surface were recovered at shallow depths; indicative of surface sherds that had been buried by shifting aeolian and alluvial surface sediments to depths reaching 20 cm. The results were further confirmed during data recovery when only additional sherds from the same vessels represented by the surface scatters were recovered from shallow depths below surface. Some lithic debitage occurred at only a few sites and no other directly associated artifacts or bone occurred at most recovered scatters. In fact, no scatters have yet been found in any proximity to other types of prehistoric sites, except at the eastern end where they occur, coincidentally, amid large lithic procurement sites.

Data recovery occurred at 14 of the ceramic scatters in direct impact zones. This included 11 different sites and three scatters recovered from the large site, CA-IMP-8314. A 1 × 1 m grid unit was staked over the center of each scatter, which usually amounted to all of the surface ceramics. Surface sherds were collected and bagged separately. The top 10 cm of silts and sands was then scraped off with a shovel and sifted through ⅛" screen to recover buried sherds. An additional 10 cm was then scraped off, continuing to progressively greater depths if sherds continued to be recovered. Shovel scrapes were then extended outside of the grid units to follow any subsurface sherd occurrence until no more ceramics were found.

Data recovery methods and results are described below from one of the three recovered scatters within a unique larger array of 16 ceramic features at CA-IMP-8314, and one representative isolated scatter, CA-IMP-8490.

CA-IMP-8314, a series of at least 16 prehistoric ceramic scatters in an area of 600 × 340 m, is located in a sandy, flat, creosote-covered area on the eastern edge of East Mesa near the Imperial Sand Dunes (Figure 1.3). This

FIGURE 1.4. Ceramic scatters at CA-IMP-8314.

site is unique in containing many scatters in relatively close proximity with no obvious functional/utilitarian explanation for their occurrence. No other artifact types were recorded within the entire complex. Most of the loci represented one or two vessels within a relatively small area (10 × 10 m each) and containing 10–50 sherds each. Colorado Beige and Black Mesa Buff were the most common ceramic types among the loci, with small numbers of Tumco Buff sherds co-occurring at all the loci. Water's (1982b) definitions were used to assign types, and for this purpose the ceramics closely matched his typology. For such a large complex, it is notable that no other artifacts or associated habitation site have been recorded here. One surface scrape unit (Locus 5, Unit 3 in the center of the site) was excavated where 173 Black Mesa Buff olla sherds were observed on the surface. The unit was excavated to a vertical depth of 30 cm below surface (cmbs) and a horizontal extent of about 3 m^2, with negative results. The excavation revealed two sedimentary strata consisting of tan, compact, fine-grained sandy silt, overlying reddish-tan, moderately compact, fine-grained sandy silt.

CA-IMP-8490 was originally recorded as a ceramic scatter (3 × 2 m) of 22 Black Mesa Buff sherds from a partially reconstructable wide-mouthed bowl (Figure 1.4). It was situated on an incipient desert pavement within a sand-mounded creosote scrub environment. One surface scrape unit (Unit 1) was excavated where 140 sherds were observed on the surface. The unit was excavated to a vertical depth of 10 cmbs and a horizontal extent of about 8 m^2. The excavation revealed two sedimentary strata consisting of tan, compact, fine-grained sandy silt overlying a caliche deposit. A total of 64 ceramics and four pieces of lithic debitage were recovered below the surface to a depth of 10 cmbs. Only portions of one large vessel were recovered.

Analyses

The landscape and spatial context of these ceramic scatters is the most compelling evidence for inferring their nonutilitarian origins. Just as compelling is the archaeological contexts derived from subsurface excavations, discussed below.

Detailed ceramic attribute analysis of the recovered ceramics cannot be overlooked, including explicit descriptions of fabric, surface treatment, and vessel shape.

TABLE 1.2. Sum of Sherd Counts from Surface and Subsurface Contexts

Site	Recovery Type	Total	% of Total
CA-IMP-6884H	general surface	32	94%
	surface scrape	2	6%
CA-IMP-6884H Total		34	100%
CA-IMP-8290	general surface	13	68%
	surface scrape	6	32%
CA-IMP-8290 Total		19	100%
CA-IMP-8293	general surface	27	54%
	surface scrape	23	46%
CA-IMP-8293 Total		50	100%
CA-IMP-8294	general surface	91	83%
	surface scrape	19	17%
CA-IMP-8294 Total		110	100%
CA-IMP-8314-2	general surface	11	15%
	surface scrape	54	85%
CA-IMP-8314-2 Total		65	100%
CA-IMP-8314-3	general surface	5	100%
CA-IMP-8314-3 Total		5	100%
CA-IMP-8314-5	general surface	173	100%
CA-IMP-8314-5 Total		173	100%
CA-IMP-8321	general surface	13	43%
	surface scrape	17	57%
CA-IMP-8321 Total		30	100%
CA-IMP-8322	general surface	34	75%
	surface scrape	11	25%
CA-IMP-8322 Total		45	100%
CA-IMP-8323	general surface	3	60%
	surface scrape	2	40%
CA-IMP-8323 Total		5	100%
CA-IMP-8357	general surface	57	44%
	surface scrape	72	56%
CA-IMP-8357 Total		129	100%
CA-IMP-8490	general surface	140	62%
	surface scrape	84	38%
CA-IMP-8490 Total		224	100%
CA-IMP-8491	general surface	11	100%
CA-IMP-8491 Total		11	100%
Grand Total		900	

Still, problems of applying standard typologies are addressed with consideration of assigning replicable types and chronologies, here made with luminescence dating of surface collections.

Archaeological Context

The questions addressed below concern the physical integrity of the recovered ceramic vessels represented at each scatter. Were whole vessels or only partial vessels and sherds left? Did natural forces disperse the sherd scatters to such an extent that our field methods failed to recover all the pieces? Were modern relic collectors or even Patayan travelers removing sherds from their original contexts, thus explaining why most scatters represent only partial vessels or scatters that did not contain rims?

The depositional context of the ceramic scatters is important to review in order to assess whether whole vessels were deposited. All of the sherd scatters occurred on flat surfaces underlain by fine sandy silts. A few scatters at the eastern end of the project occurred on a mix of sandy silts and pebble pavements. A comparison of the number and percentage of sherds recovered from the surface relative to subsurface shovel scrapes provides a sense of how much pottery can be concealed by wind-and-water-driven sediment underlaying many scatters (Table 1.2). Presumably, over time, the number of sherds visible on the surface would shift.

Most of the sites produced substantially more sherds from subsurface contexts than what appeared on the surface. The exceptions were site CA-IMP-6884H, where only 2 of 34 sherds came from subsurface contexts, and CA-IMP-8314, Feature 5, where all 173 sherds were found on the surface. A few sherds were concealed just below surface but were discovered during the surface pick-up. These results support the conclusion that surface survey data generally underestimated sherd counts in the loose sand and silts of the project area. The fine sandy-silt subsurface strata at all the sites also indicate that the velocity of wind and water action was extremely low and not likely to cause much natural displacement of sherds over time. A higher wind-and-water velocity and higher surface gradients would likely move more gravel and larger clasts. This was not the case, and the flat terrain would be expected to cause minimal sherd displacement over time. Subsurface scrapes were extended sufficiently until no other finds were discovered. There is good confidence, therefore, that all of the deposited sherds were recovered.

There was also no direct evidence that relic collectors were taking away sherds. Most of these sites are difficult to access, much less find. Relic collectors often pile up their surface finds and then select what they want. The unmistakable trace of such activity was absent at all the scatters. Although rim sherds were missing at most scatters, they were found in sufficient quantities at some scatters to indicate no prevailing pattern. Selective prehistoric sherd collecting could not be addressed for lack of evidence.

Ceramic Types

Five ceramic types were identified using 20× magnification and the Rogers/Waters Lower Colorado Buff Ware ceramic typology (Waters 1982b, 1982c). The one

Hohokam ceramic scatter is discussed in Chapter 3 of this volume. It is important to review the attributes used to distinguish each type in the current study, as Lower Colorado Buff Ware ceramic typology is not without its vagaries and has been found to be applied with great difficulty at times (see Chapter 11, this volume; Schaefer 1994b; Schaefer and Laylander 2007). This discussion is especially important for evaluating the luminescence dating of the type designations and the validity of the Patayan ceramic typology and chronology (see below).

Black Mesa Buff

Black Mesa Buff is considered to be among the earlier Lower Colorado Buff Ware types, dating to the Patayan I phase (AD 700–1000), although its occurrence throughout the Patayan I and II stratigraphic sequence at the Stallard Road sites brings that assumption into question (Hildebrand 2003). We shall see that the luminescence dating for this project also brought the assumed time range into doubt. Black Mesa Buff fabric contains large amounts of unpulverized clay, some of which may be crushed sherds. Some small, fine, rounded quartz, feldspar, and other mineral grains may occur, often only visible under high magnification or in petrographic thin section. Occasional freshwater mollusk shells may occur as well, although none were observed in this collection. Rim sherds are always direct but, even without a rim, other characteristics distinguish Black Mesa Buff body sherds from Tumco Buff, the supposed Patayan II phase counterpart that also contains unpulverized clay. Black Mesa Buff ceramics tend to be thicker and not as well finished as Tumco Buff. Uneven surfaces and crackling often occur, although not in every case. Without rim sherds, the better made Black Mesa Buff examples may be difficult to distinguish from Tumco Buff. For that reason, scatters with the characteristic direct rims were used as the comparative type specimens to identify scatters with the same ceramic attributes but no rims.

Colorado Beige

Colorado Beige is a Patayan I phase (AD 700–1050) type and also supposedly one of the earliest types on the Colorado River between the Palo Verde Valley and the Gila River. Again, the results from investigations at the Stallard Road sites suggest this type continued to be made in the Patayan II phase (Hildebrand 2003). The direct rims of Colorado Beige allegedly help to identify it and discriminate it from later types. As a presumably early type, the vessel walls can be thick, uneven, and soft. According to Waters (1982b, 1982c), Late Patayan I phase sherds have harder, even, and well smoothed walls, as do most from the AAC collection. The fabric usually contains fewer mineral inclusions and temper than Parker Buff or Topoc Buff, ranging from 5 to 55% of the fabric. The more heavily tempered examples, however, can be easily confused with Topoc Buff, although Colorado Beige possesses a softer and crumblier fabric. The grains tend to be round-to-subangular quartz, feldspar, and other colored minerals with occasional mica flakes, but no amphibole. Colorado Beige surfaces often exhibit coarse wipe marks, but a small subset of this type is actually burnished. Some of the examples from this collection display burnishing. Mineral grains always appear through the surface, but some grains also appear through the surface of Parker Buff and Topoc Buff. The smaller density of minerals, rounded grains, and greater diversity of minerals distinguish Colorado Beige from other types.

Parker Buff

Parker Buff spans the Patayan II and III phases (AD 1000–post AD 1900). According to the literature and the supposed Patayan II–III dates attributed to this type, the rims should be characteristically recurved. The recurve is more extreme on the highly decorated Ft. Mojave Variant of the historic period (Kroeber and Harner 1955; Waters 1982c). The fabric contains medium to very large amounts of poorly sorted angular to subangular crushed quartz and feldspar grains, with only traces of other minerals. Quartz, however, is the most abundant and sometimes the exclusive mineral. Although Waters (1982c:567) describes the wet-mopped surface to be so well finished that no temper shows through, in fact under high magnification (15–25×), mineral grains can be seen in some cases, although often not. Under low magnification (10×) they are less detectable or undetectable. It might be more accurate to say that minerals cannot be seen protruding through the surface when examined with a hand lens. This problem in accurately discriminating Parker Buff and Colorado Beige can lead to some difficulty when a higher-power microscope rather than a hand lens is used to examine sherds. Both types can share similar surface qualities. Colorado Beige sherds, however, always have mineral grains protruding through the surface, whereas classification with microscope observations reveals a continuum in the amount of temper protruding through the surface of Parker Buff. Other fabric attributes consequently become more important diagnostic criteria. Parker Buff temper is thought to derive from crushed rock, principally pure quartz, or granite containing quartz and feldspar; Parker Buff fabric therefore contains large quantities of poorly sorted angular to subangular grains. Colorado Beige temper, on the other hand, derives more from sands with rounded to subangular grains of quartz, feldspar, and other minerals. Thus, mineral attributes possess more primacy in distinguishing Parker Buff from Colorado Beige, if these types are valid at all, than merely surface protrusion of mineral grains.

Salton Buff

Salton Buff extends in time from the end of the Patayan I phase through the Patayan II phase (AD 950–1500). Salton Buff contains abundant well-rounded, coarse-to-fine beach sand ranging in quantity from 15% to over 50% of the fabric. Salton Buff temper on the east side of Lake Cahuilla tends to be better sorted with a predominance of large, rounded grains. Mollusk shell fragments occasionally occur but are rarely seen. Salton Buff temper on the west side of the lake tends to be less well sorted with more small grains and a variety of shapes from rounded to subrounded and even subangular. Most of the minerals (>90%) are quartz with low amounts of feldspar, black and red jasper, and other colored grains. Fracture is generally hard. The surface of Salton Buff is characteristically rough, like fine sandpaper, with many grains protruding through. Rim forms include both direct and recurved forms, with the former more common on bowls.

Tumco Buff

Tumco Buff is a Patayan II phase (AD 1000–1500) ceramic type, although examples extend into the Patayan III phase with the final infilling of Lake Cahuilla (AD 1600–1700) and the historic period. It is likely a refinement of Black Mesa Buff with the same profusion of clay chunks or crushed sherds. A few mineral grains are often only visible under high magnification or in thin section. Rim sherds are easy to distinguish by their recurved profiles, while Black Mesa Buff sherds exhibit direct rims, according to the Waters's (1982b) typology. Body sherds are therefore difficult to differentiate when sites span the Patayan and Patayan II phase, and some error may occur when distinguishing Tumco Buff from Black Mesa Buff if rims are not found. Tumco Buff sherds, however, tend to be thinner and more evenly finished, with a harder fracture, and no surface crackling. Tumco Buff cooking pots are frequently stuccoed with sandy clay to compensate for the lack of minerals in the fabric, a potential weakness when exposed to thermal shock. No stucco finishes were observed in this collection.

Type Frequencies

Figure 1.5 represents the percentage of sherds of each type in the recovered ceramic assemblage (n = 900). Table 1.3 parses that data into the distribution of sherds by type at each scatter. Of the 13 recovered scatters, nine were represented by only one ceramic type, and by examination of rims and sherd characteristics, only one vessel per scatter. Three scatters contained sherds of two vessels. In each of these cases, the second ceramic vessel was represented by only a few sherds.

At CA-IMP-6884H, the majority of sherds (n = 32) were from a single Colorado Beige vessel, with two associated Salton Buff sherds in association. At CA-IMP-8314, Feature 3, three sherds of Colorado Beige and two sherds of Tumco Buff were recovered. Black Mesa Buff was the most common ceramic type found in the entire site assemblage, occurring at five scatters and representing 59.8% of the total sherd recovery from all 13 sites. Three scatters contained Tumco Buff vessels, representing 4.0% of all sherds. Another three scatters contained Colorado Beige sherds, comprising 10.78% of the assemblage. Two sites contained Parker Buff sherds, a total of 13.44% of all. Ceramic types that were represented at only one site included Salton Buff (n = 2, 0.22%) and, most notably, Hohokam ceramics (Sacaton Red-on-buff; n = 50, 5.56%). The single Hohokam ceramic scatter was identified by application of the Museum of Northern Arizona ceramic type descriptions (Vance 2021), and informed by recent Middle Gila River Buff Ware ceramic studies (e.g., Abbott 2008, 2009; Heckman et al. 2000; Wallace 2001, 2004). It is discussed with more detail in Chapter 3.

Vessel Shapes, Rim Forms, and Completeness

Vessel shapes were inferred at those few sites possessing rim sherds (5 of 11), as most scatters contained no rim sherds or too few sherds to reconstruct shapes (Table 1.4). In most cases, however, ceramic fabric attributes indicate a single vessel was represented at most scatters. One exception is CA-IMP-8314, Locus 2, where three vessels were discriminated based on rim forms and ceramic fabrics. Also, with one exception, the number of rim sherds was inadequate to produce the complete circumference of any vessel. The finding suggests that any effort at more substantial vessel shape reconstructions would be futile at best. Two scatters contained substantial numbers of sherds, suggesting more representation of the vessel. Sherds at all other scatters were relatively few. Data on vessel forms and rim preservation are presented in Table 1.5. Drawn rim profiles are illustrated in Figure 1.6.

CA-IMP-8314, Locus 2, is one of the only scatters to contain more than one vessel. Two are Colorado Beige bowls with slightly recurved rims (Cat. No. 5, Cat. Nos. 11–12, and Cat. No. 7), and one is a Tumco Buff jar (Cat. No. 9). Waters (1982c) reports slightly recurved

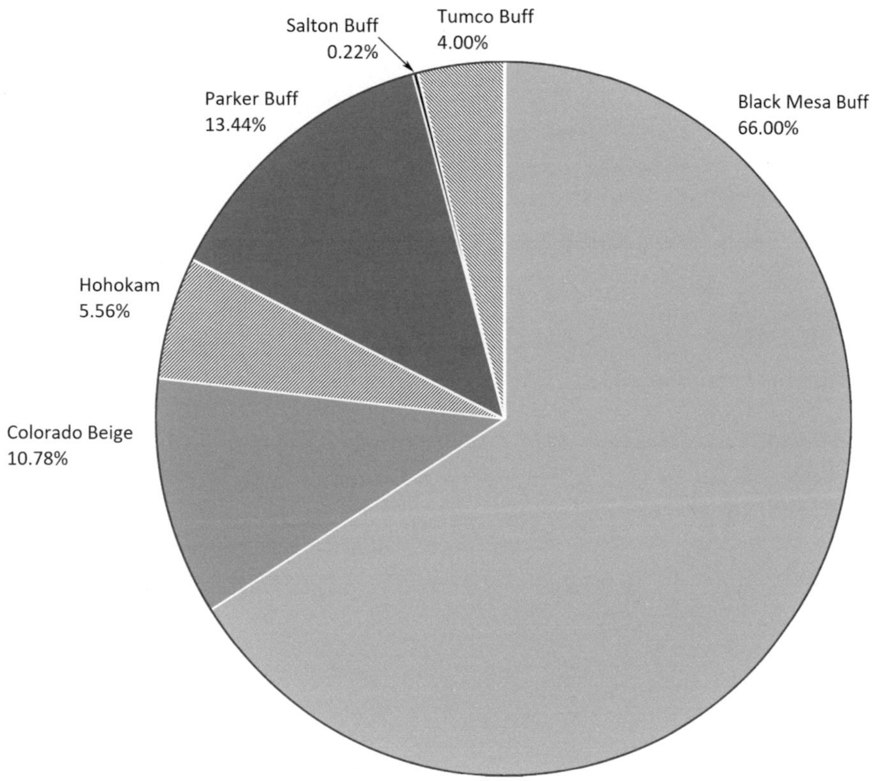

Figure 1.5. Distribution of sherds among ceramic types for the recovery assemblage (n = 900).

Table 1.3. Distribution of Sherds by Type for All Recovered Scatters

Site	Black Mesa Buff	Colorado Beige	Parker Buff	Salton Buff	Tumco Buff	Hohokam	Grand Total
CA-IMP-6884H		32		2			34
CA-IMP-8290	19						19
CA-IMP-8293						50	50
CA-IMP-8294			110				110
CA-IMP-8314-2		62			3		65
CA-IMP-8314-3		3			2		5
CA-IMP-8314-5	172				1		173
CA-IMP-8321					30		30
CA-IMP-8322	45						45
CA-IMP-8323	5						5
CA-IMP-8357	129						129
CA-IMP-8490	224						224
CA-IMP-8491			11				11
Grand Total	594	97	121	2	36	50	900

rims among Colorado Beige vessels and suggests they may date late in the Patayan I sequence or to early Patayan II times. If correctly typed and if any credence can be given to the Rogers/Waters ceramic chronology, then these three vessels from a single site represent vessels of different periods.

CA-IMP-8314, Locus 5, is a large Colorado Beige narrow-mouth olla (Figure 1.7). Approximately 85% of the partially restorable rim and neck were found, although the number of body sherds does not appear to be sufficient to reconstruct any more than half the vessel. The total sherd count for the vessel is 169 sherds,

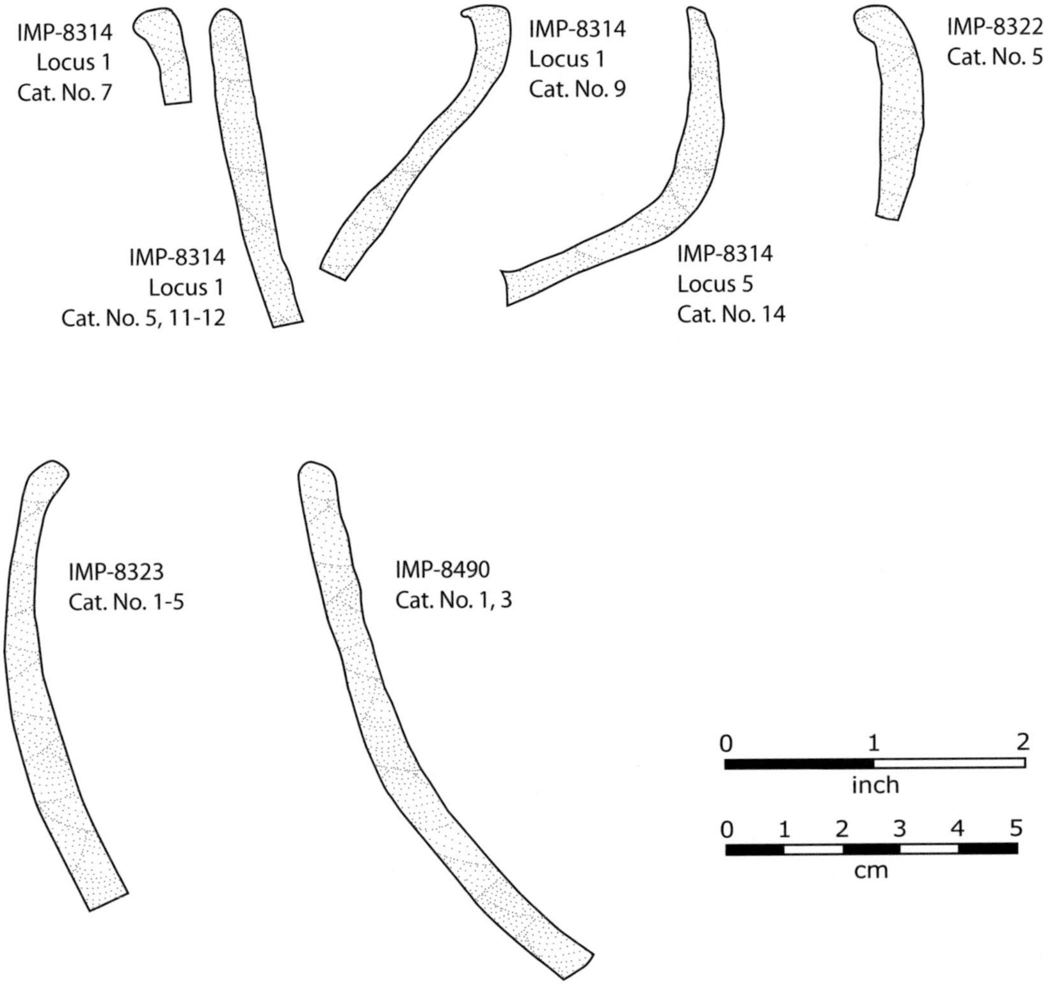

FIGURE 1.6. Rim profiles.

TABLE 1.4. Numbers of Body and Rim Sherds from Recovered Ceramic Scatters

Site Number	Body sherd	Rim sherd	Grand Total
CA-IMP-6884H	34		34
CA-IMP-8290	19		19
CA-IMP-8293	50		50
CA-IMP-8294	110		110
CA-IMP-8314-2	56	9	65
CA-IMP-8314-3	5		5
CA-IMP-8314-5	160	13	173
CA-IMP-8321	30		30
CA-IMP-8322	42	3	45
CA-IMP-8323	3	2	5
CA-IMP-8357	129		129
CA-IMP-8490	210	14	224
CA-IMP-8491	11		11
Grand Total	859	41	900

weighing 579 g. The vessel has the characteristic long, straight "chimney neck" and direct rim characteristic of Patayan I ollas (Waters 1982c). There is a substantial fire cloud on a portion of the rim where the sherds appear to be warped and do not connect. This appears to be a misfire, although it would not render the vessel unusable.

CA-IMP-8322 produced three refitted rim sherds from a Black Mesa Buff olla with a slightly recurved rim. Waters (1982c) reports that slight recurved rims occur in this Patayan I type. Although 28% of the rim is preserved, a much smaller fraction of the vessel is represented by the total number of recovered sherds (n = 45).

All five sherds from CA-IMP-8323 refit to form one straight rim sherd of a large bowl. Only 9% of the rim circumference remains. In fact, these five sherds compose the entire scatter.

CA-IMP-8490 is the only other scatter with a substantial number of sherds (n = 224) and weight

TABLE 1.5. Inventory of Ceramic Scatters with Rims and Identifiable Shapes

Cat. No.	Site (CA-IMP-)	Locus	Type	Vessel Shape	Rim Shape	Rim Diameter (cm)	% of Rim Complete
5, 11-12	8314	2	Colorado Beige	Bowl	Direct	25	22
9	8314	2	Tumco Buff	Jar	Recurved	22-32	1.5
7	8314	2	Colorado Beige	Bowl	Slight Recurved	30	3
14	8314	5	Colorado Beige	Olla	Straight	6	85
3,5	8322		Black Mesa Buff	Olla	Slight Recurved	10	28
3,5	8323		Black Mesa Buff	Bowl	Straight	26	9
1,3	8490		Black Mesa Buff	Bowl	Straight	80	15

FIGURE 1.7. Partially restored rim and neck of a Colorado Beige olla from CA-IMP-8314, Locus 5.

(1.999 kg) to seemingly represent much of a very large Black Mesa Buff bowl. Many of the rim sherds could be refitted, but they only amounted to about 15% of the circumference. This is because the rim is an astonishing 80 cm in diameter. Apparently one vessel is represented because all the straight rim sherds (n = 14) are identical in circumference, shape, and paste. Based on these metrics, the remaining sherds, although substantial in number, represent only a small fraction of an extremely large bowl. It was probably a vessel type known from Quechan ethnographic sources as a *kat'lhakem*, sometimes used to ferry goods and children across the Colorado River (Forde 1931:123–124). It would seem to be inconceivable that such a large vessel would have been transported so far into the desert. It is more likely that just a fraction of the vessel was transported (and broken?) at this location.

Chronology and Provenience

Patayan ceramic chronologies have been cast into question by the results of ceramics analysis at the Stallard Road sites in the Palo Verde Valley where presumably Patayan I ceramic types Black Mesa Buff and Colorado Beige were found to occur throughout the radiocarbon-dated Patayan I and Patayan II strata and into the sixteenth century AD (Hildebrandt 2003). The ceramics occur in what appears to be a well-dated and undisturbed colluvial stratigraphic sequence. Until these apparent chronological anomalies can be resolved, we cannot assume that the Patayan ceramic chronology has indisputable validity (Schaefer 1994a, 1994b; Waters 1982b, 1982c). If Waters's chronology is applied here, we see from the distribution of ceramic types that most scatters with Colorado Beige and Black Mesa Buff should date to the Patayan I phase between about AD 700 and

1050 (Waters 1982c). Colorado Beige, Black Mesa Buff, and Parker Buff vessels were very likely made on the Colorado River and suggest a predominant east-west movement of the people who left these scatters. The exception is site CA-IMP-6684H with two Salton Buff sherds, a Patayan II type associated with ceramic production on the Lake Cahuilla shoreline. The one Parker Buff scatter suggests some down-river exchange from the Mojave Valley/Parker Valley region in the Patayan II phase. The longest distance origin is the Hohokam scatter, which if correctly identified as Sacaton Red-on-buff, represents Hohokam Sedentary Period cultural interaction with the Patayan between AD 950 and 1150.

In light of the considerable questioning of Patayan ceramic chronology, a sherd sample and associated sediment from each scatter were submitted for Thermoluminescence (TL), Optically Stimulated Luminescence (OSL), and/or Infrared Stimulated Luminescence (ISL) dating at the University of Washington (Feathers 2016).

Although not as accurate as radiocarbon dating, TL and related luminescence dating techniques may be the next best thing for surface finds where few other dating options exist. TL dating still suffers from a lack of application in archaeological research, but it has gained more credibility in the Southwest and Great Basin by researchers who have obtained date ranges in reasonable concurrence with associated radiocarbon dates and known culture historical sequences. TL dates provide standard deviations comparable to conventional radiocarbon dating. The dating results for surface assemblages are especially good even though environmental radiation was thought to be a problem (Feathers 2000:51). Surface ceramics have not previously been recommended as candidates for luminescence dating due to greater uncertainties in determining the cosmic ray and gamma doses (Aitkens 1985, 1989). In fact, more uncertainty arises from burial environments to the extent that surface ceramics may be preferable (Dunnell and Feathers 1994).

The applicability of TL dating for surface ceramics was demonstrated by Dunnell and Feathers (1994) with Late Woodland and Mississippian ceramics from the surface of plowed sites in Southeastern Missouri. Good results were achieved, despite greater environmental fluctuations and contextual uncertainties, than the discrete surficial pot drops in the normally dry Colorado Desert. Even better results were achieved with surface ceramics in the Great Basin (Feathers and Rhode 1998).

Colorado Desert surface ceramics would seem to be excellent candidates for TL dating. Previously, surface finds have not been used because it was thought that their contexts were not as assured as buried material, however, as this study has demonstrated, most ceramic scatters in the project area appear minimally disturbed since they were deposited, except for periodic covering and exposure by shifting aeolian or alluvial surface sediments. Dry cave environments and extreme desert environments are considered excellent contexts for TL dating. Seasonal variability in moisture context and variability in depositional environment between samples will not have as uncontrollable an effect on the results as might be expected for buried sherds in temperate climates, although periodic wet and dry conditions occur throughout the year or over time in deserts. Wet ceramics absorb more radiation than dry ceramics (Dunnell and Feathers 1994:121). All of the AAC scatters are likely to have had the same general history of environmental exposure and to have remained in a fairly homogenous environmental condition.

It was expected that a proportion of the ceramics from the AAC project area would likely date to the last 300–500 years, leading to the question of whether TL dating is appropriate for late-period sites. Even if radiocarbon dating was feasible, vagaries in atmospheric carbon isotopes during the last 350 years often result in multiple intercepts when the radiocarbon years are dendro-calibrated to actual dates.

In this regard, some success has been achieved in TL-dated protohistoric Intermountain Brown Ware from surface or near surface contexts in the Great Basin where environmental conditions approximate those of the Colorado Desert (Feathers and Rhode 1998). TL dating thereby overcomes some of the uncertainties associated with protohistoric radiocarbon dates. Age ranges for the Great Basin ceramics between the fifteenth and nineteenth centuries appear appropriate, with a 5–10% uncertainty level, and with only a few exceptions conform to radiocarbon dates from organics in nearby archaeological contexts, diagnostic point types, and trade beads. The results conform well to previous estimates that Brown Ware manufacture was rare until AD 1500 but may have been introduced as early as AD 1000. The TL dates parallel typical date ranges for ceramic finds in the Great Basin, although recent discoveries of radiocarbon associations with Owens Valley Brown Ware may extend the earliest experimentation to circa AD 500–800 (Eerkens et al. 1999).

Three of the problems in luminescence dating of these younger samples include low signal output, nonlinearity in the growth curves, and determining the dose rate for surface samples. Some of these issues have specific relevance to the AAC assemblage. The coarse inclusion method of dating (Aitkens 1985), whereby particular minerals, especially quartz, are concentrated, is one solution to signal strength. Sherds were not large

TABLE 1.6. Results of Luminescence Dating

Sample	Site (CA-IMP-)	Ceramic Type	Age (ka)	% error	Calendar date (years AD)	Basis for date
UW1734	6884/H	Colorado Beige	0.640±0.040	6.6	1370±40	TL/IRSL/OSL
UW1736	8293	Sacaton Red-On-buff	1.340±0.130	9.5	670±130	OSL
UW1737	8294-A	Parker Buff	0.360±0.030	8.3	1650±30	TL/OSL
UW1738	8294-D	Parker Buff	0.530±0.030	6.1	1480±30	TL/OSL
UW1739	8314-3	Colorado Beige	0.400±0.030	7.8	1610±30	TL/IRSL/OSL
UW1735	8314-5	Black Mesa Buff	0.360±0.020	6.4	1650±20	TL/IRSL/OSL
UW1740	8321	Tumco Buff	1.000±0.120	12.4	1010±120	IRSL/OSL
			0.570±0.060	9.7	1430±60	TL
UW1741	8322	Black Mesa Buff	0.360±0.030	8.8	1650±30	IRSL/OSL
UW1742	8357	Black Mesa Buff	0.640±0.050	7.2	1370±50	TL/IRSL/OSL
UW1743	8490	Black Mesa Buff	0.470±0.030	5.9	1540±30	TL/OSL
UW1744	8491	Parker Buff	0.540±0.050	9.5	1460±50	OSL

TL = Thermoluminsence Dating
IRSL = Infrared Stimulated Luminescence Dating
OSL = Optically Stimulate Luminescence Dating

enough for this method, so the fine-grain method was applied. Obtaining sufficient crystalline material may be a problem with some of the AAC sherd scatters containing Black Mesa Buff and Tumco Buff. These two types are typically untempered but do contain natural mineral inclusions in the clay. In the Great Basin study and the current study, OSL was used as a cross-check for the TL dates.

The luminescence results for the AAC assemblage were entirely unexpected (Table 1.6). The overwhelming majority of dates were between AD 1370 and 1650 (with standard deviations between 20 and 50 years). This included all of the supposedly Patayan I (AD 700–1000) ceramic types: Colorado Beige and Black Mesa Buff. In essence, luminescence dating supported the findings at the North Stallard Road sites where dates of supposedly Patayan I types extend throughout the Patayan II period (Hildebrand 2003). The Parker Buff and Tumco Buff sherds conformed to expectations that they would date to the Patayan II period. All of these dates would appear to be contemporary with various phases of Lake Cahuilla, the last phase occurring sometime between AD 1600 and 1700 (Schaefer 1994b). This suggests that one of the major motivations for travel between the Colorado River and East Mesa was the wetland habitats of Lake Cahuilla.

Two other possibilities to consider are that the luminescence dates are in error, or the Black Mesa Buff and Colorado Beige ceramics are incorrectly typed and dated by the application of the existing typology. If we do accept these luminescence dates and the type attributions as correct, then the conclusion is obvious the established ceramic chronology as it pertains to alleged Patayan I types cannot be supported.

Interpretations and Conclusions

The collected evidence from 13 ceramic scatters supports the hypothesis that many, if not most, were intentionally left along a route of travel across East Mesa between the Colorado River and Imperial Valley/Lake Cahuilla. It should also be considered that some of the scatters may derive from people travelling north from the Colorado River Delta, particularly from the Alamo River, and then east to Imperial Valley. Care must be taken not to consider the scatters to be distributed along a narrow corridor or a single trail. That impression is only the result of the linear corridor of the AAC study area. It is more likely that travel occurred along a wide swath of territory, since the soft sandy surface of East Mesa, Buttercup Pass, and the Imperial Sand Dunes would not have preserved an enduring trace to follow, unlike trails on desert pavements. Such prominent landmarks as Pilot Knob in the east and Signal Mountain or Peninsular Ranges landmarks in the west would have guided prehistoric travelers. It is doubtful that the ceramic scatters were left like proverbial breadcrumbs to mark a route, as the scatters are not easily visible from a distance and are covered and revealed by shifting sands over time.

Nonetheless, it is worth considering that the deposition of these ceramic vessel fragments results from more profound symbolic expressions than we can appreciate. So, let us review the evidence. Very few or no other artifact types occur in direct association with the scatters, and no temporary or travel camps are associated. In fact, the creosote scrub habitat of East Mesa would appear to have offered little in the form of food resources with which to attract foragers from any direction who might dispose of ceramics during their usual subsistence activities.

None of the scatters contain enough sherds to reconstruct whole vessels, even though the flat topography of this area would not likely result in natural transport to any distance. Scatters were followed out with shovel scrapes until no additional sherds were found. Rim sherds and uniform paste characteristics of the sherds indicate that most scatters contain remains of only one vessel. Four of the 11 scatters have two vessels represented. Only CA-IMP-8314, Locus 1, contained sherds from three different vessels (three rim forms, two ceramic types). Only one nearly complete rim circumference could be reconstructed. The others contain much smaller percentages of complete rim circumferences—from 1.5 to 28%. At one scatter, CA-IMP-8490, sherds from an extremely large 80 cm diameter bowl were recovered, amounting to about 15% of the total circumference. More sherds were recovered from this scatter than anywhere else, a total of 224, weighing almost 2 kg. A complete bowl would have weighed many times more. It would be inconceivable that such a large and heavy item would have been transported whole from the Colorado River or from Lake Cahuilla or the Alamo River.

It appears that only fragments of vessels were left at each location. We cannot say if an intact portion of a vessel was left and then broken and distributed over a very delimited area by natural or human forces. Large sherds may have been left as receptacles for food offerings or rare/exotic vessel fragments left as a ritual expression. Alternatively, were already broken sherds brought to these locations and deposited on the surface? In fact, mending efforts were usually not very successful. Either way, accidental loss and breakage of complete vessels is not supported by the evidence.

We may never know all the reasons why prehistoric travelers left ceramics along routes of travel, sometimes clustered in specific areas along trails or at trail shrines. In Yuman cosmology, noncorporeal hazards exist in tandem with more mundane, earthly conditions. This was especially true for malevolent spirits of the dead who travel long the same trails (Cachora 1994). Rock alignments across trails or meandering trail alignments may thwart the movement of spirits. Trail shrines—defined as piles of rocks with ceramics and other offerings—are another archaeological manifestation of trail-related ceremonial agency. These sherd scatters are best explained, for now, as offerings to ensure safe travel across an unforgiving desert environment with both corporal and spiritual risks.

As an analogy, this type of behavior is still seen along undocumented immigrant trails across the U.S./Mexican Border. The smaller of such locations may contain all manner of votive offerings to ensure safe travel, including religious candles, coins, medals, and saints' images. These features are more site-specific than more diffuse ceramic scatters, so different symbolic meanings and cultural associations may be at play.

The symbolic meaning of ceramic scatters will never be fully comprehended, but nevertheless they can be understood to a large extent, not just as accidents, but deliberate actions within the context of prehistoric belief systems. Furthermore, they may be understood within the concept of prehistoric archaeological landscapes where geography, topography, and other aspects of the natural and cultural environment provide cultural contexts for making trailside offerings (Byrne 2011; Cleland 2005). Until empirical archaeological or ethnographic evidence can be found to explain why so many ceramic scatters occur along routes of travel or in otherwise unexplainable locations, the conclusion that they remain from nonutilitarian activity would appear to be the best explanation.

The AAC project also provided evidence that questions the currently accepted ceramic chronology. The Colorado Beige and Black Mesa Buff sherds, supposedly Patayan I ceramic types, produced luminescence dates in the same range as the Patayan II–III Tumco Buff and Parker Buff. In fact, the only (terminal) Patayan I date was produced from an IRSL/OSL-dated Tumco Buff sherd. That date has a relatively high (12.4%) error rate, and the TL date on the sherd placed it in the Patayan II phase.

How can we resolve these apparent dating anomalies of Colorado Beige and Black Mesa Buff? One may consider that the ceramics were not correctly classified, especially since Black Mesa Buff and Tumco Buff can look alike. However, several of the Black Mesa Buff dates derive from sherds with unequivocal direct rims, in addition to the other characteristics that distinguish Black Mesa Buff from Tumco Buff (thick, uneven sherds with crackled surfaces). Several Colorado Beige sherds also derive from vessels with direct rims and exhibited the more rounded and variegated mineral temper that shows through the sherd surface, unlike Parker Buff (no Parker Buff rims were recovered). Some of the slightly recurved rims of both Black Mesa Buff and Colorado Beige are presumed by Waters (1982c) to date from the terminal Patayan I, but the luminescence dates are all well into the Patayan II phase if not the Patayan III.

So, if we are to accept the luminescence dates as valid, then one or more conclusions must be considered. The Rogers/Waters Patayan ceramic typology and the chronological attribution of supposed Patayan I types require substantial reform. The AAC results support the same conclusion that has been drawn by Hildebrand (2003) from the Stallard Road sites, which had good stratigraphic associations with radiocarbon dates and also specific sherds directly dated by analysis of carbon residues (Schaefer et al. 2013).

A different source of error may lie in the luminescence dates themselves. Dr. Feathers (Feathers 2016) had to make several explicit assumptions in applying the three dating methods. These included moisture content of sherds and associated sediments, and the gamma dose rate based on the fact that these were surface manifestations, etc. However, in four samples, all three dating methods produced statistically similar results, and these were all late dates derived from Black Mesa Buff and Colorado Beige sherds. The different dating methods applied to other sherds often produced conflicting results due in large part to signal fading. In such cases, the methods with the best signals were applied. Nevertheless, a consistent range of dates was found for the entire collection. Even the early date for the Hohokam sherd, although possibly a little too early, was consistent with established dates for this ceramic type. Unless some other unrecognized technical issue remains with luminescence dating of surface ceramic scatters in the Colorado Desert, then we may need to double down on our efforts to establish a reliable lower Colorado Buff Ware classification system and chronology.

Acknowledgments

Heartfelt thanks go to the Patricia Hicks, Rene Kolvet, Laura Perry, and Mark Slaughter, archaeologists at the Bureau of Reclamation, Lower Colorado Region, for their steadfast support. I am most grateful to the Imperial Irrigation District for funding this project and for the logistical and management support of their environmental management staff, including Michael Remington and Dee Bradshaw. Zee Malas of ASM Affiliates is credited for map and figure preparation. Special thanks to Suzanne Griset for organizing the Society for California Archaeology symposium on western ceramics, spearheading this monograph, and for her draft review.

2

At the Edge of the Desert and West of the Sea

Ceramics from Anza-Borrego Desert State Park

Suzanne Griset

This chapter reports the results of an analysis conducted on the ceramic vessel collection curated by the Anza-Borrego Desert State Park (ABDSP), in the southwestern portion of the Colorado Desert of southern California (Figure 2.1). The park is located west of prehistoric Lake Cahuilla, a body of water that formed in the Salton Basin when the Colorado River changed course and emptied into the basin, rather than the Gulf of Mexico. It is tucked east of the transverse ranges making up the western boundary of the basin. ABDSP has an extensive collection of prehistoric/historic vessels gathered from across the park and curated in the Begole Archaeological Research Center (BARC) in Borrego Springs.

Project Objectives and Methods

The documentation project was funded by the Robert Begole Archaeological Research Foundation, with the objective of identifying vessels with the potential to address research questions. It was essential to examine vessels with documented provenience—even if that was a general designation such as Mine Canyon Wash—so that the distribution of vessels with different paste composition, manufacturing techniques, and vessel form could be tied to the land and examined across the southwestern Colorado desert and compared to ceramics from across southern California.

The electronic catalog maintained by the BARC is focused on providing a general description, size measurements, and storage location for each vessel. In our search for provenience data, we also examined the original specimen catalog cards begun by Robert Begole and continued by subsequent collection managers. The catalog cards often contained information not included in the electronic or printed catalogs. There have been multiple catalog numbering systems used over the years and many vessels contain more than one number written in India ink on the vessel exterior. All numbers associated with a vessel, whether on the catalog card, in the electronic inventory, or on the vessel itself were recorded.

The data from the catalog cards, a printed inventory of vessels at BARC, and a 2001 inventory of vessels at the Visitors' Center were compiled to form a list of provenienced vessels suitable for the research objectives. Eleven of the provenienced vessels recorded on the catalog cards could not be located in either the BARC or the ABDSP Visitors Center displays. In some cases, the "whole" vessel proved now to be a box of fragments due to old glue failure, and thus they were eliminated from the whole vessel assessment. Out of a preliminary list of 121 provenienced specimens, 92 vessels were documented for this project.

The project consisted of remeasuring each vessel using a measuring board and calipers; drawing a scaled profile of the vessel shape and a more detailed profile of the rim/neck area; noting whether the vessel was upright when at rest or the general angle of repose; recording observations about the manufacture, use, and post-use deposition of the vessel; assigning a pottery ware, and when feasible (especially if the paste was visible in a cracked surface/edge) a pottery type (see discussion of ware and type below). These data were recorded on a whole vessel form developed during previous research on museum collections of vessels from the cismontane area of southern California. Each vessel was digitally photographed in color in profile (at least two profiles at 0° and rotated 180°, with additional profiles when warranted), a direct view of the base, and detail photos of the rim finish and any other notable features. Special

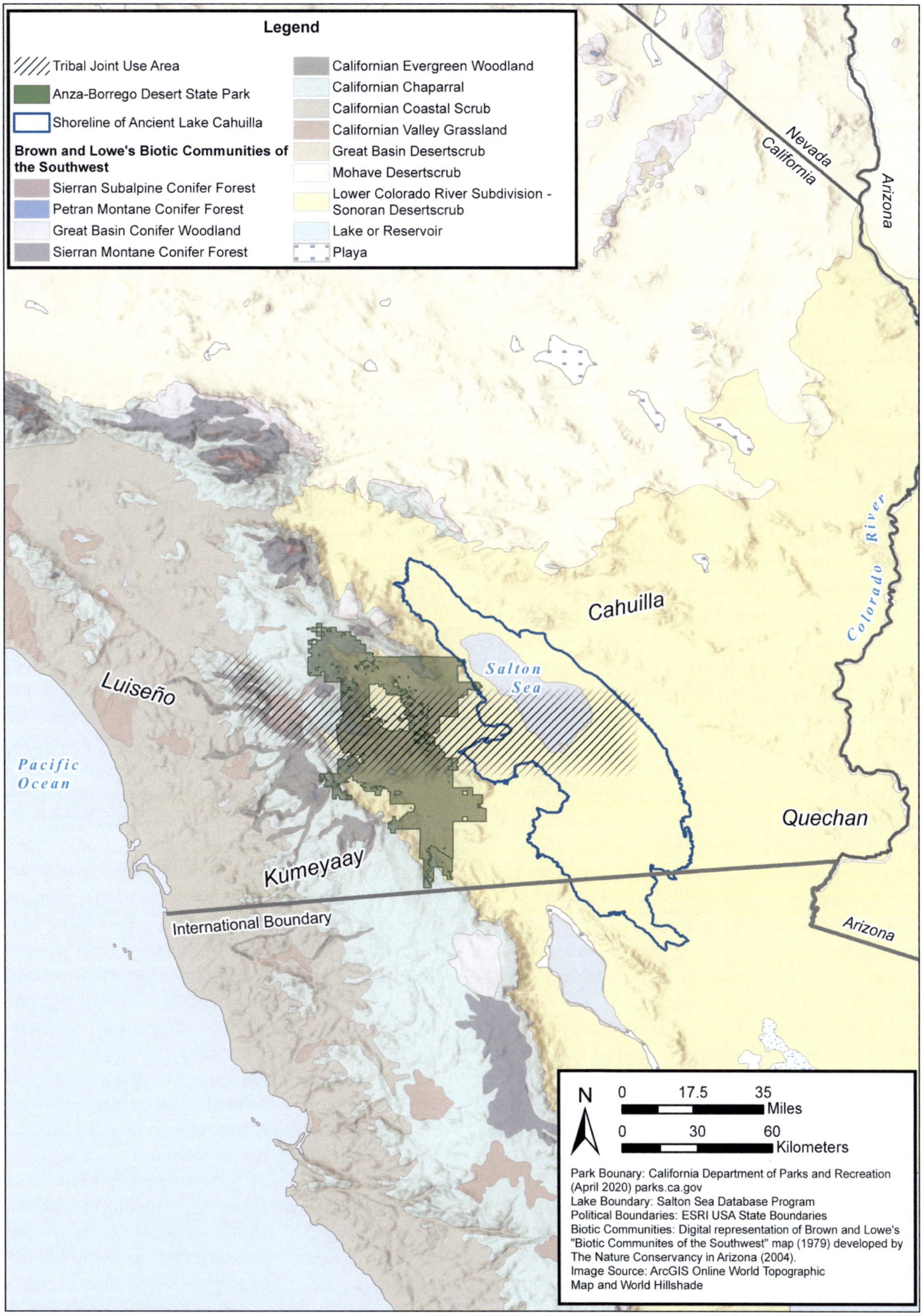

FIGURE 2.1. Location of the Anza Borrego Desert State Park (ABDSP) at the western edge of the Colorado Desert with underlying biotic communities also showing the generalized locations of tribes and a joint tribal use area in ABDSP (courtesy of Joan Schneider; map by Elizabeth Vinson).

note was made of vessels with potential residue or carbon layers that might be suitable for residue or radiocarbon analyses. ABDSP GIS expert, L. Louise Jee plotted the provenience of the vessels in the research sample and prepared a series of maps based on vessel form and pottery ware/type.

Background on Prehistoric Ceramics of Southern California

Prehistoric ceramics vessels in the cismontane and desert areas of southern California were made by a combination of initial hand modeling or forming the base on the inverted base of another pot, followed by the addition of coils of clay that were shaped and thinned using a wooden paddle on the vessel exterior opposite a stone or fired clay "anvil" held on the interior. Vessels were fired to a ceramic stage in a shallow open pit, and the vessel exteriors often exhibited variable oxidation, carbon deposits, and fire clouds.

Ethnographic data suggest that culinary pots were made by women, usually one or several vessels at a time, during the summer months. Women married into their husband's community, consequently there was considerable movement of women who likely learned potting in their natal locale(s), then married and possibly moved to other locales where they had to learn the location and attributes of local materials or acquire raw materials from sources known to them.

Southern California Ceramic Typology

Paddle-and-anvil ceramics were produced on both sides of the lower Colorado River, from the Pacific Ocean, into northern Baja California, across the Colorado and Mojave deserts, and on into northern, western, and southern Arizona and northern Sonora, Mexico. Ceramics manufactured to the north and east of this area were shaped by the coil-and-scrape method and are considered to be different ceramic traditions.

The first typology for the ceramics found throughout the desert areas of California and Arizona was compiled but never published by Rogers (1945a, 1945b); portions of his typology were modified and published by Schroeder (1958), May (1978), and Waters (1982a), and they referred to two wares—Tizon Brown Ware (TBW) and Lower Colorado Buff Ware (LCBW). TBW was first described by Euler and Dobyns (1958) for ceramics found in northwestern Arizona; others have argued that the ceramics in cismontane southern California should be designated a separate ware (Griset 1996; Lyneis 1988c; Van Kamp 1979), and they are today known more generally as Southern California Brown Ware. Waters's (1982a) Lower Colorado Buff Ware typology is most commonly used at present, with additional types added as researchers have found them to be useful. Schaefer (1996) identified Salton Brown Ware as an intermediary ware between the buff and brown, while Griset (2006) suggested a different ware name, California Desert Intermediate Brown Ware (CDIBW), to preclude confusion with Salton Brown type.

SCBW is manufactured from residual clays that weather-in-place and contain sufficient nonplastics that they do not require tempering (the purposeful addition of nonplastics) to make the clay workable. The clay body color ranges from gray brown to red brown and often exhibits mica visible on the vessel surface.

CDIBW is intermediate in that the clays have been transported by water or wind from the original mountain locations into the Colorado Desert area; they may or may not require temper, and they produce clay bodies that are lighter brown and contain less abundant mica than SCBW.

LCBW is made from sedimentary clays that have been finely sorted by fluvial or Aeolian transport; they contain few nonplastics and require tempering with sand, crushed rock, or crushed potsherds (also known as grog). The clay bodies range from tan to buff to light pinky/orange, and they often have a "scum" coat covering the vessel surfaces (Rogers 1928). The buff typology also specifies differences in vessel form and especially rim shape through time, but these have been called into question in recent studies (Hildebrand 2003).

Given the mobility of the Kumeyaay and Cahuilla peoples who inhabited the ABDSP area in the historic period and the lure of Lake Cahuilla when full, there was likely considerable movement of peoples and potters, and it is conceivable that individual potters used different clays depending on their proximity to clay sources or the type of vessel that was being produced. Archaeologists would classify these as different types or wares depending on where the clays were obtained. Some clays were renowned for their specific properties, and potters travelled or traded to obtain these clays. A prime example close to ABDSP is the micaceous clay found in the Jacumba area. Davis (1961) reported that potters in the early twentieth century would travel extensive distances to obtain this clay as it was reputed to make superior cooking pots. The flat muscovite grains become aligned parallel to the vessel walls when the vessel is shaped with the paddle-and-anvil technique, increasing resistance to thermal fracture.

Thus, ceramic typologies are heuristic devices that assist in classifying and analyzing a large body of data and facilitate the identification of patterns and/or anomalies that might reveal the human behavior represented by the pots. Their replicability from one analyst

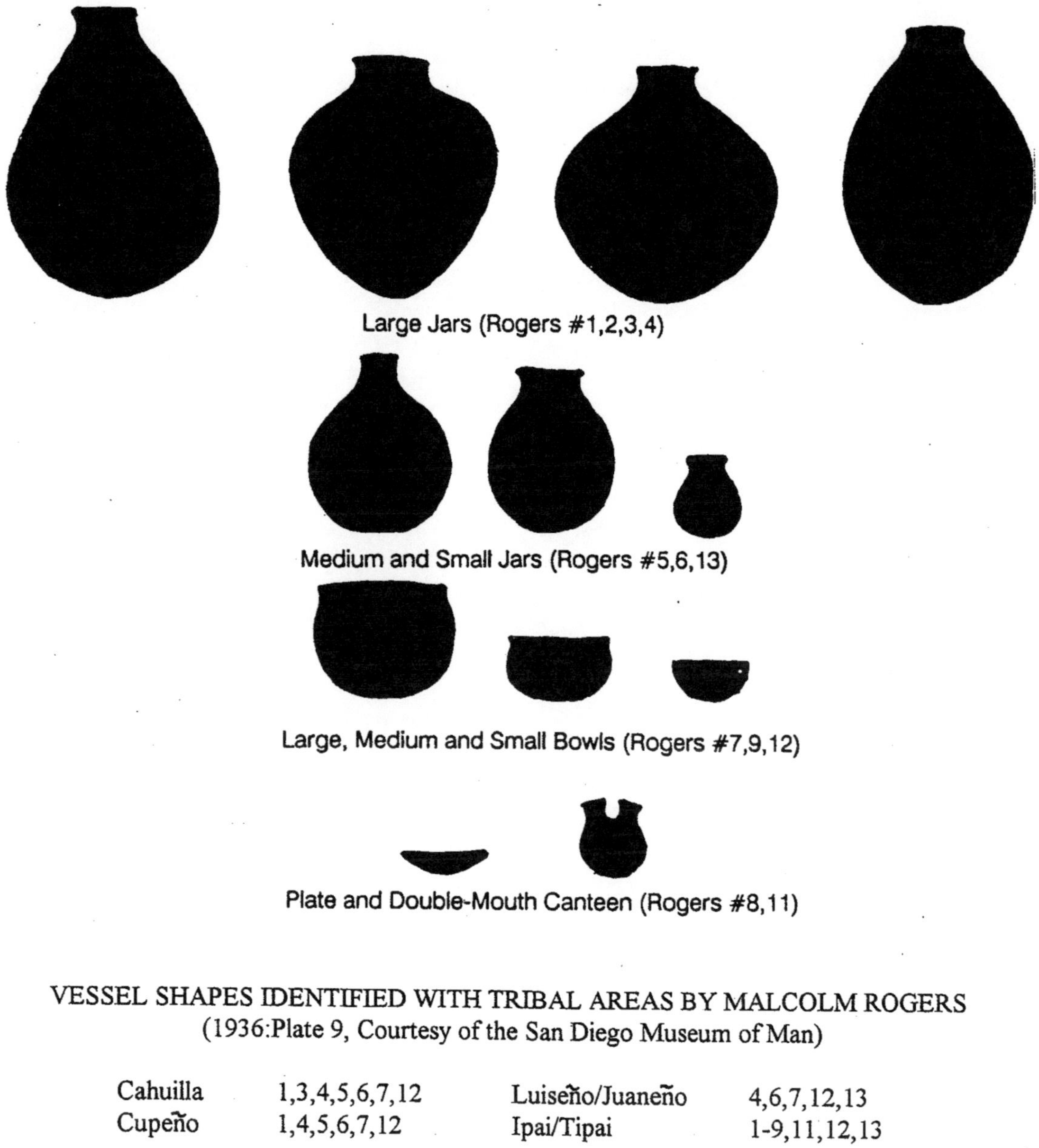

FIGURE 2.2. Compilation of Malcolm Rogers' southern California prehistoric vessel shapes (Griset 1990:Figure 2, revised from Rogers 1936b:Plate 9).

to another is sometimes problematical (see Laylander, Chapter 11 this volume).

The typology used for the ABDSP whole vessel examination is a combination of previous typologies and types that appear best suited to the ceramics found in ABDSP (Griset 2017:Appendix E).

Vessel Forms and Functions

Two primary vessel forms occur throughout southern California: Jars (often interchangeably referred to by the Spanish term "olla") and bowls. These were made in a range of sizes and shapes. For this study, vessels were classified as jars when their rim diameter:height ratio was <1:1, and as bowls when the ratios were 1:1 or >1:1. Within these two forms, there are further discriminations of shape based on the rim shape, vessel aperture size, and vessel size classes.

The size classes (miniature, small, medium, large, and extra-large), are based on distributions observed in other prehistoric southern California ceramic assemblages and on ethnographic evidence (Griset 1996, 2012; Rogers 1936; Waters 1982a). Figure 2.2 is a compilation of Malcolm Rogers's 1936 summary of Southern California vessel shapes (Rogers 1936). The vessel form typology used in this study is described below and includes ethnographic examples of the functions of each form class.

Jars

Narrow mouth (NM) jars have rim diameters of 6.0 cm or less; medium-wide mouth (MWM) rim diameters are >6–12 cm; and wide mouth (WM) diameters are >12 cm.

Functions for these size classes are drawn from the ethnographic literature for southern California and from archaeological examples of vessels with contents or residues, as well as comparisons with worldwide ethnographic samples (Griset 1996). Small NM jars were generally used as personal canteens or small storage jars. Medium NM jars were used to transport contents, especially water or seeds. Large NM jars were quite heavy when filled and usually served as fixed storage vessels cached among boulder outcrops, distant from residential sites.

Medium-wide mouth (MWM) jars permit easier access while still restricting the contents; most are medium- to large-size and were used for short-term transport (especially water jars) or storage, but small versions were also used to boil tinctures. Medium and large versions were used to store or process foods and other items such as ceremonial regalia or cremated human remains. They could be covered with an everted bowl, animal hide, a large flat boulder, or a large potsherd that could be affixed with an adhesive.

Wide mouth (WM) jars provide the easiest access; large WM jars were often used as the water jar at the residence and were filled with water transported by NM or MW jars. When cached distant from the home, they could store large quantities of foodstuffs or materials.

Water jars, both MWM and WM, were recycled as cooking pots when their pores became saturated with natural salts residues from water evaporation. WM jars, similar to large bowls, were also used to process other materials, such as soaking basketry fibers while weaving, or to prepare foods.

Bowls

Bowls were classified as miniature (<5 cm diameter), small (>5–10 cm rim diameter), medium (>10–20 cm diameter and <15 cm height), large (>20 cm diameter and >15 cm height), and extra-large (>30 cm diameter and >15 cm height). When appropriate, bowls were additionally designated as shallow, elliptical, or hemispherical. Special note was also made of bowls with undulating rims, as this is a common form in the California Desert. Large shallow bowls served as trays. Teardrop-shape bowls are designated as "scoops" and resemble the shape of bisected gourds used to dip water or other materials out of bowls.

Bowls were primarily used to serve food, process other materials, hold tobacco for ceremonies, and also to cover jars. The size suited the number of people being or the quantity of goods being processed. Occasionally, large jar sherds (from the base or wall of a large jar) were ground and recycled as shallow bowls.

Miniatures

There is conflicting evidence whether miniature jars and bowls were toys, funerary offerings, children's attempts to mimic their female relatives' potting, or a combination of uses (Griset 2012). They are generally hand-modeled, not shaped by paddle-and-anvil, and often low-fired, suggesting they may have been made and fired in the cooking fire rather than a pottery firing pit. Incipient ceramic traditions often include "baked clay" forms that are hand-modeled, low-fired, and not a true "ceramic" vessel capable of repeated heating and cooling cycles.

Other Forms

Several other vessel forms were produced in limited numbers and include an elliptical scoop (similar in shape to scoops made from split gourds) and rare effigy pots, found principally in the Colorado Desert.

According E. H. Davis's 1935 manuscript on Indian basketry and pottery, a small, double mouth olla was used to transport water and could be suspended by threading a buckskin thong through both mouths. His drawing shows a round-bottom vessel with two direct, small diameter mouths. This aboriginal vessel form was modified by early twentieth century potters to make it more attractive to a non-native audience. The base of the vessel was flattened so that it could sit on a shelf, the two spouts were enlarged greatly, and red designs such as butterflies and flowers were painted on the exterior; it became a decorative collector's piece rather than a utilitarian piece of pottery.

Historic Forms

Many of the prehistoric vessel forms continued to be made until the early twentieth century; some were modified to suit modern conditions and to reach a non-native market. Prehistoric pots had rounded or conical/pointed bases because they were used on uneven surfaces. When used for cooking, they were inserted base first on their sides into the coals of a fire or placed on cobble trivets above the fire. Flat bases, handles, and thicker vessel walls typify vessels made in the late nineteenth/early twentieth century (Griset 1990).

Ceramic Assemblage

Ceramic analysts often try to reconstruct the ceramic assemblage produced and used at an individual site and extrapolate from that to the larger cultural group. The number of different vessel shapes and sizes can suggest possible activities and estimated family/group size based on vessel size; however, pots made and used by mobile groups were also used away from the residence and left (cached) in distant gathering sites, along trails, or cached in secret locations. As might be expected, the cached vessels are usually different from those found in residential contexts. Cached vessels tend to be larger jars used to store food, supplies, or ceremonial regalia. Some have suggested that jars were used to store water, but given the porous nature of southern California pottery, water would have quickly evaporated (see Griset 1996:Appendix D). Cached vessels also may include cremations.

Within residential sites, the primary vessels are medium size, WM jars used to cook foods and to transport water; large WM jars to store water in residences; and bowls for cooking, serving, or processing materials. Sometimes jars and bowls were reused to store cremated human remains in a cemetery area associated with larger residential sites. Individual sherds from broken vessels were often reused; they were ground and shaped into tools such as scrapers and disk vessel covers, or game pieces, and rarely, pendants.

Ceramics found in residential contexts are usually sherds that have been trampled to less than 2–3 cm in size; few whole vessels are found within residential middens. In contrast, whole vessels are generally found cached at some distance from residential sites, or stashed near temporary campsites beneath boulders, near bedrock mortars, in rock shelters, along trails, or hidden in vegetation. This pattern holds true in the desert as well as in the cismontane regions.

Results of the ABDSP Whole Vessel Documentation

The results of the analysis are discussed below by the following topics: composition of the collection by vessel form, types of locations where vessels were cached or collected and their physical distribution by form and ceramic type, which vessel forms by ceramic type were found together, types of decoration and repair, contents and residues found in the collection, new radiocarbon dates, and a discussion of the chronological implications from the vessels in this collection.

Composition of the Sample

The documented ABDSP whole vessel collection consists of 75 jars and 17 bowls for a total of 92 vessels. Most of the whole vessels were found by state employees or by ABDSP visitors while hiking in the canyons or camping in campgrounds. Several were found by fire crews after an area burned (622-1-19, 622-1-20, 622-1-1014); their surface color may have been affected by the fire, leaving it with new carbon deposits or oxidized areas depending on the temperature of the fire and the fuel present near the pot.

Table 2.1. Distribution of Whole Vessels by General Locale

General Locale	Jars	Bowls	Totals
Cached	53 (71.6%)	7 (41.2%)	59 (65%)
Unknown	21 (28.4%)	10 (58.8%)	32 (35%)
Totals	74 (100%)	17 (100%)	91 (100%)

One vessel in the collection, 622-023-0001b, is a heavy double-spouted, flat-bottomed canteen with red-painted rims, reported as being from Ramona. It has no additional provenience data. The flat bottom, the type of decoration, and the general shape suggest that it was likely made in the early twentieth century when similar vessels were being made for sale to non-natives. It was documented but excluded from the following analyses of 91 vessels.

The sample comprised 74 jars (82% of the total sample) and 17 bowls (18%); no scoops were curated among the whole vessel collection. As seen in Table 2.1, 65% of the vessels were recovered from a variety of cached contexts; 35% were from unknown or unreported contexts and simply noted as being from a specific drainage or area.

Nearly three-quarters of the jars were cached, and it is likely that this number is higher as many vessels from unidentified contexts contained evidence of pack rats having used the vessel, which suggests the vessel was hidden in some manner. The pattern is reversed for bowls—only 41% were cached, and two of these were cached as covers over jars. Bowls are but one type of lid for cached jars (other lids include baskets—see spec. 622-1-889; flat rocks; or shaped ceramic sherds), so it is not surprising that they are only about half as frequent as cached jars.

Assignment of site numbers to the vessels has been spotty (n = 38; 41.8%), even for those vessels with a fairly specific locale. Even spottier is the assignment of site type. Table 2.2 shows the distribution of vessel shapes by site type when mentioned in the accession records. For the purposes of this analysis, we identified residential (village) sites, temporary campsites, rock shelters (includes caves), boulders (and crevices), along a trail, among dunes, and unknown. Unfortunately, the ABDSP site record database does not uniformly include site type. When this information becomes available as sites are revisited and site records updated, it will be possible to use GIS to examine the distribution of vessels with point-specific locations and designate a location for general regional distributions.

As predicted, most of the vessels in the sample were found cached away from residential sites. In some cases, they were cached in boulders or crevices near campsites or bedrock mortars.

A few vessels were photographed in situ (Figure 2.3). Many collectors remarked that the vessels had been hidden; however, in several cases, the jar was found sitting on the ground or in vegetation but was not visible from the adjacent trail. In one case, the vessel may have rolled from its original cache spot or the vegetation significantly changed over the past hundreds of years, as the vessel was found out in the open.

TABLE 2.2. Distribution of Whole Vessels with Recorded Site Type

Site Type (per catalog card)	Jars	Bowls	Totals
Residential Village	1	—	1 (1.2%)
Campsite	4	—	4 (4.1%)
Cache-Rock shelter	14	3	17 (18.7%)
Cache-Amongst Boulders	21	3	23 (25.2%)
Cache-Generic	10	1	11 (12.1%)
Cache-Along trail	3	—	3 (3.3%)
Among Dunes	4	1	5 (5.5%)
Unknown	17	9	26 (28.6%)
Totals	74	17	91 (100%)

FIGURE 2.3. Vessels in situ: at top, extra-large medium-wide mouth Colorado Red-on-buff storage olla (#622-1-182) found with basket covering mouth, in Carrizo Badlands mudflats; at bottom, Plum Canyon large medium-wide mouth San Diego Brown storage olla, cached on side of steep ridge (behind green agave).

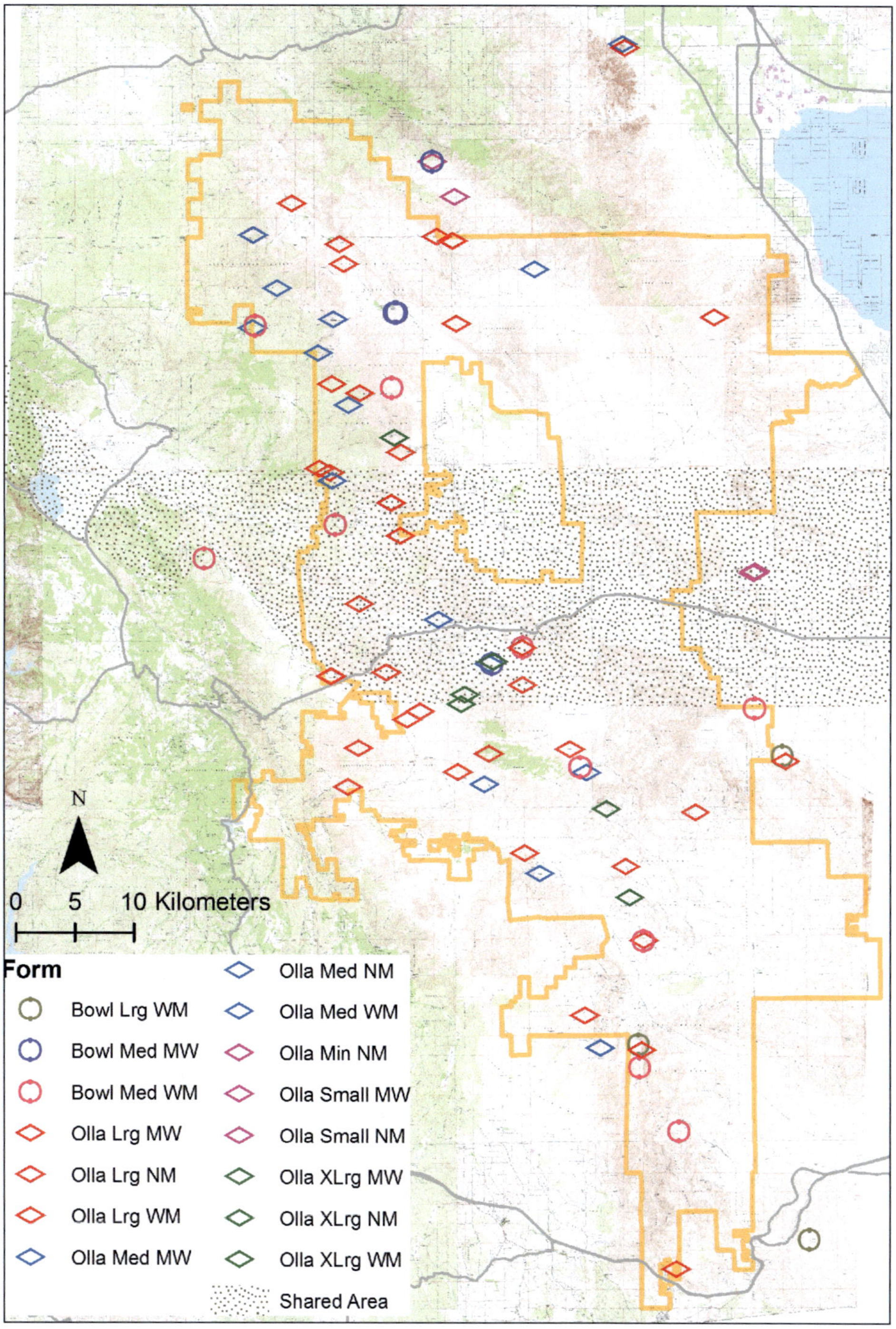

FIGURE 2.4. Map showing distribution of Anza Borrego Desert State Park whole vessel forms; stippled area indicates area shared by Cahuilla (to the north) and Kumeyaay (to the south).

Distribution by Form and Ceramic Type

The sample was fairly random in that only whole or nearly whole vessels were examined, and only those with at least a regional provenience were included in the sample. The distributions of vessel forms and ceramic types are provided in Figures 2.4 and 2.5. As might be expected, the brownware types plot closer to the transverse ranges, while the buff types are to the east, in the Salton Basin.

Table 2.3 lists the distribution of bowls by form, size, and identified ceramic type and ware. Bowls were recovered in medium and large sizes; no miniature, small, or extra-large bowls were among the sample. Apertures

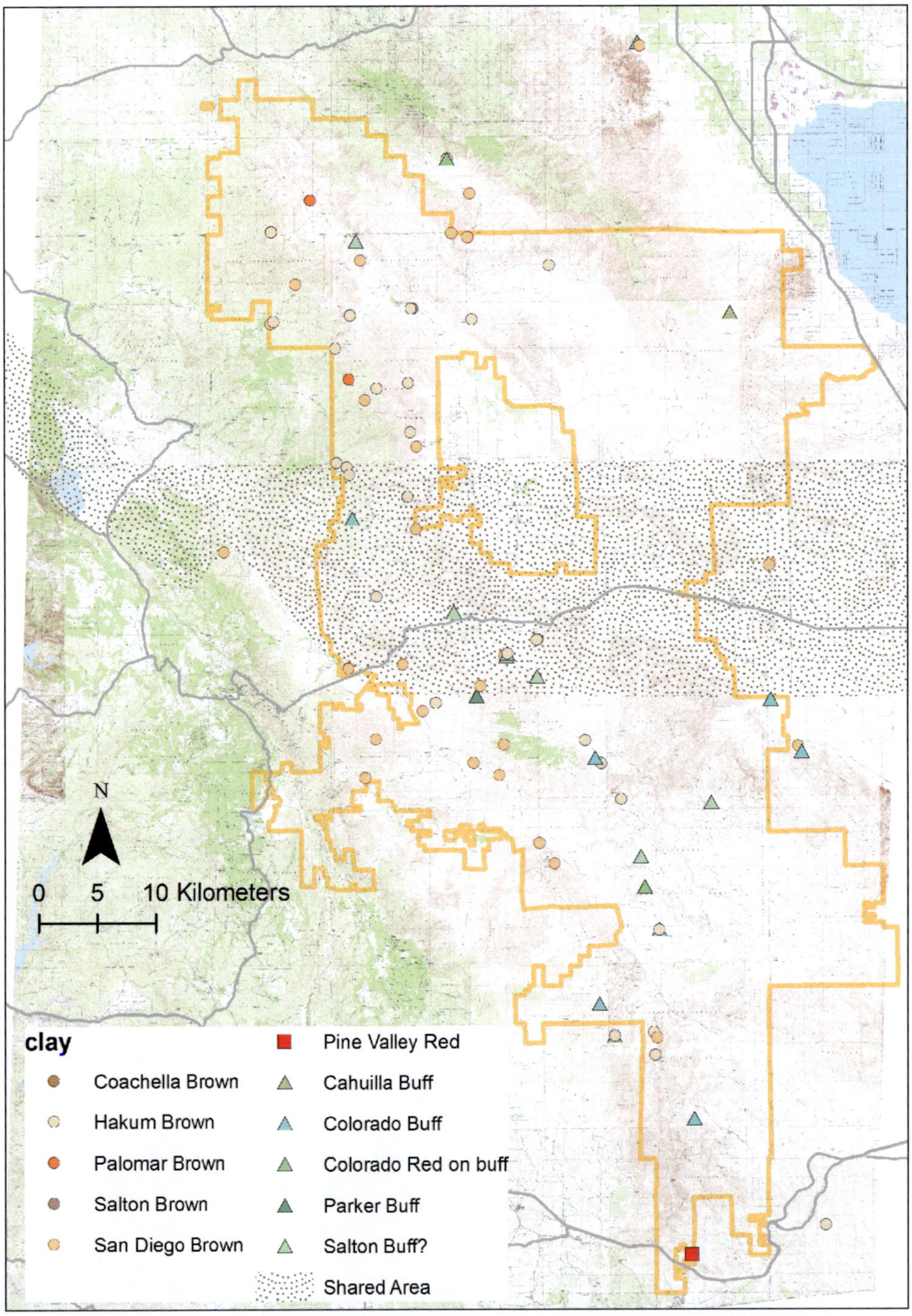

FIGURE 2.5. Map showing distribution of Anza Borrego Desert State Park vessels by pottery type; stippled area indicates area shared by Cahuilla (to the north) and Kumeyaay (to the south).

were MWM or WM. Medium-sized bowls constitute 82.3% of the bowls; over half of the sample consisted of medium size, WM bowls. Only six ceramic types were identified with Hakum Brown the predominant type (n = 7), followed by Colorado Buff and its decorated version, Colorado Red-on-buff (n = 5). All of these types were made in the southern portion of the Colorado Desert with the browns originating in the mountains to the west, Colorado Buff along the river to the east, and the Salton types in between.

Table 2.4 presents similar data for jars. A total of 71 jars were assigned a ceramic type, and all were coded for their vessel form. Two additional vessels not included in Table 2.7 are miniatures ollas: one was typed as a San Diego Brown miniature NM jar and the other as likely NM miniature jar from the Santa Rosa Mountains.

TABLE 2.3. Distribution of Bowl Forms and Size by Ceramic Type and Ware

Ceramic Ware and Type		Medium Bowls		Large Bowls		Totals by	Totals by
Ware	Type	MWM	WM	MWM	WM	type # (%)	ware # (%)
SCBW							10 (58.8)
	San Diego Brown	1	1	—	1	3 (17.6)	
	Hakum Brown	1	4	—	2	7 (41.2)	
CDIBW							1 (5.9)
	Salton Brown	1	—	—	—	1 (5.9)	
LCBW							6 (35.3)
	Salton Buff	1				1 (5.9)	
	Colorado Buff	—	4	—	—	4 (23.5)	
	Colorado Red-on-buff	1	—	—	—	1 (5.9)	
Totals # (%)		5 (29.4)	9 (52.9)	—	3 (17.6)	17 (100)	17 (100)

TABLE 2.4. Distribution of Jar Forms and Sizes by Ceramic Type and Ware

	Small Jars			Medium Jars			Large Jars			Extra-large Jars			Totals			Totals
Ceramic Type	NM	MWM	WM	NM	MWM	WM	NM	MWM	WM	NM	MWM	WM	NM	MWM	WM	by Ware and Type
SCBW																54 (76%)
Palomar Brown	—	—	—	—	—	—	—	1	—	—	—	—	—	1	—	1
San Diego Brown	1	2	—	1	1	2	—	9	9	—	—	1	2	12	12	26
San Diego Red-on-brown	—	—	—	—	—	2	—	—	—	—	—	—	—	—	2	2
Hakum Brown	—	—	—	1	4	4	—	8	4	—	1	2	1	13	10	24
Hakum Red-on-brown	1	—	—	—	—	—	—	—	—	—	—	—	1	—	—	1
CDIBW																3 (4%)
Salton Brown	—	—	—	—	—	—	—	—	—	—	—	—	—	—		—
Pine Valley Red	—	—	—	—	—	—	—	2	—	—	—	—	—	2	—	2
Coachella Brown	—	—	—	—	—	—	—	1	—	—	—	—	—	1	—	1
LCBW																14 (20%)
Cahuilla Buff	—	—	—	1	—	—	—	—	—	—	—	—	1	—	—	1
Salton Buff?	—	—	—	1	—	—	—	4	—	—	—	—	1	4	—	5
Colorado Buff	—	—	—	—	1	—	2	1	1	—	—	1	2	2	2	6
Colorado Red-on-buff	—	—	—	—	—	—	—	1	—	—	—	—	—	1	—	1
Parker Buff	—	—	—	—	—	—	1	—	—	—	—	—	1	—	—	1
Totals # (%)	2	2	—	4	6	8	3	27	14	—	1	4	9	36	26	71 (100%)

Not unexpectedly, three-fourths (76%) of the jars were classified as SCB: 28 jars (52%) were San Diego Brown (including two red-decorated) and 26 (48%) were Hakum Brown (including one red-decorated), which indicates that the clay sources are located in the mountains to the west and southwest. Only one jar was identified as Palomar Brown, suggesting a deciduous clay from the general area of Palomar Mountain to the northwest. Twenty percent of the jars are LCBW; only 4% were identified as made from intermediary clays.

By far, large jars are the most numerous jar size class at 62% of the jars, and they constitute more than double the next numerous size, medium-size jars at 25%. Extra-large jars represent 7% of the assemblage, and small jars

TABLE 2.5. Distribution of Cached Jars by Aperture and Size

Narrow Mouth				Medium-wide Mouth				Wide Mouth			
Small	Medium	Large	X-Large	Small	Medium	Large	X-Large	Small	Medium	Large	X-Large
1	2	1	1	1	6	20	1	—	8	6	3
5 (10%)				28 (56%)				17 (34%)			

constitute 5%. MWM jars dominate the sample at 50% of the jar apertures; WM jars constitute 37% of the assemblage; and NM jars account for 13%.

If examining only those jars known to have been cached, 48 jars constitute 87% of the 55 cached vessels, with the most numerous form by far, the large size, MWM jar (Table 2.5). The extra-large jars of any size aperture would have been very heavy when full, and likely remained in place once they had been cached. They could have been filled and refilled multiple times, providing long-term storage in a fixed place. The width of the opening likely corresponded to the size of the materials stored in them and the need for easy or restricted access to those materials.

In contrast, the most numerous form, the large size MWM jar (aperture of 6–12 cm) would likely have been transportable using a tumpline and carrying net, and was easily filled and emptied, yet could be sealed to protect the contents between uses. This would be an ideal form for storing prepared pieces of agave, mesquite pods, piñon and acorn nuts, basketry materials, regalia, etc.

Interestingly, few NM jars were recovered. This is the form most likely used to store small-sized contents such as seeds and grains. Others have argued they were used to cache water; however, the results of evaporation experiments suggest that these porous vessels retain water for no more than a few days (Griset 1996:Appendix D). Only three vessels could be interpreted as canteens for transporting water, or, when cached, storing small-sized contents. Davis (1928) reported that the large narrow mouthed ollas were used historically to store grains or seeds such as mesquite and piñon.

Upright Versus Not

One of the attributes noted during the analysis was whether the vessel sat upright or leaned. Upright is designated as 90°, and a deviation to the left of 90° was measured using a protractor. Jars are particularly susceptible to being made off-center, and this is likely an intended trait, even in vessels that are symmetrical in all other aspects. To measure the orientation, the vessel was placed in an upright position, then the supporting hands slowly removed (but kept near) while the vessel sought its natural resting point. Many of the vessels had physical restrictions that precluded measuring whether they were upright—they were cracked, fragile, or missing the original portions that constituted their original resting point. None of the extra-large vessels were measured as they were too unwieldy, although based on their shape, it is likely a good guess that none rests upright.

Table 2.6 shows the distribution of degrees of variation from upright, by jar size and aperture. Thirty of the 45 vessels (two-thirds of the sample) for which measurements are available, are large size. Twenty-one percent of the 45 vessels rest upright, 37% cluster between 110° and 115°, and six jars (13%) cluster at 130° to 145°. Two pots found together in Hell Hole Canyon (622-1-014 and 622-1-015) lay on their sides at 180°; they may be pots made by a single potter and were designed specifically to rest in this manner. One additional medium size, MWM jar (622-1-870) from Rockhouse Basin (not shown in the chart) rests at 240° on the shoulder of the vessel, which is a very unusual orientation.

Distribution by Specific Locale

Figure 2.4 provides a generalized plot of the locations of the vessel forms. Given the randomized nature of the sample due to the criteria of reconstructible dimensions and recorded provenience, the distributions on the map fit the expected pattern of vessels cached along the edge of the Transverse Range, with occasional vessels found on the flats between the mountains and Lake Cahuilla. When more detailed information is available about each of the recovery locations, GIS can be used for finer comparisons of ceramic type, vessel shape and size, contrasted with other factors such as trail systems, distance to water, vegetation types, etc.

Vessels Co-Located

In 17 instances, two or more vessels were found together (Table 2.7). Bowls were found in seven instances (a little more than one-third of the total): in one instance, two bowls co-occurred; and in the other six cases, one bowl occurred with one jar. Generally, the co-occurrences include a mixture of vessel forms and types, even in the same cache. In most cases (13 out of 17, or 76.4%), the vessels also represent a mixture of functions.

In more than half of the instances (10 of 17, or 58.8%), the vessel ceramic types are different within a single cache. Whether these vessels were deposited by the

Table 2.6. Degrees of Variation from Upright (90°) for Measurable ABDSP Jars

	Narrow Mouth			Medium-wide Mouth			Wide Mouth			
Degrees	Small	Medium	Large	Small	Medium	Large	Small	Medium	Large	Totals # (%)
90					3	1		4	2	10 (21)
95						1			2	3 (7)
100	1			1						2 (4)
105						2				2 (4)
110		1	1			3		1	2	8 (17)
115				1	1	3		2	2	9 (20)
120						2			1	3 (7)
125										—
130									1	1 (2)
135									1	1 (2)
140					1	2				3 (7)
145						1				1 (2)
150										—
155										—
160										—
165										—
170						1				1 (2)
175										—
180						2				2 (4)
Totals	1	1	1	2	5	18	—	7	11	46 (100)

same person who had access to or made vessels from different clays, or less likely, were deposited by multiple individuals, is not something we can discern.

In seven instances, the clay sources are widely separated as the vessels are brown and buff types, perhaps indicating that the cache location was used to stash vessels as the same group passed through, going west to the mountains and coast, or returning east to the desert.

Decorated Vessels

Only seven, possibly six, of the 91 vessels (less than 9%) were decorated: seven had red painted designs on the vessel exterior; one had a diagonally incised lip (Table 2.8). All but one of the vessels are jars and two of those are extra-large jars, extremely heavy even when empty. The extra-large jars are the long-term storage vessels likely cached permanently; the others appear to be vessels cached for later use. Their functions include two canteens for water transport, two cooking pots, one serving jar, and one serving bowl. One of the medium WM cooking vessels was found near a pictograph and shows evidence of having been laid on its side and the bottom inserted in the fire. It may have served a ceremonial purpose.

The single example of a vessel with an incised design is a San Diego Brown extra-large WM storage vessel with seven lines incised diagonally across the lip of the rim.

Vessel Contents

Only a few of the cached vessels retained original contents; most had been converted to pack rat dens, any organic materials were consumed, and rat urine impregnated the vessel walls, making them unsuitable for residue analysis. Two exceptions include:

- 622-1-71/72: "small short reeds" tentatively identified as split galleta grass (*Pleuraphis Torr.*).
- 622-1-182/181: found lying on side with inverted basket cover, covered in mud, hole in basket, and unidentified grain inside. This vessel is on display in the Visitors Center in a sealed plexiglass display case and it is unknown whether it retains any of the "grain."

Thirteen vessels were noted during the analysis as having potential residues on interior surfaces that might be suitable for gas chromatography or other elemental analyses. The specimens with potential residues suitable for analyses are: 622-1-0012; 622-1-0017; 622-1-0019; 622-1-0020; 622-1-0100; 622-1-0117; 622-1-0122; 622-1-0185; 622-1-0887; 622-1-1048; 622-1-1051; 622-11-0001a; and 625-11-0001.

Vessel Repairs

Four methods of repairing cracked or missing pieces of vessels were observed on ten vessels (about 10% of the total examined; Table 2.9). Four vessels exhibited

Table 2.7. Vessels Cached Together

Specimen #s	Vessel Forms	Ceramic Type	Location	Function
622-1-0012	Bowl Lrg WM	Hakum Brown	Carrizo Gorge	Cooking
622-1-0013	Bowl Med WM	Hakum Brown		Water?
622-1-0014	Jar Lrg MWM	Coachella Brown	Ridge Trail between Dry and Hell Hole Cyn	Storage
622-1-0015	Jar Lrg MWM	Hakum Brown		Storage
622-1-0017	Jar Med WM	Hakum Brown	Flat above Hapaha Flats	Cooking
622-1-0042	Bowl Med WM	Colorado Buff		Serving
622-1-0019	Jar Med WM	San Diego Red-on-br	Lost Valley	Cooking
622-1-0020	Bowl Med WM	Hakum Brown		Cooking
622-1-0071	Jar Lrg MWM	Hakum Brown	San Ysidro Mts	Storage
622-1-0072	Jar Lrg MWM	Hakum Brown		Cooking
622-1-0073	Jar Med NM	Hakum Brown		Storage
622-1-0100	Jar Med WM	Hakum Brown	Carrizo Cyn	Cooking
622-1-0101	Jar Med NM	Cahuilla Buff	Historic camp; pots cached nearby	Water transport (canteen with wire handle)
622-1-0114	Jar Lrg WM	Hakum Brown	Upper Alder Cyn	Water jar
622-1-0115	Jar Lrg MWM	San Diego Brown		Storage
622-1-0116	Jar Lrg MWM	San Diego Brown		Water jar
622-1-0117	Jar Small MWM	San Diego Brown		Serving
622-1-0119	Jar Lrg WM	Hakum Brown		Water jar/cooking
622-1-0120	Jar Lrg MWM	San Diego Brown		Storage
622-1-0122	Jar Med MWM	Hakum Brown		Cooking
622-1-0181	Basket bowl	Kumeyaay	Arroyo Hueso	Inverted over jar
622-1-0182	Jar XLrg MWM	Colorado Red-on-buff		Storage
622-1-0186	Jar Sm NM	Hakum Red-on-br	Rockhouse Cyn	Water transport (canteen)
622-1-0187	Bowl Med MWM	Colorado Red-on-buff		Serving
622-1-0789	Jar Lrg MWM	Hakum Brown	Sheep Cyn	Cooking
622-1-0790	Jar Med MWM	Hakum Brown		Storage
622-1-0831	Jar Lrg WM	Hakum Brown	Rockhouse Basin	Water storage/Cooking
622-1-0870	Jar Med MWM	Hakum Brown		Water transport/Storage
622-1-0867	Jar Lrg NM	Colorado Buff	Vallecito Creek	Water? storage
622-1-0868	Bowl Med WM	Hakum Brown		Serving
622-12-0001a	Jar Lrg WM	San Diego Brown	Butterfield Stage Sta spring	Water storage/Cooking
622-12-0001b	Jar Lrg MWM	San Diego Brown		Cooking
622-13-0001a	Bowl Lrg WM	San Diego Brown	Fish Cr Mts	Cooking
622-13-0001b	Jar Lrg WM	Colorado Buff		Water Storage?
622-25-0001h	Jar XLrg WM	Colorado Buff	Mine Wash Ridge; 2 caches near site	Storage
622-25-0001i	Jar XLrg WM	Hakum Brown		Storage
622-25-0001j	Jar Lrg WM	San Diego Brown	Rockhouse Cyn Ridge	Water transport/Storage
622-25-0001k	Jar Lrg WM	San Diego Brown		Water transport/Storage
622-27-0001a	Jar Med MWM	Colorado Buff	Fish Traps	Water transport
622-27-0001b	Jar Lrg WM	San Diego Brown		Water storage

TABLE 2.8. Decorated Vessels

Red Painted Designs			Incised
Hakum Red/Brown	San Diego Red/Brown	Colorado Red/Buff	San Diego Brown
Jar Small NM (canteen) (622-001-0186)[a]	Jar Med WM (cooking) (622-001-0185)	Jar XLrg MWM (storage) 622-001-0182)	Jar XLrg WM (storage) (622-34-0001a)
	Jar Med WM (cooking) (622-001-0020)	Bowl Med MWM (serving) (622-001-0187)[a]	
	Jar Small MWM (serving) (622-010-0001d)		
	Jar Small NM (canteen)[b] (622-010-0001e)		

[a] found together
[b] possibly decorated

TABLE 2.9. Vessel Repairs

Type of Repair	Specimen No.	Ceramic Ware	Ceramic Type	Vessel Form
Crack-lace Mending	622-1-1015	LCB	Salton Buff?	Olla Large MWM
	622-25-1d	LCB	Salton Buff?	Bowl Medium MWM
	622-25-1h	LCB	Colorado Buff	Olla XL WM
	622-25-1i	SCB	Hakum Brown	Olla XL WM
Crack-lace & Clay Patch	622-22-1a	SCB	San Diego Brown	Olla Large WM
	622-22-1a	SCB	San Diego Brown	Olla Large WM
Clay Patch	622-13-1a[a]	SCB	San Diego Brown	Bowl Large WM
Pitch along Crack	622-23-1a	SCB	Hakum Brown	Olla Large MWM
Neck Edge Ground to make Rim	622-20-4	LCB	Salton Buff?	Olla Large MWM
	622-28-1a	SCB	San Diego Brown	Olla Large MWM

[a] Information from catalog card; no longer present in bowl interior

crack-lace mending, where paired holes are drilled along either side of a crack, and a rawhide thong or strong fiber was strung through the holes and tied to hold the crack together. One bowl was reputed to have had clay "patches" over holes or cracks on its interior—the information was recorded on the catalog card; the patches are no longer extant in the vessel. Two vessels had both crack-lace and clay patches. One large olla had "pitch" (substance has not been tested to verify its contents) along a crack. Two ollas whose rim and upper neck had broken, had been reground at the middle of the neck (the aperture) to form a new rim.

Two of the ten vessels were bowls, one brown and one buff. Seven large jars (four with medium-wide mouths and two with wide mouths) had been repaired; and two extra-large jars, both with wide mouths, had crack-lace mending. The repairs occurred on four buff vessels and on six brown ware vessels: crack-lace mending and edge grinding were common to both wares. Clay patches and pitch were only found on brownwares; however, the sample size is small.

Chronology

Previous investigations of the chronology of ceramic use and manufacture throughout southern California were based first on relative dates (dates provided by associated datable artifacts); within the past 40 years, direct radiocarbon dating has been attempted on carbon residues on vessels. The general picture painted by both of these dating sources suggests that ceramics were in use as early as AD 900 and manufactured widely by AD 1400–1500 (Griset 1996).

Griset (1996) also submitted several sherds from Indian Hill Rock Shelter (CA-SDI-2537), one of the few ABDSP sites with deep cultural deposits, for radiocarbon dating. Two of the dates were run on a single sherd to test whether there were differences in the dates obtained from the interior surface versus the exterior of the sherd. If sherds are recovered from subsurface deposits that have not been subjected to repeated wildfires, then the interiors are thought to contain residues from burnt food materials, while exterior carbon derives from firewood that may include "old wood" collected from desert surfaces. In fact, the two surfaces of the sherd produced mean calibrated dates of AD 1105 on the vessel exterior and AD 1365 on the interior, a 263-year difference (Griset 1996:249). This is likely a prime example of the "old wood" problem identified by Schiffer (1986), especially in arid deserts where old wood could be used for campfires. This cautionary tale suggested that carbon deposits from sherd interiors were the most likely to produce dates associated with the use of the ceramic. The interior date of AD 1365 fits well within the other three directly dated ceramics from Indian Hill, which all fit between AD 1300 and 1400 dates (Griset 1996:255).

Excavated samples curated at BARC were examined as part of this research to obtain additional direct dates of ceramic usage. Unfortunately, excavated ceramic samples from ABDSP are few, and suitable specimens are even rarer. Three sherds with interior carbon deposits were submitted to Beta Analytic for radiocarbon Accelerator Mass Spectrometer (AMS) radiocarbon dating: (1) a sherd excavated from the 45.7–61.0 cm (18–24 in) level below ground surface in Unit M27 at Bow Willow #9, (CA-SDI-10573); (2) a sherd from a pot cached in Sheep Canyon that had been reconstructed and glued; and (3) loose dark colored residue collected from the inside of a vessel cached in Alcoholic Pass.

Only the Bow Willow sherd (Specimen P1571-31) was deemed suitable for analysis. Bow Willow #9 is a campsite located on a level bench above Bow Willow Wash, south-southeast of Mt. Laguna, and above the highest stand of Lake Cahuilla. The site was excavated in 1959 by Wallace who noted that the surface was "littered with potsherds, broken rock and stone artifacts" (Wallace 1962:2). The submitted sherd was from a small bowl, 10 cm diameter at the mouth and an estimated 9 cm high. It had a direct, rounded, undulating rim with a roughly smoothed exterior, cracks from the original drying of the paste, and a heat spall on the exterior of the bowl. The paste was micaceous with embedded carbon that was used as a bulk sample (the sherd was crushed and all carbon retained for the dating). It produced two dates—AD 905–920 and AD 965–025—calibrated at the first sigma. Interestingly, Wallace (1962:5) judged the site to have been occupied within the "closing phase of native occupation...from 1000 AD to modern times." The radiocarbon date suggests a slightly earlier use of pots in the earliest levels of the site. The micaceous clay was typed as Hakum Brown and suggests local manufacture of pottery at that time period.

Several of the vessels have attributes dating them to the Historic period. Some were recovered from sites identified as historic due to the presence of historical artifacts, for example 622-1-100. Another, specimen 622-1-101, from Rockhouse Canyon, is a buff canteen (medium NM olla) with bailing wire wrapped around the neck and extending in a loop to permit suspension of the vessel. Other vessels such as 622-1-114, a large WM jar from Upper Alder Canyon, or 622-25-001b, a medium WM bowl that was covering a large MWM jar (622-25-001c) cached in a cave above Pinyon Canyon, were noted as looking "unused," suggesting they either had not been well used or had been cached for a shorter period of time than many of the other vessels. Other vessels that are asymmetrical, thick-walled, and/or have semi-flattened bases permitting the vessel to sit upright, may also date to the Historic period (see discussion in Griset 1990).

Discussion

By selecting only those vessels with provenience data, we essentially randomized the sample of whole vessels in the ABDSP collection. As anticipated from previous examinations of museum collections, whole vessels tend to be found distant from village sites or camp sites, primarily in protected circumstances such as large boulders or rock shelters/caves, and occasionally among dunes and along trails. This must be kept in mind when trying to reconstruct the ceramic assemblage—vessels at residential sites have been trampled and vessel form is often difficult to reconstruct, especially when projected from a recurved rim that could belong to a bowl or jar of unknown size. One would expect more cooking jars and serving bowls at residences, and fewer storage vessels.

Eighty-two percent of cached vessels are jars; bowls represent only 18% of the sample and most were found as lids for the jars. Surprisingly, NM jars represent only 10% of the sample; the vast majority (56%) have medium-wide mouths, and 34% have wide mouths. All three aperture sizes include extra-large jars, though the majority are WM. This suggests long-term placement of a "granary" within a resource area, to which the contents can be added and subtracted, as needed. Decorated jars are few, and surprisingly, the two largest vessels are heavily decorated with red paint.

Fifty-nine percent of the bowls are SCBW and all large bowls are SCBW. CDIBW accounts for 6% of the bowls; 35% are LCBW, with five of those six LCBW bowls typed as Colorado Buff. Most bowls (over 82%) are medium size with 53% WM and 29% MWM. Four medium size WM bowls are Hakum Brown; four are Colorado Buff.

The typological analysis demonstrates a clear predominance of SCBW (76% of the whole vessels) over CDIBW and LCBW. The SCBW constitutes 76% of the jars and is nearly evenly divided between San Diego Brown and Hakum Brown, both made of clays from the

Transverse Range west and southwest of ABDSP. Surprisingly, CDIBW represents only 4% of the sample, while LCBW represents 20%. The LCBW includes two vessels from distant areas along the Colorado River—a Colorado Red-on-buff (the extra-large WM jar) and a Parker Buff.

Cracked vessels were repaired with crack-lace mending, clay patches fired over the hole, or application of a "pitch" to seal the crack. The repairs occurred on four buff vessels and on six brownware vessels. Crack-lace mending and edge grinding were common to both wares; clay patches and pitch were only found on brownwares. Two broken recurved rim vessels were reground so that the middle of the "neck" aperture became the new rim.

Residue analysis is problematical due to the presence of rat urine and feces in cached vessels. Curated vessels have undergone a number of processes that may also affect their suitability for residue analysis, for example, the interiors have been washed and a variety of adhesives used for repairs. Residues may yet be present in vessel walls, but curators tend to frown on compromising intact vessels. Hopefully new techniques will work around these issues.

Although several vessels were identified as potential sources of carbonized materials for radiocarbon dating, the single date obtained during the whole vessel collection was run on a sherd from the Bow Willow Canyon #9 archaeological site (CA-SDI-10573), which lacked whole vessels. Two dates—AD 905–920 and AD 965–1025, calibrated at the first sigma—were obtained on the sherd. Dates obtained previously from another ABDSP archaeological site, Indian Hill Rock Shelter (CA-SDI-2537), produced a date of AD 1365. Both of these dates fit within the pattern observed previously (Griset 1996): that ceramics were in use as early as AD 900 and manufactured widely by AD 1400–1500.

Future research using the whole vessels will hopefully build on this initial investigation. GIS analysis of correlations of vessels with specific vegetation plots, site types, and landforms must await completion of the ABDSP site record database. Site type definitions need to be standardized and all site forms reviewed to ensure that resources with similar attributes are coded consistently in the database.

Another research topic suggested by the current study is more detailed characterization of SCBW Hakum Brown type. When looking at the distribution of ceramic types (see Figure 2.5), an immediately apparent pattern is the widespread distribution of Hakum Brown vessels. Since all highly micaceous vessels were typed as Hakum, this may be an erroneous pattern, particularly in light of the micaceous residual clays still used in the Santa Rosa Mountains, to the north of ABDSP in Cahuilla territory. Were the micaceous pots found in the northern portion of ABDSP part of the same pottery tradition as the southern micaceous pots made in Kumeyaay territory in the Late Prehistoric period? Can XRF or INAA, coupled with petrographic thin sectioning discriminate between multiple clay sources along the transverse range? Preliminary tests using portable XRF were conducted under a previous Begole grant (Quinn and Burton 2008, 2009; Quinn et al. 2013); this investigation should be expanded systematically along the western border of ABDSP.

Acknowledgments

My thanks to the Robert Begole Archaeological Research Fund for supporting this research with grants in 2011 and 2012. This research also benefitted greatly from the unstinting contributions of several key individuals: Joan Schneider encouraged me to apply for the funds and shared her knowledge of the collection and of ABDSP's archaeological resources. Astrid Webb volunteered many hours and assisted me in understanding how the collection and documentation are organized and stored; she became my assistant in recording data and enabled the research to continue despite the retirement and loss of curators and archaeologists during the analysis period. Sue Wade, former ABDSP archaeologist and herself a recognized southern California ceramic analyst, shared her knowledge of the collection, the archaeology, and the data gaps. L. Louise Jee greatly assisted in organizing the GIS data and helping me to understand its current limits. Sam Webb shared photography expertise and regional knowledge. Chuck Bennett, Carol Black, and Susan Gilliland were unfailingly supportive and interested in ceramic analysis. The project report, data, and photographs are curated at the Anza Borrego Desert State Park's Begole Archaeological Research Center in Borrego Springs.

3 Patayan Transport of Hohokam Ceramics to the Colorado Desert, California

Jerry Schaefer

A small number of Hohokam ceramic scatters and other ceramic finds in the Colorado Desert, California, bear witness to the geographical extent of Patayan/Hohokam interaction in the far Southwest. Face-to-face interaction, and sometimes cohabitation around Gila Bend, the Papaquería, and further east in the Salt-Gila Basin were opportunities for ceramic exchange and, with that, the transport of Hohokam ceramics across the Colorado River to southern California. In several cases, their landscape and archaeological contexts suggest agency instead of accident. Hohokam artifacts appear to have been prized to the extent that they reached late prehistoric sites on the California coast and Channel Islands.

A Hohokam Ceramic Scatter at CA-IMP-8293

The detailed analysis and dating of a rare Sacaton Red-on-buff ceramic scatter at site CA-IMP-8293 on East Mesa, Imperial County, California, highlights the fact that the Patayan/Hohokam interaction sphere extended far west of the Hohokam homeland. This interaction sphere was most active and far-reaching in the Colonial and Sedentary periods of Hohokam expansion between AD 800 and 1150 (Ahlstrom and Roberts 2002; Doyel 2008; Fish 1989). By the beginning of the Classic Period (AD 1150–1450), there was a geographical retreat of the Hohokam from the Gila Bend area—their western territorial.

Hohokam ceramics may have been symbols of prestige or status for the Patayan bearer, denoting their access to rare trade goods or wider cultural contacts. The small number of ceramic finds occurring without other associated Hohokam artifact types, rock art, or archaeological features suggests that Hohokam ceramics reached the Colorado Desert through trade, travel, and direct cultural contacts in Arizona. These ceramic finds were not likely from the travel or migration of Hohokam people themselves in any great numbers, as no distinctive Hohokam assemblages or cultural features have been found in California. Hohokam ceramics and other artifact types do appear at habitation sites as far west as Orange and Los Angeles counties and the Channel Islands, where trade in such items as shell beads and soapstone was important. Hohokam artifacts, rarity suggests they had prestige value in California.

One of the only Hohokam ceramic scatters to be studied in detail and within the context of the surrounding East Mesa archaeological landscape is CA-IMP-8293. A total of 50 sherds from a single jar were recovered although only 10% of the vessel was likely represented in the scatter. All were body sherds, with no rim sherds present. A total of 27 sherds derived from a 15 m^2 surface area. A surface scrape of a larger area to a depth of 10 cm followed the subsurface distribution of sherds until no more were found, producing another 23 sherds, and including five red-on-buff painted sherds in unmistakable Hohokam style (Figure 3.1). No evidence of a Gila shoulder was found among the recovered sherds.

The ceramic paste contains abundant, well-sorted, angular quartz and feldspar grains, calcium carbonate, and smaller amounts of biotite, some of which were attached to quartz grains. These mineral constituents bear some of the hallmarks characterizing Hohokam Red-on-buff ceramic types. The sherds, however, have none of the compositional or surface characteristics of crushed

FIGURE 3.1. Painted sherds from a Sacaton Red-on-buff vessel at CA-IMP-8293.

mica or schist tempering that might indicate a more eastern Hohokam origination, in the Salt-Gila or Tucson basins. By the time of the Early-Middle Sacaton Phase of the Sedentary Period (AD 950–1150), Hohokam ceramics were made by specialists for local and long-distance markets (Abbott 2000, 2008, 2009). Crushed mica and schist tempering was almost universal, although some local variations do occur. More likely, this vessel was made from clays in the Lower Gila River area near Gila Bend or some other outlying area of Hohokam culture, and without the addition of crushed mica or schist.

With regard to surface decoration, the integrated interlocking scrolls and opposing thick serrated lines probably covered the entirety of the upper portion of the large vessel exterior. Unpainted sherds with the same fabric at CA-IMP-8293 suggest that the base or lower body was undecorated. The painted design motif differs markedly from prehistoric Patayan ceramic decoration, which usually includes widely dispersed or vertically arranged, simply drawn, geometric elements. Only in the ethnohistoric Patayan III phase on the Colorado River are ceramic decorations found to be organized as integrated design elements across the entirety of the vessel surface, but none of the published examples in any way resembles the sherds from CA-IMP-8293 (Kroeber and Harner 1955; Waters 1982b). In fact, opposing serrated line design elements do occur rarely on Patayan ceramics, but interlocking scrolls have never been recorded (Waters 1982b). Both elements often occur together on Hohokam jars, usually covering the entire surface (Amsden 1938). Closest to East Mesa, this motif is found in profusion on Gila Butte Red-on-buff (Colonial Period: AD 550–900) and Sacaton Red-on-buff vessels (Sedentary Period: AD 900–1110) at sites around Painted Rocks Reservoir and Gila Bend, some 206 km east of Yuma (Wasley and Johnson 1965).

The well-executed 4 mm line work and thick opposing serrated line elements also conform better to Sacaton Red-on-buff, specifically Early-Middle Sacaton Phase (AD 950–1050; Aaron Wright and Henry Wallace, personal communication 2016). Such a designation would place the CA-IMP-8293 find within the time range of the other Patayan ceramic scatters found in the All American Canal (AAC) project area (see Chapter 1, this volume). Optically Stimulated Luminescence (OSL) dating, however, yielded a date of AD 670±130 years (Feathers 2016), spanning the Pioneer and Colonial periods and ostensibly placing the ceramic too early for the style. This is the oldest OSL date among 11 samples from the AAC project, the others all being Lower Colorado Buff Ware types. If the date is correct, hardly a certainty, then perhaps an attribution as Gila Butte Red-on-buff or Santa

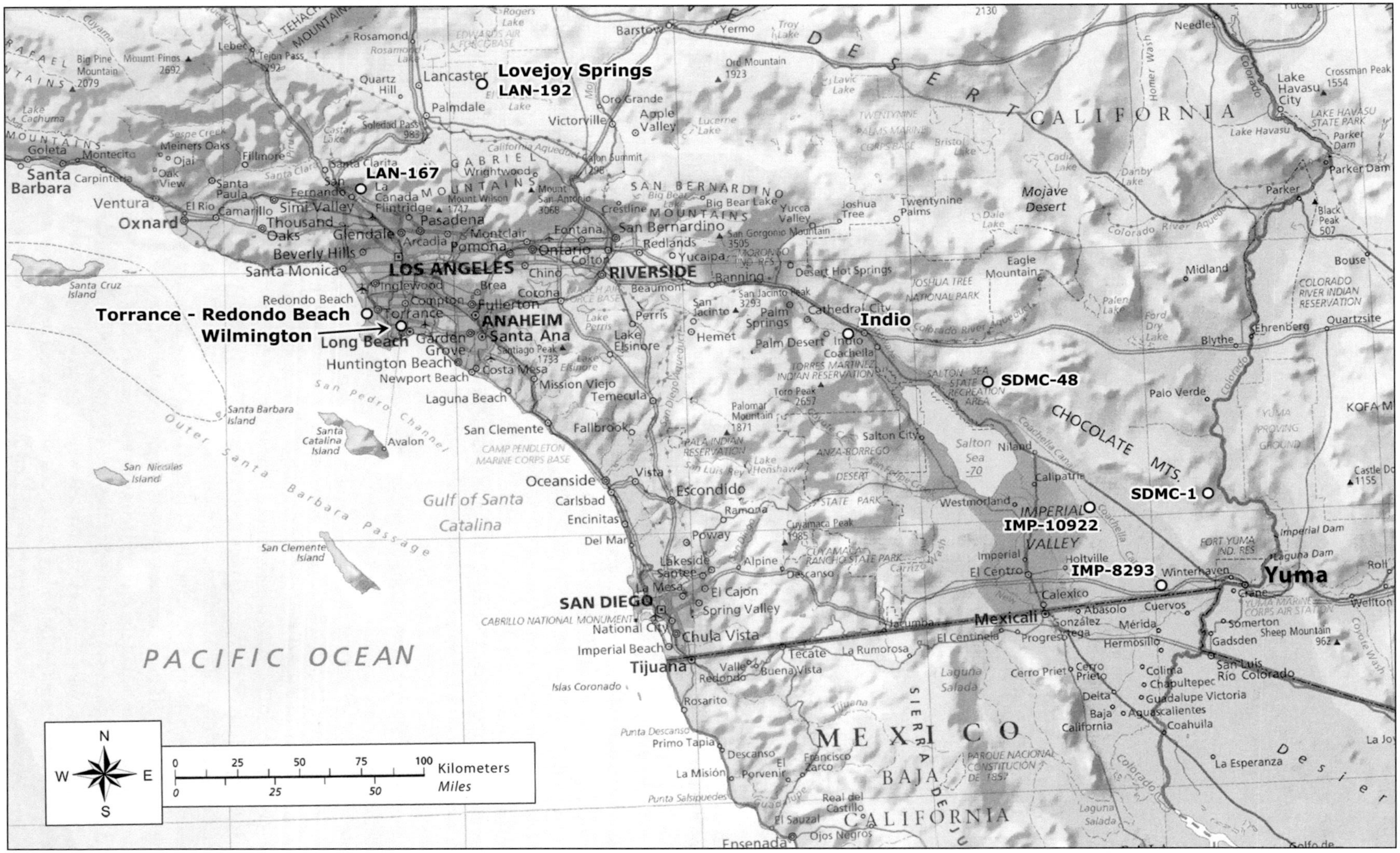

FIGURE 3.2. Location of reported Hohokam ceramic scatters in southern California.

Cruz Red-on-buff would be more appropriate, although I am reluctant to attribute a stylistic type based solely on an OSL date. The sherds also lack the very thin side walls that characterize Santa Cruz Red-on-buff. Therefore, Sacaton Red-on-buff would appear to be the most convincing type attribution based on stylistic elements (Wallace 2001, 2004). The similarity between these two types has led Ahlstrom (2008) among others to consider a combined Santa Cruz/Sacaton category, both typologically and chronologically.

Taken on face value, could the Hohokam scatter actually represent an earlier occurrence than the other scatters? Alternatively, could sherds from an heirloom vessel have been deposited? As with so many other scatters, the vessel is far from complete, missing all rim sherds, and may have been a portion of an old vessel acquired by a traveler in Arizona and purposely deposited on East Mesa, California

This Hohokam ceramic scatter is one of the few documented cases in eastern Imperial County, and proof that Patayan groups in California, either directly or indirectly, participated in cultural interaction with the Hohokam (Figure 3.2). One site previously excavated by Malcolm Rogers, SDM C-1, included a trail shrine (Waters 1982d) near Black Mesa and Indian Pass. It contained purported Santa Cruz Red-on-buff Hohokam ceramics. Rogers recovered another Hohokam sherd at an unspecified location along a different trail in the general region, SDM C-70 (Waters 1982c). Like other ceramic finds discussed below, assigned Hohokam ceramic types should be viewed with caution, given recent efforts to distinguish Sacaton from Santa Cruz Red-on-buff.

Another Hohokam ceramic occurrence in eastern Imperial County is a Sacaton or Santa Cruz Red-on-buff scatter (CA-IMP-10922) found some 4.5 km east of the Lake Cahuilla shoreline in the general area of a profusion of Patayan scatters (Andrews and Schaefer 2010). The Hohokam sherds included a single volcanic flake and scattered mammal bone, much of which appeared to have been calcified but not burned. Of 26 sherds noted, at least 10 were painted, four of those refit, and a minimum of two vessels were represented.

Further afield, sherds representing a complete reconstructable Hohokam Red-on-buff jar of unspecified type were recovered from a sand dune near Indio (Schaefer 1994a). Malcolm Rogers also recovered Hohokam sherds (identified by Waters 1982b) from three trails in southeastern California: two from north-south trending trails in eastern Imperial County, one of which is relatively close to the current discovery; and the third is from the southern branch of the Coco-Maricopa Trail along Salt Creek, not far from the north shore of Lake Cahuilla in southeastern Riverside County.

Hohokam sherds have been reported as far away as the Los Angeles area (see Figure 3.2; Ruby and Blackburn 1964). They include a single Red-on-buff sherd from the surface of CA-LAN-192 at Lovejoy Spring, a site in the Antelope Valley in the far western Mojave Desert (Griset 2013). The item was likely carried down the Mojave River travel corridor from the Colorado River, as were many associated Lower Colorado Buff Ware ceramics. Other finds identified as Sacaton Red-on-buff were found closer to the coast at CA-LAN-167 in the Tujunga–Redondo Beach area (Walker 1951), Wilmington, and Torrance areas (Boxt and Dillon 2013).

To find the likely source of these ceramics, one must look to Gila Bend and an area extending perhaps 16 km (10 mi) to the west along the Gila River. This was the closest and most principal point of major cultural interaction between the Hohokam and Patayan peoples. Evidence includes the co-occurrence of their respective ceramic types and rock art styles, and the western-most location of major Hohokam settlements (Shaul and Andresen 1989; Shaul and Hill 1998; Wasley and Johnson 1965). Hohokam ceramics occur on the surface in noticeable amounts as far west of Gila Bend as Agua Caliente Mountain near the Yuma County/Maricopa County line, about 132 km east of Yuma along the Gila River (Vivian 1965:138).

The interaction sphere appears to extend south and east through the Papaguería along Growler Valley to the Gulf of California, as seen in the regional distribution of Hohokam and Patayan ceramics on the Barry M. Goldwater Range and what may be described as a broad travel corridor, marked by sites with Hohokam ceramics and rock art. Growler Valley was apparently used to transport marine shell from the Gulf of California to the Salt-Gila basin.

Although Hohokam ceramics do appear to diminish in quantity west of this boundary, Patayan ceramics continue to occur with considerable frequency to the east, albeit at much lower numbers compared to Hohokam ceramics (Ahlstrom and Roberts 2002:127ff.; Ezell 1955). This may be, in part, attributable to the more highly mobile settlement and subsistence patterns of the Patayan, enabling more Patayan intrusion into Hohokam occupation areas with their irrigation systems, ball courts, and platform mounds than vice versa. Among the most interesting archaeological manifestations of this interaction is a Patayan residential enclave (House Group XVII) identified through ceramics at the major Hohokam village of Las Colinas near Phoenix (Beckwith 1988).

Another habitation site of Hohokam/Patayan co-residence is AZ T:13:18 (ASM) at Gillespie Dam, located just north of Gila Bend (Watkins and Rice 2010). Two contemporary cemetery areas, dated between AD 950 and 1040, were found at about a 30 m distance from each other. One cremation ground contained Sacaton Phase Hohokam ceramic offerings, while the other contained Patayan I phase ceramics. The investigators posit four modes of Hohokam/Patayan interaction, several of which find support at different sites throughout the Lower and Middle Gila River areas, and on the Salt River. The first is through long-distance trade and exchange. The second is through a symbiotic relationship between the more sedentary agricultural Hohokam and the more mobile mixed hunter-gatherer/horticultural Patayan. The latter likely established residences at the periphery of Hohokam settlements for the purpose of exchanging their products for Hohokam cultigens and material culture. Under these and more intensive interaction scenarios, there was likely Patayan participation in Hohokam cultural activities. The third interaction mode is through Patayan sharecroppers working on Hohokam land. The fourth mode is fully integrated co-residence, with Patayan households establishing themselves within Hohokam villages. Patayan ceramic-producing women might marry into Hohokam families and Patayan people would have participated in the cultural, economic, and political life of the Hohokam. This co-residence would have altered both cultural traditions in the Gila Bend area.

Further west of Gila Bend, small numbers of Santa Cruz Red-on-buff and Gila Plain (Wingate Variety) ceramics occur among more numerous Patayan ceramics at White Tanks, located 35 km north of the Gila River and 81 km east of the Colorado River (Schaefer et al. 1993:45). Obsidian from the Tank Mountain source located in east-central Yuma County, Arizona also occurs at Classic period Hohokam sites as far east as Phoenix (Shackley 1991). *Laevicardium* sp. shells found at Patayan sites, including many locations near the Lake Cahuilla shoreline, suggest possible Patayan-Hohokam interaction related to important shell-collecting areas on the Gulf of Mexico. Branching trade networks extended both into the Hohokam heartland and into the Colorado Desert. *Laevicardium* is much more common at Patayan sites, while *Glycymeris* appears to have been preferred by the Hohokam. Nevertheless, unmistakable Hohokam *Glycymeris* bracelet fragments or whole specimens have been recovered in very small numbers from village sites CA-ORA-57[-77], CA-ORA-58, and CA-ORA-225 near Newport Bay in Orange County, California, and another bracelet was purportedly recovered from Santa Catalina Island (Koerper 1996; Koerper and Desautels 2002).

Very rare three-quarter grooved polished stone axes have been found in southern California as well, including examples from the soapstone quarries on Catalina Island and from the turquoise quarries at Halloran Springs in the Mojave Desert (Heizer 1945). They could derive either from the Hohokam or Ancestral Puebloans (the latter most likely at Halloran Springs). All of these items probably reached the San Pedro region of the southern section of the Southern California Bight through down-the-line trade in *Olivella* shell beads, steatite, and other items. These exchange networks were both a product of, and contribution to, the cultural complexity of this region (Glassow et al. 2007).

The very long and finely made notched projectile points found in some burials in the Imperial and Coachella valleys also bear a close similarity to those found in ceremonial contexts at Hohokam sites in the Gila Bend area (Smith and Fauvelle 2015). Finally, Hedges (1973) has observed similarities between Patayan clay figurines with coffee bean eyes and Hohokam figurines, although Patayan flat paddle-shaped figurines of the so-called Southern Tradition do not otherwise resemble the modelled Hohokam versions. These lines of evidence all suggest considerable trade or cultural interaction of more highly mobile bands, possibly from both cultural affiliations (Beck 2006, 2008; Beck and Neff 2007).

Conclusion

A suite of evidence suggests a sphere of interaction between the Patayan and the Hohokam people likely residing in the Gila Bend and Salt-Gila Basin areas. Site and ceramic distributions suggest that the expansion of the Hohokam into their western frontier at Gila Bend likely began in an ephemeral way during the Formative (Pioneer) period (AD 1–750) but really intensified during the Gila Butte phase (AD 750–850) of the Colonial period. This would be contemporary with the early Patayan I phase. Hohokam settlement continued to grow through the Santa Cruz phase (AD 850–950) and Sacaton phase (AD 950–1150), which span the Colonial-to-Sedentary periods. Soon after the beginning of the Classic Period (AD 1500), the Hohokam retreated from Gila Bend back into their heartlands in the Phoenix and Tucson basins. Patayan/Hohokam interaction had likely diminished by then.

Although we cannot put too much significance into the rare and widely dispersed occurrences of Hohokam ceramics in California, we can surmise that the Patayan people who brought these ceramics with them may also have brought other items, including perishable goods, and more importantly, new ideas and experiences from their contacts with the more complex Hohokam cultural tradition.

4 Evidence of Long-Distance Exchange from the Robbers Mountain Region, West-Central Mojave Desert

Helen F. Wells

Between 2007 and 2016, field classes from California State University, Los Angeles (CalStateLA), tested sites, mainly rock shelters, that are widely distributed across the South Range of the Naval Air Weapons Station, China Lake (NAWS; Figure 4.1). This area is distinct in both environment and archaeology from the North Range, which is known for its obsidian quarries and the rock art-filled canyons of the Coso Mountains. The South Range also falls into a gap in the prevailing organizational schemes for the archaeology of the northern Mojave Desert: it lies between the Western Mojave archaeological area, as defined by Sutton (1989, 1996), Gardner (2007), and their colleagues, and the Central Mojave as described by Basgall and Hall (1992) for Ft. Irwin.

Most of the shelters we have investigated appear to have been used as temporary camps by small groups who were either seeking seasonally available resources or traveling through the area en route to other destinations. A few of the larger shelters, however, have yielded evidence of more intensive use and of ritual activity. Comparative data from early excavations at these other sites, notably those in the Bierman Caves complex and at Seep Spring, have been incorporated into our research.

Although earlier components are present, use of the South Range appears to have been most frequent during the Rose Spring (ca. 1500–1000 BP) and Late Prehistoric (ca. 1000 BP–historic contact) periods (Walsh and Backes 2005a; Wells and Backes 2010a). This inference is based on a few radiocarbon dates and obsidian hydration readings as well as on diagnostic artifacts, which include both projectile points and ceramics.

Some of the ceramics originated in locations far from the South Range, and in each instance the find consists of one to three sherds of each type. Their origins range from southern Nevada to central Arizona; thus, they represent contact, direct or indirect, between different peoples and cultures.

The Robbers Mountain Region

The slopes of Robbers Mountain, which is located south of Pilot Knob Valley in the western part of the South Range, are riddled with rock shelters and overhangs, some of which provided shelter for prehistoric foragers. In the late 1940s, Agnes Bierman and Albert Mohr recorded and excavated sites here and in other areas of the South Range. In 2004, the previously identified Robbers Mountain sites were revisited, and the archived collections were reviewed (Wells and Backes 2007). Three years later CalStateLA began test excavations in this area.

Nonlocal ceramics have been recovered from three of the Robbers Mountain sites: Bandit Spring A, the Lead Pipe Spring site (CA-SBR-43/H), and Agnes Bierman Cave (CA-SBR-8; Figure 4.2). Bandit Spring A is the northernmost and the smallest of the three sites. It is located at a small spring that emerges from a steep slope overlooking a narrow alluvial valley. Part of the site lies on a flat surface sheltered by a shallow overhang, but much of the deposit is scattered over the slope below.

The valley below Bandit Spring terminates at a high ridge formation 0.5 km to the south. Directly north of that ridge is Lead Pipe Spring, the major water source in the vicinity of Robbers Mountain. Surrounding the spring itself is a large, open site, CA-SBR-43/H, that includes two boulders with cupules. Beyond the ridgeline to the south, but with easy access to the spring, lies Agnes

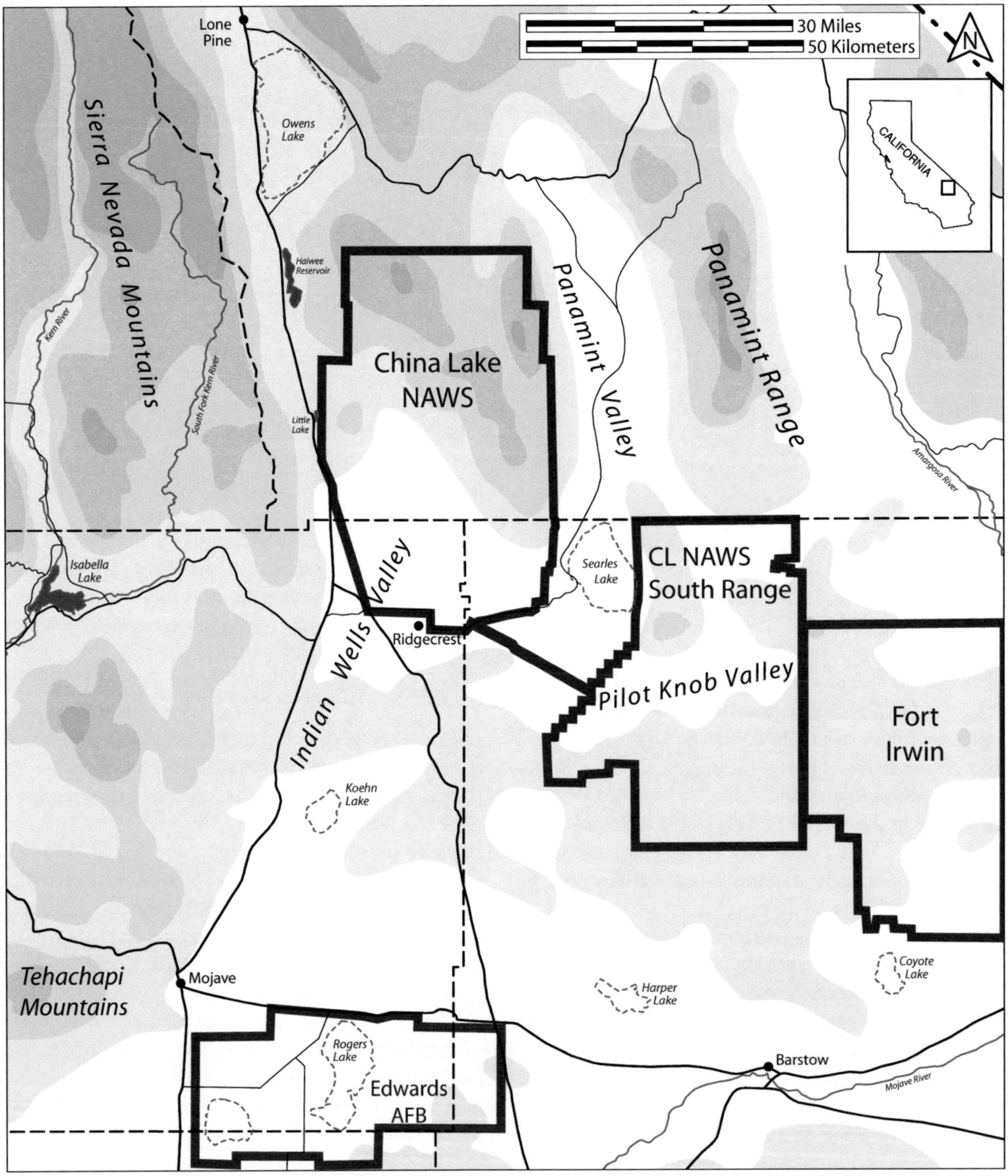

FIGURE 4.1. Location of the South Range Study Area, Naval Air Weapons Center, China Lake, California.

Bierman Cave (CA-SBR-8), named after one of the original excavators. It is the most prominent feature in the cluster of sites known as the Bierman Caves complex.

Ceramics from Bandit Spring

CalStateLA excavated test units at Bandit Spring A in 2010, recovering flaked and ground stone artifacts from the shallow deposit. Temporal indicators from this site include one Rose Spring Corner-notched point and one Desert Side-notched point, representing the Rose Spring and Late Prehistoric periods, respectively.

The surface collection from the apron of the shelter yielded nine ceramic sherds. Four of these, along with 11 specimens from three other sites we had tested, were examined by Margaret Lyneis. Lyneis classified some of these as Great Basin Brown Ware and others as paddle and anvil-thinned, or Patayan, ceramics (Lyneis, personal communication 2011).

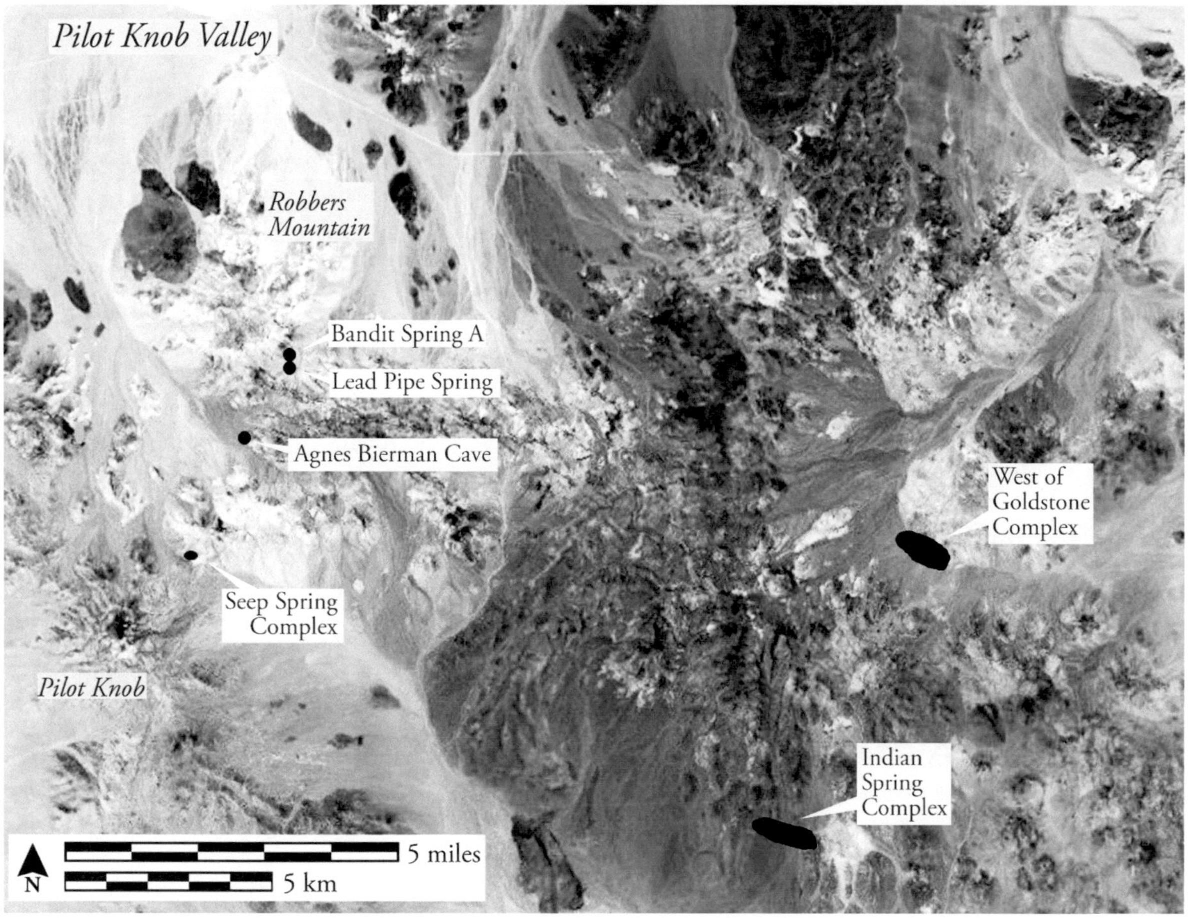

FIGURE 4.2. Locations of South Range site complexes.

Most previous site records and reports from South Range sites, including ours, refer to all finds of undecorated pottery simply as brown ware, or sometimes more specifically as Owens Valley Brown Ware, the latter implying both a manufacturing technique and an origin that have not been documented. As early as 1989, however, Lyneis identified both Great Basin Brown Ware and paddle and anvil-thinned ceramics at three sites in the eastern part of the South Range adjacent to Fort Irwin (Lyneis 1989). Lyneis previously identified both wares at sites to the east in the Drinkwater Basin and Tiefort Basin on Ft. Irwin itself (Lyneis 1988a). In Tiefort Basin she classified the majority of the sherds as paddle and anvil-thinned (Lyneis 1988b).

Using criteria explained by Lyneis (Lyneis 1988c), we distinguish between these two wares in our assemblages, at least for the larger specimens. Although there is some variation in color, we found that the attribute alone cannot be used to distinguish between wares. Patayan and Great Basin Brown Wares co-occur at five of the South Range sites we have tested. Both are present as well in the archived collections from sites at Seep Spring and at Pothunter Spring (Saldaña 2012), located about 5 km south and southwest, respectively, of Robbers Mountain.

By far the most interesting sherd we have recovered on the South Range is a decorated specimen from Bandit Spring A (Figure 4.3). Lyneis identified this as Sosi Black-on-white pottery, which was produced in the Hopi Mesa region of northern Arizona. According to Earle (2005), Hopi Mesa was an important destination for shell beads manufactured on the Pacific coast. The date range for Sosi Black-on-white in Arizona is AD 1070–1180 (Northern Arizona University 2001), corresponding to the Late Prehistoric period in the west-central Mojave Desert.

Ceramics from Agnes Bierman Cave

Lyneis also examined 12 sherds that Bierman and Mohr had excavated from Agnes Bierman Cave (CA-SBR-8) in the 1940s. Measuring 20 m wide by 8 m deep with an excavated depth of 1.2 m, this is one of the largest rock shelters in the Robbers Mountain region. The back wall of the shelter exhibits more than 77 pictographs, some of which appear to represent the distinctive Kawaiisu style that has been documented in the Tehachapi Mountain

FIGURE 4.3. Sosi Black-on-white sherd from Bandit Spring A.

region to the west. Obsidian hydration data indicate use of the site from approximately 2000 BP to 250 BP (Wells and Backes 2007). Diagnostic projectile points include one Elko series point in the Bierman and Mohr collection and one Cottonwood point recovered by Monastero (2007).

We had noted the sherds in the Bierman and Mohr collection while rerecording the site in 2004. In 2011, with a renewed interest in South Range ceramics, we sent the artifacts to Lyneis, who identified specimens of both Patayan and Great Basin Brown wares. But she also noted six specimens that we had not expected to find in the west-central Mojave Desert. Like the Sosi Black-on-white specimen recovered from Bandit Spring A, these sherds originated far to the east. Four of the six, two of which are from the same vessel, are Moapa Gray Ware, distinguished by its temper containing olivine. This pottery was made near Mt. Trumbull on the Arizona Strip north of the Grand Canyon, and, according to Lyneis, was widely distributed in the Moapa Valley of southern Nevada, where it was supplied to the Pueblo settlements on the Muddy and lower Virgin rivers (Lyneis 2008b; Lyneis and Hays-Gilpin 2008). The ware has a time range in the Southwest from about Basketmaker III to Late Pueblo II (AD 500 to AD 1200), overlapping the Rose Spring period in the west-central Mojave. The ware includes two types, Boulder Gray and Moapa Corrugated, both of which are represented in this small assemblage: three are Boulder Gray and one is Moapa Corrugated.

One of the CA-SBR-8 sherds, likewise classified by Lyneis, is Tusayan Gray Ware, Virgin Series, a sand-tempered ware widely produced west of Kanab Creek in western Utah and occurring in Moapa Valley sites (Allison 2000, cited in Lyneis and Hays-Gilpin 2008). The type is North Creek Corrugated. Lyneis tentatively identified the final specimen, a spall, as Tusayan White Ware, Virgin Series.

These are not the first sherds of Puebloan pottery reported from the South Range and adjacent areas, and by no means are they the first nonlocal ceramics to be recorded from southern California sites (see Koerper and Hedges 1996). During investigations of the China Lake-Fort Irwin Joint Land Use Area, two sherds of North Creek Black-on-gray pottery were recovered from CA-SBR-1429 (Lyneis 1989). Puebloan sherds were also collected from sites directly east of our study area on Fort Irwin. In Tiefort Basin, one site reportedly yielded several sherds of Verde Black-on-gray and another yielded a single sherd described as Anasazi Black-on-gray (Lyneis 1988a:E30). In Drinkwater Basin, two sherds of Tusayan Gray Ware and a single sherd of North Creek Black-on-gray were recovered from one site (Lyneis 1988b:E12).

Southwestern sherds have been found, not surprisingly, at the Seep Spring complex 5 km south of Robbers

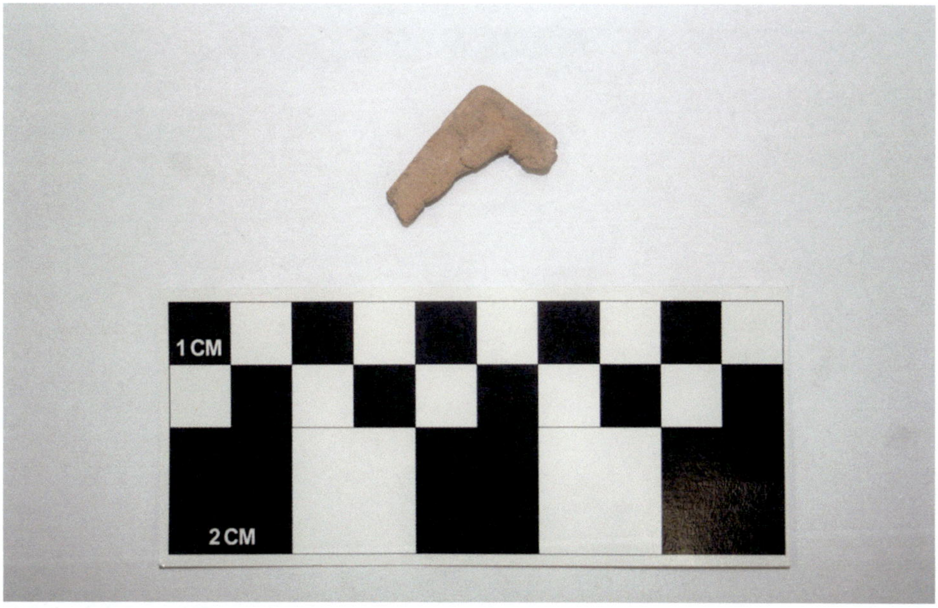

FIGURE 4.4. Clay figurine fragment from Lead Pipe Spring.

Mountain as well. Seep Spring, which is dominated by a large semicircular rock formation containing shelters, ledges, and free-standing boulders, exhibits several features that appear to be ritual-associated (Wells 2014). The rock art at Seep Spring also suggests multiple cultural affiliations (Walsh and Backes 2005a, 2005b), and as Clarus Backes and I have argued, it may have been a ritual site that was a destination for groups coming from different areas (Wells and Backes 2010a, 2010b).

In the 1950s, Peck and Smith (1957) reported the recovery of two black on white sherds from Cave 1 at Seep Spring and one red on gray sherd from a different locus at Seep Spring. Their provenience data are imprecise. More recently, Walsh and Backes recorded a black sherd with a flared recurved rim on the surface of Locus L at Seep Spring. Walsh classified this specimen as "Anasazi" (Walsh and Backes 2005a).

Ceramics from the Lead Pipe Spring Site

Our 2007 test excavation at the Lead Pipe Spring site (CA-SBR-43/H) recovered no sherds, but it did produce two nonlocal artifacts that are unique for this region. The disturbed deposit is horizontally extensive but shallow; it yielded only one-time sensitive artifact: a Rose Spring projectile point. Obsidian hydration readings from the subsurface assemblage suggest a Late Prehistoric age, but these were derived from non-Coso obsidian, precluding secure conversion to calendar dates (Wells, Saldaña, and Stosel 2011; Wells, Stosel, and Backes 2008).

The assemblage from the Lead Spring site includes two baked clay artifacts, found in the 10–20 cm level of unit 8. These are pinkish-buff in color (Munsell 5YR7/4) with no visible temper. Specimen CLNAWS-1525-135 (Figure 4.4) is a flat L-shaped fragment, possibly part of a pendant, or, more likely, of a limb from a figurine or even a doll. This is not the only probable figurine fragment found in the Robbers Mountain region. Schroth and Kearney (2007:32) describe a "figurine ceramic fragment" from the SBCM-160 collection curated at San Bernardino County Museum and now in the Curation Facility at NAWS. The San Bernardino County Museum site number probably refers to a large area that includes at least one of the rock shelters located in the general vicinity of Lead Pipe Spring. Schroth and Kearney note the specimen's similarity both to ceramic dolls sold by Mohave Indians to tourists in the early 1900s and to figurines from the Hohokam culture of Arizona, but they reject the former identification, based on the assumption that Mojave dolls were not manufactured during prehistoric times. According to Furst (2001:79), the Mohave also made ceramic effigies of both humans and animals, which were "unfired or only partially fired." Although there are no known archaeological examples of these effigies, she suggests that their absence may reflect the Mohave practice of burning the belongings of the deceased.

The SBCM-160 artifact is gray in color, in contrast to the pinkish-buff specimen from unit 8 at CA-SBR-43/H. Bierman and Mohr's (1947–1949) field notes from CA-SBR-2 (Lead Spring Cave), one of the rock shelters they excavated in the Robbers Mountain area, describe "modeled, smoothed objects of a fine untempered grey clay," which they tentatively identify as figurine fragments.

Comparisons of the CA-SBR-43/H find with illustrations and descriptions from elsewhere in California,

FIGURE 4.5. Clay bead from Lead Pipe Spring. Dimensions are 0.49–0.52 cm in diameter by 0.18 cm thick.

the Southwest, and southern Nevada, have been inconclusive (e.g., Haury 1937; Hedges 1973; Heizer and Beardsley 1943; Koerper and Hedges 1996; Morss 1954; Treganza 1942; Tuohy 2000). Its recovery in association with the second baked clay artifact does, however, support the possibility of a central Arizona origin.

The other clay artifact, also found in the 10–20 cm level of unit 8, is a small bead (specimen CLNAWS-1525-134) with shallow lines on one face (Figure 4.5). It measures 4.9–5.2 mm in diameter and 1.8 mm in thickness. Ceramic beads are apparently rare in southern California. I have found no references to similar clay beads from other sites in southern California or from Nevada. Sutton and colleagues (2016) report two baked clay beads from the surface of CA-KER-4220, located on the shore of Buena Vista Lake in the southern San Joaquin Valley. These are much larger, however, than the specimen from Lead Pipe Spring, measuring 17.8 by 11.4 mm and 20.6 by 8.7 mm, respectively (Sutton et al. 2016:53). According to the authors, "They may actually be buttons rather than beads as both appear to be historic, perhaps even modern" (Sutton et al. 2016:49).

Beads similar to the Lead Pipe Spring specimen have been reported from central Arizona. More than 80 years ago, Haury (1931:84–85) described and illustrated beads of clay, stone, and shell from the Salt-Gila River region of Arizona that were then curated at the Casa Grande Museum. Attempts to locate the collection for comparative purposes have been unsuccessful. Some of the clay beads are similar in size and appearance to the specimen from CA-SBR-43/H. The manufacturing technique described by Haury includes wrapping the clay around plant fiber, which burns away when the bead is fired, leaving the hole.

Based on a recent examination of more than 13,000 disk beads from mortuary contexts at three Hohokam sites in the Tucson Basin, Adams and Ownby (2018) update Haury's observations on manufacturing techniques. They furthermore describe methods for distinguishing fired clay beads from similar specimens of stone and shell.

Other reports of small clay beads, which provide less detailed descriptions, include an assemblage of 370 specimens associated with a cremation from the Grand

Canal Ruins in Phoenix (Mitchell 1989), as well as a few occurrences at other central Arizona sites (Foster 1994; Mabry 1997; Vokes 2001).

Obsidian sourcing data from the Lead Pipe Spring site point to the same direction as the nonlocal ceramics. While more than 90% of the obsidian from the site was sourced to the Coso Volcanic Field, located approximately 100 km to the northwest, seven of the flakes are of material originating at quarries far to the east. Four of these are from Hackberry and/or Hole-in-the-Wall in eastern San Bernardino County, near the Nevada border, two are from Shoshone Mountain in southern Nye County, Nevada, and one sourced to Devil Peak West, located in the Spring Mountains of southwestern Clark County, Nevada (Hughes 2010; Saldaña 2010).

Other non-Coso sources represented on the South Range are diverse. Most of the obsidian from CA-SBR-14, a rock shelter tested by CalStateLA in 2015, sourced to the Coso Volcanic field, but the site also yielded one flake from Casa Diablo, and two other non-Coso specimens not yet identified to source. Data from other projects on the South Range include one specimen from Seep Spring sourced to Hackberry (Giambastiani et al. 2009). Farther north, LaPierre's investigation of CA-SBR-12134/H, a ritual-associated rock feature on the shore of Searles Lake near the northern boundary of the South Range, yielded one specimen from Buck Mountain in northern California and one from Wild Horse Canyon, Utah (LaPierre 2012).

Ethnographic Territories and Movements

Given the evidence of use of the South Range during the Late Prehistoric period and possibly even more recently, it is appropriate to consider ethnographic territories and movements. Our study area is within the mapped territory of the Kawaiisu, specifically of the Desert Kawaiisu (Underwood 2006). Ethnographic sources state the Kawaiisu traveled from winter villages in the Tehachapi Mountains west of our Study Area to use the Mojave Desert seasonally (Kroeber 1925; Steward 1938; Zigmond 1986). Ethnographic data suggest that the area within what is now the South Range was also used by others, including the Shoshone, who co-occupied settlements with the Kawaiisu in the Panamint Valley and the Trona area, just north of our Study Area (Steward 1938). The western boundary of Chemehuevi territory is nearby as well.

Mohave travelers and traders may have traversed the South Range en route from the Colorado River to the coast. The role of the Mohave in moving goods between the Southwest and southern California has been documented in ethnographic and historic accounts, as summarized by Koerper and Hedges (1996:213–214), who trace a potential route between the Colorado River and Orange County, California, well south of the South Range. Using ethnohistorical data, however, Earle suggests routes that are closer to our study area. Basing his research largely on John P. Harrington's notes, Earle (2003, 2005:13) identifies landmarks between the Colorado River and the coast that held mythic significance for the Mohave, including locations on what is now Edwards Air Force Base and in the Tehachapi Mountains. Earle (2003) also discusses several historic routes that may follow aboriginal trails. One of these follows the natural east-west corridor through Pilot Knob Valley just north of our Robbers Mountain sites and extends eastward to Leach Spring located on present-day Fort Irwin. This route is part of a late nineteenth-century historic road that continues on from Leach Spring to Death Valley. It is identified in the NAWS cultural resources database as Nadeau's Death Valley Road or the Randsburg to Death Valley Road (Baker and Maniery 2010:100, Figure 24). As shown on an 1871 map (Figure 4.6; U.S. Army Corps of Topographical Engineers 1871), the route connects to Saratoga Spring at the southern end of Death Valley with a road that continues eastward to Salt Spring. From there, it diverges in three directions, one of which extends northeast into the Spring Mountains of southern Nevada, the same range where the Devil Peak obsidian source is located.

Discussion

The significance of these finds is less about trade than about how we may view prehistoric use of this area in general. The sites discussed here were used on a temporary, perhaps seasonal, basis, and they were used repeatedly before, during, and possibly after Late Prehistoric times. While some people were there to target desert resources, others may have been passing through. The large and unusual rock formation associated with Seep Spring may have served as a landmark or even as an interim destination drawing long distance travelers who gathered there for rituals (Wells 2014; Wells and Backes 2010a).

There are locations in the east Mohave that offered the same critical resources of shelter and nearby water that some of our South Range sites provided. Puebloan and Patayan ceramics co-occur at many rock shelter sites in southern Nevada (e.g., Slaughter et al. 2005); these sites are situated in areas that were probably used by more than one cultural group.

In 1980, test excavations were conducted at the Bird Spring site (26CK-1), a rock shelter in the Spring Mountains of southern Nevada, (Clewlow and Wells 1980; Wells and Clewlow 1981). Ceramics from the Bird Spring site include a mix of Great Basin Brown Ware and paddle

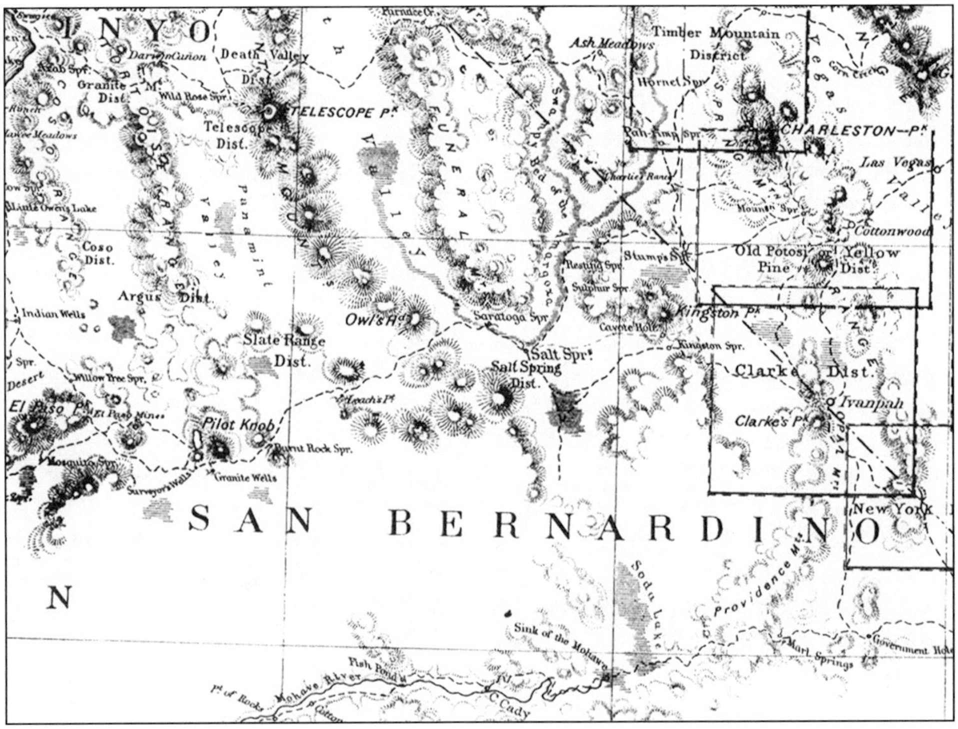

FIGURE 4.6. 1871 Map of Explorations and Surveys South of the Central Pacific Railroad. U.S. Army Corps of Topographical Engineers (Courtesy of University of Nevada, Las Vegas, Libraries Special Collections).

and anvil finished pottery, along with a variety of Puebloan sherds (Olson 1980), but the assemblage is much larger than any recovered from our South Range sites. At Bird Spring we concluded that the mix of wares most likely resulted from use of the shelter by different peoples.

Recent research suggests, however, that in southern Nevada, a single group may have made more than one of the non-Puebloan wares. Roberts and Ahlstrom (2012) describe the co-occurrence of brown and buff wares at several rock shelters in the Las Vegas Valley. They suggest that this may represent the merging of Southern Paiute and Mohave peoples in the Las Vegas region in the Late Ceramic period. Citing Isabel Kelly's ethnographic data, they consider the possibility that both wares may have been made by individuals within the same groups: some Las Vegas Paiutes and Chemehuevi made brown ware, some made buff ware, and others made both (Roberts and Ahlstrom 2012:224). According to Harry and Sachiko (this volume), though, Puebloan people made brown ware pottery as well, which is not easily distinguished from that made by the Southern Paiute.

We cannot determine who made the Great Basin Brown Ware and Patayan ceramics in our assemblages, but the emerging data from the South Range, which also include a puzzling variety of rock art styles, suggest that people with different cultural affiliations moved through this area. For some, use of plant and animal resources may have been opportunistic, rather than targeted. That some of the people who camped on the South Range had connections northward to the Coso Volcanic Field and westward to the coast, directly or indirectly, has been well established. These connections are based, respectively, on obsidian sourcing data and on the presence of *Olivella* shell beads, which occur at a few sites.

Identification of obsidian from southern Nevada and the California-Nevada border region along with ceramics from Arizona has simply broadened the reach of external connections and has directed our attention to sites such as those presented here as stopovers for people coming from southern Nevada, the Arizona strip, or the California/Arizona border region. These people may have included Mohave Indians, who were known to travel for the purpose of visiting other regions as well as to engage in trade (Kroeber 1925). Perhaps other Yuman, or even Numic groups, may have brought artifacts from outside the region. Given the requirement for both shelter and water in this harsh environment, people of whatever cultural affiliation who were moving through the area would have selected the same locations to make their camps. They would have carried some good quality toolstone along with them, rather than depending on finding it along the way.

Pots or Fragments?

But were they carrying only whole pots or were they also carrying sherds that represented economic, cultural, or symbolic connections between peoples, cultures, and even specific places? Fragmentation studies undertaken in Europe (Chapman 2000; Chapman and Gaydarska 2007) address the movement of pieces of broken artifacts prior to their deposition in archaeological sites. Fragments of a vessel may be dispersed across the landscape, resulting in the occurrence of "orphan sherds" in individual sites; they cannot be refitted with other sherds from the same site but may refit with fragments from other sites. For farming communities in southeastern Europe, these represent "one of the most important social practices through which enchained relations were maintained at the local and sometimes wider level" (Chapman and Gaydarska 2007:111).

Even a complete excavation of the South Range sites where the Sosi Black-on white sherd and other single occurrences of nonlocal specimens were found, might not allow us to classify the isolates as "orphan sherds." The rest of the pot may be there somewhere, or it may be scattered across the open desert. Nevertheless, we can consider the possibility that the Southwestern sherds were carried to the South Range as fragments that conveyed some meaning.

Acknowledgments

This paper would not have been possible without the contributions of Margaret Lyneis, who identified the 27 sherds we sent her and taught us how to distinguish between the two main pottery wares that occur on the South Range. Michael Baskerville, Installation Cultural Resource Manager, Naval Air Weapons Station, China Lake, has supported and participated in our field school and research project since 2007. He found the Sosi Black-on-white sherd on the last afternoon of our last field weekend in 2010. The field school that year was partially funded by a Cotsen Grant through the California State University, Los Angeles, Foundation, for which I thank James Brady. Clarus Backes prepared the graphics for this paper, and Melanie Saldaña has contributed to all aspects of the research.

5

Geochemical and Luminescence Insights into the Cultural Transmission of Clay and Temper Recipes in Southern Owens Valley, California

Jelmer W. Eerkens, Jeffrey R. Ferguson, and Carl P. Lipo

Tracking long-term trends in human behavior, particularly material culture, has long been a strength of archaeological studies. In the 1800s and a good portion of the 1900s, a major focus of archaeological research centered on tracing changes in material culture over large geographic regions. The emphasis was generally on phenomena such as architecture, projectile point shape, and pottery decoration styles (e.g., Phillips et al. 1951; Rouse 1939). These studies used multidimensional classes of cultural variability to measure patterns of cultural inheritance at the scale of regions, an approach generally referred to as "culture history" (Lyman and O'Brien 2001; Steward 1942).

Today, using archaeometric techniques (e.g., microwear analyses, organic residue analysis, trace-element studies), we can measure changes in material culture using additional and more fine-grained attributes. This approach allows us to track variation over smaller units of space and through narrower windows of time, providing greater discrimination on the structure of past social interactions. Thus, we can focus our studies on exploring the evolution of particular technologies *within* a given sociocultural setting. This approach is generally referred to as the study of "cultural transmission" or "learning strategies."

The current study investigates such an evolutionary process for one form of technology, fired-clay vessels, in one small area of the world, southern Owens Valley, California, and for one cultural group, the hunter-gatherer ancestors of modern-day Owens Valley Paiute. Judging by the relative number of sherds found in prehistoric deposits and the investment in time and energy they represent, fired-clay pots (pottery) played a significant role in the lives of ancient peoples in the region. Previous studies have documented a pattern in which, over time, there is a significant increase in the number of pottery vessel fragments relative to other kinds of artifacts (Eerkens and Lipo 2013, 2014). This increase in relative abundance suggests that the use of pottery vessels and their manufacturing technology spread over time and space and was used by an increasingly large portion of the population. Yet, the details of the transmission of this technological information are not well understood. For example, we do not know whether ceramic vessel manufacturing increased through time because of improved performance, or due to a reduced cost of pottery relative to other technologies, or some combination of these or other factors. Nor do we know whether pottery played an essential role in changing subsistence strategies, were part of practices that are related to increased populations (e.g., increased the nutritional content of food allowing people to grow family size), or whether fired clay vessels are simply concomitant with broader changes in subsistence practices.

In this study, we combine two archaeometric databases, one concerning age (measured through optically stimulated luminescence dating), the other concerning clay composition (determined with element geochemistry), to trace fine-scaled changes in pottery technology in southern Owens Valley (see Figure 5.1). Given relatively constant firing technology and similar depositional histories, we assume that clay composition information largely reflects the choices potters made in gathering the raw materials necessary for forming pots. By dating individual sherds, in which each sample represents a different vessel, we can use clay geochemistry

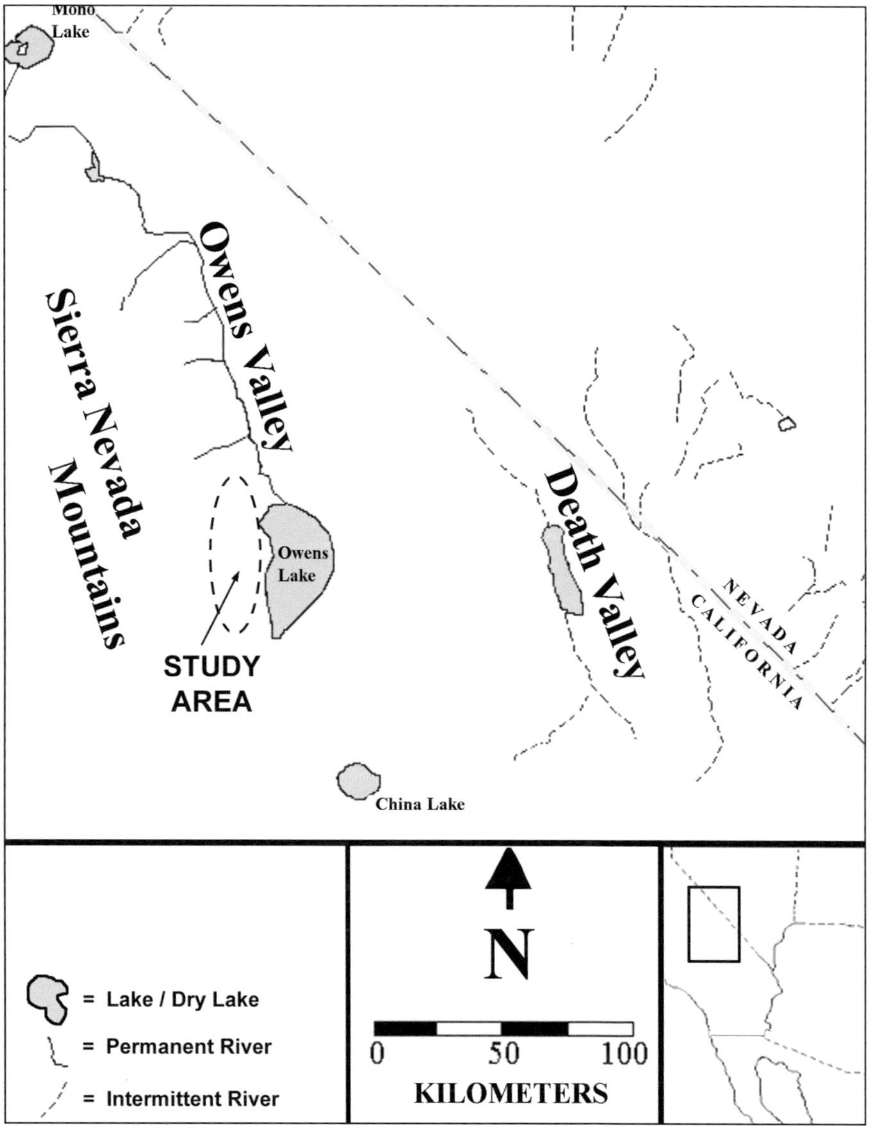

FIGURE 5.1. Map of region showing location of study area.

to trace the ways in which potters chose clay and nonplastic or temper materials over time. It is not our goal to "source" ceramics and identify the geolocation of particular clay deposits, but rather to study the range of variation exhibited among the practices of potters over time. In this way, our study of mineralogy and clay sources provides insight into the actions and behaviors of ancient potters.

Pottery in Owens Valley

While the oldest pot sherds in Owens Valley date to AD 750 or earlier (Eerkens et al. 1999), the vast majority of pottery dates to after AD 1350 (Eerkens and Lipo 2014; Pippin 1986; Rhode 1994). There is some variance in shape and size, but most ceramic vessels from the region are medium-sized (ca. 15–25 cm high and 18–25 cm wide at the mouth) and V-shaped (i.e., conical) cook pots. Small numbers of more spherical bowls with recurved rims are also present (Bettinger 1986, 1989; Hunt 1960; Lyneis 1988c; Pippin 1986; Prince 1986; Touhy 1990; Touhy and Strawn 1986; Wallace 1986). The majority of the ceramic vessels are undecorated, with only 5–20% of the samples exhibiting embellishment with rows of fingernail or punctate designs on or below the rim. Vessel walls are generally thin: wall thickness varies between 4 and 9 mm at points just below the rim. Based on preserved organic residues collected from the cores of sherds, high temperature boiling of seeds and stews seems to have been a major function (Eerkens 2005).

Research also shows that the steps involved in vessel formation were not static but changed slowly over time (Eerkens 2003). There appears to be experimentation and innovation in pot formation practices throughout the last 650 years. Pots predating AD 1500 are generally over 7.0 mm thick, often contain biotite mica, more frequently have organic temper, and are usually smoothed on their exterior surfaces. In addition, there is less variation in rim shape and mouth diameter than vessels found later in prehistory. Between AD 1500 and 1650, pots become somewhat thinner (ca. 6.5 mm), contain less biotite mica, and are less frequently smoothed on their exterior surfaces. After AD 1650, assemblages contain the thinnest sherds, usually less than 5.5 mm, have only small amounts of biotite mica or organic temper present, and are more often rough on their exterior and interior surfaces. These pots are also more variable in size and shape, suggesting a diversification of the context of vessel use and/or increased numbers of craftworkers producing vessels.

For this study, we are interested in studying geochemical variation in pots over time. Fired-clay vessels are composed of two main fractions, fine-grained clay and coarse-grained nonplastics (often referred to as temper). In terms of geochemistry, different combinations and abundances of elements characterize each of these two components. Clays contain high concentrations of aluminosilicate minerals and also adsorb a number of minor elements, especially the Rare Earth Elements (REE). For this reason, we focus especially on REE signatures in ancient pots to study changes in the clay component of ancient pots.

By contrast, nonplastics can come in a number of forms. Organic temper, especially plant material, was commonly added or already present in clays in Owens Valley. This organic temper is represented today as voids in the clay matrix and/or plant impressions made in the green clay prior to firing. Because plant material is burned out during firing, it does not contribute to geochemical signatures within sherds. Of interest in the present study are mineral nonplastic materials. In Owens Valley brownware, the main nonplastic minerals consist of those available in the granitic bedrock that dominates the region, including mainly feldspar and quartz, with smaller numbers of hematite, biotite, hornblende, apatite, and titanite, as well as other rarer minerals (e.g., zircons). These could have been added as temper or have been present in the clays naturally.

As an example of the geochemical and mineralogical variability that exists within a single ceramic sample, Figure 5.2 shows results of electron microprobe mapping of a thin section of one of the sherds included in this analysis. The figure shows separate plots for overall backscattered electrons (upper left), and then the distribution of Fe, Al, and Na in successive panels (clockwise). Warmer (orange-red) colors indicate higher concentrations at a particular spot while cooler colors (blue-black) indicate lower concentrations. From the element map, we can examine how an element is distributed across the volume of a sherd, for example, whether it is highest in the nonplastic or clay component.

The upper right part of the figure shows that Fe occurs in high concentrations in small, rounded grains, 20–50 times higher than within the clay matrix, and in intermediate levels in many elongated grains, and is not detectable in black areas. The small grains are hematite (Fe_2O_3) particles comprising approximately 5% by volume of the total nonplastics. The intermediate Fe levels in the elongated particles show grains of biotite mica ($K\{Mg,Fe\}_3AlSi_3O_{10}\{OH\}_2$), that consist of about 10% of the total nonplastics.

Likewise, the Na map shows that sodium is also concentrated in discrete grains. These particles are slightly more angular in form, and include a range of different feldspar minerals ($\{Na, K\,Ca\}Al_2Si_2O_8$), some higher and others lower in Na. Feldspar grains comprise roughly 60% of the total nonplastics by volume. The hematite and biotite mica grains highlighted in the Fe map appear as black in the Na map, indicating there is no detectable sodium in hematite and biotite mica. The clay fraction of the sherd likewise has low levels of Na.

Finally, the Al map shows this element more evenly distributed across the sherd, occurring primarily in the clay and feldspar components, but also in low concentrations in the biotite mica. It does not occur within the hematite grains highlighted in the Fe map. Additionally, note that many of the larger rounded black areas in the Al map that are not hematite are grains of quartz (SiO_2), while elongated linear black areas are small vugs (likely formed by burned-out organics) or cracks within the sherd. Maps for minor elements, including REEs, are generally black because these elements occur in concentrations below the limits of detection for electron microprobe mapping.

Analysis of these chemical maps, as well as additional targeted microprobe analyses on particular spots, helps determine how different elements are distributed across a sherd. Upon examination of many similar maps, we find that the major elements, such as Na, K, Ca, Fe, and Mg are found primarily in the nonplastic component of pots, while clays have lower concentrations relative to the nonplastics. By contrast, REEs are found mostly in the clay fraction of pots, although they also occur in low levels in nonplastic particles. As a result, we can use signatures in REEs as a proxy for the clay component. By contrasting variation in the major elements with those of the REEs, we can gain information about nonplastics

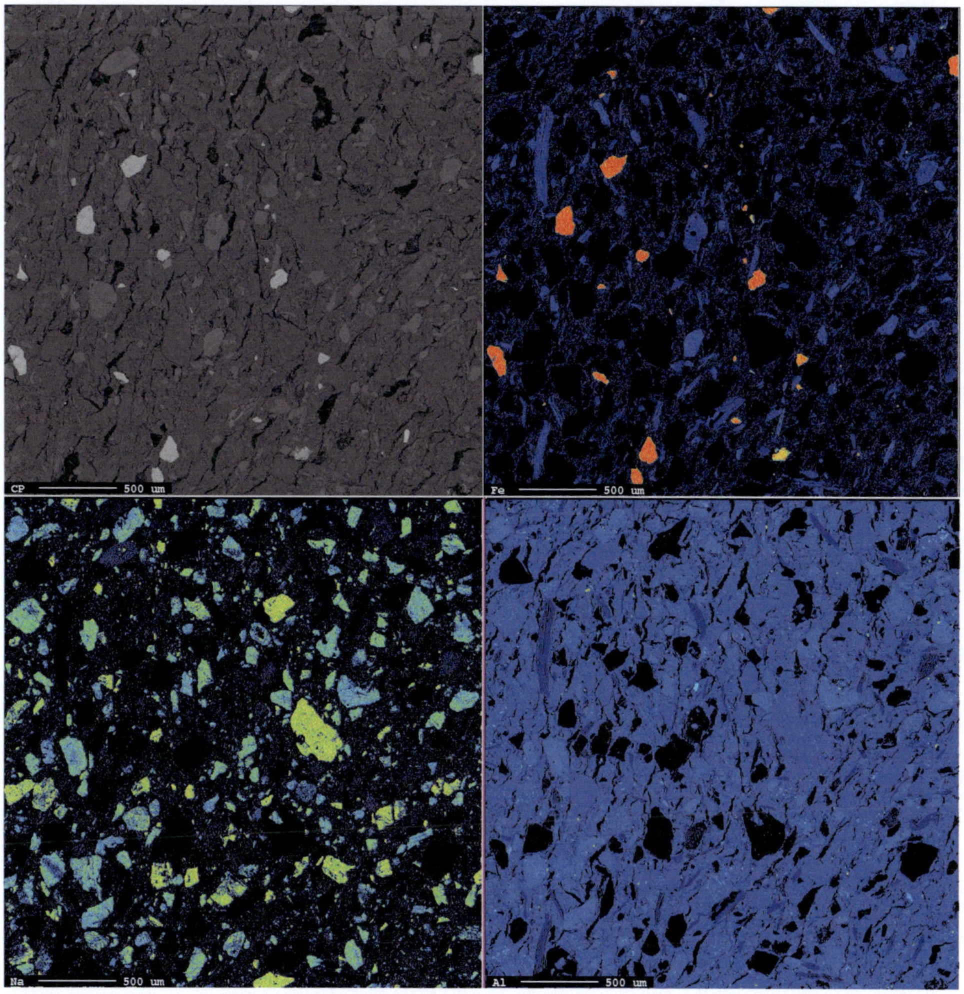

FIGURE 5.2. Electron microprobe maps for one sherd (JEC085 from CA-INY-5207) showing backscattered electrons (*upper left*), distribution of iron (*upper right*), distribution of sodium (*lower left*), and distribution of aluminum (*lower right*). Warmer colors indicate higher concentrations.

versus clay of pots, and overall recipes that potters used. Other elements, especially Si and Al, are found in both the clay and nonplastic components.

Hypotheses

We tested two hypotheses regarding the transmission of pottery technology among the prehistoric populations of the Southern Owens Valley. First, as potting technologies became more widely used, we expected to see an increase in the relative abundance of pottery found in archaeological assemblages combined with evidence for an increasing number of clay sources exploited to meet growing material demands. Clay is a heavy material that exists in variable but relatively abundant amounts across the landscape. Cross-cultural studies show it is typically acquired within a short distance of where pots are made and used (Arnold 1985). Thus, unless there was a strong performance advantage in choosing a remote clay source with specific properties offsetting the costs of transportation, potters would likely have made use of more local clay sources.

As clays are formed from locally weathered bedrock, different regional sources generally vary in their underlying composition. Accordingly, as pottery technology spreads, and more potters engage in the craft, we predicted that we would see increasing geochemical variation over time (due to the expansion of pottery technology and not due to long distance travel for resources). In particular, we predicted that the expansion of pottery use over time would lead to increasing variation in elements associated with the clay component of pottery (vs. nonplastics), especially REEs, and perhaps other minor elements. There is, of course, the possibility that potters selected better sources of clay. In such a case, more sudden shifts in the REE composition of pots, marking periods of innovation in clay use, with abandonment of older inferior sources, and exploitation of superior clay sources would be seen.

Second, as knowledge and experience accrued among potters and information transmitted across generations, potters would likely have varied the combinations of clays and nonplastics to more finely match local performance needs. Because REEs tend to occur within clay particles, it is not possible for potters to directly choose REEs, or easily alter their concentration, in their pots. Further, because they are rare and not visible in clay, potters could not have known anything about possible performance characteristics of these elements. Thus, REEs will tend to vary in a more haphazard way, corresponding to local sources of clay. By contrast, we expected that particular types of added temper (e.g., feldspar-poor or mica-rich sand) were more readily observable in their composition, and hence, people could more easily manipulate their presence and abundance and observe performance outcomes. As a result, we expected increasing manipulation of the nonplastic component of pottery through the selection *of specific temper* sources (or clays with naturally occurring minerals), and hence, stable or decreasing variation in the elements that contribute to major nonplastic minerals.

Methods

We characterized the geochemistry of pottery vessel fragments using neutron activation analysis (NAA) at the University of Missouri Research Reactor Center (MURR). MURR's analysis provides measures of the abundance of 32 elements comprising major rock forming elements (Al, Ca, Fe, K, Mn, Na), semimetals (As, Sb), alkali earths (Ba, Sr), alkali metals (Cs, Rb), transition metals (Co, Cr, Hf, Sc, Ta, Ti, V, Zn, Zr), REE's (Dy, Lu, Tb, Yb, Ce, Eu, La, Nd, Sm), and actinide elements (Th, U). We prepared the samples according the standard MURR procedure (see Glascock 2002; Neff 1992). In short, this involves weighing 200 mg of crushed powder from each sample into a polyethylene vial and irradiating the sample for 5 seconds at a flux of 8 × 1,013 n/cm^2/sec. Following irradiation, the sample is placed at a fixed distance from a high-resolution germanium detector to collect a spectrum of emitted gamma rays. This first irradiation allows determination of nine short-lived elements. A second irradiation involves placing 200 mg of each sample into a high-purity quartz vial and irradiating at the same flux for a period of 24 hours. This second irradiation allows determination of the remaining 23 elements using two separate counts. Standards of SRM-1633a Flyash and SRM-688 Basalt Rock were used for quantification of the elemental concentrations in the unknowns, and samples of Ohio Red Clay were run as quality controls with each batch of samples.

For luminescence dating, all of the sherds discussed here were previously reported in Eerkens and Lipo (2013, 2014). In short, optically stimulated luminescence (OSL) measurements were made on coarse grains (90–120 μ) within each sherd using an automated Risø TL/OS 12B/C reader that incorporates calibrated beta (^{90}Sr) radioactive sources for evaluating the rate of luminescence signal accumulation. We employed blue-light OSL (BOSL) stimulation with single aliquot regenerative dose (SAR) protocol outlined by Feathers (2003; Murray and Wintle 2000). Blue-light LED on the Risø TL/OS 12B/C stimulate samples in the 400–550 nm range (centered at 470 ± 30 nm). A double-IR wash was employed to help eliminate contribution of feldspar contaminants (Banerjee et al. 2001). For this step, the samples were stimulated using infrared diodes in the 800–900 nm transmission range. A U-340 filter was used to eliminate spillover from stimulation blue light.

To calibrate the internal dose, we used a GBC Opti-Mass 8000 ICP Time of Flight Mass Spectrometer attached to a New Wave Research UP-213 Laser Ablation system (LA-TOF-ICP-MS). The sample was ball-milled to ~5 μm and thoroughly mixed with 40 ppm indium internal standard and briquetting additive before being pressed into a pellet using a 15-ton geological sample press. The resulting pellet was analyzed for U, Th, and K concentrations using laser ablation ICP-MS. Replicates of 5-second acquisitions were averaged and the standard error of each analysis was reported with the sample averages. All intensity counts were normalized to the internal standard and calibration curves for each element and were generated using external calibration standards. These data were used to calculate the years necessary to account for the OSL signal measured given the radiation activity in the local environment of deposition. Our measurements and calculations estimate the amount of time elapsed since the last zeroing event, the event in which there was sufficient energy to release the accumulated electrons previously captured in the crystalline structure of the mineral grains. Using the blue-light LED as a stimulus, we measured an OSL signal that was invariant to the relatively low-level heating events related to cooking, thus providing measurements that reflect the time since the event of manufacture.

Results

Our results are summarized in Table 5.1. Trends in the variation of particular elements were examined and categorized as either increasing, stable, or decreasing over time. To accomplish this task, we calculated a running

TABLE 5.1. Trends in variation (increasing, stable, or decreasing) of different element groups over time. The numbers indicate the number of individual elements conforming to that trend.

	Actinide	Alkali Earth	Alkali Metal	REE	Rock-Forming	Semi Metal	Trans Metal	Total
Increase	2	0	2	7	0	0	3	14
Stable	0	1	0	2	4	2	6	15
Decrease	0	1	0	0	2	0	0	3

standard deviation by first sorting the sherds by the median OSL date, and then calculating the standard deviation across the temporally preceding seven, and temporally succeeding seven samples, for each particular element (n = 15 samples for each measure of standard deviation; this number was arbitrarily chosen). This computation is not possible for the youngest seven and oldest seven sherds (because there are no longer seven younger or seven older sherds to calculate to make a sample of 15), but overall provides estimates of running variation for all sherds in between.

Table 5.1 shows that a clear majority of elements either display relatively stable variation over time (n = 15) or increase noticeably in variation (n = 14). In particular, nearly all of the REEs (7 of 9), actinides (2 of 2), and alkali metals (2 of 2) increase in variation. Figure 5.3 depicts two such elements, Lanthanum (La; top), a REE, and Thorium (Th; bottom), an actinide. The running standard deviation is plotted as a black line above the data points. As shown, variation for La and Th is initially low between AD 1200 and 1530, but starts to increase markedly thereafter, more than doubling by AD 1750. Nearly all the REEs show a similar pattern.

By contrast, none of the rock-forming, alkali earth, and semimetal elements, and only three of the nine transition metals, increase in variation. For these groups of elements, variation is typically stable (unchanging) or fluctuating slightly up and down over time. Only three elements (Al, Fe, and Ba) show decreasing variation over time. Figure 5.4 plots Al and Fe. As shown, each graph depicts overall dropping standard deviation throughout the temporal sequence, with the least variation at the end, around AD 1880. For Fe, there is also a slight trend toward lower ppm over time. As biotite mica has Fe in its mineralogical formula, this finding is consistent with decreasing use of biotite mica as a component of nonplastics over time, as noted previously (Eerkens 2003).

Discussion

Together, the data reveal important clues about changing potting practices in the Owens Valley. Variation in the majority of rock-forming elements remains stable or decreases. This pattern is consistent with our hypothesis that, over time, potters refined their knowledge about pottery manufacture to best suit the requirements of their local environments. In other words, potters made choices about clay and temper recipes, noted the performance of ensuing pots, and transmitted this information to neighboring people and/or the next generation.

The main elements that can be attributed to the nonplastic component of Owens Valley pots, namely Ca, Na, K, Al, and Fe, did not increase in variation over time. To account for this pattern, we posit that the relative amounts of feldspar (for Ca, Na, and K) and hematite (for Fe) added to, or naturally present in, the raw clay (i.e., pot recipes) was fairly established to produce a pot with desired performance characteristics. This information was transmitted across generations in a consistent manner. The composition of nonplastics is known to have major effects on pot performance characteristics and impacts properties such as heating efficiency and resistance to formation of internal cracks that lead to breakage (e.g., Braun 1983:122–125; Bronitsky and Hamer 1986; Feathers 1989, 2006; London 1981; Reid 1984; Rye 1976; Sampson and Vobel 1996; Shepard 1968:24–31; Skibo et al. 1989). In this respect, the effects of nonplastics would have been visible to potters and are likely to have been under selection due to their effects on performance. In the case of Fe, reduction in the density of biotite mica may have led to decreasing concentrations, and decreasing variation, in Fe within sherds.

Likewise, variation in relative abundance of aluminum, one of the major elements in clay, decreased over time. While feldspars also contain Al, and the standardization could be due to processes similarly affecting Ca, Na, and K, it may also indicate standardized amounts of clay relative to nonplastics that comprise pots. The clay/nonplastic ratio would have had obvious effects on pot performance. Indeed, for Al and Fe, variation appears to decrease over time, suggesting increasing standardization in these two components of pottery technology.

By contrast, the abundance of minor elements, especially REEs, Actinides, and Alkali metals, generally increased in variation over time. As discussed, these minor elements are mainly components of the clay fraction, rather than mineral grains in the nonplastic component.

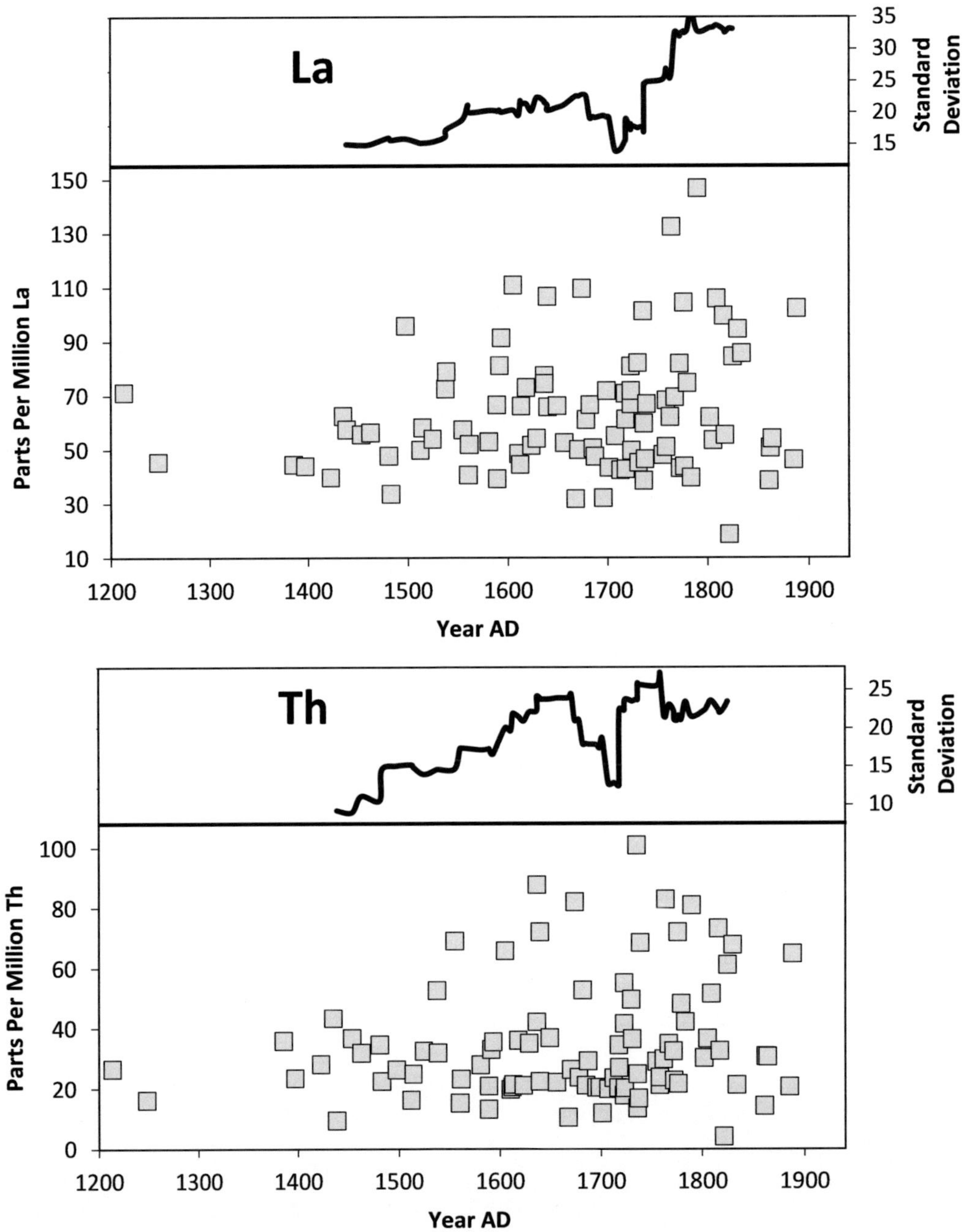

FIGURE 5.3. Concentrations (in ppm) of La (top) and Th (lower) over time in Southern Owens Valley sherds, along with a running measure of standard deviation (black line), showing increasing variation over time.

Being present only in trace amounts, these elements have a negligent effect on the functional properties of fired-clay vessels. Further, being embedded primarily within the clay fraction, they are not easily controlled or modified by potters. As a result, they are less likely to have been under selection.

We suggest that the increasing variation in these elements is a by-product of an increasing number of clay sources exploited by regional potters over time. As potting technology spread and became more common (see Eerkens and Lipo 2014), we expect that the demand for clay grew. Potters had to experiment with an increasing number of local clay deposits to find suitable sources of materials for their vessels, rather than carry heavy clay from known sources over long distances. It is also possible that "good" sources of clay were owned by groups of potters, forcing new adopters of the technology to seek out alternative sources. Each of these clay sources

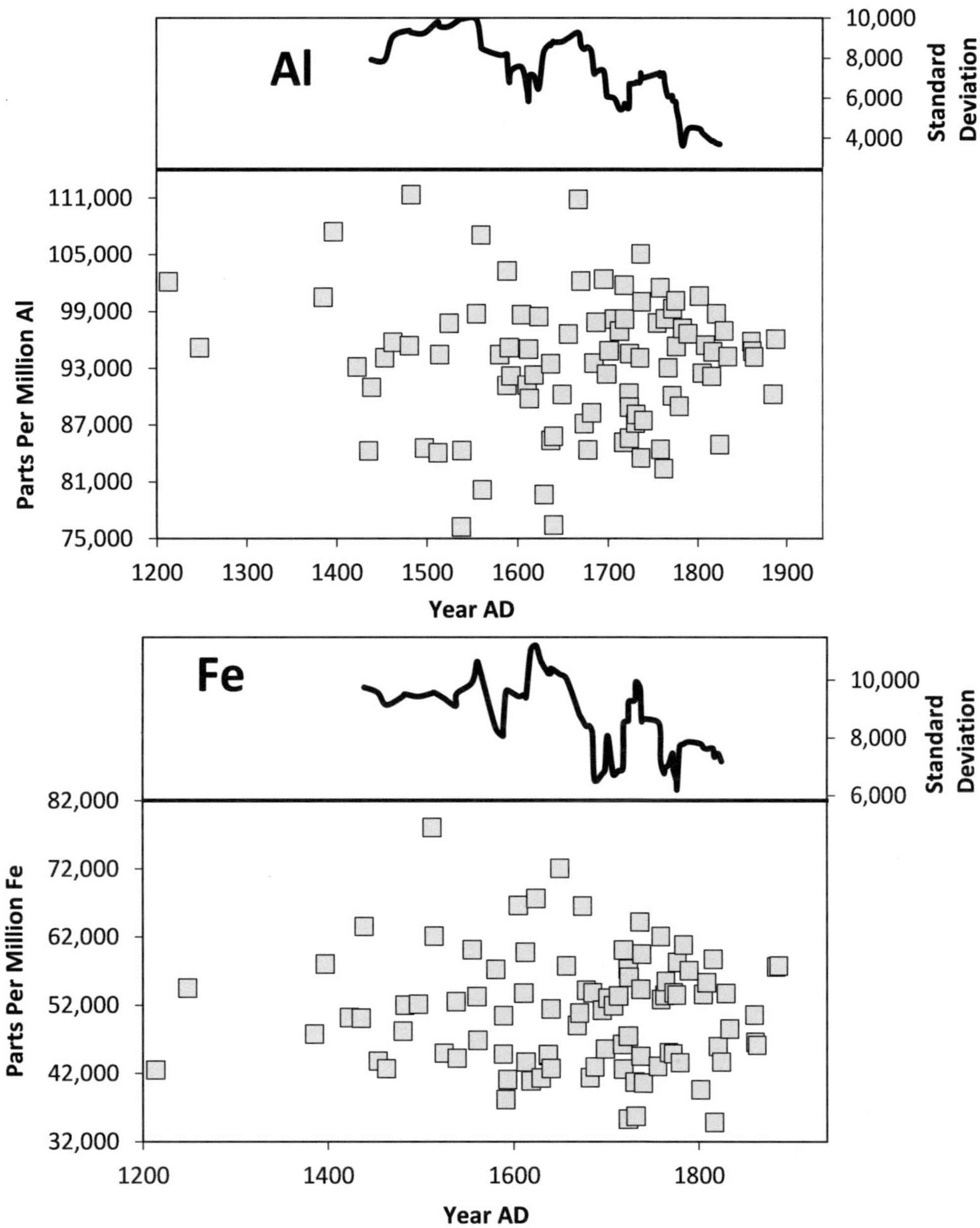

FIGURE 5.4. PPM of aluminum (top) and iron (bottom, showing decreasing variation over time.

may have varied slightly in the concentration of minor elements, thereby contributing to greater intersherd variation over time.

Conclusions

Results from the analyses are consistent with our original hypotheses. We found increasing variation in REEs associated with the clay fraction of ceramic vessels over time, a finding supportive of our explanatory model in which rising numbers of potters were exploiting increasing numbers of clay sources across Southern Owens Valley. By contrast, we found stable or decreasing variation in elements that reflect nonplastics, supportive of our model that particular clay/temper recipes became standardized over time.

This finding for precontact pots is somewhat at odds with ethnographic observations made by Steward (1933: 266), who suggested that a small number of women were more or less specialist potters and supplied others in the community with vessels, and that they owned clay sources. Under Steward's model, we would expect to find a small and relatively consistent degree of variability in relative abundance of elemental composition of clays over time. In contrast, our finding suggests that many clay sources were likely exploited, and that this number increased slowly over several centuries. Of course, dramatic changes to Owens Valley Paiute lifeways, including the introduction of metal containers, may have changed the demands for earthenware pots and the popularity of this craft in the 1900s when Steward conducted his studies (see also Griset 1990 for a similar process in Southern California). Thus, the potters Steward interviewed may have been practicing their craft in a different manner than in precontact times, and his model may not be appropriate for understanding the dynamics of more ancient technologies.

Our geochemical result is consistent with previous analyses of southern Owens Valley sherds examining metrical variation in pot size and rim shape (Eerkens 2003). That study also showed increasing variation over time, which can be explained as the byproduct of increasing technological experimentation by a growing number of potters. Thus, experimentation with new clay sources seems to have covaried with experimentation in vessel form and size.

Our data likewise provide support for our second hypothesis of increasing standardization in basic clay/nonplastic recipes over time. In these analyses, we find that the major rock-forming elements comprising the majority of the geochemical signature in nonplastics did not increase in variation, but either stayed stable or decreased over time. This pattern is consistent with the interpretation that potters constrained the ways pots were produced due to inherent performance requirements of pottery vessels. Knowledge about outcomes was then passed on to subsequent generations, who perfected a recipe suiting their potting needs. This transmission of information resulted in the removal of particular recipes that did not produce desired performance outcomes, causing overall variation to decrease. Part of the pattern in the youngest sherds may also relate to a transformation and consolidation of pottery technologies among a restricted number of specialists (e.g., Griset 1990), as recorded in ethnographic studies.

Together, the findings support the notion that cultural transmission processes for particular artifact categories, such as pottery, can have many different vectors of change. Variation in some attributes can increase, while variation in others can simultaneously decrease or stay stable. In order to trace these ancient transmission processes, we can link particular human behaviors, such as accessing clay, to particular artifact attributes, such as REE geochemistry, to population-level characteristics, such as increasing or decreasing population levels.

Acknowledgments

This material is based upon work supported by the National Science Foundation under grant BCS-0723484 and BCS-0723857, to JWE and CLP. Additional NSF support provided to the MURR Archaeometry Group, including the most recent grant BCS 1415403 to Jeffrey Ferguson and Michael Glascock. We thank the many individuals who made this research possible, including access to collections (Lisa Deitz, Amy Gilreath, and Bill Hildebrandt) and preparation of samples (Sachiko Sakai).

6 Using Luminescence Dating to Address the Chronology and Cultural Affiliation of Brownware Ceramics in the Virgin Branch Puebloan Region

Karen G. Harry and Sachiko Sakai

The Virgin Branch Puebloan (VBP) culture encompassed the easternmost portions of the Mojave Desert and the westernmost edges of the Colorado Plateau between about AD 300–1200/1250. During prehistoric and early historic times, a variety of ceramics were produced in this area by potters associated with Puebloan, Yuman-speaking, and Numic-speaking cultures. The wares associated with each of these three groups are, in theory, easily distinguishable: Puebloan pottery is typically described as a gray or whiteware; Yuman pottery is identified as a buffware; and the pottery of the Numic-speakers is characterized as a brownware. It is with the brownwares that this paper is concerned.

In the VBP region brownware ceramics are traditionally interpreted as evidence for the presence of Numic-speaking populations. Because the timing of the Numic arrival into the southern Great Basin is subject to considerable debate, in recent years there have been several attempts to directly date these ceramics. Most studies have yielded dates that fall within the late prehistoric and historic periods, though a handful of earlier dates have been obtained. These dates obviously have important implications for understanding the spread of Numic speakers into the region. Tying the dates to Numic expansion, however, depends on two assumptions: first, that the dates are correct; and second, that the identification of the ceramics with Numic-speaking potters is accurate. In this paper, we discuss dates obtained from brownware and other ceramics recovered from the northwestern edge of the Colorado Plateau, and consider their implications for understanding Numic expansion.

Brownware Ceramics in the VBP Region

Like other Puebloan groups, the VBP people produced primarily gray and white ware ceramics, and it is these ceramics that comprise the vast majority of region's indigenous pottery. The occurrence of brownware pottery was first recognized by Baldwin (1950), who referred to the ceramics as Southern Paiute Utility Ware in recognition of their similarity to that made by the historic Paiute. Today, this pottery is often referred to as Intermountain Brown Ware (Pippin 1986; Tuohy 1990:97–98) and is one of three recognized brownwares made by Great Basin tribes (the other two being Shoshone Brown Ware and Owens Valley Brown Ware, made to the north and west of the VBP region, respectively). Like the other Great Basin wares, Intermountain Brown Ware ceramics were produced by residentially mobile people who are known to have occupied the area during the historic period. Evidence suggests that use of the pottery also occurred during the prehistoric period, though it is unknown how far back in time it extended.

Reflecting their production by residentially mobile people, Intermountain Brown Ware ceramics were more expediently produced and crudely made than those of their more sedentary Puebloan neighbors. Intermountain Brown Ware ceramics are typically characterized as having thick walls and coarse, crumbly textures. Surface colors vary but usually range from very dark brown to black, and the sherds have dark gray to black carbon cores. The ceramics contain poorly sorted, coarse sands, which may be naturally occurring or added as temper. Conical jars with pointed or semipointed bases comprise the most common vessel form. Surface decoration may be present and consists of incising, fingernail impressions, or occasionally, corrugation (Baldwin 1950; Betensen 2005; Seymour and Perry 1998:65–66).

When first identified by Baldwin, Southern Paiute Utility Ware (referred to as Intermountain Brown Ware hereafter) were the only brown ceramics known to occur in the VBP region.

Shortly thereafter Colton (1952:73) identified a second type that he termed Moapa Brown. Like Intermountain Brown Ware, this ware was described has having a brown surface color and a dark gray core; however, unlike the former it contained olivine rather than sand temper. Olivine temper also occurs in the better known and more common Moapa White and Gray wares, both belonging to the Virgin Branch sequence, and today most archaeologists consider the so-called Moapa Brown Wares to be a variant of Moapa Gray rather than a separate ware (Lyneis 2008b). Though superficially similar to Intermountain Brown Ware, these ceramics easily can be distinguished by their unique green olivine inclusions and by their lighter hues and finer pastes (Seymour and Perry 1998:58). Although Moapa White and Gray wares were produced throughout the VBP sequence, Schroeder (1955) suggested that the brown olivine-tempered ceramics were limited to the Basketmaker III and Pueblo I periods, a suggestion echoed by more recent archaeologists (Lyneis 2008a).

In the late 1980s, Margaret Lyneis (1992) identified a third brown-colored ceramic in the VBP region. This ceramic differed from both the Intermountain Brown Ware and the so-called Moapa Brown Ware by its ground sherd, or grog, temper. Common at Pueblo II period sites in the Moapa Valley, Lyneis suggested that this ceramic was made by VBP potters living on the Shivwits Plateau, the landform located on the westernmost edge of the Colorado Plateau. Lyneis named the newly identified pottery Shivwits Ware.

Thus, there are three ceramic wares in the VBP region with brown pastes. Two of these (Moapa Brown and Shivwits Ware) are associated with the Virgin Branch Puebloan people, and one of these (Intermountain Brown Ware) is associated with the Southern Paiute or their Numic-speaking ancestors. By convention, however, today only the Intermountain Brown Ware ceramics are referred to as "brownwares." Because of the close association of the term with Numic-speaking people, archaeologists currently working in the VBP region avoid classifying either Shivwits Ware ceramics or the brown olivine-tempered pottery as brownwares.

Dating of Appearance of Intermountain Brown Wares in the VBP Region

The chronological relationship between the makers of the Intermountain Brown Ware ceramics and the VBP people has been vigorously contested by archaeologists. In a review of the issue, Roberts (2012:165) observed that "today, most archaeologists support a model of Virgin Branch Puebloan abandonment of the region by AD 1300, followed by a Numic migration into the area from somewhere near Owens Valley." But despite general support for this viewpoint, she notes that there is a growing body of evidence suggesting that the two populations may have overlapped temporally. This evidence includes (a) the co-occurrence of brownware and grayware sherds in archaeological contexts, and (b) luminescence dates obtained directly on brownware ceramics.

Shutler (1961) was one of the first archaeologists to propose that the Southern Paiute and the VBP occupations overlapped in the Moapa Valley. This conclusion was based on his observation of what he thought was Southern Paiute pottery on VBP sites. However, these ceramics were subsequently reexamined by Lyneis (1994), who determined them to be Virgin Branch Shivwits Wares rather than Southern Paiute pottery. Since that time there have been additional reports from other areas of the Great Basin of the co-occurrence of brownware and grayware pottery. Yet, because most are from mixed or otherwise problematic contexts, they fall short of being able to prove the coexistence of the two populations (Lyneis 1994; Pippen 1986; Rhode 1994:126).

Due to problems in associating brownwares with other artifacts, archaeologists in recent years have turned to luminescence dating to directly date the ceramics themselves. Table 6.1 summarizes the 66 luminescence dates obtained on brownware ceramics in the Great Basin; these include four from sherds recovered in the VBP region and 62 from areas outside of the region. Of the 66 luminescence dates obtained, all but three have 2-sigma ranges that postdate the presumed circa AD 1250 abandonment of the region by the VBP people. The three earlier dates are from the Conway Shelter of southeastern Nevada (dated to AD 612–1032), Yucca Mountain of south-central Nevada (AD 881–1281), and Owens Valley of southeastern California (AD 965–1045).

Taken together, the luminescence dates suggest Numic-speakers most likely entered the area shortly after AD 1300 (Figure 6.1). The three earlier dates nonetheless raise the possibility that some Numic-speakers may have been in the Great Basin centuries before that

TABLE 6.1. Previous Luminescence Dating of Brownware Pottery

Provenience or Project	2-Sigma Date	Midpoint	Reference
Yamashita (Moapa Valley, southeastern Nevada)	AD 1158–1466	1312	Lyneis 2012
	AD 1403–1639	1521	
26CK2954 Data Recovery (Moapa Valley, southeastern Nevada)	AD 1749–1837	1793	Harper 2006
	AD 1716–1924	1820	
Conaway Shelter (southeastern Nevada)	AD 612–1032	822	Rhode 1994
Fortymile Canyon (south-central Nevada)	AD 1410–1558	1484	Rhode 1994
	AD 1503–1647	1575	
	AD 1521–1641	1581	
	AD 1784–1840	1812	
Yucca Mountain (south-central Nevada)	AD 881–1281	1081	Rhode 1994
	AD 1426–1566	1496	
	AD 1476–1588	1532	
	AD 1786–1842	1814	
	AD 1798–1874	1836	
Owens Valley (east-central California)	AD 1598–1710	1654	Rhode 1994
	AD 1564–1760	1662	
Hogup Cave (northwest Utah)	AD 1802–1847	1827	Rhode 1994
Nevada Test Site (south-central Nevada)	AD 1292–1608	1450	Feathers and Rhode 1998
	AD 1366–1586	1476	
	AD 1442–1638	1540	
	AD 1468–1808	1638	
	AD 1720–1804	1762	
	AD 1796–1960	1787	
	AD 1788–1892	1840	
Kern River 2003 Expansion Project (southwest Utah)	AD 1209–1467	1338	Friel 2005
	AD 1314–1428	1371	
	AD 1554–1660	1607	
	AD 1592–1738	1665	
	AD 1604–1780	1697	
	AD 1685–1759	1722	
	AD 1726–1744	1735	
	AD 1570–1910	1740	
	AD 1726–1774	1750	
	AD 1730–1868	1799	
	AD 1730–1868	1799	
	AD 1802–1860	1831	
	AD 1802–1860	1831	
	AD 1775–1903	1839	
	AD 1836–1858	1847	
	AD 1836–1874	1855	
	AD 1836–1874	1855	
	AD 1840–1870	1855	
	AD 1814–1846	1830	
Kern River 2003 Expansion Project (southwest Utah)	AD 1612–1662	1637	Friel 2005
	AD 1630–1694	1662	
	AD 1793–1843	1818	
	AD 1749–1837		

TABLE 6.1. (cont'd.) Previous Luminescence Dating of Brownware Pottery

Provenience or Project	2-Sigma Date	Midpoint	Reference
Owens Valley (southeastern California)	AD 965–1045[a]	1005	Eerkens and Lipo 2013
	AD 1489–1580 (8 sherds)[a]	n/a	
	ca. AD 1630–1685 (2 sherds)[a]	n/a	
Death Valley (southeastern California)	AD 1790–1900 (6 sherds)[b]	n/a	Eerkens and Lipo 2013
	ca. AD 1420–1675 (4 sherds)[b]	n/a	

[a] Eerkens and Lipo analyzed 11 sherds from Owen Valley. Of these, specific dates were provided for only one sherd. That sherd had a midpoint date of AD 1005; and a 2-sigma date range of AD 965–1045. Another eight sherds were reported to date within the interval of AD 1489 and 1580, and the dates of the remaining two sherds appear to fall between about AD 1630 and 1685 (as extrapolated from Eerkens and Lipo 2013:Figure 3).

[b] Eerkens and Lipo analyzed 10 sherds from Death Valley. Specific dates were not provided for each sherd, but they report that six of the dates fall within the range of 1790 to 1900. The dates of the four remaining sherds are widely distributed, but appear to fall between about AD 1420 and 1675 (as extrapolated from Eerkens and Lipo 2013:Figure 3).

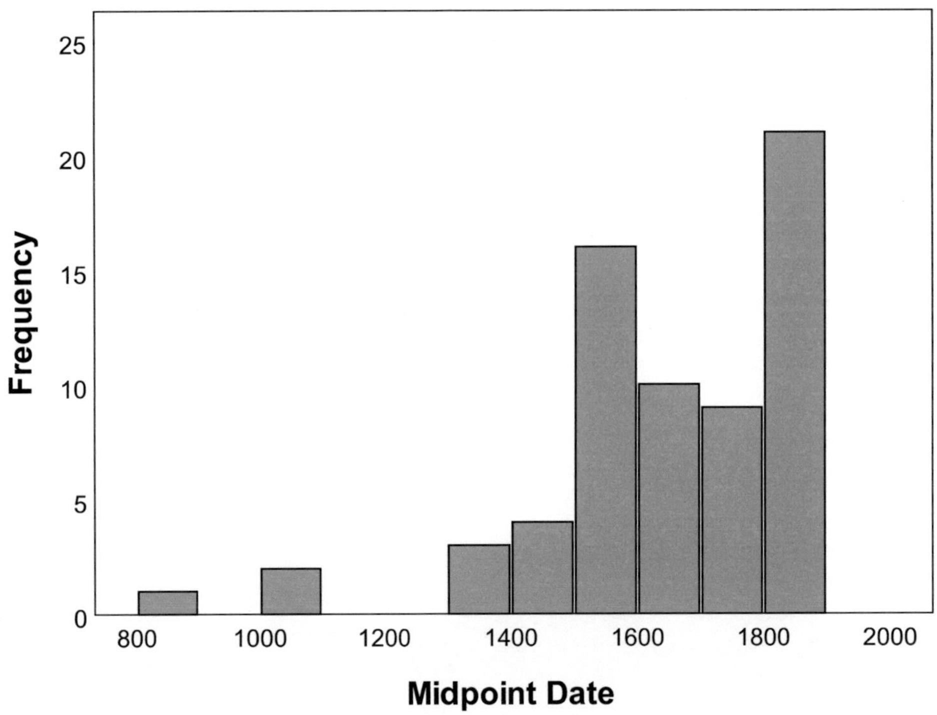

FIGURE 6.1. Graph of midpoint dates obtained from brownware ceramics in the Virgin Branch Puebloan region and Great Basin (data from Table 6.1).

time. This possibility was further raised when we discovered sand-tempered brown ceramics commingled with grayware ceramics at Pete's Pocket, a VBP site located on Shivwits Plateau (Figure 6.2).

In the VBP region, the proportion of corrugated ceramics is commonly used to chronologically sequence sites and features. In this area, corrugation first appears during the Middle II period (i.e., at about AD 1050) and steadily increases in time thereafter (Lyneis 1995:209). Sites having no corrugated ceramics, therefore, are assumed to date to the Early Pueblo II period or earlier; those having between 1 and 10% to the Middle Pueblo II; those with between 11 and 39% to the Late Pueblo II; and those with more than 40% to the Early Pueblo III.

The Pete's Pocket Site

The Pete's Pocket site, located about 300 m north of the Grand Canyon rim, contains eight dispersed rooms and a dispersed artifact scatter. Fieldwork was conducted at the site by the University of Nevada Las Vegas' Department

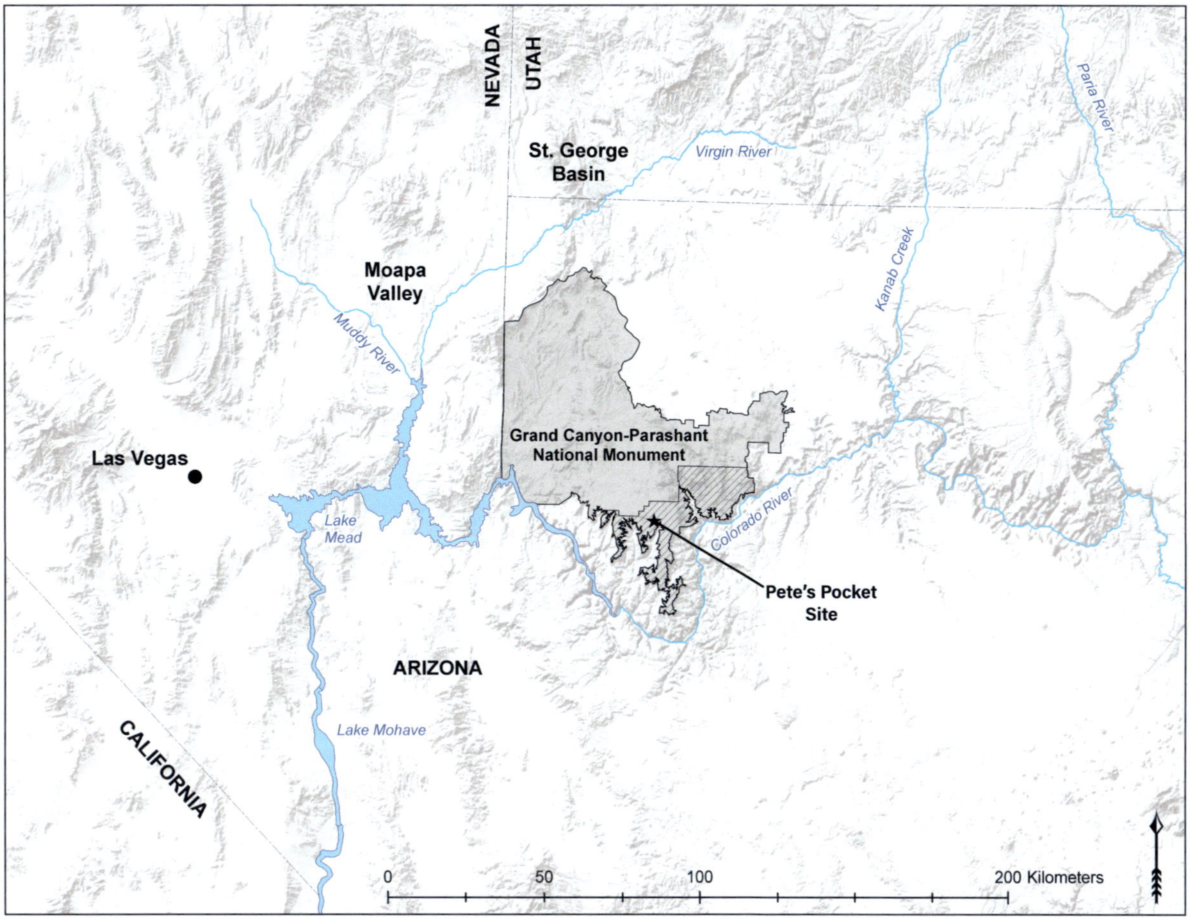

FIGURE 6.2. Location of Pete's Pocket site.

of Anthropology (UNLV) in the summers of 2012 and 2015 (Harry and Ferguson 2015). The results of the fieldwork indicate the site was constructed and used by the VBP people, although the distribution of ceramics suggests not all rooms were contemporaneous. Corrugated ceramics comprised about 10% of the Pete's Pocket ceramic collection; however, this proportion varied widely across the site. Ceramic collections associated with the various rooms suggest that of the eight rooms, four likely date to the Pueblo II period, two to the late Pueblo II period, and one to the early Pueblo III period. The ceramic collection obtained from the eighth room contained no corrugated ceramics, raising the possibility that it dates to the Pueblo I or early Pueblo II period, though the small number of ceramics recovered (n = 42) make this interpretation tentative (Table 6.2).

About 50 m northeast of the edge of Pete's Pocket is LAKE 12-038, a site comprised of four large roasting pit features. Initially thought to be associated with the VBP occupation at Pete's Pocket, test units were placed within two of the features by UNLV archaeologists in the summers of 2013 and 2014. Three radiocarbon dates obtained from the features indicate that they were used sometime between the early eighteenth and early twentieth centuries (Harry and Berkebile 2015). The historic dates suggest that they were associated with the Paiute Indians, who are known to have hunted and gathered in the area historically during the late summer and early fall (Kelly 1976). Macrobotanical remains recovered from the roasting pits are consistent with this interpretation and include cheno-am, purslane, sunflower, and grass seeds, all of which would have been available during the late summer to early fall (Harry and Berkebile 2015).

Pete's Pocket Ceramic Collection

Compared to ceramic collections recovered from other VBP sites on the Shivwits Plateau, the ceramics from Pete's Pocket are unusually diverse and exhibit substantial technological variability. Since 2006, Harry has overseen excavations at ten sites on the plateau and has conducted in-field analyses at countless others. This research indicates that most VBP ceramic assemblages on the Shivwits Plateau are dominated by three types of wares: Shivwits Ware, Moapa Ware, and Tusayan Ware-Virgin series ceramics. To recap, Shivwits Ware ceramics

Table 6.2. Chronological Information from Pete's Pocket

	Surface Ceramic Collection		Subsurface Ceramic Collection		
Room	Percent Corrugated	Total No. Ceramics	Percent Corrugated	Total No. Ceramics	Chronological Placement
1 and 2[a]	17.8	565	16.7	211	Late Pueblo II
3, 4, and 5[a]	20.7	125	5.8	69	Middle Pueblo II (note: date is based on the subsurface collection; because these rooms are within 25 m of Rooms 1 and 2, both of which were associated with an unusually dense artifact scatter, it is likely that their surface collections contain ceramics associated with the occupation of those two rooms)
6	0.5	219	1.3	398	Middle Pueblo II (note: this date is supported by a radiocarbon date of AD 1020–1160 obtained from an upright beam recovered from the structure's floor)
7	0	42	—	—	Possibly Pueblo I or Early Pueblo II (though the small sample size makes this conclusion tentative)
8	50.0	32	41.9	74	Early Pueblo III

[a] Because these rooms are contiguous and share walls, they are considered contemporaneous.

Table 6.3. Pete's Pocket Ceramic Assemblage

Ware	Count	Percent
Tusayan Ware, Virgin Series (sand-tempered)		
Gray or white	307	14.5
Brown	145	6.8
(Total Virgin Series)	*(452)*	*(21.3)*
Moapa Ware (olivine-tempered)		
Gray or white	457	21.5
Brown	164	7.7
(Total Moapa Ware)	*(621)*	*(29.3)*
Shivwits Ware (sherd-tempered with brown paste)	935	44.0
Intermountain Brown Ware (sand-tempered with dark brown paste)	6	0.3
Other/Indeterminate	109	5.1
Total	2,123	100.0

are dark brown and sherd-tempered ceramics, while Moapa Ware ceramics are gray or white and olivine-tempered. Tusayan Ware-Virgin series ceramics, in contrast, are sand-tempered and gray or white in color. Because of the different paste colors and tempering materials, the three wares can generally be distinguished quite easily both from one another and from Intermountain Brown Wares.

As with the other sites we have studied on the Shivwits Plateau, the Pete's Pocket ceramic collection was dominated by pottery identified as either Shivwits Ware, Moapa Ware, or Tusayan Ware-Virgin Series (Table 6.3). However, unlike the other sites, many of the Moapa Ware and Tusayan Ware-Virgin series ceramics contained brown, rather than white or gray, pastes. These brown varieties comprised more than a quarter of the Moapa Ware ceramics and nearly a third of the Virgin Series. Six sherds having brown pastes and sand tempers were identified as Intermountain Brown Ware.

The recovery of such large numbers of olivine-tempered and sand-tempered brown ceramics was unexpected. The olivine-tempered brown sherds, which ranged in color from light brown to very dark brown, exhibited coarser and more poorly prepared pastes compared to their gray counterparts (Figure 6.3). These sherds, though unusual, matched Colton's description

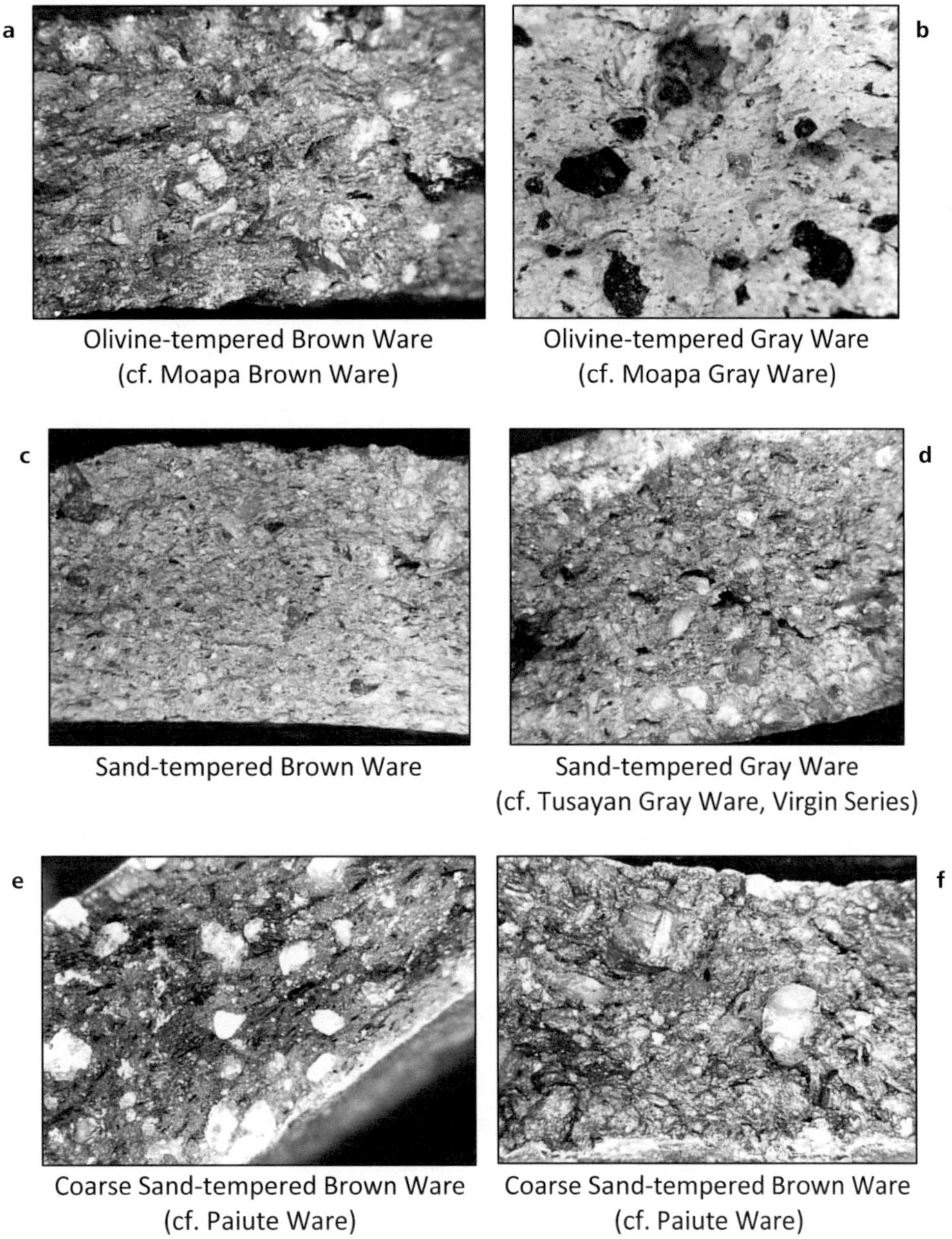

FIGURE 6.3. Cross sections of ceramic wares discussed in this paper.

for Moapa Brown Ware. Because Moapa Brown Ware was thought to occur only during the early part of the VBP sequence, this suggested that the sherds might be an early variant of Moapa Gray Ware. Assuming Schroeder (1955) was correct in assigning these ceramics to the early part of the VBP sequence, their presence would lend support to the Pueblo I period occupation suggested by the radiocarbon dates.

In addition to the brown-colored, olivine-tempered sherds, we also recovered numerous brown sherds tempered with quartz sands. Although brown sand-tempered sherds are traditionally associated with Numic-speaking groups such as the Paiute, other attributes of the sherds did not match those of the Numic Intermountain Brown Ware pottery. Compared to the latter, most of the brown sand-tempered ceramics at Pete's Pocket contained smaller inclusions and exhibited more homogenous and less crumbly pastes. In texture and temper size they were similar to the Tusayan Gray Ware-Virgin series ceramics, and for this reason they were considered to be a variant of that series (see Figures 6.3c and 6.3d). They were less vitrified than the gray sand-tempered sherds, however, suggesting that they had been fired at lower temperatures.

Finally, six darker-brown, more coarsely textured, sand-tempered sherds were recovered that we tentatively classified as Intermountain Brown Ware. These ceramics contained coarse, poorly sorted quartz sand tempers and exhibited dark black, almost oily looking, cross sections (see Figure 6.3e and 6.3f). Compared to the other ceramics at the site, their pastes were coarser and appear to have been poorly prepared.

Research Goals

The recovery of the brown ceramics raised several questions regarding the age and cultural affiliation of both the pottery and the site. In particular, we wished to determine whether the six sherds tentatively identified as Intermountain Brown Ware were contemporaneous with the roasting pits located just outside of the Pete's Pocket site. If so, these would represent the first undisputed Paiute sherds found on the Shivwits Plateau. The previous lack of reports for these sherds appears to reflect a region-wide trend in which the Paiute utilized the western Colorado Plateau but seemingly left behind no ceramic artifacts (Euler 1964).

A second goal was to determine when the brown olivine-tempered and Virgin series sand-tempered ceramics were produced. Was the olivine-tempered brown pottery produced during the Pueblo I period, as previous archaeologists have suggested? If so, were the sand-tempered brown ceramics also an early variety, contemporaneous with the olivine-tempered brownwares? Or, were these brown VBP ceramics produced later during the sequence—perhaps during the middle Pueblo II or early Pueblo III period, when the majority of the site appears to have been occupied?

Research Methods

To address these questions, we conducted Optically Stimulated Luminescence (OSL) dating on fourteen sherds from Pete's Pocket. These included three of the brown olivine-tempered sherds (those similar to the Moapa Brown Ware), three of the sand-tempered medium brown sherds (considered to be a variant of the Tusayan Ware-Virgin series sherds), and two dark brown sherds (identified as probable Intermountain Brown Ware). In addition, for comparative purposes, three Moapa Gray Ware and three Tusayan Gray Ware, Virgin series sherds were analyzed.

OSL dating works by measuring the amount of light (luminescence) given off by crystalline material (in this case, the quartz grains contained in the ceramic pastes) when sufficient energy is applied. The resulting luminescence is generated by trapped electrons that have accumulated over time from naturally occurring radiation in the environment. Thus, the greater amount of time that has elapsed since the electrons have started to accumulate, the greater will be the amount of emitted light. However, when the material is exposed to sufficient heat or sunlight, such as that which occurs during the manufacture or firing of the ceramic vessel, the charged particles will be released and the luminescence clock "reset." In the case of ceramics, then, it is possible to determine the amount of time since the vessel was fired by measuring the amount of emitted light from quartz inclusions. (More detailed explanations of the technique can be found in Feathers 2003 and Malainey 2011:121–129.)

The OSL analyses were carried out on coarse-grained (90–120 µ) quartz particles removed from the interior of sherd samples. All work was conducted at the Luminescence Dating Laboratory in the IIRMES Laboratory, California State University, Long Beach. Luminescence signals were measured by an automated Risø TL/OS 12B/C reader with calibrated beta sources (^{90}Sr) to evaluate the rate of luminescence signal accumulation. Blue-light OSL (BOSL) stimulation was used with a single aliquot regenerative dose (SAR) protocol (Murray and Wintle 2000). (The general methods used follow the procedures outlined by Sakai 2014, and the reader is referred to that resource for additional information.)

Table 6.4. Results of OSL Dating

Ware	2σ date range	Midpoint Date
cf. Paiute Ware	AD 534–818	AD 676
cf. Paiute Ware	AD 1166–1334	AD 1250
Virgin series, gray	AD 845–1089	AD 967
Virgin series, gray	AD 1044–1236	AD 1140
Virgin series, gray	AD 1634–1714	AD 1674
cf. Virgin series, brown	AD 1076–1224	AD 1150
cf. Virgin series, brown	AD 1094–1266	AD 1180
cf. Virgin series, brown	AD 1102–1298	AD 1200
Moapa Ware, gray	AD 773–1153	AD 963
Moapa Ware, gray	AD 1149–1381	AD 1265
Moapa Ware, gray	AD 1200–1404	AD 1302
cf. Moapa Brown	AD 534–830	AD 682
cf. Moapa Brown	AD 952–1156	AD 1054
cf. Moapa Brown	AD 1689–1745	AD 1717

Results

The results of the OSL dating are presented in Table 6.4 and graphically illustrated in Figure 6.4. These data indicate that the sherds tentatively identified as Intermountain Brown Ware predate the use of the two roasting pits that were dated by radiocarbon dating, and even more significant, they substantially predate the time when the Paiute were known to have used the Shivwits Plateau.

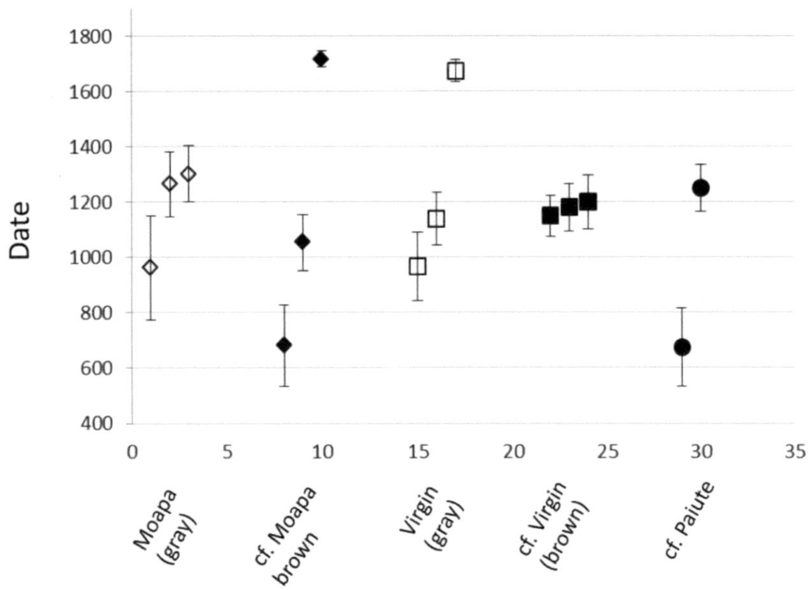

FIGURE 6.4. OSL dates obtained on analyzed ceramics. Icons represent the midpoint dates and the bars the 95% confidence intervals. Triangles represent olivine-tempered ceramics (Moapa Wares), squares represent sand-tempered ceramics (Virgin series), and circles represent coarse sand-textured sherds (cf. Intermountain Brown Ware). Shaded icons represent brown ceramics and unshaded icons represent gray ceramics.

The most recent sherd dates to AD 1166–1334, which encompasses the time period that the Southern Paiute are thought to have entered the region. The earlier sherd dates to AD 534–818 and, if truly produced by Numic-speaking people, would represent the earliest such ceramic to be recovered this far to the east.

The dates of the brown olivine-tempered ceramics are widely distributed, ranging from the Basketmaker III or Pueblo I period (AD 534–830), the Pueblo II period (AD 952–1156), and the historic period (AD 1689–1745). They do not cluster to the Basketmaker III or Pueblo I periods, as would have been predicted by their distributions at other sites. The brown so-called Virgin Series ceramics also do not date to this early period, but cluster rather tightly to the middle Pueblo II or early Pueblo III periods. The dates on these two ceramics suggest that, at the Pete's Pocket site, VBP potters produced brown as well as gray and white ceramics until the end or nearly the end of the VBP sequence.

The two historic period dates (obtained for a Virgin series gray sherd and a Virgin series brown sherd) are likely anomalous. All available evidence suggests that the VBP people abandoned the Shivwits Plateau and adjacent regions by the late thirteenth century. Thus, the dates on these ceramics must either (a) not reflect the time of their manufacture, or (b) our assumptions about their cultural affiliation must be wrong. The most likely explanation is that the dates do not reflect the time when the vessels were fired and used. Because OSL dates the last time that the sherd was fired, if these ceramics were subjected to a postdepositional firing event (such as a forest fire or a campfire created by a later visitor to the site) then the date would reflect that later event.

Discussion

The OSL dates from the Pete's Pocket ceramic collection suggest that, unlike most Virgin Branch potters, the inhabitants there produced or used ceramics with brown pastes. As with the gray wares, some ceramics were tempered with olivine and others with sand. Given their temporal overlap with their gray counterparts, we consider the brown sherds to be local variants of Moapa Ware and Tusayan Ware-Virgin series ceramics.

Most of the sand-tempered ceramics exhibited well-prepared pastes and medium to fine sands, but a very small number exhibited coarse pastes and textures like those that typically characterize Intermountain Brown Ware. Given the early OSL dates obtained for these sherds and given the presence of the other brown ceramics, however, we believe that they were not produced by Numic-speaking people. Instead, we suggest that these coarse brown ceramics represent atypically coarse ceramics produced by VBP potters.

These findings have implications for interpreting other early dates obtained from brownware ceramics. As discussed earlier, the majority of luminescence dates from such ceramics postdate AD 1300. However, at least three dates fall before this time period, and these dates have been used to suggest that the Southern Paiute may have overlapped with the VBP people for several centuries. The data presented here, though, suggest that while not common, some VBP people did produce brown sand-tempered ceramics. The data further suggest that, despite the common assumption that the pottery of Numic speakers can be distinguished easily from that produced by Ancestral Puebloan groups, attributes of the two wares can overlap in some instances. As a result, archaeologists are urged not to assume all sand-tempered brown ceramics from the eastern Great Basin and western Colorado Plateau are Numic in origin. Rather, the specific attributes of the ceramics must be taken into consideration as well as the context from which they were recovered. In particular, ceramics for which unexpectedly early dates are obtained should be carefully examined to ensure they exhibit attributes (such as incised decorations or pointed bases) not found in Puebloan vessels.

7

A Functional Analysis of Upland and Lowland Virgin Branch Ceramics through Residue Analysis

Brenna Wilkerson, Karen G. Harry, and Spencer M. Steinberg

Food is a fundamental component of human life, and the decisions that people make regarding what foods to eat and how they are to be procured can affect more than just health and nutrition; they can also shape how people interact both with one another (e.g., through exchange relationships and distribution networks) and with the surrounding environment and landscape. Diet, subsistence strategies, and the role of food in human societies have long been important topics in archaeological research; however, relatively little work on these subjects has been conducted within the Virgin Branch Puebloan (VBP) region. This study explores VBP diet and subsistence strategies by using gas chromatography-mass spectrometry (GC-MS) to examine food residues embedded within VBP ceramics. Used in this analysis were ceramics dating to the middle Pueblo II period (ca. AD 1050–1100) and recovered from sites located in the lowland and upland regions.

Environmental Setting

The VBP culture spanned parts of northern Arizona, southern Nevada, and southern Utah from approximately 300 BC to AD 1200 (Figure 7.1). The area can be divided into three geographic and ecological zones: (1) the plateaus, located within the Colorado Plateau physiographic province, (2) the St. George Basin, and (3) the Moapa Valley lowlands. Both the St. George Basin and the Moapa Valley lowlands are located within the Basin and Range physiographic province (Lyneis 1996). These areas have significantly different environments and climates that affect the types of wild plant and animal resources available, as well as the conditions for agriculture. This study focused on two of the zones, the upland plateaus and the lowlands.

The Plateaus

The upland region, situated on the western portion of the Colorado Plateau, is comprised of a series of north-south trending plateaus (Lyneis 1995). This study focuses on the westernmost of these, the Shivwits Plateau. Near its southern edge, where the ceramics used in this study were recovered, elevation averages between 1,890 and 1,980 m (6,200–6,500 ft) above sea level and the growing season lasts about 150 days. Permanent water sources are lacking, and few springs exist in the area. Precipitation, which averages between 23 and 33 cm (10–15 in) annually, follows a bimodal pattern with about 60% falling during the winter and the majority of the remainder during the summer. The timing of the precipitation would have created challenges for prehistoric farmers. To avoid losing crops to late spring or early fall frosts, planting would have had to been done between the middle of May and the middle of June. Unfortunately, this is also the driest period of the year, making the risk of germination failure high.

Vegetation on the southern end of the Shivwits Plateau includes pinyon-juniper woodlands, ponderosa pines (*Pinus ponderosa*), and sagebrush (*Artemesia* sp.). Other wild resources include sunflower seeds (*Helianthus*), buckwheat (*Eriogonum* sp.), globemallow (*Sphaeralcea* sp.), and groundcherry (*Physalis* sp.). Several varieties of cacti, including prickly pear (*Opuntia* sp.), are present. Agave can also be found at and just beneath the rim of the Grand Canyon. Large mammals

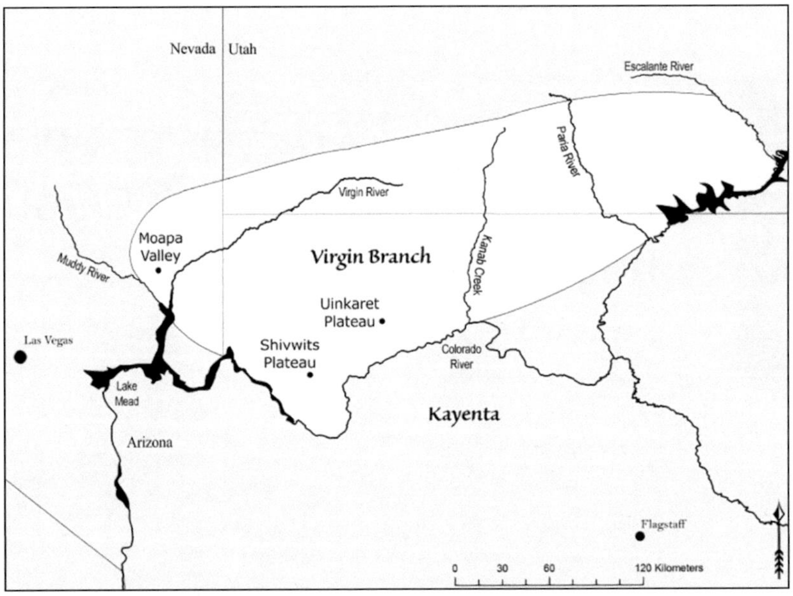

FIGURE 7.1. Map of locations discussed in text: Moapa Valley; Shivwits Plateau; and Uinkaret Plateau.

such as mule deer (*Odocoileus hemionus*) are abundant, as are jackrabbits (*Lepus* sp.) and cottontails (*Silvilagus* sp.; Lyneis 1995; Wells 1991).

The Lowlands

The lowland area is located in the Moapa Valley of southern Nevada, where the Muddy and the Virgin Rivers meet. Elevation ranges from between 250 and 500 m (1,150 to 1,640 ft) above sea level and the growing season averages 180 days. Mean precipitation is 10 cm (4 in) per year, far too little to have supported dry farming. However, the reliable and sluggish flow of the spring-fed Muddy River is ideal for irrigation (Larson and Michaelsen 1990; Lyneis 1995). Due to the reliability of the river and the long growing season, irrigation farming in the Moapa Valley would have been far less risky than the dry farming that was practiced on the Shivwits Plateau.

Wild plant resources in the lowlands vary based on topography. Valley floors contain creosote (*Larrea tridentata*), cholla (*Cylindropuntia* sp.), beavertail cactus (*Opuntia basilaris*), and bursage (*Ambrosia dumosa*), and the floodplain supports riparian species such as mesquite, cattails, and various grasses (Allison 2000; Lyneis 1995). On Mormon Mesa, which overlooks the floodplain to the east, desert lily (*Eromocrinum albomarginatum*) grows in abundance (Duke and Rice 2016: 38, personal communication 2016). Small mammals and reptiles are present and fish could have been obtained from the river. Large game animals do not inhabit the immediate vicinity, though bighorn sheep could have been found in rock outcrops located some 13 km (8 mi) to the west of the floodplain and deer from the Virgin Mountains about 32 km (20 mi) to the east.

Cultural Setting

Compared to other areas of the American Southwest, the prehistory of the VBP region is poorly understood. The archaeological sequence is known primarily from large-scale surveys and excavations that took place in the Moapa Valley between 1925 and 1941 (Shutler 1961). Less work has been conducted in the uplands, though unpublished information is available from a series of field schools conducted on the southern end of the plateau by the University of Nevada, Las Vegas.

Available information indicates that the inhabitants of the two regions incorporated both wild resources and domesticated crops (maize, beans, and squash) into their diet. There is substantial disagreement, however, about the role agriculture played in VBP society. Some researchers have argued that VBP inhabitants were heavily dependent on maize agriculture, and that wild resources comprised only a small part of their diet (Allison 1990:114; Martin 1999; McFadden 1996). In contrast, others have proposed that they were essentially horticulturalists who incorporated only small amounts of cultivated foods into a diet based primarily on wild resources.

Similarly, it is unknown to what degree subsistence patterns differed between the two regions. Based on data from the lowlands of the St. George Basin, Dalley and McFadden (1988:288) have suggested that hunting played only a minor role, and Harrington (1927) and Hayden (1930) likewise commented on the rarity of animal bone at sites in the Moapa Valley. Large game, though, would have been far more abundant on the plateau. It is therefore possible hunting, and therefore meat, was more important in that area. As well, due to the greater risk of farming in the upland region, wild plants may have comprised a larger part of the upland diet.

Another possibility is that foodstuffs were transported between the two regions to offset the different resources available in each area. We know the areas were linked economically and that nonfoodstuffs were transferred between the two regions. The evidence for this comes primarily from the distribution of ceramics. Three wares comprise the overwhelming majority of most VBP ceramic assemblages. These are Moapa Ware ceramics, believed to have been produced in the upland region on the Uinkaret Plateau (Allison 2000; Lyneis 1992, 1995; Sakai 2014); Shivwits Ware ceramics, believed to have been produced on the southern end of the Shivwits Plateau (Harry et al. 2013); and Tusayan Ware Virgin series ceramics believed to have been produced widely in the VBP region (Allison 2000; Ferguson 2014, 2016; Lyneis 1992:43). Evidence of the ceramic distribution network comes primarily from the Moapa Valley, where as much as half of the ceramic collections at some sites consist of the upland-produced Moapa and Shivwits Wares. This ceramic distribution network began as early as the Basketmaker III period (i.e., around AD 500), and reached its peak during the middle Pueblo II period (i.e., at around AD 1050–1100; Harry 2005; Lyneis 1992).

Research Goals

To investigate issues relating to the subsistence practices of the VPB people, residue analysis was conducted on plain jar sherds recovered from the upland and lowland regions. This analysis was conducted with three goals in mind. First, we wished to explore the general diet of the VBP people—are the residues contained within the vessels primarily those of domesticated crops, suggesting that they relied on agricultural foods; or are they primarily those of wild resources, suggesting that agricultural played only a limited role in their diet?

Second, we hoped to examine whether the diet of the upland and lowland inhabitants differed. Relating to this goal, we specifically wished to investigate (a) whether the upland region had evidence for a greater dependence on wild resources compared to the lowland region; (b) whether different resources were utilized in each area (e.g., a greater dependence on large mammals or pinyon nuts in the upland areas, vs. a greater dependence on fish and desert lily bulbs in the lowlands); and (c) whether there was evidence for food exchange between the two regions. The latter possibility would be suggested if the residues of resources found only in one region were recovered from the ceramics obtained in the other region. For example, if fish residues were found in pottery collected from upland sites, this would suggest that fish had been transported into the area (either through trade or direct procurement) since no permanent streams or lakes are present in the latter area.

Finally, we hoped to investigate whether different wares contained different residues. In a study on modern Kalinga groups, Skibo (1992, 2013:77) found that vessels with different forms served different functions; pots used to cook vegetables and meats were shorter with flared rims and large openings, while rice-cooking pots were taller with smaller openings and less flared rims. Likewise, Eerkens (2005:97) found that different types of pots in the western Great Basin were used to cook specific types of foods. The three wares used in the present study are made with different types of clays and tempers, attributes that would have affected their performance characteristics. A previous study by Anderson (2011) suggests the Moapa and Shivwits Ware ceramics would have been more resistant to thermal shock than the Tusayan Ware Virgin series ceramics. Perhaps then, the former ceramics were used more frequently to boil foods or cook foods at higher temperatures than were the Virgin series ceramics. If the different wares were used to prepare different categories of food, this practice should be reflected in the types of residues absorbed into the walls of the ceramics.

Issues in Archaeological Residue Analysis

To address the questions raised above, gas chromatography-mass spectrometry (GC-MS) was used to identify the types of lipids present in ceramics recovered from upland and lowland sites. These data were used to infer broad categories of food cooked, stored, or prepared in the ceramic vessels.

Plant and animal residues are made of a wide variety of lipids, proteins, carbohydrates, and other chemicals compounds, and these residues can be absorbed into the walls of a ceramic vessel during cooking (Evershed 1993; Heron and Evershed 1993). One of the advantages of GC-MS is that it enables archaeologists to separate and identify specific chemical compounds (Heron and Evershed 1993). The current study focuses on identifying lipids since they are present in a variety of plant and animal residues (Heron and Evershed 1993), tend to preserve better than other types of molecules (Evershed 1993, 2008; Heron and Evershed 1993), and are unlikely to have been contaminated by the sherd being buried in the soil (Evershed 1993).

Another advantage of GC-MS is that it can often detect foods unable to be detected by other methods, such as flotation or pollen analysis or the analysis of faunal remains. For example, foods such as the desert lily tubers found in the VBP lowland region are unlikely to preserve (Munson et al. 1971), making it difficult to find evidence of them during excavation. Furthermore, prehistoric storage and disposal practices can affect the types of food and animal remains recovered. These and other formation processes can bias our understanding of diet and subsistence strategies by emphasizing those foods (such as maize) that preserve well. By providing evidence of less easily preserved and recovered remains such as greens, roots, and tubers, residue analysis can contribute to a better understanding of prehistoric diet and subsistence strategies.

The technique does, however, have some drawbacks. First, it should be recognized that the identified residues do not represent all of the foods cooked, stored, or processed in the vessel. Instead, the residues are likely to reflect only those foods present during the vessel's initial uses. This is because the initial residues will quickly clog the vessel pores; effectively sealing the ceramic off from any residues produced during subsequent uses (Eerkens 2005).

Second, determining the origin of even these initial residues is not a straightforward process. This is because lipids (including fatty acids) are subject to degradation from exposure to heat (Eerkens 2005:87; Malainey 1997), which can affect both the type and amount of fatty acids present. Since most or all of the ceramics used in the present study likely came from cooking vessels, the residues have likely been degraded. Interpretation is further complicated by the fact that fatty acids degrade at different rates. Because unsaturated fatty acids break down more rapidly than saturated ones, residues from archaeological contexts will contain lower relative percentages of polyunsaturated fatty acids compared to fresh, undegraded samples (Eerkens 2005:87; Malainey 1997). It can also be difficult to pinpoint specific foods because similar lipids can occur in a wide variety of plants and animals. Although some species leave behind specific biomarkers, in the present study no such biomarkers were found. Finally, if multiple foods were cooked together (as will often have been the case), the mixture of residues can further confound interpretation.

Methods

Despite the complicating factors discussed above, residue analysis can provide information relevant to understanding general patterns of subsistence and food preparation practices. In this section, we describe the methods used to conduct the GC-MS analysis and to interpret the resulting data.

Table 7.1. Summary of Sample Size Based on Ware and Site

Ceramic	Moapa Valley	Shivwits Plateau	Total
Moapa Ware	5	5	10
Shivwits Ware	5	5	10
Virgin series	5	5	10
Total	15	15	30

Sampling Strategy

Thirty ceramics representing the three ceramic wares and the two environmental areas were analyzed for this study (Table 7.1). All sherds selected for analysis were from plain, undecorated jars. This was done to increase the likelihood that they came from vessels used in daily cooking, storage, and food preparation activities. Because painted ceramics were often used to store or serve dry foodstuffs or other materials, they were considered to have a lower likelihood of yielding food residues. Additionally, ceramics were selected from proveniences widely separated in space to decrease the likelihood that sherds from the same vessel would be sampled.

Only body sherds thought to come from the upper portions of the vessel were used in the analysis. As with the decision to sample only unpainted sherds, this decision was made to maximize the likelihood that food residues would be recovered. Previous studies have shown that during cooking, the highest concentration of residues tends to accumulate near the vessel's rim and the lowest concentrations near the base (Charters et al. 1993; Malainey 2011).

Finally, only sherds larger than 3 cm were selected. Because GC-MS analysis requires the destruction of a small (approximately 1 × 1 cm) portion of the sherd, sherds smaller than this size were avoided in order to ensure that the entire sherd was not destroyed. By retaining a portion of each sherd, further analysis will be possible in the future.

Two upland and two lowland sites were represented in the analysis. Both sites date to the middle Pueblo II period, the time when the ceramic distribution network was at its height. This time period was selected in order to evaluate whether foods, as well as the pottery, were transferred between the two regions. The lowland ceramics come from sites MRS 73-5 and MRS 73-34 in the Moapa Valley (see Figure 7.1) and were collected during a 1973 surface survey of the sites. The upland sites were Granary House (AZ A:14:46) and Site 232 (AZ A:14:232), both of which are located on the Shivwits Plateau and were excavated between 2006 and 2011 by the University of Nevada, Las Vegas. Additional information regarding these sites can be found in Wilkerson (2016).

TABLE 7.2. Criteria Used to Distinguish Food Types based on Fatty Acid Ratios (reproduced from Eerkens 2005:Table 2)

Ratio	State	Terrestrial Mammals	Fish	Roots	Greens	Seeds and Nuts	Berries
(C15:0+C17:0)/C18:0	Fresh	<0.2	0.2–0.5	>0.2	0.1–1.0	<0.6	<0.2
	Degraded	<0.2	0.2–0.5	>0.2	0.1–1.0	<0.6	<0.2
C16:1/C18:1	Fresh	0.02–0.2	0.2–0.5	0.05–0.7	>0.7	<0.3	<0.08
	Degraded	0.08–0.8	0.8–2.0	0.2–2.8	>2.8	<1.2	<0.32
C16:0/C18:0	Fresh	<3.5	4–6	3–12	5–12	0–9	2–6
	Degraded	<7	8–12	6–24	10–24	0–18	4–12
C12:0/C14:0	Fresh	<0.15	<0.15	>0.15	>0.05	>0.15	>0.15
	Degraded	<0.15	<0.15	>0.15	>0.05	>0.15	>0.15

Sample Preparation

To prepare the sample, a rock saw was used to remove a 1 × 1 cm section of each sherd. Distilled water was sprayed on the sherd and blade during the cutting process to allow for easier cutting. After the sherd dried, the outer 1 mm of all surfaces was sanded down and removed to reduce the likelihood of surface contamination (Eerkens 2001). Once the sherd was completely dry, it was ground into a fine powder using a porcelain mortar and pestle. The sherd powder was then transferred to a sterile cryovial for temporary storage until it could be analyzed. Nitrile gloves were worn when handling sherds to prevent contamination from the oils present on the skin, particularly cholesterol™ (Evershed 1993; Heron and Evershed 1993). All tools were washed with soap, rinsed with distilled water, and coated with methanol after each use.

The GC-MS analysis was carried out by Spencer Steinberg at the University of Nevada Las Vegas' Department of Chemistry, similar to the method reported in Steinberg and colleagues (2008). Fatty acids were detected and quantified using chemolysis (pyrolysis with methylation), whereby complex organic mixtures are thermally degraded (pyrolysis) and simultaneously derivatized. Chemolysis was conducted using a CDS Pyroprobe 2000 equipped with a CDS model 1500 GC interface. The pyroprobe was installed on a Varian model 3800 gas chromatograph equipped with a model 1039 injector that was in turn interfaced to a Varian 2200 mass spectrometer. Aliquots of the sample (25 to 35 mg) were packed into precombusted (1,100°C) open quartz tubes (2 cm × 2 mm), and the sample was held in place with precombusted quartz wool. The quartz wool was combusted at 900°C for 18 hours before use.

Tetramethylammonium hydroxide (TMAH; 20 μL of 25% in methanol) was added to the sample with a syringe. The TMAH effects alkaline degradation of food residues and also methylates many polar pyrolysis and degradation products that would otherwise be insufficiently volatile for GC–MS analysis. The ground sherd sample was dried for 30 seconds at 90°C to remove the methanol and then ballistically heated to 800°C for 10 seconds (600°C also tried) effecting simultaneous saponification and methylation of fatty acid to produce volatile methyl esters.

The model 1039 injector was set to a 10:1 split ratio during the chemolysis step. The chemolysis products were separated by gas chromatography using a Restek Rtx-5ms column with dimensions of 30 m × 0.25 mm. The column phase thickness was 0.25 um. The gas chromatograph oven was initially held at 40°C for 6 min and then ramped at 10°C min-1 to 280°C, where it was held for 10 min. The carrier gas (He) flow rate was electronically regulated to 1.00 mL/min. Blanks were run in between samples to minimize cross contamination.

Chemopyrolysis products were identified by comparison of their mass spectra with standard compounds and by comparing collected mass spectra with the National Institute of Standards and Technology (NIST 2002) mass spectral library.

Data Reduction and Analysis

Three techniques were used to aid in the interpretation of the data obtained from GC-MS analysis. These include the calculation of fatty acid ratios, the calculation of relative percentages of fatty acids, and cluster analysis.

The calculation of fatty acid ratios is based on the work of Jelmer Eerkens (2001, 2002, 2005). To avoid interpretative problems caused by the fact that different types of fatty acids degrade at different rates, Eerkens proposes that archaeologists base their analyses on fatty acids that degrade at similar rates. Specifically, he suggests four ratios for interpreting archaeological residues: (1) C16:1/C18:1, (2) C16:0/C18:0, (3) C12:0/C14:0, and (4) (C15:0 + C17:0)/C18:0. Eerkens uses these ratios to categorize residues into six broad categories: seeds/nuts, roots, berries, greens, fish, and terrestrial mammal. The value ranges for each ratio by food type is presented in

TABLE 7.3. Relative Percentages of Fatty Acids used to Identify Archaeological Residues (Malainey et al. 1999:100)

Identification	Medium Chain	C18:0	C18:1 isomers
Large herbivore	≤15%	≥27.5%	≤15%
Large herbivore with plant or bone marrow	Low	≥25%	15%≤x≤25%
Plant with large herbivore	≥15%	≥25%	No data
Beaver	Low	Low	>25%
Fish or corn	Low	≤25%	15%≤x≤27.5%
Fish or corn with plant	≥15%	≤25%	15%≤x≤27.5%
Plant (except corn)	≥10%	≤27.5%	≤15%

Table 7.2. The table lists two ranges for each ratio by food type: fresh and degraded. The fresh values come from experimental work done on modern foods; the degraded values are derived from research on the long-term decomposition rates of the foods. Because our analyses are based on archaeological samples, we compared our results against the degraded values in Table 7.2.

A second method used to interpret the results was based on the work of Mary Malainey (1997; Malainey et al. 1999) and relies on the calculation of the relative percentages of certain fatty acids. To identify the proportion of fatty acids represented by different foods, Malainey cooked various foods in ceramic containers and then heated the ceramic samples to mimic degradation over time. Principal component analysis was then used to characterize the types of residues present in the experimental samples. Based on this information, she created criteria for identifying seven categories of residues: large herbivore, large herbivore with plant *or* bone marrow, plant with large herbivore, beaver, fish or corn, fish *or* corn with plant, and plant (except corn). Table 7.3 lists the criteria used to identify these categories based on the relative percentages of C18:0, C18:1, and medium chain fatty acids (C12:0, C14:0, and C15:0).

The above two methods provide the means to assign residues into food categories. Categorization is not absolute and not without error, however. For example, Eerkens' technique of using the fatty acid ratios often leads to samples being placed in more than one category, because of the overlap that can occur in fatty acid ratios. A value of 10 for C16:0/C18:0, for instance, would fall into the degraded categories for fish, roots, greens, seeds/nuts, and berries (see Table 7.2). Further, though the method greatly improves the accuracy of classification over that which would occur from chance alone, errors in classification do nonetheless still occur. In a discriminant analysis of the data, Eerkens (2005:91) reports that 65% of the samples were correctly classified, a substantial improvement over the 17% that would have been correctly classified by chance alone. Despite this improvement, however, more than a third of the samples were nonetheless incorrectly identified. There is no similar evaluation for Malainey's technique, but we can expect that some errors might similarly be expected. Because of the likelihood of errors on individual samples, we elected to conduct a hierarchical cluster analysis (using Ward's method) on the data to look for grouping patterns. Once groups were identified, they were compared against the individual assignments made using both Eerkens' and Malainey's technique. Thus, while it was assumed any individual sample might have been misclassified using the latter methods, it was considered unlikely that the majority of the identifications were incorrect. Eerkens's and Malainey's techniques, therefore, were used to help interpret the identified clusters but were not used to absolutely interpret individual specimens.

RESULTS

Fatty acids were detected in all of the samples, with most of the residues being medium chain or long chain fatty acids from C12:0 to C18:1. The majority were saturated, but two monounsaturated fatty acids, C16:1 and C18:1, were also present (Figures 7.2 and 7.3). Only two samples contained any polyunsaturated acids, both of which included the long-chain fatty acid C18:2. Blanks were run in between samples; however, the amount of background fatty acids in the blanks was extremely small, so approximate integrated peak areas were used for this analysis. The resulting data can be found in Wilkerson 2016:Table A.1

Cluster Analysis Results

Once the integrated peak areas for the fatty acids were obtained, the relative percentages of fatty acids (Table 7.4) and the fatty acid ratios (Table 7.5) were calculated for each sample. These data were then examined to look for any grouping tendencies. Two cluster analyses were run: one using only Malainey's relative percentages of

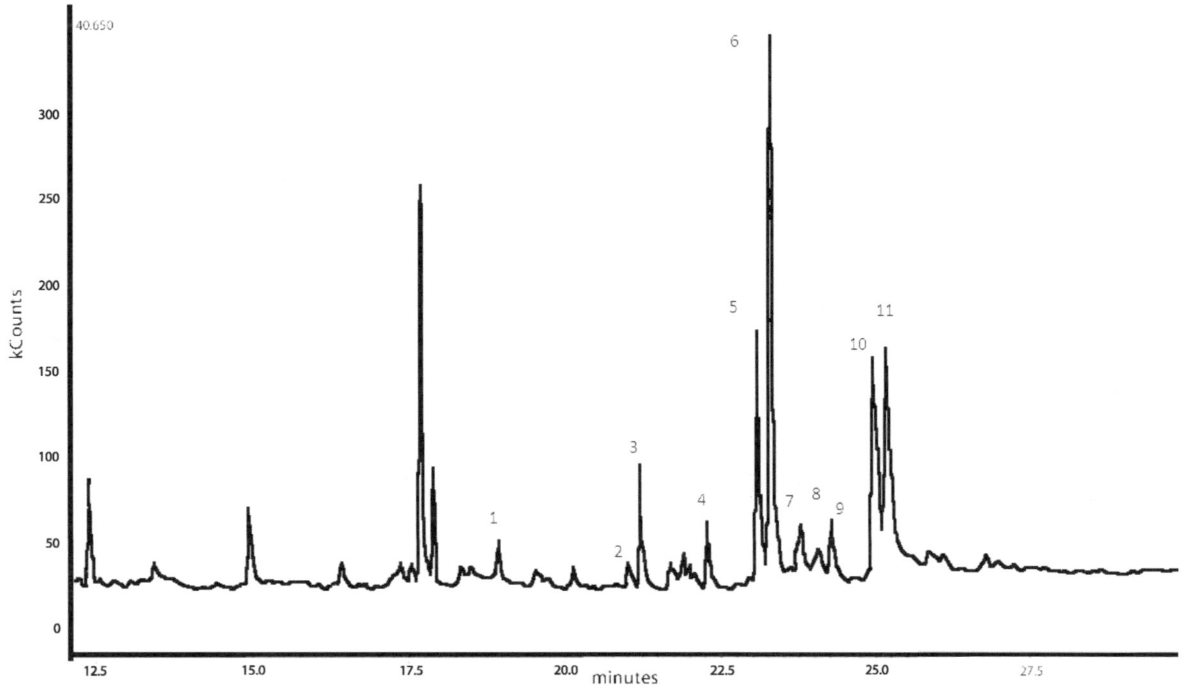

FIGURE 7.2. The total ion chromatogram for sample A103-1: fatty acid methyl esters identified are 1 = C12:0, 2 = C14:1, 3 = C14:0, 4 = C15:0, 5 = C16:1, 6 = C16:0, 7 = isomeric C17:0, 8 = C17:1, 9 = C17, 10 = C18:1, and 11 = C18:0.

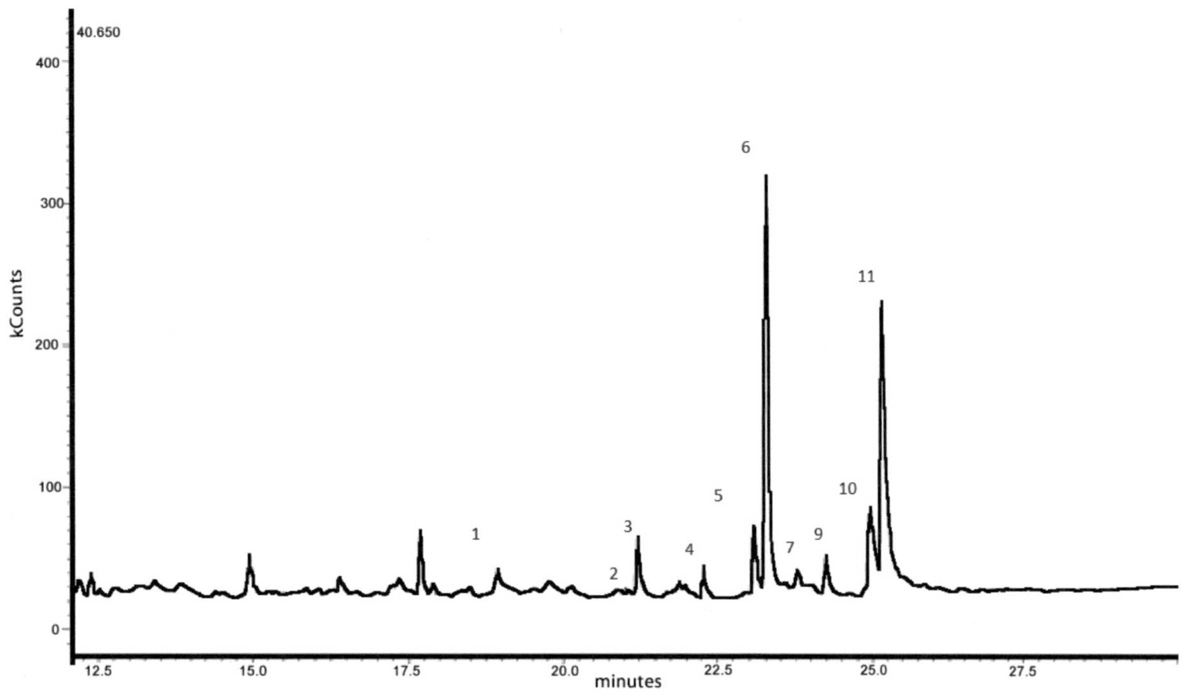

FIGURE 7.3. The total ion chromatogram for sample A103-37: fatty acid methyl esters identified are 1 = C12:0, 2 = C14:1, 3 = C14:0, 4 = C15:0, 5 = C16:1, 6 = C16:0, 7 = isomeric C17:0, 8 = C17:1 (not found), 9 = C17, 10 = C18:1, and 11 = C18:0.

TABLE 7.4. Calculated Relative Percentages of Fatty Acids Present in Samples

Sample	Location	Ware	Medium Chain %	C18:1%	C18:0%
A103-17	Moapa Valley	Moapa Ware	13.7	18.0	15.0
A103-58	Moapa Valley	Moapa Ware	15.6	13.2	22.4
A103-89	Moapa Valley	Moapa Ware	10.8	17.8	26.7
A105-1	Moapa Valley	Moapa Ware	9.5	22.6	26.9
A105-29	Moapa Valley	Moapa Ware	19.3	15.0	16.7
A105-33	Moapa Valley	Shivwits Ware	23.7	14.1	17.2
A105-42	Moapa Valley	Shivwits Ware	10.4	9.2	42.7
A105-46A	Moapa Valley	Shivwits Ware	9.6	8.1	40.2
A105-46B	Moapa Valley	Shivwits Ware	21.5	6.6	29.5
A105-54	Moapa Valley	Shivwits Ware	16.4	17.0	23.6
A103-37	Moapa Valley	Virgin series	10.4	10.4	32.3
A103-69A	Moapa Valley	Virgin series	11.6	22.8	19.4
A103-69B	Moapa Valley	Virgin series	16.5	9.4	27.9
A103-7A	Moapa Valley	Virgin series	16.8	14.9	23.9
A103-7B	Moapa Valley	Virgin series	14.2	14.1	26.6
LAKE 20334A	Shivwits Plateau	Moapa Ware	4.5	4.2	56.9
LAKE 20334B	Shivwits Plateau	Moapa Ware	8.7	21.5	25.3
LAKE 20335	Shivwits Plateau	Moapa Ware	12.9	7.9	36.7
LAKE 20362	Shivwits Plateau	Moapa Ware	13.8	2.3	29.6
LAKE 30708	Shivwits Plateau	Moapa Ware	17.1	5.6	22.7
LAKE 20890A	Shivwits Plateau	Shivwits Ware	7.4	31.2	26.2
LAKE 20890B	Shivwits Plateau	Shivwits Ware	18.0	6.9	22.3
LAKE 20897	Shivwits Plateau	Shivwits Ware	10.1	23.8	25.2
LAKE 20923A	Shivwits Plateau	Shivwits Ware	5.7	54.0	12.8
LAKE 20923B	Shivwits Plateau	Shivwits Ware	6.7	20.4	36.8
LAKE 20321	Shivwits Plateau	Virgin series	10.7	5.8	43.2
LAKE 20334	Shivwits Plateau	Virgin series	13.5	2.9	38.2
LAKE 303707	Shivwits Plateau	Virgin series	9.4	12.0	36.6
LAKE 30707	Shivwits Plateau	Virgin series	10.8	10.3	30.5
LAKE 307076	Shivwits Plateau	Virgin series	12.5	5.5	38.7

TABLE 7.5. Calculated Values for Fatty Acid Ratios

Catalog #	(C15:0+C17:0) / C18:0	C16:1 / C18:1	C16:0 / C18:0	C12:0 / C14:0
A103-58	0.8069	0.7372	1.5367	0.3360
A103-17	1.4817	0.9138	2.1530	0.2625
A103-89	0.8064	0.5976	1.0981	0.4072
A105-1	0.9670	0.3611	1.0678	0.3475
A105-29	1.2113	0.5310	2.1509	0.2276
A105-33	1.1254	0.5875	1.7333	0.4110
A105-42	0.2692	0.5566	0.6853	0.8864
A105-46A	0.2673	0.5361	0.8562	0.2882
A105-46B	0.4380	0.5689	1.1270	0.4060
A105-54	0.8595	0.3044	1.2600	0.4339
A103-37	0.4190	0.6345	1.1192	0.3632
A103-69A	1.3597	0.5071	1.5968	0.6452
A103-69B	0.5157	0.6995	1.2691	0.4298
A103-7A	0.8650	0.4423	1.2535	0.9584
A103-7B	0.7058	0.5496	1.1600	0.6367
LAKE 20334A	0.0458	0.4696	0.5411	0.3406
LAKE 20334B	0.7441	0.2257	0.9049	0.8868
LAKE 20335	0.1422	0.9500	0.8934	0.3700
LAKE 20362	0.1852	1.4355	1.5994	0.3328
LAKE 30708	0.4339	1.4683	1.8114	0.1343
LAKE 20890A	0.1215	0.2468	0.9715	0.4985
LAKE 20890B	0.3281	1.0776	1.8918	0.2807
LAKE 20897	0.1767	0.4700	1.0976	0.3268
LAKE 20923A	0.2270	0.1596	1.3633	0.6120
LAKE 20923B	0.0685	0.2067	0.8310	0.6022
LAKE 20321	0.1105	0.9285	0.7625	0.3355
LAKE 20334	0.1386	1.1286	1.0463	0.2604
LAKE 303707	0.1492	0.5389	0.9096	0.4943
LAKE 30707	0.1815	1.0883	1.1522	0.3250
LAKE 307076	0.1407	1.1069	0.8980	0.3086

Table 7.6. Group Assignments based on Cluster Analysis

Sample No.	Location	Ceramic	Group Assignment: Relative % of Fatty Acids Data	Group Assignment: Using Fatty Acid Ratio Data	Group Assignment: Final
A103-17	Moapa Valley	Moapa Ware	1	1	1
A103-58	Moapa Valley	Moapa Ware	1	1	1
A103-89	Moapa Valley	Moapa Ware	1	1	1
A105-1	Moapa Valley	Moapa Ware	1	1	1
A105-29	Moapa Valley	Moapa Ware	1	1	1
A105-33	Moapa Valley	Shivwits Ware	1	1	1
A105-42	Moapa Valley	Shivwits Ware	2	2	2
A105-46A	Moapa Valley	Shivwits Ware	2	2	2
A105-46B	Moapa Valley	Shivwits Ware	1	2	n/a
A105-54	Moapa Valley	Shivwits Ware	1	1	1
A103-37	Moapa Valley	Virgin series	2	2	2
A103-69A	Moapa Valley	Virgin series	1	1	1
A103-69B	Moapa Valley	Virgin series	1	2	n/a
A103-7A	Moapa Valley	Virgin series	1	1	1
A103-7B	Moapa Valley	Virgin series	1	1	1
LAKE 20334A	Shivwits Plateau	Moapa Ware	2	2	2
LAKE 20334B	Shivwits Plateau	Moapa Ware	1	1	1
LAKE 20335	Shivwits Plateau	Moapa Ware	2	2	2
LAKE 20362	Shivwits Plateau	Moapa Ware	1	2	n/a
LAKE 30708	Shivwits Plateau	Moapa Ware	1	2	n/a
LAKE 20890A	Shivwits Plateau	Shivwits Ware	1	2	n/a
LAKE 20890B	Shivwits Plateau	Shivwits Ware	1	2	n/a
LAKE 20897	Shivwits Plateau	Shivwits Ware	1	2	n/a
LAKE 20923A	Shivwits Plateau	Shivwits Ware	1	2	n/a
LAKE 20923B	Shivwits Plateau	Shivwits Ware	2	2	2
LAKE 20321	Shivwits Plateau	Virgin series	2	2	2
LAKE 20334	Shivwits Plateau	Virgin series	2	2	2
LAKE 303707	Shivwits Plateau	Virgin series	2	2	2
LAKE 30707	Shivwits Plateau	Virgin series	2	2	2
LAKE 307076	Shivwits Plateau	Virgin series	2	2	2

fatty acids (i.e., the data in Table 7.4) and one using only Eerkens's fatty acid ratios (i.e., the data in Table 7.5). Malainey's and Eerkens's results agreed 80% of the time. Based on these results, each sample was assigned to a final group assignment. In those cases where the two cluster analyses agreed, the sample was assigned to the agreed-upon group. When the two methods resulted in different assignments, no final group assignment was made (Table 7.6).

Relative Percentages of Fatty Acids

To aid in the interpretation of the residue groups, the identification of the residues contained in each sample was determined using Malainey's relative percentages of fatty acids method (Table 7.7). These data indicate that all of the Group 2 samples contained residues identified as large herbivores, whereas only two of the Group 1 samples did. Of the remaining samples in Group 2, three contained residues consistent with a plant other than corn, one contained residues identical to those produced from either fish or from corn and another plant, and three contained residues that could not be identified.

Fatty Acid Ratio Results

A comparison of the fatty acid ratios between the two groups indicates that Group 1 has elevated (C15:0 + C17:0)/C18:0 and C16:0/C18:0 ratios compared to Group 2 (Figure 7.4). A Mann Whitney *U*-test indicates that the differences for these ratios are statistically significant, but that the differences between the two groups in the values for C16:1/C18:1 or C12:0/C14 are not significant (Table 7.8). According to Eerkens (2005; see Table 2), elevated concentrations of (C15:0 + C17:0)/C18:0 can indicate residues from greens and/or roots,

Table 7.7. Identification of Sample Residues based on Relative Percentages

Cluster	Sample	Location	Identification
1	A103-17	Moapa Valley	n/a
1	A103-58	Moapa Valley	Plant (except corn)
1	A103-69A	Moapa Valley	n/a
1	A103-7A	Moapa Valley	Plant (except corn)
1	A103-7B	Moapa Valley	Plant (except corn)
1	A103-89	Moapa Valley	n/a
1	A105-1	Moapa Valley	Large herbivore w/ plant or bone marrow
1	A105-29	Moapa Valley	Plant (except corn)
1	A105-33	Moapa Valley	Plant (except corn)
1	A105-54	Moapa Valley	Fish or corn w/ plant
1	LAKE 20334B	Shivwits Plateau	Large herbivore w/ plant or bone marrow
2	A103-37	Moapa Valley	Large herbivore
2	A105-42	Moapa Valley	Large herbivore
2	A105-46A	Moapa Valley	Large herbivore
2	LAKE 20321	Shivwits Plateau	Large herbivore
2	LAKE 20334	Shivwits Plateau	Large herbivore
2	LAKE 20334A	Shivwits Plateau	Large herbivore
2	LAKE 20335	Shivwits Plateau	Large herbivore
2	LAKE 20923B	Shivwits Plateau	Large herbivore w/ plant or bone marrow
2	LAKE 303707	Shivwits Plateau	Large herbivore
2	LAKE 30707	Shivwits Plateau	Large herbivore
2	LAKE 307076	Shivwits Plateau	Large herbivore
n/a	A103-69B	Moapa Valley	Plant with large herbivore
n/a	A105-46B	Moapa Valley	Plant with large herbivore
n/a	LAKE 20362	Shivwits Plateau	Large herbivore
n/a	LAKE 20890A	Shivwits Plateau	n/a
n/a	LAKE 20890B	Shivwits Plateau	Plant (except corn)
n/a	LAKE 20897	Shivwits Plateau	n/a
n/a	LAKE 20923A	Shivwits Plateau	n/a
n/a	LAKE 30708	Shivwits Plateau	Plant (except corn)

Table 7.8. Comparison of Fatty Acid Ratios between Groups 1 and 2

Ratio	Mean and Standard Deviation	*U*	Sig. (2-tailed)
$\frac{(C15:0+C17:0)}{C18:0}$	Group 1: $= 1.0; \bar{x} = 0.3$	0	0.000
	Group 2: $= 0.2; \bar{x} = 0.1$		
$\frac{C16:1}{C18:1}$	Group 1: $= 0.5; \bar{x} = 0.2$	34	0.088
	Group 2: $= 0.7; \bar{x} = 0.3$		
$\frac{C16:0}{C18:0}$	Group 1: $= 1.4; \bar{x} = 0.4$	8	0.000
	Group 2: $= 0.9; \bar{x} = 0.2$		
$\frac{C12:0}{C14:0}$	Group 1: $= 0.5; \bar{x} = 0.2$	43	0.270
	Group 2: $= 0.4; \bar{x} = 0.2$		

and lower concentrations of C16:0/C18:0 can indicate the presence of terrestrial mammals.

Biplots of the samples against the fatty acid ratios are shown in Figures 7.5 and 7.6. In Figure 7.5, the samples fall mainly in the ellipses for the roots category and the seeds and nuts category. In Figure 7.6, the samples fall predominantly in the category for seeds and nuts. Examples of foods in the roots category include agave roots and desert lily bulbs. Examples of seeds and nuts include maize, pinyon nuts, chia seeds, amaranth seeds, and mesquite seed pods.

Research Questions Revisited

With the data obtained from the residue analyses in mind, we now turn our attention to the three research questions that were outlined at the beginning of this chapter.

Evaluation of the VBP Diet

As is often the case with residue analysis, our data did not pattern neatly into specific food groups. Our inability to firmly identify the specific foods that created the residues in each sample likely results from the mixture of foods that created the residues (i.e., from cooking a mixture of foods in the containers), from the differential

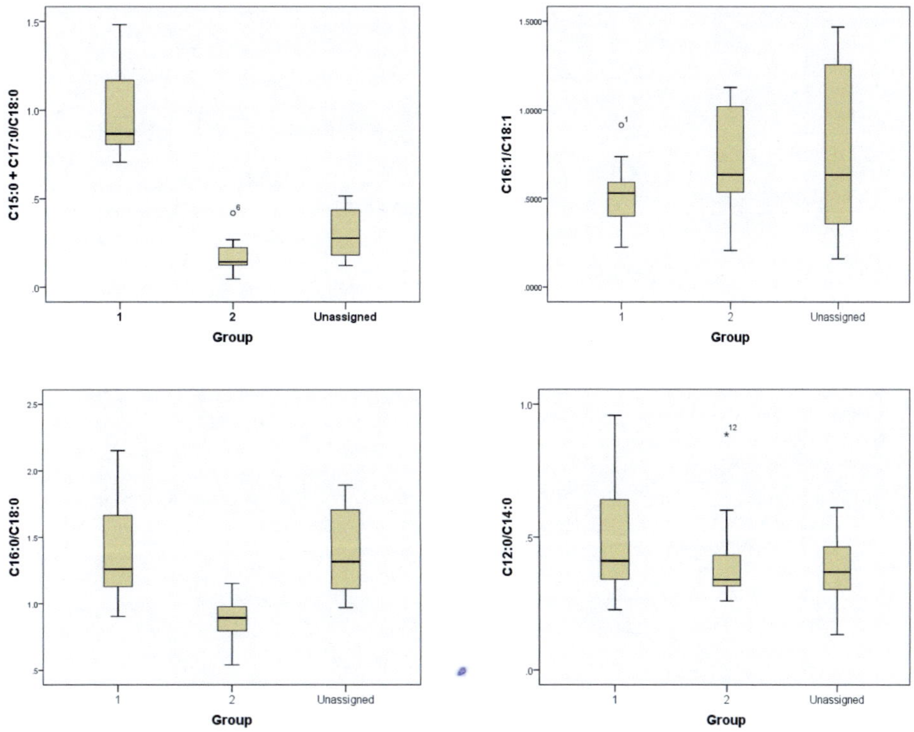

FIGURE 7.4. Boxplots of fatty acid ratios by residue group.

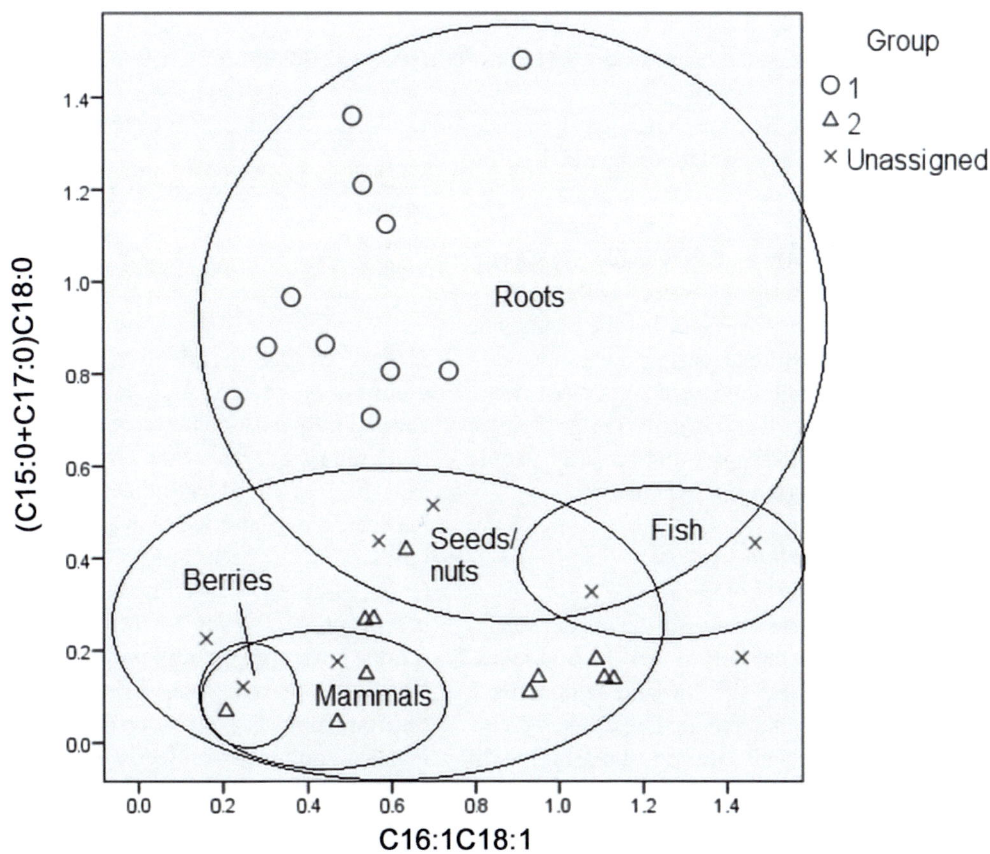

FIGURE 7.5. Samples plotted by fatty acid ratios C16:1/C18:1 and (C15:0 + C17:0)/C18:0.

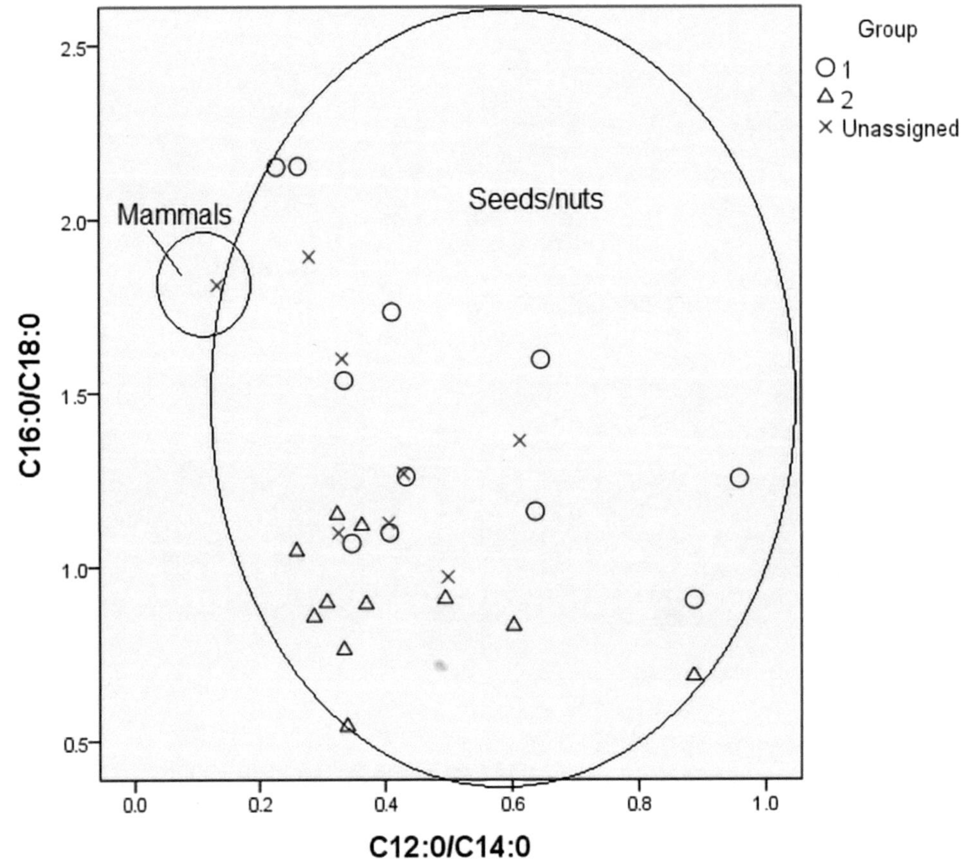

FIGURE 7.6. Samples plotted by fatty acid ratios C12:0/C14:0 and C16:0/C18:0.

degradation of the residues in archaeological context, and perhaps from the presence of foods for which we do not yet know the fatty acid signatures.

Nonetheless, certain patterns are apparent. The relative percentage of fatty acids (see Table 7.7) suggest that both herbivores and plants were regularly eaten. The fatty acid ratios further suggest that the plants may have included some mixture of maize, pinyon nuts, chia seeds, amaranth seeds, mesquite seed pods, agave roots, and desert lily bulbs. Although these food groups are broadly defined, they do suggest that the VBP people relied on both domesticated and wild resources.

Comparison of Upland and Lowland Regions

In contrast to the first research issue, the residue analysis provides a clearer answer to our second question—whether the upland and lowland regions were characterized by dietary differences. The residue groups are strongly correlated with location (Table 7.9), with Group 1 found disproportionately in sherds from the Moapa Valley and Group 2 in sherds from the Shivwits Plateau. Despite the identical group sizes of the two groups, more than 90% of the Group 1 sherds were recovered from the Moapa Valley, compared to just slightly more than a quarter of the Group 2 sherds. A Fisher's exact test of the data indicates that the correlation between group and location is statistically significant ($p = 0.008$).

TABLE 7.9. Residue Groups by Location

Location	Group 1	Group 2	Unassigned	Total
Moapa Valley	10	3	2	15
Shivwits Plateau	1	8	6	15
Total	11	11	8	30

As discussed above, though it is difficult to know precisely the full complement of foods creating the two residue groups, the relative proportion of fatty acids and fatty acid ratio data suggest that Group 2, represented disproportionately by the ceramics from the Shivwits Plateau, contained residues produced by the cooking of large herbivores. This suggests that hunting played a greater role in the upland regions than it did in the lowland regions. Consistent with the low proportions of faunal remains discovered in the lowlands, large herbivores appear to have played a much smaller role in the lowland diet. The paucity of meat observed in the lowland diet may have been responsible for the iron deficiency anemia observed in that region (Martin and Thompson 2008; Roberts 1997).

The higher values for the (C15:0 + C17:0)/C18:0 ratio in Group 1, the group disproportionately associated with the Moapa Valley, suggests there may have been a greater emphasis on greens and/or roots in that region. Although we cannot be sure what specific plants might be represented, agave and desert lily tubers are possibilities.

Finally, while we cannot rule out the possibility that any foodstuffs were transported between the region, the differences between the residue patterns of the two areas suggest that, if food transport did occur, it was insufficient to obscure the dietary differences between the two regions. The most parsimonious interpretation of the residue data is that the inhabitants of both regions ate a similar range of foods, but that the relative proportions of the foods eaten differed between the two regions, and that this reflected the differential availability of food resources in each area.

Comparison of Wares

Our final research question had to do with whether or not different foods were cooked, stored, or prepared in the different wares. A comparison of the residue groups by ware category indicates no strong correlations between these two variables, and a Fisher's exact test (using the Freeman-Halton extension) further indicates that the relationship between residue group and ceramic ware is not statistically significant ($p = 0.23$). This information suggests there were no patterned differences in the ways that vessels from the ware categories were used (Table 7.10).

TABLE 7.10. Residue Groups by Ware

Ware	Group 1	Group 2	Unassigned	Total
Moapa Ware	3	6	1	10
Shivwits Ware	2	3	5	10
Tusayan Ware Virgin series	6	2	2	10
Total	11	11	8	30

Discussion

Although less precise than we would wish, the data presented in this study demonstrate that GC-MS has the potential to contribute to our understanding of prehistoric subsistence patterns. A combination of factors—including the practice by cooks of preparing multiple foods in the same vessel and the postdepositional degradation of fatty acids—can obfuscate the residue patterns and make it difficult to connect residue data with specific foods, yet GC-MS can nonetheless provide useful information for archaeologists. By way of example, the data presented here provide the first evidence that large herbivores played a major role in the upland VBP diet. Despite numerous excavations conducted in that area, the role of hunting previously could not be evaluated due to a lack of faunal remains. This lack, in turn, was caused not by an absence of hunting in prehistory, but by the trash disposal practices of the prehistoric people. In the upland area, trash is found in deflated middens on the ground surface. The prehistoric practice of discarding the trash on the ground surface means faunal remains originally discarded have long been obliterated by scavenging coyotes and by decay caused by millennia of exposure.

Currently, there is very little research on VBP diet and subsistence strategies, especially on the Shivwits Plateau, but this study has helped identify possible sources of organic residues cooked, prepared, and stored in VBP ceramic vessels. The study has also demonstrated that GC-MS holds promise for identifying the types of foods prehistoric groups cooked, prepared, and stored in VBP ceramics.

8

A Regional Analysis of Brownware in Colonial Period Chumash Sites

Catherine Bailey

Colonial-era deposits in Chumash village sites are marked by the introduction of new materials and introduced technologies, including metal objects, glass beads, and both porcelain and low-fired brownware ceramics. Historical documents tell us that utilitarian brownware was produced locally at the coastal missions in Chumash territory, but we lack any direct written evidence regarding the production or use of ceramics by the Chumash people either in the missions or in their villages. This chapter addresses new petrographic analyses of brownware ceramics recovered from ten Chumash occupation sites that better illuminate patterns of its production, transport, and use by Chumash people during the colonial period (AD 1776–1846).

Petrographic analyses of brownware sherds recovered from these sites as well as from coastal Spanish outposts yield distinct groupings deepening our understanding of evolving Historic period Chumash social networks. These data support the hypothesis that sherds from coastal villages match the petrographic signature of brownware produced at the missions of Santa Barbara and San Buenaventura; however, brownware recovered from inland sites, appear to have been produced locally and likely represent a native ceramic tradition originating from interior groups. Taken together with ethnohistorical evidence, the findings help to refine our understanding of how Chumash social networks and technology shifted across the landscape during a period of rapid cultural and economic change.

Intervillage Relationships in the Colonial Period

When the Spanish arrived in California, they encountered a Chumash economy built upon extensive trade networks linking the islands to mainland villages and to neighboring groups, including the Yokuts, Kitanemuk, and Gabrieliño. Craft specialization, increased trade in nonessential goods, and social stratification followed the development of the *tomol* (plank canoe) in the Channel Islands region in the late first and early second millennium AD (Arnold 2007; Arnold and Graesch 2004). The development of ocean-going technology in the form of the *tomol* permitted more reliable communication between island and mainland populations across the channel (Arnold 2007; Arnold and Bernard 2005). It also enabled the intensification of highly specialized shell bead production on the islands, which connected the Channel Islands through trade to mainland sites as far away as the American Southwest.

Populations rose steadily on the islands and along the mainland coast during the Middle period (600 BC–1150 AD), with notably large populations for hunter-gatherer groups by AD 750 and a peak between 1300 and 1500 (Arnold 2001a; Rick 2004:99). As island populations increased, so did the need to import certain terrestrial resources from the mainland for subsistence in exchange for abundant marine resources and manufactured goods such as *Olivella* shell beads (Arnold 1992). Mainland coastal villages with immediate access to high-yield supplies of marine food as well as rich arrays of terrestrial plants and animals had the region's largest populations and still produced enough surplus to support extensive trade relations inland across the channel.

By the AD 1200s–1300s, social stratification along the mainland coast and islands produced chiefdom-level societies (Arnold 2001a, 2001b). Although there is some evidence that social stratification existed in the interior villages (Horne 1981; Johnson 1988), the Chumash people in the interior foothills and mountains lived in smaller settlements spaced farther apart. The people in these communities moved seasonally from their base settlements to camps at higher and lower elevations where

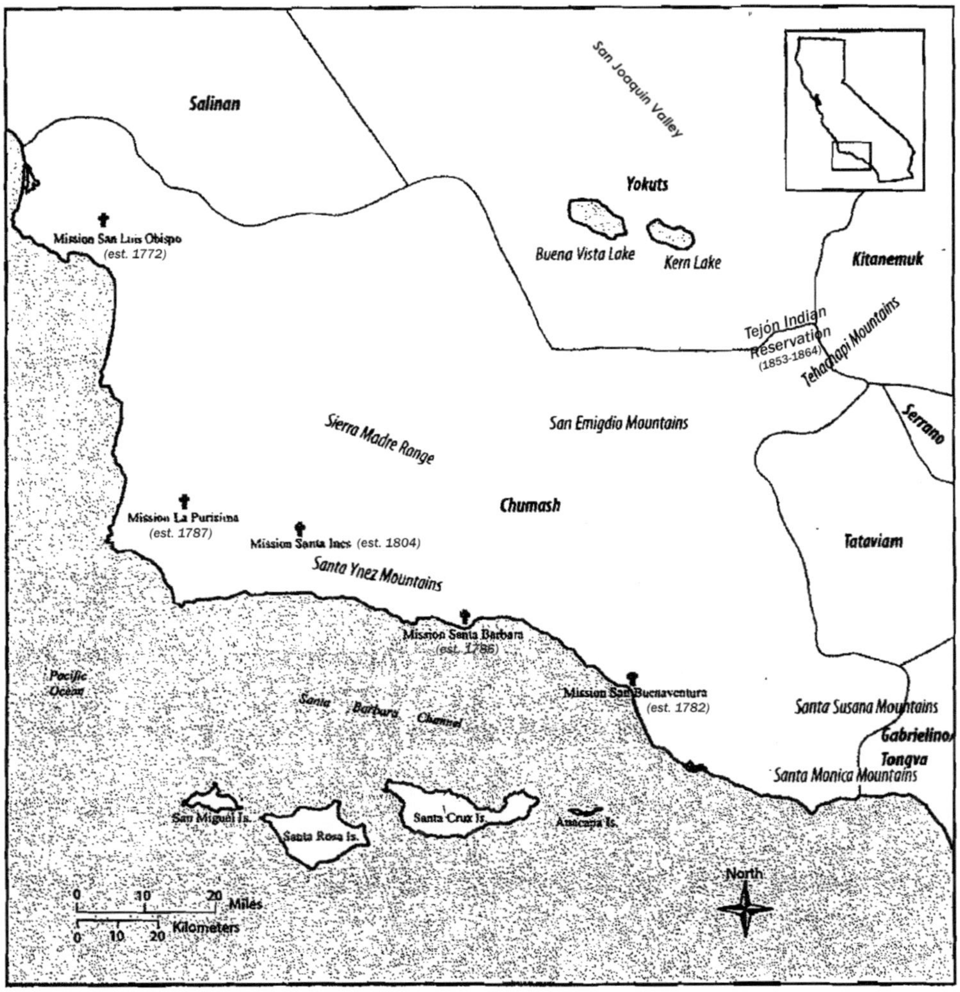

FIGURE 8.1. Map of Chumash region (after Bernard 2008).

they could exploit resource-rich hunting and gathering areas (Horne 1981:50; Robinson 2006:71). Interior Chumash traded their local resources, such as seeds, nuts, and hides, to the coastal villages in exchange for marine resources and shell beads (Hudson and Blackburn 1987; King 1976; Robinson 2006).

Early colonial accounts describe several distinct ethnolinguistic groups living in the northeastern hills and mountains of Chumash territory, an area stretching south to the Santa Susana Mountains and north into the San Joaquin Valley (Figure 8.1; Bernard 2008:143; Kroeber 1925; McLendon and Johnson 1999). This interior region was a cultural borderland encompassing Uto-Aztecan, Yokuts, and Chumash language groups (Golla 2011:197; Kroeber 1925). The Central Valley and southern foothills, from the Emidgiano and Tehachapi Mountains, through the Yokuts territory, and as far north as Sacramento, served as a refuge for coastal groups and individuals avoiding or fleeing the missions (Bernard 2008; Heizer 1941; Horne 1981; Robinson 2006). The San Joaquin Valley and the mountains along its southern border remained beyond the control of Spanish settlers clustered near the coast. By the 1820s, one official cautioned that the region could become a second Apachería and urged missionary and military action to bring it under control (Heizer 1941:104). Firsthand accounts of regional politics are rare, and as relatively few members of the far interior populations joined the missions during the early colonial period, we have relatively little data on interior demography or village organization during the late eighteenth and early nineteenth centuries.

In the early 1800s, Spanish writers passing through the southern Yokuts and northeastern Chumash territories recorded that each group had enemies between themselves and the coast, whose territory they took care to avoid (Robinson 2006:83). Periodic conflicts and cooperative relations may have occurred at the level of families or villages and not exclusively along ethnolinguistic lines. One account of an interethnic alliance, derived from records of a 1790 expedition to capture a runaway neophyte from San Buenaventura, recounts a war party of men from Yokuts, Chumash, and Kitanemuk groups who banded together to attack a Spanish military party sent after an escaped neophyte (Johnson 2007:91).

In the colonial hinterlands, indigenous political and economic autonomy persisted—at least in the mountains—for two to three generations after the founding of the first channel-coast Chumash mission in 1782, but along the mainland coast, traditional village life came to an end by 1804 (Johnson 1988). It is in this window of approximately 20 years that most colonial period artifacts were deposited in the indigenous mainland villages. Trade items and gifts came from colonists at the mission and presidio, as well as occasionally from the trading ships mooring along the Santa Barbara Channel (Costello 1990; Love and Resnik 1983; Perisnotto 1998).

Coastal Chumash villages failed by the early 1800s, and villagers abandoned their homes for the missions or interior villages (Johnson 1984, 1989). This collapse reverberated inland, and, as points along both middle- and long-distance trade networks were abandoned, village alliances shifted and fractured along different paths across the region. Following the breakdown of large villages on the coast and given the relative isolation of the islanders, reliable supplies of marine resources and shell beads ceased to flow into the interior. Judging from later colonial accounts of interethnic alliances and communities, as well as from archaeological evidence, Chumash families and villages in the interior may have struck up new ties or strengthened old ones with neighboring groups farther to the east, north, and south (Arkush 1993; Bernard 2008; Robinson 2006). The collapse of old trade networks, concurrent with the addition of new materials to exchange such as glass beads and horses, likely provided the motivation to increase interior trade with neighboring indigenous groups.

Chumash descendants of the mission communities recalled accounts of family members using and producing pottery in the early 1800s (Benson 1997), and one report describes indigenous people procuring clay in the hills at the edge of the town of Santa Barbara for making pots (Hudson and Blackburn 1987:195). It appears that locally manufactured utilitarian pottery in the Chumash region fell out of circulation fairly quickly after the 1850s with the increased availability of metal containers (Hudson and Blackburn 1987:196). This brief period of pottery production lasted approximately from the 1780s to the 1850s. Chumash pottery made during this period left few traces in the material and ethnographic records, and researchers have not yet determined its relationship to the native brownware traditions to the east and south of Chumash territory or to the utilitarian pottery produced in the coastal missions and presidios of California.

Precolonial Ceramic Traditions

While the Chumash did not have an indigenous ceramic tradition, people in southern and eastern California had well-established traditions predating Spanish intrusion into the area in the late eighteenth century. Brownware ceramics were produced along the southern California coast from south of Los Angeles into northern Baja California, while the sedimentary clays found in the interior desert areas were used to produce buffwares. The wares in southern and Baja California were produced by the paddle-and-anvil technique, similar to those made in southern Arizona/northern Sonora.

Many of the neighboring cultural groups to the east of Chumash territory also produced pottery, using the coil-and-scrape technique. Few well-documented excavations have been conducted in the borderland where southern Yokuts, Kitanemuk, Gabrielino, and Tataviam cultures met around the Tehachapi Mountains. However, archaeological and ethnographic data suggest that all of these groups produced pottery by the Late period, and they continued to interact with the coastal villages and Spanish settlements into the nineteenth century (Arkush 1993:620; Horne 1981; Jackson 1990:160).

Several brownware sherds have been found in the Chumash portion of the Cuyama Valley and the Sierra Madre range, and more appear in poorly documented excavations from the early twentieth century in Yokuts territory to the northeast of Cuyama near Buena Vista Lake (Horne 1981). Excavations at Yokuts sites have recorded eight sherds of low-fired pottery in the upper layers of middens (Wedel 1941:47). Another occupation area located on Kern Lake yielded 20 thick-walled brownware sherds, and 16 were found along the shores of nearby Tulare Lake (Gifford and Schenck 1926:55). By the colonial period, it is likely that many of these villages included a mix of individuals tied through kinship and material trade across ethnographically defined culture areas (Johnson 1978).

Mission Ceramics

Mission neophytes from the mountains and coastal areas of parts of southern California carried their ceramic tradition into the missions. Potsherds virtually indistinguishable from precontact samples are found in missions and presidios from San Diego to San Francisco (Skowronek et al. 2001). In the south, this reflects continuity with existing native traditions; north of Los Angeles, however, interesting questions remain regarding the identity of the potters, the transmission of ceramic technology, and the movement of vessels from production sites.

Spanish records attest that indigenous pottery producers from Baja and southern Alta California, as well as mestizo and European-trained potters, were brought to missions in areas lacking a native ceramic tradition (Hoover and Costello 1985; Skowronek et al. 2009).

Archaeologists concerned with cross-cultural interaction and neophyte identity in the missions and presidios highlight the potential for locally produced pottery to act as a sensitive indicator of cultural change or persistence (Allen 1995:195; Deetz 1963:44; Evans 1969; Hoover and Costello 1985; Walsh 1988). Locally manufactured pottery from the presidio of Santa Barbara is described in one report as "a hybrid of several aboriginal forms, with perhaps regional and idiosyncratic variations" (Walsh 1988:3). The sherds included low-temperature oxidized, sand-tempered earthenware with both indigenous and European forms and styles, including basket-impressions, folded rims, wheel-thrown bases, plate rims with cavetto, and punctate patterns (Walsh 1988:10). Rather than distinguish specific types for the presidio sherds, Walsh acknowledges a wide range of influences and highlights the plurality of mission pottery technologies.

For the 1976 report on San Buenaventura Mission, ceramicist Ronald May created a detailed typology of locally fired earthenware and linked it to chronology by relative dating of majolica sherds in each context. May was the first to suggest native potters produced vessels at Chumash missions.

Written records do not identify the ethnic background or number of native potters in the missions and presidios immediately north of Los Angeles, nor do they indicate whether neophytes were formally apprenticed to mestizo potters or informally taught by other native people. During the 1790s, California officials requested Mexican artisans to teach California laborers skills like carpentry and masonry (Webb 1952:126), but ceramic production is never mentioned in accounts of neophyte industries. In 1790, the governor at the Santa Barbara Presidio petitioned Mexico for a professional potter to work for a brief period to supply the fort, and four years later, documents record the construction of a pottery kiln at the Santa Barbara Presidio ahead of the potter's long-awaited arrival (Whitehead 1996:141, 148).

Evidence from eighteenth- and nineteenth-century occupations at Chumash villages indicates that distinctions in ceramic technology are both socially and temporally significant. Much of the brownware found at Chumash villages parallels the technological attributes of coiled plain ware used by laborers and soldiers at the ranchos, missions, and presidios along the coast, but no wheel-made pottery appears in the village contexts. Thus, it may be that the early production of pottery in the missions and presidios was exclusively coiled or pinched, with wheel-made wares appearing around the time that most coastal villages were abandoned.

Petrographic analyses of brownware sherds recovered from colonial-era Chumash villages builds on existing ceramic research and provides a more nuanced view of ceramic production and use by native people living outside of Spanish outposts. Comparing the petrographic signatures of Chumash village brownware to the signatures of sherds recovered from contemporary colonial contexts in nearby missions and presidios further illuminates patterns of native ceramic production and use during this period in coastal and interior settlements.

Sampling Procedure

This project has relied on brownware pottery from Chumash sites in existing collections at the University of California in Santa Barbara, Los Angeles, and Berkeley; the Natural History Museum of Los Angeles County; the Ventura County Archaeological Society; and the Santa Barbara Museum of Natural History. These institutions hold the major collections from archaeological investigations of Chumash sites to date.

Overall, 31% of the sherds were sampled, taking care to ensure that at least one of each visible variant from each village's assemblage was included in this initial selection (Table 8.1). The sherds were grouped according to relevant morphological characteristics, such as surface treatment and variations in mineral inclusions visible under a 20× binocular microscope.

Sites include the coastal villages of Helo' (CA-SBA-45 and CA-SBA-46), Mikiw (CA-SBA-78), and Syuxtun (CA-SBA-28); mountain sites of Saq'ka'ya (CA-SBA-823), He'lxman (CA-SBA-485), and Santa Cruz Creek (CA-SBA-1283); and the interior sites of Kashtiq (CA-KER-307), Pinwheel rock shelter (CA-SBA-5836), and a cache at Salisbury Potrero (CA-SBA-1279) in the Sierra Madre Range (Figure 8.2). All brownware potsherds occurred either on the surface or within the upper 25–30 cm, in historic period graves, and/or in association with other imported objects such as porcelain or majolica, iron, and glass. Although the recorded contexts and documentation for these collections are as a whole highly variable, relative chronology for each site dates pottery to the Spanish Colonial and Mexican periods.

To test whether the Santa Barbara and San Buenaventura mission localities contain petrographically distinct or overlapping signatures, a representative sample of low-fired brownware was drawn from each site, and

TABLE 8.1. Provenience of Sherds Selected for Investigation

Village (Site: CA-)	Total Sherds From Site	Sherds from Site Selected For Physical Analysis	Sherds from Physical Analysis Selected For Petrographic Analysis
Coastal			
He'l.xman (SBA-485)	1	1	1
So.xtonocmu' (SBA-167)	3	0	0
Muwu (VEN-11)	14	0	0
Saq'ka 'ya (SBA-823)	4	4	3
Mikiw (SBA-78)	50	22	7
Helo' (SBA-45 and SBA-46)	15	8	5
Xalam (SBA-205)	1	1	1
Svu.xtun (SBA-28)	3	3	3
Kayiwish (VEN-71)	2	2	0
Teqepsh (SBA-477)	3	0	0
S'a.xpilil (SBA-60)	I	0	0
Santa Cruz Creek (SBA-1283)	1	1	1
Island			
Xa.xas (SCRI-240 and SCRI-147)	6	0	0
Interior			
Kashtɨq (KER-307)	179	41	13
Salisbury Potrero (SBA-1279)	1	1	1
Pinwheel (SBA-5836)	5	5	2
Total	289	89	37

TABLE 8.2. Sample of Mission Sherds Investigated

Mission or Presidio	Total Sherds from Site	Sherds from Site Selected for Physical Analysis	Sherds from Physical Analysis Selected for Petrographic Analysis
Mission Santa Barbara (CA-SBA-25)	9	3	2
Santa Barbara Presidio (P711-89DX)	337	21	13
Mission San Buenaventura (CA-VEN-1222H)	2	19	11
Mission Purisima Vieja (CA-SBA-520 and CA-SBA-521)	3	3	3
Mission Santa Ines (CA-SBA-518)	2	2	1
Total	383	48	30

more limited samples from Mission Santa Inés and La Purisima Mission provided comparative material (Table 8.2). A roughly homogeneous signature within each site would tend to indicate production at each location.[1]

Similar geological conditions at multiple sites may make it difficult to petrographically distinguish pottery manufactured at specific sites.[2] Both Santa Barbara and Ventura are sandwiched between the Transverse Ranges and the Pacific Ocean. Clays and sands underlying both locations stem from Holocene weathering and redeposition of earlier sedimentary deposits (Dibblee 1986, 1988). Sedimentary clay deposits from these formations are rich in quartz and feldspar, but limited silt-size grains of mica are present in some layers (Compton 1991:461). Culturally prescribed methods of processing raw materials, such as adding or subtracting sand grains or organic temper, can shift proportions of mineral inclusions. Barring the introduction of imported mineral temper, however, sherds produced from local materials along the southern Chumash coastline should contain primarily quartz and feldspar sand grains indicative of local formations.

Pottery was produced at both the mission and the presidio at Santa Barbara, and because they are located within 3.2 km (2 mi) of each other along Mission Creek, potters at the two locations likely shared access to the

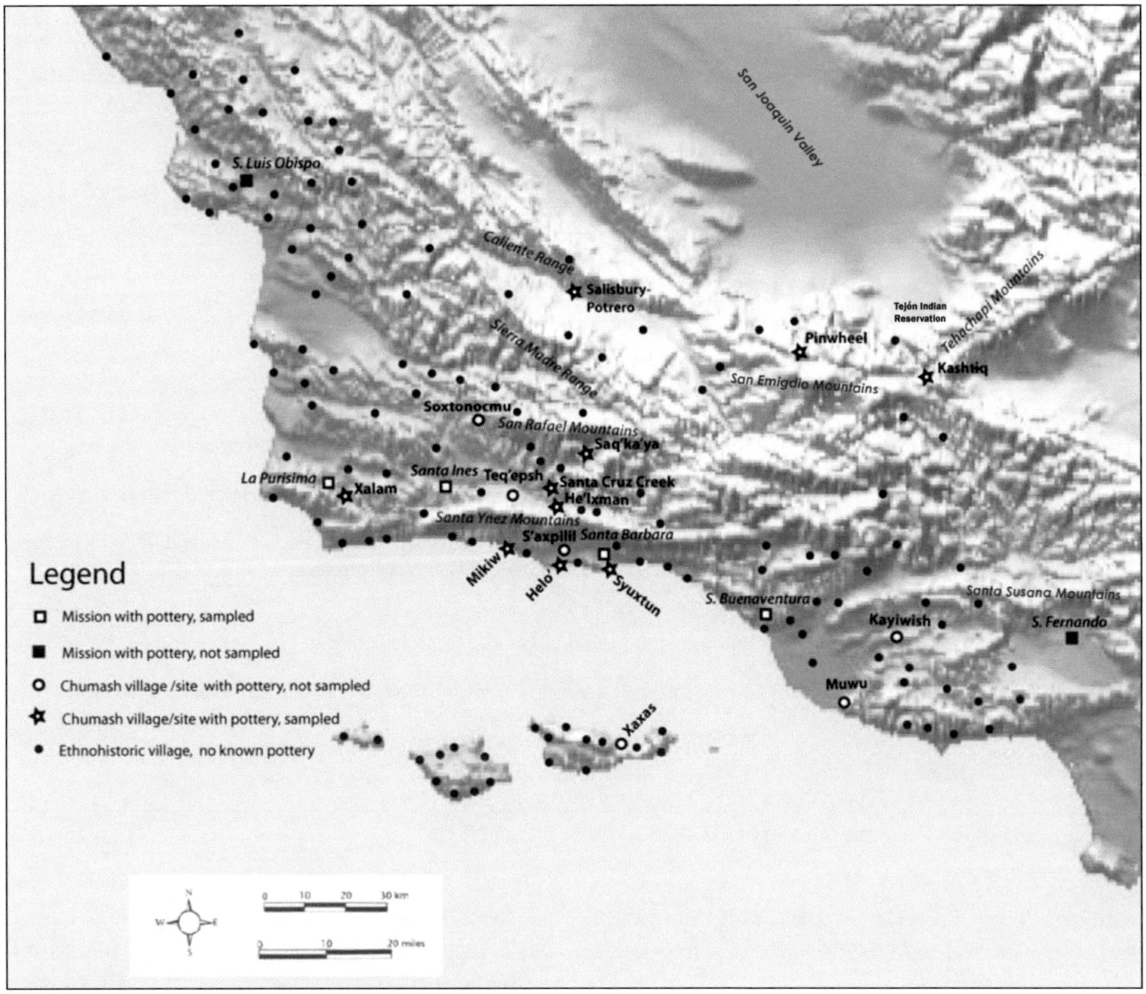

FIGURE 8.2. Missions and villages in Chumash territory.

same raw materials. Assuming similar (or no) transformations of raw material at the two sites, the potsherds should reflect similar petrographic signatures. Little excavation has been conducted at the mission, so to maximize the available sample size of ceramics from the Santa Barbara area, three sherds were selected for physical analysis from the mission and 21 from the presidio. Of these, two and 11, respectively, were chosen for petrographic analysis. Nineteen sherds from San Buenaventura were selected for physical analysis in this study, and from those, 11 sherds were analyzed petrographically. Table 8.3 provides the abbreviations used to indicate the source of each sherd investigated.

Methods

Two methods were employed: (1) sherd classification based on physical analysis (Table 8.4), and (2) petrographic analysis based on pointcounting procedures. Each site was treated as an independent sampling pool, and homogeneity was not assumed within any one

TABLE 8.3. Abbreviations Used in Coding Sample

Abbreviation	Site Name
SBP	Santa Barbara Presidio
BV	San Buenaventura Mission
PM	Purisima Mission
SBM	Santa Barabra Mission
IM	Santa Ines Mission
M	*Mikiw*
SX	Saq'ka'ya
J	*Xalam*
SP	Salisbury Potrero
H	*Helo'*
SC	Santa Cruz Creek
EX	*He'lxman*
PN	Pinwheel
SY	*Syuxtun*
K	*Kashtɨq*

TABLE 8.4. Terms Used to Describe Pastes

Mineral or Lithic Type	Abbreviation	Description
Quartz	Q	All quartz types
Plagioclase Feldspar	Fp	Etched, often with albite twinning, occasional Carlsbad Twinning
Potassium Feldspar	Fk	Alkali feldspar; etched and stained yellow, perthite, antiperthite, as well as microcline with polysynthetic (cross-hatch) twinning
Micas	M	Sand-sized mica, including biotite and muscovite
Dense Minerals	D	Dense, slow cooling igneous materials, such as pyroxene, amphibole, and epidote
Volcanic Lithic	Lv	One or more cemented mineral grains, including microphenocrysts of quartz and feldspar, as well as dense and mafic minerals
Sedimentary Lithic	Ls	Granular aggregates of subrounded, silt-sized or sand-sized grains
Metamorphic Lithic	Lm	One or more cemented mineral grains transformed by heat and pressure
Grog	G	Rounded clay inclusions, ranging from zero to several silt- or sand-sized inclusions; it is unknown whether this material derives from recycled bits of crushed ceramic or if it is a natural occurrence
Matrix	M	Clay matrix encasing independent mineral grains
Pore	P	Cavities formed by trapped air or from organic material that burned away
Calcareous	C	Lithics or monomineralic grains high in calcium, such as dolomite, calcite, and caliche
Unknown	?	Unidentified grains

Note: Table modified from Miksa and Heidke 1995:158

assemblage. From intrasite samples, point counts of paste constituents were compiled to create a petrographic database to look for patterns among sites.

Classification

Existing ceramic analyses in colonial period California have followed a variety of approaches to lumping or splitting brownware based on factors such as texture, surface treatment, and color, but few researchers have attempted to look beyond small assemblages to engage in intersite comparisons (Costello 1989; Felton 2006; May 1976). Chemical analyses recently undertaken using specimens collected at the presidios and missions in coastal California allow us to look at regional patterns. But these studies do not combine instrumental neutron activation analysis (INAA) results with discussion of petrographic or attribute variability in brownware (see Skowronek et al. 2001). It therefore remains uncertain whether brownware petrographic signatures covary with macroscopic features used in some of the California typological constructs. In this study, each village, presidio, and mission assemblage was divided into subtypes to ensure that samples represent the maximum petrographic variety present in the sampled assemblage.

Establishing intrasite typological groups based on paste types both reduces the potential for sampling error and furthers the preservation of ceramic material. Taking one thin section from every sherd would provide the most complete measure of intrasite variation, but such exhaustive testing is prohibitively expensive and unnecessarily destructive. However, with larger sample assemblages, sampling error decreases, as does the potential to miss rare categories or variants (McCartney and Glass 1990:523; Neff 1993:29). Magnification using a 20× binocular microscope provides an expedient and reasonably accurate method for quickly separating different paste types by examining the texture of inclusions present in each sherd (Shepard 1968:141).

For each site, only those samples that appeared to be hand-formed or coiled rather than wheel-thrown were selected. The small size of many of the potsherds available for this study often made it difficult to positively identify the method of production; however, no clearly wheel-thrown sherds were selected for petrographic analysis.

Primary emphasis was placed on identifying organic inclusions and lithic sand grains—visible using a binocular microscope. The goal was to identify variation

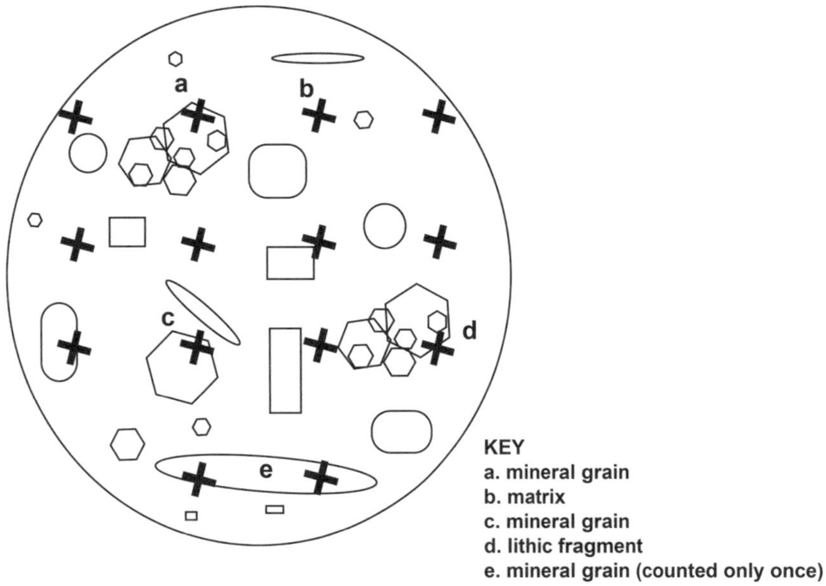

FIGURE 8.3. Gazzi-Dickinson Model. Each *x* represents the crosshairs landing at fixed increments across each thin section. Each spot where it lands is counted as matrix, mineral grain, or lithic fragment. This figure represents a partial view of a thin section as viewed through the microscope. For each thin section, I count a minimum of 100 mineral grains and lithic fragments.

in temper, so sherds were grouped according to textural variation. This difference in texture, whether due to raw materials or technological choices, provides the best predictor for identifying petrographic groups. Texture is used here to refer to grain size, the types of inclusions and voids, and their orientation in the clay matrix, as discussed in Rye (1981:50). Voids or pores are quite common in low-fired brownware at every site sampled here and include air bubbles from improperly kneaded clay as well as cavities left over from the combustion of organic material (Rye 1981:62). In nearly every sherd, pores tended to be randomly distributed, indicative of a coiling rather than wheel-thrown or drawn technique (Rye 1981:62). Pores from the combustion of straw or chaff frequently co-occurred with other textural characteristics, and although these pores occur in most sherds from the Chumash area, organic inclusions did not serve as the sole tempering agent in any specimen.

Using the classification scheme established for the assemblage, 68 sherds were submitted to the thin-section lab at UCLA for preparation using standard petrographic thin-section methods. A standardized, systematic point-counting method (Ingersoll et al. 1984; Middleton et al. 1985; Miksa and Heidke 1995; Stoltman 1989) was used to measure the proportions of specific inclusion types, clay matrix, and pores in the thin sections (Figure 8.3; see Bailey 2009 for details).

Results

To explore patterns in the point count data, cluster analysis and principal component analysis (PCA) were employed. Running the counts through two varieties of cluster analysis (Ward's linkage hierarchical clustering and k-means spatial clustering) provided slight variations in the petrographic groups or clusters created, and the degree of similarity or difference among these outputs provided a measure of the archaeological significance of those groups. Clustering in this case overlapped quite well among hierarchical and nonhierarchical clustering methods, and consistency between these clusters and groups suggested by PCA permits a high level of confidence in the validity of the groups presented below.

The four groups identified by cluster analysis are: Santa Barbara (a group of sherds primarily from Santa Barbara Presidio and the coastal villages); San Buenaventura (a group of primarily San Buenaventura sherds); Kashtɨq (a group of interior sherds, mostly from Kashtɨq);[3] and Interior/Unknown (a smaller group from interior village sites and from coastal sites).

These groups correspond with expected geological constituents for each area. Based on the known abundance of sedimentary minerals, such as quartz and feldspar, along the coast and of metamorphic minerals near Tejón Pass (Dibblee 1986, 1988), we can tentatively associate each petrographic group with corresponding

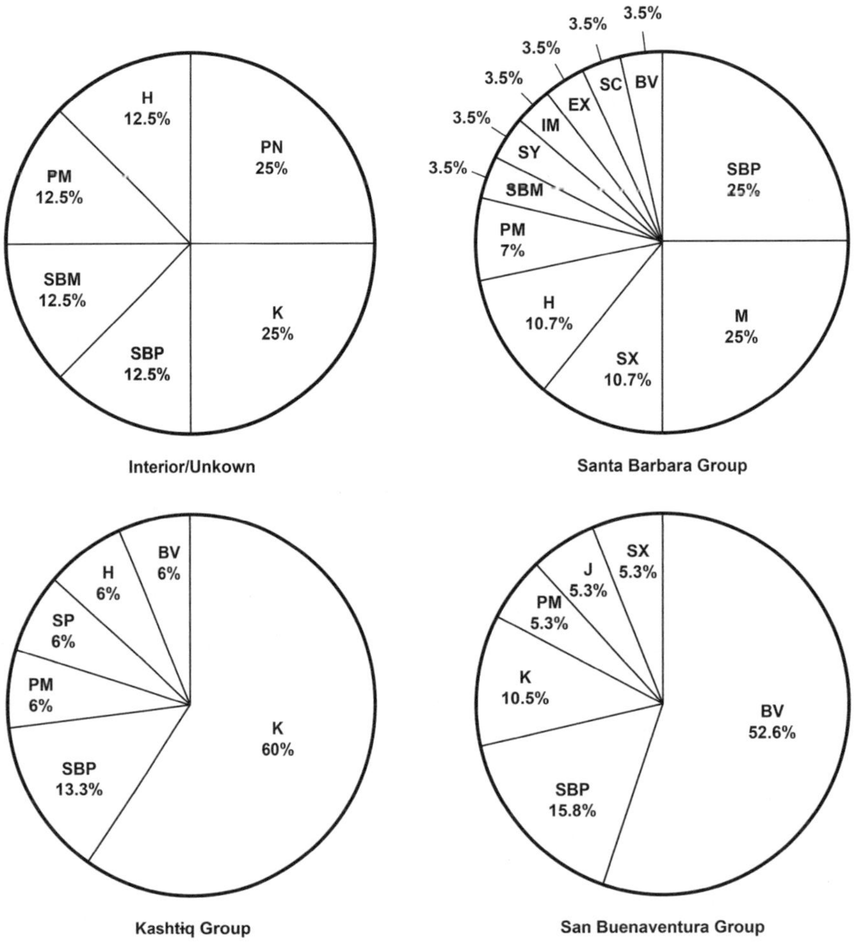

FIGURE 8.4. Percentage of each site in the petrographic groups. K = Kashti-q; SY = Syuxtun; PN = Pinwheel; EX = He'lxman; SC = Santa Cruz Creek; H = Helo'; SP = Salisbury Potrero; J = Jalam; SX = Saq'ka'ya; M = Mikiw; IM = Mission Santa Ines; SBM = Santa Barbara Mission; PM = Purisima Mission; BV = San Buenaventura; SBP = Santa Barbara Presidio

geological formations across the region. For the Kashtiq group this includes a high percentage of dense minerals and mica associated with metamorphic and volcanic activity.[4]

The Santa Barbara and Interior groups contain high proportions of quartz and feldspar and low percentages of clay matrix relative to mineral and lithic inclusions. The San Buenaventura group contains similar mineral inclusions but a high percentage of matrix relative to inclusions (Figure 8.4). Sherds from Pinwheel (PNl and PN2) fall within the smaller Interior/Unknown group that includes two samples from Kashtiq, which are low in dense minerals and mica content. This small group of Pinwheel and Kashtiq sherds is notably higher in plagioclase feldspar and slightly higher in potassium feldspar than the Santa Barbara sedimentary group, suggesting a petrographically distinct clay source and production area in the interior.

Principal components analysis collapses multiple variables into fewer ones that approximate the variation in the original (Shennan 1997:269). These data are visible in two dimensions and reflect the structure of the data in a way that maximizes the differences between samples. Factors typically decrease in the amount of variation explained, so that the first and second factors typically explain variance of more samples than do the third and fourth, and so on. In this case, Factors 1 and 2 account for 57.32% of the total variation in the data.

Factor 1 is negatively correlated with dense minerals, mica, and metamorphic lithic fragments, and is positively correlated with quartz, feldspar, and porosity. Factor 1 separates Kashtiq from the other sedimentary groups. Factor 2 is negatively correlated with matrix, and it separates San Buenaventura from the other groups.

To see whether the PCA analysis divided samples based on the same criteria as clustering, each of the four

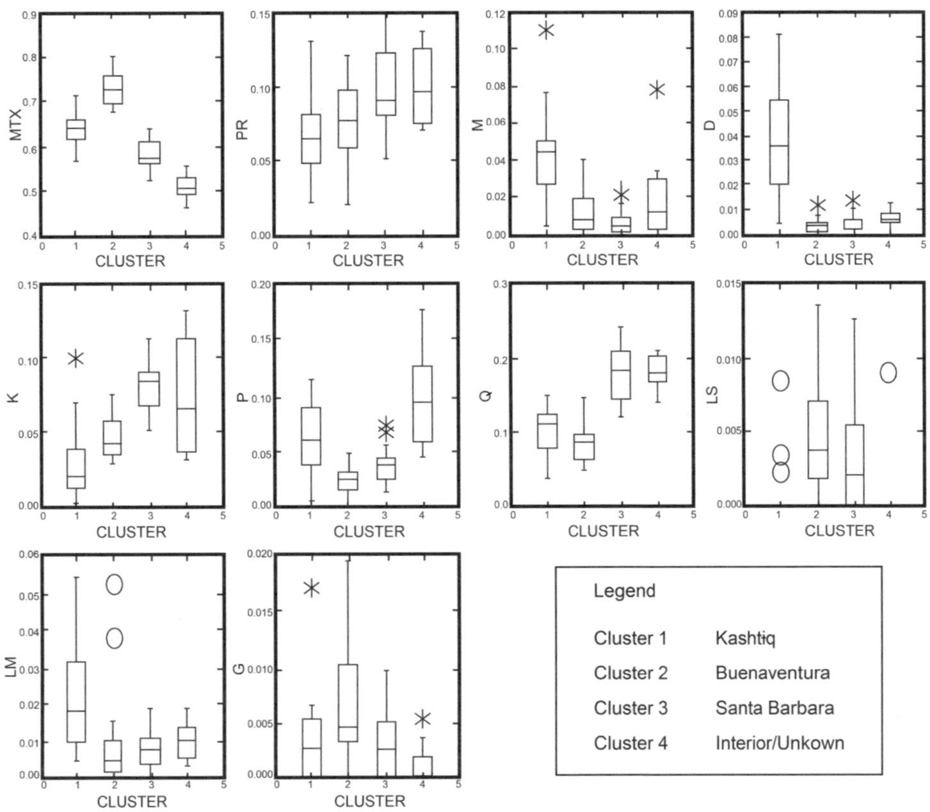

FIGURE 8.5. The box-plots display the mean and range of mineral and lithic constituents characterizing the petrographic groups identified through k-means cluster analysis. Circles and asterisks on the plots represent sherd outliers for that cluster, which fall outside of the mean. MTX = clay matrix; PR = pore; M = mica; D = dense mineral; K = potassium feldspar; P = plagioclase feldspar; Q = quartz; LS = sedimentary lithic fragment; LM = metamorphic lithic fragments; G = grog. Here, grog refers to rounded clay inclusions which likely occur as natural inclusions in the clay matrix.

clusters was plotted against the factor results for PCA (Baxter 1994). A graphic representation of K-means cluster analysis and Factors 1 and 2 (Figures 8.5 and 8.6, respectively) displays distinct groups corresponding with those created through each method independently.

Discussion

The brownware from Chumash territory fit within the four broad petrographic groups described above. Within each group, assemblage variability at coastal and interior sites is tied to localized historical and archaeological contexts.

Santa Barbara and San Buenaventura Petrographic Groups

The baptismal records indicate that individuals from the coastal villages included in this study interacted with populations at the missions and had mostly relocated to the Santa Barbara and San Buenaventura Missions by 1804 (Johnson 1989). The baptism of villagers from Helo', Syuxtun, Mikiw, He'lxman, and Saq'ka'ya took place at Santa Barbara Mission. Samples from each of these villages, with the exception of two sherds found at Syuxtun,[5] fall within the Santa Barbara group, along with samples from Santa Barbara Presidio and Santa Barbara Mission (Table 8.5). The small number of pottery sherds found in these villages likely indicates that production occurred not in the villages but at the mission and presidio, with finished vessels traveling out to the communities where some native individuals integrated pottery into the household economy (Hudson and Blackburn 1987:195).

Three samples from the Santa Barbara petrographic group appear to be exceptions to the mission-to-village pathway for pottery exchange in coastal sites. Sample K10 was found at the village of Kashtiq and may represent vessels moving with individuals from the coast to the interior. Two sherds (SBP11, SBP12) from the Santa Barbara Presidio site diverge from the other coastal wares. Both contain a high proportion of mica and are linked to the Kashtiq petrographic group. This pottery may have moved from the interior to the coast, but it is also possible that pottery with high quantities of mica was derived from a source near a mission or presidio

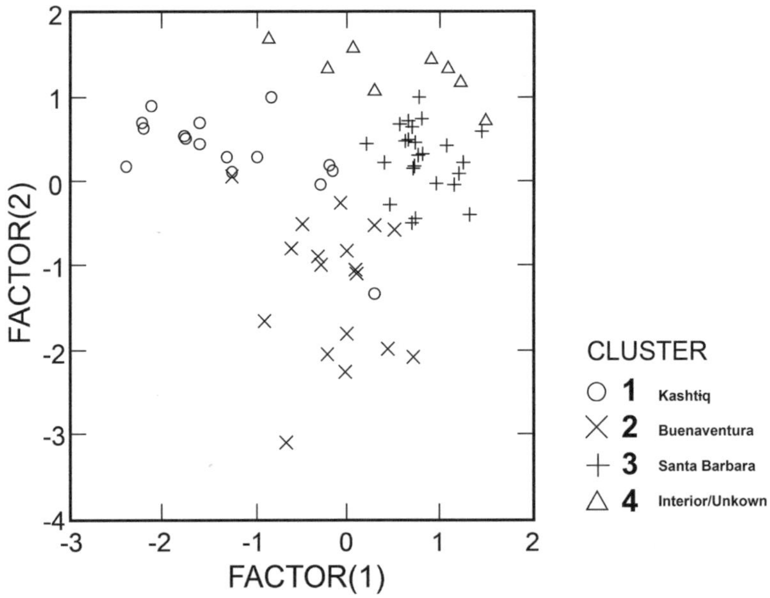

FIGURE 8.6. This graph shows individual samples as they fall into the four groups created through cluster analysis and plotted against PCA Factors 1 and 2.

TABLE 8.5. Distribution of Investigated Samples

Santa Barbara	San Buenaventura	Kashtɨq	Interior/Unknown
SBPI, SBP3, SBP4, SBP7, SBP8, SBPIO, SBP13, BV7, PMI, PM3, IMI, SBM2, MI, M2, M3, M4, M5, M6, M7, SXI, SX2, SX4, H2, H3, SCI, EXI, SYI	SBP2, SBPS, SBP14, BVI, BV2, BV3, BV4, BVS, BV6, BV7, BV8, BV9, BVI 1, PM2, SX3, JI, H4, K6, KIO	SBPI 1, SBP12, BVIO, PMI, SPI, HS, KI, K2, K3, K4, KS, K7, K8, K9, KII	SBP6, PM3, SBMI, HI, PNI, PN2, KI 2, K13

farther east or west along the coast. Resolving this with certainty is beyond the scope of the present study.

The San Buenaventura group largely consists of pottery excavated from the mission site itself, and although ceramic morphology, including surface treatment, appears similar for the San Buenaventura and Santa Barbara groups, the petrographic signatures are distinct. Sample sherds from coastal villages whose members were baptized primarily at San Buenaventura Mission were not identified for use in this study, and the lack of coastal village sherds in the San Buenaventura petrographic group fits with the hypothesis that pottery moved primarily from the missions to the villages of constituent neophytes.

One sherd each from two of the coastal villages linked by baptism to Santa Barbara Mission, Helo' and Saq'ka'ya, cluster with the San Buenaventura group. This could indicate pottery moving from San Buenaventura into these villages through neophyte visitation. This is possible but unlikely, given that only two individuals from Helo' appear on the San Buenaventura baptismal registers and the rest of the village appears on the registers at Santa Barbara (John R. Johnson, personal communication 2008). Alternatively, limited quantities of pottery may have been carried from San Buenaventura to Santa Barbara and from there to the villages. The few individuals from Kashtɨq who appear in baptismal records went to San Buenaventura Mission (John R. Johnson, personal communication 2008), but petrographic data do not provide evidence for a significant quantity of pottery moving into Kashtɨq from the coast or vice versa. One sherd from the village of Kashtɨq clusters with the San Buenaventura group, and one sherd from San Buenaventura Mission can be assigned to the Kashtɨq group. It is possible that a few vessels moved from the coast to the interior, but if so, this seems to have occurred rarely.

Kashtɨq and Interior/Unknown Petrographic Groups

The village of Kashtɨq, located approximately 64 km from the coast near Tejón Pass, yielded 179 sherds that were recovered from limited excavation (Jennings 1976).

Unlike brownware sherds from coastal sites, a number of Kashtɨq sherds examined in this study retain visible coils on the interior of the vessel walls where potters did not completely smooth the coils prior to firing. Four sherds collected from the surface include punctate patterning and basketry impressions, and all the decorated sherds may have come from two vessels.[6]

The abundance of dense minerals and mica in the pottery found at Kashtɨq matches the local mineral composition on site, which, together with the large quantity of potsherds found at Kashtɨq suggests that ceramic production occurred in or around the village.

Two sherds from Santa Barbara Presidio and one sherd from San Buenaventura fall within the Kashtɨq petrographic group. These sherds may come from an interior source near Kashtɨq, but perhaps more likely, given the relative isolation of interior villages during the mission period, they may derive from another mission beyond the sampling area. One source could have been a site located near metamorphic and volcanic deposits to the south, such as San Fernando Mission or San Gabriel Mission.

The Interior/Unknown petrographic group includes eight specimens: two from Pinwheel shelter, two from Kashtɨq, and four coastal sherds, one each from Santa Barbara Presidio, Santa Barbara Mission, Purisima Mission, and Helo'. The sherds from Pinwheel suffer from abrasion, and surface treatment was not clearly identifiable. The two Interior/Unknown-grouped sherds from the village of Kashtɨq (K12, K13) appear closer in color to the Pinwheel sherds, a gray 5YR 4/1, than to the shades of brown and red seen on the other Kashtɨq sherds, and no coils remain visible on either sample. It appears that these two sherds from the village of Kashtɨq derive from another noncoastal production site, but determining whether or not this source is the same as that of the Pinwheel sherds would require analysis of additional samples of pottery and of local clay sources.

Pinwheel Shelter is situated near a seed-processing site located approximately 64 km from the coast in the San Emigdio Mountains. No baptisms are associated with this site because it cannot be linked to a documented village (Robinson 2006). Few Chumash from this area moved to the missions or appear in the baptismal records, and those who did were recorded a decade or more after the 1803–1804 abandonments of coastal communities and immigration to the neophyte villages at the missions of Santa Ines, Santa Barbara, La Purisima, and San Buenaventura (Johnson 1989; John R. Johnson, personal communication 2007). The petrographic data suggest the production of "Interior" pottery from local sedimentary deposits. Sherds in the Interior group contain sedimentary material, but they differ from Santa Barbara and San Buenaventura group sherds in that they have a higher proportion of plagioclase feldspar. Runaway neophytes who learned to produce pottery at the missions could have produced pottery from local materials in the San Emigdio Mountains, but the presence of Yokuts or Yokuts-influenced pottery production offers a simpler explanation for these Interior ceramics in an area we know to have been a cultural and economic crossroads between Chumash territory and the Central Valley.

Analysis of Intrasite Variability

Each petrographic group consists of internally cohesive clusters based on the temper constituents of ceramic samples. These four petrographic groups are organized roughly by region, but the villages and sites from whence the samples derive may contain samples that fit in more than one petrographic group. Intrasite variability has implications for interpreting who produced pottery and how it moved among sites. However, with small sample sizes, it is difficult to decide whether the variability captured is representative of the variation throughout the entire site.

Small samples recovered as a surface collection, as at Saq'ka'ya, or over the course of limited or poorly documented excavation, as at Syuxtun, require interpretive caution. For sites represented by only a small sample, internal variability solely indicates that source variability exists at the site; it does not necessarily reveal how much variation exists. Syuxtun, for example, yielded three sherds from poorly documented contexts, each containing different inclusions, clay, and surface treatment. Two of the sherds (SY1, SY2) contain extraordinarily high quantities of calcareous inclusions not present in more than trace amounts in any other sample, while the third (SY3) clusters with the San Buenaventura group. Two of the three Syuxtun sherds come from outside the study area. It may be true that if a village contains mostly sherds from local source material as well as two or three from some other source, the evidence would point to the arrival of individuals with their own vessels but no further production. On the other hand, this pattern might indicate sporadic exchange.

The presence of two buffware pottery sherds in colonial period deposits at Mikiw and Muwu near Santa Barbara (Harrison 1965; Love and Resnik 1983) suggests neophytes born to the east of present-day Los Angeles may have brought their indigenous pottery with them. Historical records also describe the presence of indigenous immigrants and mestizos from farther south in Mexico who traveled north with the missionaries to Santa Barbara and San Buenaventura. In contrast, the proximity of the interior sites in this sample to known pottery-producing Yokuts and Kitanemuk peoples suggests a local connection linking interior Chumash pottery to eastern brownware traditions akin to those of the Owens Valley and the Colorado River regions.

In sum, it appears likely that neophytes trained by potters south and east of Los Angeles may have traveled north where they either produced or taught Chumash locals to produce brownware pottery in the Patayan and/or mestizo tradition at San Buenaventura and Santa Barbara missions. The pottery at the village of Kashtiq, however, represents a separate ceramic tradition related to the coil-and-scrape techniques of Owens Valley Brown Ware. The visibly unsmoothed coils differ from the morphology of the brownware found at coastal Chumash villages, the presidio, and the missions, and a separate petrographic signature matching local minerals at Kashtiq further supports this distinction. As early as the late eighteenth century, Spanish colonists described the area as a haven for runaway neophytes (Johnson 2007:91) and as a region where Yokuts and Kitanemuk individuals joined on raids and in long-distance trade to the San Joaquin Valley (Arkush 1993; Bernard 2008; Johnson 2007). On the coast, this pottery entered the archaeological record of indigenous village sites sometime before their abandonment, that is, sometime before circa 1804. In the interior, this material could have been deposited any time between the late 1700s and the early American period when indigenous people continued to live in villages on and near the Tejón Indian Reservation in the southern San Joaquin River Valley and the surrounding hills of the Tehachapi and San Emigdio Mountains.

Conclusions

Petrographic analysis of brownware pottery in the colonial period Chumash villages confirms localized production and use. This mirrors patterns of brownware use and distribution observed in other sourcing studies at mission communities along the California coast and of precontact indigenous pottery production in eastern and southern California (Eerkens 2001; Gallucci 2001; Hildebrand et al. 2002; Skowronek et al. 2001; Skowronek, Blackman, Bishop, and Koons 2005; Skowronek, Blackman, Bishop, and Rosas 2005; Skowronek, Blackman, Bishop, and Tsukiji 2005; Skowronek, Blackman, Bishop, and White 2005). Brownware appeared sporadically across Chumash territory in the colonial period, from the Channel Islands to the Interior, and its presence is best read within the context of a given site's proximity to known brownware production sites (both European and indigenous), and based on historic evidence of how and why native villagers may have accessed brownware technology.

Ceramic technology spreads into new territory via temporary or permanent migration, trade, and intermarriage. Frequently, these relationships overlap, and brownware moved along social and economic exchange routes alongside other commodity trade items, such as painted porcelain and glass. Brownware produced from a local clay source indicates that the associated site was inhabited by at least one individual familiar with the process of procuring, preparing, forming, and firing the clay to produce vessels used in household tasks. The brownware found in coastal Chumash villages may have been deposited there when mission neophytes returned to visit their homes, or it may have been obtained through direct exchange with nearby Spanish outposts.

Although trade items of European origin do appear in Channel Islands Chumash villages, few brownware sherds have been recovered from island village excavations relative to the quantities excavated from the larger mainland villages along the coast. Utilitarian technology such as pottery did not move as frequently across the channel as did more coveted commodities such as glass beads and iron needles.

Future researchers should seek to enlarge the present sample size by drawing on material excavated from additional sites not included in this study. Locating this pottery will require additional archival and collections research on existing sites at institutions such as the Smithsonian and the Hearst Museum at Berkeley. Ideally these samples will include villages linked through baptism to missions other than Santa Barbara to test the patterning described here. Ceramic material procured from additional survey and excavation at sites associated with the Yokuts, Kitanemuk, Interior Chumash, and other groups extending to the Antelope Valley will refine our understanding of ceramic movement among villages. More pottery samples will also enhance our understanding of morphological variation and the intersection between ceramic technology and regional petrographic groups tied to particular ceramic traditions such as Numic and Patayan pottery in eastern and southern California, respectively.

With European incursions, settlement shifts occurred across the region. Villagers from different ethnic and linguistic backgrounds came together in the coastal missions, and native families and neophytes fleeing the missions traveled into the northern and eastern borders of Chumash territory to form new settlements or join existing communities in the mountains and valleys bordering the southwestern San Joaquin Valley. Finally, after the secularization of the missions, native communities were formed on or near inland reservations like that at Tejón (Beeler and Klar 1977; Phillips 2004). These multiethnic communities housed many of the informants interviewed by ethnographers in the late nineteenth and early twentieth centuries on subjects ranging from material culture and technology to the cultural and linguistic geography of Chumash territory. A better understanding of how these communities emerged helps to illuminate community change, interethnic interaction, and processes of material culture change in California.

Notes

1. Due to the small sample size of sherds available for analysis and the undifferentiated nature of each sherd (i.e., few distinguishing features), there is the possibility that a signature might be overrepresented in this study.
2. This study does not attempt to identify a specific clay source for the brownware pottery sampled here. All of the sherds are analyzed and grouped relative to one another. The noted correspondence between the composition of brownware temper and the geological composition of the regions from which they were excavated must be tested to confirm or disprove.
3. The Interior Chumash village of Kashtiq is located alongside Castac Lake, near Tejón Pass, and is distinct from other Chumash settlements alongside Castaic Creek (Johnson 1978)
4. None of the decorated sherds are included in the petrographic analysis due to curatorial concern.
5. These two sherds (SY2 and SY3) were removed from the cluster listings in Table 4 in order to eliminate outlier signatures.
6. The Tejón Indian Reservation, located at the southwestern point of the San Joaquin River Valley where it meets the Tehachapi Mountains, was founded by the United States government in 1853 and was closed in 1864 (Phillips 2004).

9

The Brownware Ceramic Traditions at Mission San Gabriel Archángel

Suzanne Griset

Ceramic Background

Although the missions in Alta California were managed as a single system, local foods and native technologies greatly influenced the development of each mission and how the Native systems were incorporated, modified, or rejected by the Spanish missionaries. Native ceramics, defined here as culinary containers capable of sustained heating and repeated cooling cycles, were not universally used or produced in prehispanic Native California. Only the south coast and interior desert of Alta California and the northern portion of Baja California had extensive ceramic traditions of nearly 700 years duration before the Spanish intrusion in the last quarter of the eighteenth century.

The native ceramic tradition in southern California included small, hand-modeled vessels (small bowls and scoops) and disks and pipes, and a variety of larger bowls and jar vessels made by the coil/paddle-and-anvil technique (Rogers 1936). These culinary vessels were begun with a circular base hand-formed or molded over an extant vessel base. The walls were built by adding coils of clay that were pinched together, then thinned and shaped with a ceramic or stone anvil held on the interior, and a wood paddle used on the exterior. Traditional southern California vessel forms included bowls and jars in small, medium, and large sizes, with apertures also ranging from narrow, to medium-wide, to wide mouth. These vessels were used to collect, process, serve, and store foods and other goods, and many were ultimately repurposed to hold cremated human remains.

Other ceramic traditions in prehistoric California consisted of coiled-and-scraped Owens Valley Brown Ware made along the eastern escarpment of the southern Sierra Nevada Mountains, which blends into the Intermountain Brown Ware of the Great Basin. A relatively late tradition of small hand-modeled, flat-based bowls was made among the Yokuts and Western Mono (Monache) on the western flank of the southern Sierra Nevadas and was likely a result of Spanish mission influence.

The ceramics discussed here were recovered from excavations at Mission San Gabriel Archángel in the northern Los Angeles basin. This mission was first established in 1771 to baptize the surrounding Tongva (a.k.a., Gabrielino) villages. The Tongva inhabited the Los Angeles Basin, the eastern portion of the San Fernando Valley, and three of the Channel Islands—San Clemente, Santa Catalina, and San Nicolas, which had rich marine resources and renowned soapstone deposits. The Tongva, like their Chumash neighbors to the northwest, used stone bowls carved from soapstone, granite, or sandstone. Ethnologists reported that ceramics were not produced by the Tongva (Bean and Smith 1978; Johnston 1962; Kroeber 1925; McCawley 1996). Archaeologists, however, have recently excavated small numbers of ceramic sherds at late prehistoric sites in Orange County, suggesting ceramics were just beginning to be used and possibly produced in the southern portion of the Tongva area where it abutted the pottery-making Juaneño/Luiseño (Boxt and Dillon 2013).

A flood in 1775 destroyed the fields and much of the mission building. The mission was relocated 8 km (5 mi) to the north, closer to the San Gabriel Mountains near the village of *Shevaanga*, and continued drawing Tongva converts from an ever-widening radius. By 1800, the San

Gabriel mission population had reached 1,000. By 1805, the missionaries were forced to draw from non-Tongva tribes to the east and northeast, among the Pass and Mountain Cahuilla, the Serrano in the San Bernardino Mountains and the Mohave Valley, and from the Luiseño to the south. All of these people were paddle-and-anvil pottery makers. By the 1820s, four natal languages were spoken by mission residents—Western and Eastern Gabrielino, Serrano, Cahuilla, and Luiseño; however, the majority of the population by that time was Serrano and Cahuilla (NEA and King 2004:40).

For the first 30 years of Mission San Gabriel's existence, its neophytes derived from areas lacking native ceramic traditions. Potters were imported from missions to the south where native people had been making ceramics for more than 500 years (Griset 1996); or were artisans from Mexico; or found among the soldiers and colonists associated with each mission. Mariano Vallejo (a Californio military and political leader in the first half of the nineteenth century) remembered:

> It was between 1792 and 1795, as I have heard, that the governor brought a number of artisans from Mexico, and every Mission wanted them, but there were not enough to go around. There were masons, millwrights, tanners, shoemakers, saddlers, potters, a ribbonmaker, and several weavers (Vallejo 1890).

In the case of San Gabriel, the soldiers and colonists who settled the mission and the nearby pueblo of Los Angeles, were immigrants from Sonora, Mexico and were a mixture of Hispanic, black, Native, and mestizo peoples who brought their own ceramic traditions including wheel-thrown, molded (where liquid clay is poured into forms then hand-finished), paddle-and-anvil, or hand-modeled vessels.

The Spanish also introduced new foods, new cooking techniques, and vessel forms that altered and augmented the traditional bowl/olla forms of southern California. Wheat, barley, corn, and beans replaced acorn and native seeds as the principal crops. Forms such as cups (for drinking hot chocolate), comals to make tortillas, casuelas to cook beans, and handled pitchers were introduced along with the cuisine; rounded vessel bases were replaced by flat bases that could sit on a table (Griset 1990). Vessel shapes made during the early years of Mission San Gabriel were those of the introduced pottery traditions, made with a combination of introduced technologies.

The mission system was terminated in 1834, the priests were recalled, and the abandoned neophytes returned to their natal villages or found new residences. Hugo Reid, whose wife was a Tongva neophyte from Mission San Gabriel, reported in 1852 that most of the Serrano and Cahuilla who had been living at Mission San Gabriel, returned to their home villages in the mountains and deserts, while the Tongva from the Los Angeles Basin moved northward because their home villages had been granted or sold to non-native ranchers (Heizer 1968). Only a few local Tongva families remained living on small parcels immediately surrounding the mission.

Also, in 1852 Indian Agent B. D. Wilson reported that the natives who returned to mountain villages manufactured "a kind of urn to hold water and keep it cool in summer (called olla)" for sale to non-native customers (Caughey 1952). Greenwood and colleagues (1983) observed a gradual decline in the number of native ceramics present at Los Angeles ranchos by 1860, as other types of imported ceramic and metal vessels became more readily available. Nevertheless, traditional Native ceramic forms—especially ollas for transporting and holding household drinking water and small bowls for ceremonial purposes—continued to be produced at native villages for use well into the early twentieth century (Griset 1990, 1996).

From the inception of the mission at its present location in 1775 until approximately 1805, the Tongva neophytes at Mission San Gabriel likely had no existing ceramic tradition and would have been taught how to make ceramics. After 1805, the Cahuilla and Serrano brought to the mission may have advocated for continuing their traditional paddle-and-anvil manufacturing techniques, unless forced to do otherwise. Also after 1805, the ceramic assemblage may have included more of the traditional bowl and jar shapes typically produced by potters brought from villages to the northeast, east, and south of the mission.

Mission San Gabriel Ceramic Sample

With this background in mind, brownware ceramics from Mission San Gabriel were examined from two samples derived from data recovery excavations and construction monitoring by SWCA Environmental Consultants for the California Department of Transportation's San Gabriel Trench Grade Separation Project (Dietler et al. 2015; Griset 2015, 2018). Ten functional designations assigned to areas within the two investigations (Figure 9.1) contained significant ceramic samples that were analyzed (Griset 2015, 2018). The data recovery included: portions of the mission garden; a midden area divided into north and south areas by the Southern Pacific Railroad; a granary area; a stone reservoir; and the Chapman's Mill millrace. During construction

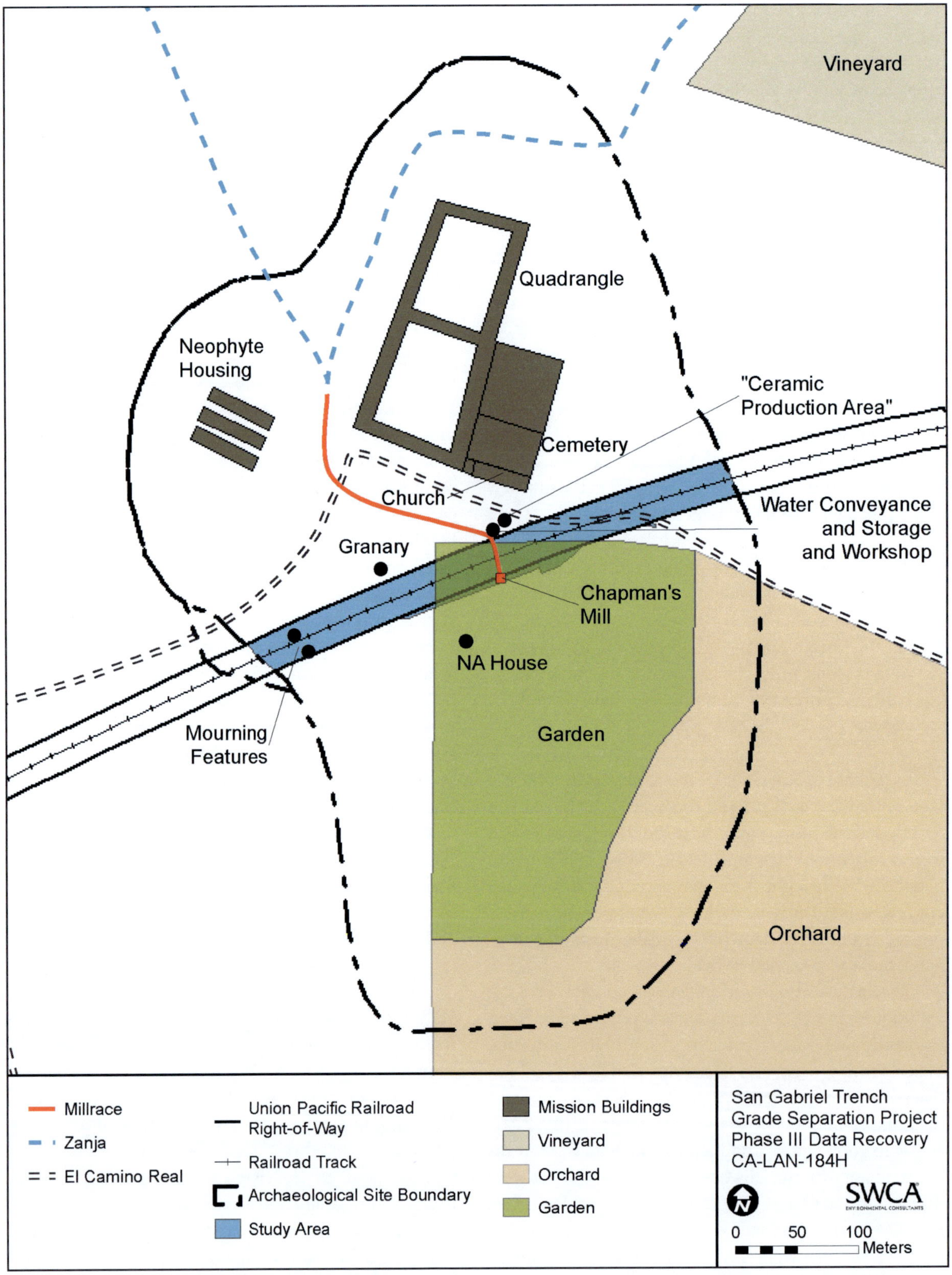

FIGURE 9.1. Locations of ceramic sample from Mission San Gabriel: data recovery included mission garden, midden, granary, stone reservoir, Chapman's Mill millrace; construction monitoring included Native American house, mourning area, ceramic production area, water storage/conveyance, and workshop. (Map by Lara Mitchell, SWCA, based on Dietler et al. 2015, 2018).

FIGURE 9.2. Example of grass vugs on the interior of a hand-modeled cup, apparent on many of the MSGB sherd surfaces and cores.

monitoring, ceramic grab samples were collected as features were exposed in the following areas: a Native American house; a mourning area with a compacted (dance?) surface; a possible ceramic production area; a water conveyance and storage area (with a feature near the wall of another reservoir, a plastered surface near the garden wall, and a water channel); and a row of adobe rooms designated as a workshop. Except for the Native American house located in what became the western portion of the mission garden, none of these areas overlapped. The monitoring grab samples were used to augment the observations on ceramics recovered from the data recovery excavation units.

Four samples of clays present on or adjacent to the site were collected; briquettes were made and fired in a kettle barbeque to simulate open-pit firing. All appear silty gray in texture and color and contain small grass vugs on the surfaces and/or in the core (Figure 9.2). These local clays appear to be the clay used to make what was identified as Mission San Gabriel Brown (MSGB) type (summarized below and described formally in Griset 2015), as well as roof tiles (tejás) and floor tiles (ladrillos; Dietler et al. 2015).

Archaeological ceramic typologies for traditional prehistoric pottery divide southern California native ceramics into brown, buff, and intermediate wares, based on the color of the paste and presumed regions where the clays originated: *Southern California Brown Ware* (SCBW; formerly Tizon Brown Ware of southern California) is made of self-tempered residual clays collected near their place of origin in mountainous areas. These clays contain angular to subangular nonplastics and fire orangey to red brown, brown, and gray brown due to the amount of iron oxides present in the clay and the degree of oxidation achieved in open pit firings. Residual clays often contain varying amounts of naturally occurring mica visible on the sherd surfaces.

Lower Colorado Buff Ware (LCBW) is crafted from finely sorted sedimentary clays transported by fluvial or aeolian forces from mountain ranges on either side of the lower Colorado River down into desert basins. These sedimentary clays contain finely sorted and

TABLE 9.1. Distribution of Pottery Wares in Data Recovery Sample from Mission San Gabriel

	MSGB	SGBW	CDIBW	LCBW	Puebloan	Indeterminate	Totals
Number of Sherds	833	191	35	4	1	182	1,246
Percent of Total	66.9	15.3	2.8	0.3	<0.1	14.6	100

rounded nonplastics, when present, or in some cases, purposely crushed potsherds—aka grog. Nonplastics typically must be added to "temper" the clay to give it sufficient strength during vessel forming. Buff clays fire pink, salmon, beige, buff, tan and cream colors due to the lack of iron oxides in the sedimentary clays.

California Desert Intermediate Brown Ware (CDIBW) is just that—made of clays that burn lighter brown, contain semirounded nonplastics that have been transported some distance from their mountain origins, and may also contain additional nonplastics added as temper.

Mission Brown Ware (MBW) is a fourth southern California ceramic tradition that was restricted to the historic period. It was first identified by Ron May's analysis of sherds from Mission San Buenaventura (May 1976) as being distinct from traditional prehistoric pottery made by native peoples of southern California. Mission San Gabriel Brown (MSGB) is a newly identified type within MBW; it was formally described during the analysis of the data recovery investigation at Mission San Gabriel (Griset 2015), and is the predominant type found in the data recovery and monitoring collections from Mission San Gabriel.

Analytical Methods and Results

The analysis of the San Gabriel ceramic samples assigned a ceramic ware and type to each sherd greater than 10 × 10 mm in size, noted evidence of manufacturing technique (hand-modeled, coil-and-scrape, paddle-and-anvil, wheel-thrown or wheel- finished), surface treatment, and presence/location of any carbon or residues that could identify vessel uses or postdeposition contexts. Sherds that conjoined or had similar paste were recorded as individual vessels. Rim sherd analysis focused on reconstructing vessel dimensions, likely form, and noting any evidence of use.

Both ceramic samples contained low numbers of SCBW, LCBW, and CDIBW. A single Puebloan Black-on-white jar sherd from the Four Corners area of the Southwest was present in each sample. By far, the preponderance of the analyzed ceramics proved to be locally made MSGB type identified in the data recovery ceramic sample (Table 9.1).

MSGB, as presently defined (Griset 2015), incorporates a combination of manufacturing techniques and may in fact be better termed "wheel fashioning." In some cases, it appears that a vessel was begun with hand modeling and a slow wheel was used to shape and finish it, thereby producing a variety of surface finishes.

MSGB vessels were typed as "MSGB wheel" when there was ample evidence of the vessel having been wheel thrown—widely spaced horizontal "coils" or rills on either or both surfaces (Figure 9.3). These ranged from partially to completely smoothed, although the latter still left a rippled effect on the vessel surface. An alternate explanation for the rippled exteriors may be provided by three small basket-impressed sherds found in EU 154, east of the millrace, and likely from the same vessel. All three sherd exteriors contained clear impressions from the base of a flat coiled basket (tray?). The impressions were left unsmoothed and suggest that vessels (trays?) were formed by covering basket interiors with a layer of clay that was removed once it had dried sufficiently. If the coil impressions were smoothed before the clay dried to the leather hard stage, they also would leave a horizontally rippled surface.

There were a few examples of completely smoothed and sometimes polished sherds that would be typed as SCBW had they not been made from the local clays. This suggests that potters with native ceramic traditions used the local clays to make vessels, and likely dates the sherds to post-1805. Several examples of small, hand-modeled vessels were also made with the local clays (see Figure 9.4).

While the majority of the MSGB sherds have a silty gray-brown appearance, a small subset consists of highly oxidized sherds; whether they were oxidized by firing or use, is unclear. These oxidized sherds also tend to lack the grass vugs so prevalent on the wheel-finished vessels and may represent a better prepared local clay or even a change in the manufacturing techniques as the potters became more experienced (see Ceramic Production Area below).

SCBW sherds were identified by surface treatment (well smoothed and occasionally the presence of an anvil mark on the interior), and by the difference in clays—MSGB lacks the "silty" appearance, has more abundant angular granitics, and lacks the distinctive abundant grass vugs on the surfaces or in the core.

LCBW sherds were made from sedimentary clays and were typed as Parker Buff, Cahuilla Buff, Hedges

FIGURE 9.3. Examples of wiping marks, footring, and definitive wheel rills on vessel sherds of MSGB clay.

Buff, and Colorado Buff based on the clay color and the presence/absence and type of nonplastics (see Griset 2015:Table 10.7 for the description of the attributes of the ceramic wares and types used in this study).

CONTEXTS OF THE CERAMICS

Most of the sherds were discarded in transformed (churned) secondary deposits, making stratigraphic chronological assessment difficult. Only one context could be tentatively dated. The Native American house contained a mixture of historic/prehistoric artifact types deposited in two distinct layers suggesting an early Mission period time range, in the late eighteenth century shortly after the creation of the mission.

Although nine functional areas were identified during the two investigations, the data recovery analysis focused on the area with the most concentrated samples—the millrace/stone reservoir. Most of the ceramic sample collected during construction monitoring consisted of grab samples representative of the variety of sherds observed in each area. Two exceptions were the hand-excavated samples from: Groups A and B of the mourning area; and the Native American house, which had two distinct deposits (Dietler et al. 2018).

Unique ceramics found in these functional areas are described below, followed by summary observations on the combined samples.

Mill Race/Stone Reservoir

Four examples of individual candlestick holders, hand-modeled from local clay, were identified in the trash deposits around the exterior of the reservoir. One example (conjoining specimens #11964.02, #11964.03, and #7403.01) was found 100–110 cmbd in adjacent units 223 and 224 along the north wall of the reservoir (Figure 9.4). A very similar candlestick holder (#13380.01 and #13380.03) was found east of the reservoir at 140–150 cmbd in Unit 235; the third small fragment was also

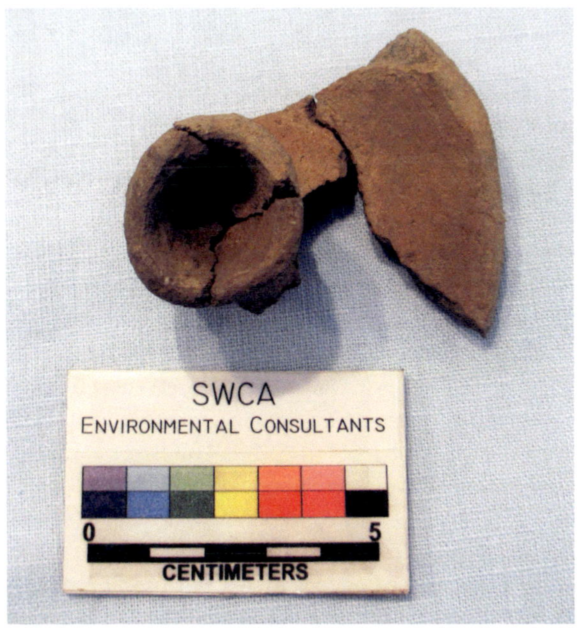

FIGURE 9.4. Candlestick holder, 10–11 cm in diameter with very irregular rounded rim/lip. The "dish" is approximately 5 cm deep, with the candle holder diameter 1.9 × 2.1 cm and projecting 2.3 cm above the interior of the dish. The fine silty clay has extensive fine vugs indicative of clay that was not well prepared.

FIGURE 9.5. Miniature olla, height 8.5 cm, rim diameter 6.5–7.0cm, maximum diameter 8.6–8.8 cm; found with 1 needle-drilled shell bead and 2 carbonized seeds; hole in base due to construction activities during monitoring.

found along the north wall in Unit 206, at 120–140 cmbd; and a fourth example (Specimen 6035.01) was recovered from Unit 106 at 140–150 cmbd. The latter specimen was distinctive in having a smaller diameter, estimated at 7 cm, while the first candlestick holder had a diameter of 10–11 cm, the second was not measurable, and the third was 16 cm in diameter. All have shallow dishes with flattened bases and a single candle holder in the middle of the dish; insufficient portions remain to determine whether they had handles. No other candlesticks were found elsewhere in either ceramic sample.

Mourning Area

The only complete vessel recovered from either investigation was a flat-bottomed, hand-modeled, miniature MSGB jar found 3 m below a compacted (dance?) area. Edward Davis's description of a Luiseño mourning ceremony describes similar small ollas:

> During this time, some of the calcined bones of the dead were pounded up in the mortars to a fine powder, diluted and drunk out of small ollas by the relatives, thereby insuring [ensuring] long life free from sickness, and endowing themselves with the virtues and characteristics of the dead, in accordance with the ancient ritual. (Edward Davis in Quinn and Quinn 1965:101; cited in Bean 2017:51, footnote 62)

After the missionaries banned cremation in favor of inhumation, later versions of the mourning ceremony substituted the water from the washing the deceased's clothes for the powdered cremains. The flattened base on the miniature olla also affirms that it dates to the historic period (Griset 1990).

Native American House

The Native American house (Feature 13254) was the feature with the most intact deposits; it contained two distinctive cultural strata (Stratum III, the upper cultural layer, and Stratum VIII, the lower) separated by largely sterile layers. Both strata contained historical period materials expected at the beginning of the Mission era—adobe brick fragments, small majolica and Galera sherds, and glass beads—however, no metal or glass fragments or whiteware ceramics were found in this feature, which suggests that it dates to the early historic period. Traditional native materials in the house deposits included flaked stone, faunal remains (including marine shell and a sea mammal bone), and marine shell beads.

With one exception, the native sherds were typed as MSGB produced from the local silty clays, with roughly smoothed surfaces and often with horizontal wiping marks and evidence of grass and seed vugs. These are interpreted as remnant from vessels formed and finished on a slow wheel—the wiping marks on the surface are not uniformly parallel or evenly spaced and are more haphazard.

Stratum VIII contained the most numerous and most diverse vessel assemblage with 16 of the 22 vessels recovered from the house: 3 jar/bowls, 3 jars, 9 bowls, and 1 cup/bowl (see Vessel Assemblage below for vessel dimensions and shapes). The bowl rims tend to be 15 or 20 cm in diameter with a single rim at 18 cm in diameter. Each rim was sufficiently different in dimensions and surface treatment that it was identified as a separate vessel; however, given the apparent lack of consistency in the surface treatment and shaping of MSGB vessels, some may, in fact, derive from the same vessel.

Stratum III contained five vessels: a cup, a small cup/bowl(?), a medium bowl, a medium-wide jar, and a wide-mouth jar. All these vessels are for personal serving or family-sized cooking/water transporting tasks.

TABLE 9.2. Worked Sherd Disks from the Native American House

Specimen No.	Depth (cmbd)	Strata	Diameter × thickness (cm)	Percent Present	Drilled from	Description of Sherd
42848.01	1–16	I	9.0 × 0.6	10	Exterior	MSGB, roughly smoothed surfaces
43205.01	31–40	I	6.0 × 0.45	9	Exterior	MSGB-silty gray; roughly smoothed surfaces; carbon on interior
42928.01	65–85	III	5.5 × 0.5	9	n/a	MSGB, roughly smoothed surfaces; carbon on both surfaces
43000.01	65–77	III	4.5 × 0.8–0.85	30	Exterior	MSGB-silty gray, roughly smoothed surfaces
43001.01	65–77	III	3.5 × 0.5–0.6	30	Exterior	MSGB-silty gray, roughly smoothed surfaces
43041.01	87	III	8.0 × 1.0	8	Exterior	MSGB-silty gray, roughly smoothed surfaces; fugitive red wash on both surfaces and on ground edge
42986.01	74–92	III	5.0 × 0.6	10	Exterior?	MSGB-silty gray; rough exterior with carbon; roughly smoothed interior
43419.01	—	III	5.0 × 0.55–0.6	15	Exterior	MSGB-silty gray; roughly smoothed surfaces
43369.01	76	III	4.0 × 0.75–0.95	50	Interior	Mexican Majolica with glazed interior; rough exterior
43138.01	56	III	4.5 × 0.55–0.75	50	Biconical?	MSGB-silty gray; roughly smoothed surfaces; soot on exterior
43243.01	66–95	VIII	Est. 9.0 × 0.6–0.7	25	Interior	MSGB-silty gray; roughly smoothed exterior; roughly shaped, began to drill, broke
43302.01	n/a	n/a	6.0 × 0.65–0.7	21	Interior	MSGB-silty gray; roughly smoothed surfaces; carbon on exterior
43303.01	n/a	n/a	7.0 × 0.5	11	Exterior	MSGB-silty gray; smoothed both surfaces; carbon on exterior
43294.01	n/a	n/a	Est. 6.0 × 0.5	10	Interior	MSGB-silty gray; roughly smoothed surfaces; faint carbon both surfaces
43294.02[a]	n/a	n/a	Est. 10.0 × 0.5 mm	5	n/a	MSGB-silty gray, roughly smoothed surfaces, faint carbon exterior
43294.03[a]	n/a	n/a	Est. 2.0 × 0.5–0.6	25	n/a	MSGB-silty gray, roughly smoothed surfaces, carbon on exterior

[a] Two additional sherds from 43294 are likely initial attempts to grind and perforate MSGB sherds

No narrow- or medium-wide-mouth storage jars were recovered from the house, nor were there any large communal serving vessels.

Stratum III also contained 8 of the 16 perforated disk fragments found in the house and two MSGB amorphous-shape worked sherds, which suggests this stratum is related to the use, manufacture, or discard of the disks (Table 9.2; Figure 9.6). The eight disks consist of 7 MSGB and one majolica fragment. Only one disk was found in the lower cultural stratum (VIII); two were found in the upper disturbed layer; and five did not have a provenience recorded when they were collected during the monitoring.

None of the disk fragments conjoin and none resemble another. Each disk is a unique fragment, and their remainders were not recovered from the excavated portion of the house. Most are fairly well shaped, which suggests that they were at the end stage of manufacture when the hole was being drilled *OR* that the activity in which they were being used caused them to fragment. Dietler and colleagues (2018:139) interpret the disks as spindle whorls related to the production of cloth at the mission by native women, which would suggest that the cloth was being made within individual houses rather than a workshop. Whatever the function, one would expect to find conjoins or multiple pieces of the fragmented disks within the house.

Some of the disks are decorative in that unusual sherds were used—for example, the Majolica example or one with a fugitive red wash on both surfaces and on the ground edge (indicating that it was purposefully decorated). Most disks, however, were made from wall sherds of cooking vessels and evidenced abrasion and carbon deposits associated with their previous uses.

FIGURE 9.6. Examples of disk fragments recovered from the Native American house.

Only five disk preforms (unfinished and undrilled) were found elsewhere in the combined investigations of Mission San Gabriel, corroborating the unique nature of the disks in the deposit associated with the lower house floor.

Optically Stimulated Luminescence (OSL) dating was attempted for this feature; unfortunately, the results are not in stratigraphic order and contradict the dates attributed to the other artifacts found in association with the sherds. Based on the lack of metal, glass, and later historic ceramics, and the presence of trade beads, majolica, and locally and roughly made MSGB, with traditional materials such as faunal, lithics, and shell, it is likely that the house feature dates to the early Mission period. It may even be the location of the village of *Shevaanga* where the missionaries moved Mission San Gabriel in 1775 after being flooded out of the 1771 mission. Within that four-year interval, villages surrounding the original church would have been aware of the new technologies and goods brought by the missionaries and participated in exchange networks moving those goods throughout the Los Angeles Basin.

Ceramic Production Area

During the construction monitoring, one feature (11024) was designated as a possible ceramic production area. A ladrillo brick-and-mortar walled rectangular enclosure with a roughly 4.0 × 2.1 m (13 × 7 ft) ladrillo floor, was excavated west of the garden, with a single southeast-northwest course of ladrillo bricks separating the room into one-third/two-thirds. A deposit of clay capped the floor and included brownware, burned and unburned faunal bone, glass fragments, unmodified shell, non-diagnostic metal fragments, one of two ceramic kiln stilts found in the room, one metal cabinet knob, ladrillo fragments, tejá brick fragments, mortar fragments, and a roughly ground *Olivella* wall bead.

Most of the 41 vessel sherds found in the clay deposit in this feature are small fragments (average 2–7 g) and include 10 MSGB (undiagnostic), 4 MSGB Wheel sherds, 3 MSGB Wheel (oxidized) sherds, 16 SCBW, 6 LCBW-Parker Buff, and 1 indeterminate sherd. This feature clearly had an atypical assemblage in that the local MSGB comprised only 23% of the assemblage while the most numerous sherds were SCBW (35%) and 14% were LCBW. Six sherds were recovered from unknown depths: two are large conjoining sherds (weighing a total of 328.9 g) forming a portion of a large wheel-thrown vessel (bowl? Amphora?) with wall thickness of 7 cm toward the incurving rim (the rim is missing) and expanding to 12 cm thick by presumably mid-vessel. A third unprovenienced sherd is from this same very heavy-walled bowl.

Two ceramic Y-shaped kiln stilts (used as kiln furniture to separate items so that they did not fuse during firing) were found in ladrillo feature as well. Both were hand-modeled of very fine clay with subangular nonplastics. They were likely cut in the 3-pointed star shape (using a form?) as the underside of the stilt body is flat; they were hand-smoothed on the sides of each arm and the tip was bent downward to provide additional space and air flow along the bottom of the stilt (Figure 9.7). Similarly shaped and sized kiln stilts are still manufactured today.

A sample of the clay layer was collected. It is a fine silty gray brown to the naked eye (Munsell: 10YR 5/4

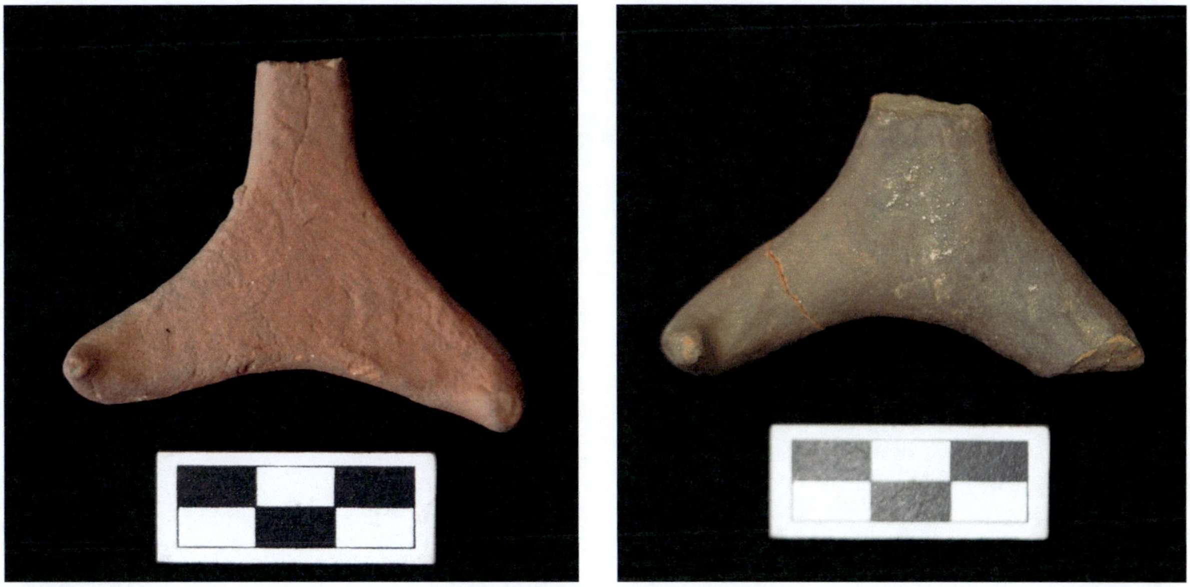

FIGURE 9.7. Kiln stilts from the ceramic production area (Dietler et al. 2018:Figure 6.26).

yellowish brown) with very few inclusions, and those are small and well rounded. The clay may have been levigated to remove organics and larger nonplastics. It appears to be the same clay used for MSGB, but more refined, possibly for wheel-thrown vessels.

The presence of the kiln stilts and the clay deposit was interpreted by the construction monitors as an indication that the room had some part in ceramic production; however, the sparse presence of sherds, many of which were imported wares, suggest that it was likely not the production room, rather a materials storage or clay preparation area.

San Gabriel Mission Vessel Assemblage

The traditional prehistoric vessel assemblage consisted primarily of jars and bowls that can be grouped into small, medium, and large forms based on the exterior diameter at the rim. Although the rim diameters are not a measure of the height and volume of the vessels, they provide a means of sorting vessels into size classes.

Jars are classed as narrow mouth (diameter of <6 cm), medium-wide mouth (6–12 cm diameter), and wide mouth (>12 cm). Bowls are classed as small (5–10 cm diameter), medium (>10–20 cm), and large (>20 cm and height greater than 15 cm). Small bowls in historic sites may be cups, but the sherds in this sample were too small to determine more than the diameter at the rim. Miniature versions of these forms were also made prehistorically and historically.

Table 9.3 summarizes the distribution of vessel forms reconstructed from 106 rim sherds from the data recovery and construction monitoring samples; Table 9.4 provides the detailed information for each reconstructed vessel. In both samples, bowls predominate the ceramic assemblage (62.7%), compared to jars (28%) and platter/trays (9.3%). Medium bowls, likely used for serving or processing family-size quantities, are the most prevalent (24.2%); wide mouth jars and large bowls are the next most prevalent, each at 14.2%, and may represent communal cooking/serving. Two-thirds of the large bowls and jars were found in the mourning area, confirming that this was an area devoted to communal activities.

The construction monitoring sample did not contain the plates, trays, and scoops found in the data recovery sample. This may be due to the nature of the deposits and the collection method: the data recovery deposits are interpreted primarily as churned trash deposits likely containing the full range of vessel forms and sizes made and used at the mission. In contrast, nearly 60% of the monitoring sample was collected from the mourning area, which is interpreted as a communal area with ceremonial functions.

The largest number of vessels was concentrated in three areas. The combined mourning area loci had the most vessels (29 vessels, 27.4% of the vessel assemblage) and the largest fragments of vessels; the next largest sample derived from smaller rim sherds found in the trash deposited along the east exterior of the millrace (25 vessels, 23.6%); and finally, the Native American house contained 23 vessels (21.7%). Together, these three areas produced nearly three-quarters of the identified vessels.

Table 9.3. Summary of Vessel Forms Reconstructed from Rimsherds, by Mission Area and Ceramic Tradition

	Vessel Form						
		Bowls					
Mission Area	**Platter/Tray**	**Cup**	**Small**	**Medium**	**Large**	**Very Large**	**Unknown**
Data Recovery Sample							
Millrace East Exterior	3 M	2 M	2 M	8 M	3 M		1 M 1 M bowl/plate/scoop
Millrace NE Exterior	1 M	1 M cup/ comal?					1 MWh bowl/plate/ scoop
Reservoir Interior					1 M		
Garden	2 M tray/shallow bowl? 1 MWh? tray/shallow bowl			1 SC	1 M		1M bowl/plate/tray
Construction Monitoring							
Mourning Area Group A			1 M*	1 M 3 MWh	2 M 4 MWh 1 M/SC?	1 MWh	
Mourning Area Group B			1 M*	1 M			
Mourning Area Adjacent							
NA House Strat I							
NA House Strat III		1M* 1 MWh Cup?		1 M			
NA House Strat VIII		1 M*		5 M 4 MWh			
NA House Unknown							
Water Conveyance (W.C.) – Wall				2 MWh	1 M	1 MWh	3 M 1 MWh
WC – Water Channel							
WC – Workshop					2 MWh?		
WC – Plastered Area							
Totals (%)	7 (6.6)	6 (5.7)	4 (3.8)	26 (24.5)	15 (14.2)	2 (1.9)	8 (7.5)
M M* MWh M/SC SC SC/CD?	6 M 1 MWh?	3 M 2 M* 1 MWh	2 M 2 M*	16 M 9 MWh 1 SC	8 M 6 MWh 1 M/SC	 2 MWh	6 M 2 MWh

M – Mission San Gabriel Brown
M* – hand-modeled
MWh – Mission San Gabriel Brown – wheel thrown?
SC – Southern California Brown Ware
CD – California Desert Intermediate Brown Ware

TABLE 9.3. (cont'd.) Summary of Vessel Forms Reconstructed from Rimsherds, by Mission Area and Ceramic Tradition

Vessel Form						Totals by Ceramic Tradition	Number of Vessels (%)
Jar/Bowl		Jars					
Medium-wide	Wide Mouth	Miniature	Medium-wide	Wide mouth	Very Large		
	1 MWh	1 M	2 M 1 MWh?			23 M 2 MWh	25 (23.6)
	1 M			1 SC		3 M 1 MWh 1 SC	5 (4.7)
1 M			1 MWh			2 M 1 MWh	3 (2.8)
	1 SC			1 SC		4 M 1 MWh? 3 SC	8 (7.5)
	2 MWh			2 M 2 MWh 2 SC/CD?		5 M 1 M* 12 MWh 1 M/SC? 2 SC/CD?	21 (19.8)
				1 M/SC? 2 MWh		1 M 1 M* 2 MWh 1 M/SC?	5 (0.7)
1 M		1 M*		1 MWh		1 M 1 M* 1 MWh	3 (2.8)
1 MWh						1 MWh	1 (0.9)
			1 M	1 M		3 M 1 M* 1 MWh	5 (4.7)
1 M 1 MWh	1 M			2 M	1 M	10 M 1 M* 5 MWh	16 (15.1)
1 MWh						1 MWh	1 (0.9)
	1 MWh					4 M 5 MWh	9 (8.5)
	1 MWh					1 MWh	1 (0.9)
						2 MWh?	2 (1.9)
1 SC?						1 SC?	1 (0.9)
7 (6.6)	8 (7.5)	2 (1.9)	5 (4.7)	15 (14.2)	1 (.9)	106	100.0
3 M	2 M	1 M	3 M	5 M	1 M	56 M	52.8
		1 M*				5 M*	4.7
3 MWh	5 MWh		2 MWh	5 MWh		36 MWh	33.9
				1 M/SC?		2 M/SC	1.9
1 SC?	1 SC			2 SC		5 SC	4.7
				2 SC/CD?		2 SC/CD?	1.9

TABLE 9.4. Descriptive Data for Reconstructed Vessel Forms

Project Location	Exc. Unit	Depth (cmbd)[a]	Catalog Number[b]	Ceramic Type[c]	Form and Size Class	Rim Form
Millrace East Exterior	105	50–60	03015.01	MSGB	Tray, shallow	Direct, Slightly everted
		70–80	03267.01	MSGB	Bowl?, medium	Direct
		100–110	04871.01 & .02	MSGB-WT?	Jar, MW	Direct
			04871.03	MSGB	Bowl, medium, shallow Tray?	Direct, Everted, Undulating
		110–120	04827.01	MSGB	Tray/plate, large	Direct, Everted
		120–130	04681.01/ 05858.01	MSGB	Jar, WM	Recurved
			05858.02	MSGB	Bowl	Direct, Slightly recurved
			05858.04	MSGB	Bowl, medium	Direct, Slightly inverted
		130–140	05367.02 & 05916.03	MSGB	Bowl, medium	Direct, Slightly inverted, Undulating
		140–150	05557.09 & similar 05557.04 & .11	MSGB	Cup	Direct, Slightly inverted
		140–150	06139.01	MSGB	Bowl, medium (25% present)	Direct, Slightly inverted
			06139.02	MSGB	Jar, MW	Slightly recurved
			06139.03	MSGB	Bowl/Plate/Scoop?	Direct
			06139.04	MSGB	Bowl	Direct, Inverted
			06139.05	MSGB	Bowl, small	Direct, Inverted
			06139.07	MSGB	Miniature jar	Direct, Slightly Recurved
		150–160	05916.01	WT	Jar, WM	Slightly recurved
			05916.02	MSGB	Bowl, medium	Direct, Inverted
			05916.03	MSGB	Bowl, medium	Direct, Inverted
			05916.04/ 06133.06	MSGB	Bowl, medium, shallow	Direct, Slightly everted
			06133.01/.04	MSGB	Bowl, large	Direct, Slightly everted
			06133.02/05	MSGB	Bowl, large	Direct
			06133.03	MSGB	Tray/plate	Direct, Everted, Slightly recurved
			06133.06	MSGB	Bowl, small	Direct, Slightly everted
			06133.07 &.15	MSGB	Bowl, large	Direct

TABLE 9.4. (cont'd.) Descriptive Data for Reconstructed Vessel Form

Lip Form, Thickness (mm)	Base Form, Thickness (mm)	Dimensions (cm)[d]	Wall Thickness (mm)	Function	Comments
Beveled on exterior, 6.0–7.0	n/a	D: 20–22	8.00	Serving	Slow wheel?
Rounded (lip folded over), 7.0	n/a	D: 12	5.5–6.6	Serving?	Salts on lip
B interior, 5.5	n/a	D: 10	6.5	Serving	Collared
Rounded, 6.5	n/a	D: 12–14	8.0	Serving?	Slow wheel; both surfaces are very uneven and undulate
Rounded Flat, 4.5–5.0	n/a	D: >38	7.0–8.0	Serving	Tiny black deposits (manganese?) on both surfaces
Rounded, 4.0	n/a	D: 16 N: 3 Min: 14 at 1.5	6.0	Storage/ Transport	Broken before deposited; yellowish deposit on all surfaces; burnish on both surfaces of rim/neck
Rounded, 4.5 Lip incised with line parallel to vessel walls	n/a	n/a	6.0	Serving?	Interior surface not entirely smoothed; if orientation is incorrect, may be a restricted bowl
Rounded Flat, 4.0	n/a	D: 14 Max: 16 @ 2	6.0–6.5	Serving?	Very uneven exterior; yellowish deposits especially on interior
Rounded, 4.0–7.0	n/a	D: 20	8.0–10.0	Cooking	Specimens do not conjoin, but derive from same vessel. Undulating exterior; carbon on exterior below rim; distinctive chunks of feldspar
Rounded, 4.0	n/a	D: 4	7.0	Serving	None
Rounded, 3.5	Rounded, 14	D: 12 Max: 14 @ 3 H: 7.5 B: 4	9.0–15.0	Serving	Pinch pot; salts on lip; chipped on rim interior; poorly smoothed
Beveled, Rounded, 7.0	n/a	D: 10 N: 3.2 Min: 9 at 3.5	12.0	Storage/ Transport	Slow wheel; lip poorly smoothed and chipped; exterior surface undulating with grass vugs; interior grass vugs
Rounded, 5.0	n/a	D: >18	6.5	Serving	Grass vugs both surfaces; possibly slipped
Rounded Flat, 3.0	n/a	D: 12?	7.5	Serving	None
Rounded Flat, 7.0	n/a	D: 10	5.5	Serving	None
Rounded, 3.0	n/a	D: 5–6	n/a	?	None
Rounded, 4.5–6.0	n/a	D: 16 Min: 15 at 1.5	8.5	Storage/ Transport	Exterior undulating with grass vugs; interior wheel marks with grass vugs
R, 3.5–4.5	n/a	D: 13 Max: 16 at 3	13.0	Serving	Grass vugs both surfaces
R, U, 6	n/a	D: 13 Max: 15 at 3.5	8.0	Serving	Both surfaces uneven
R, 4–5	n/a	D: 11 H: est. 3–4	5.5	Serving	Grass vugs both surfaces
R, U, 8–10	n/a	D: 24	zz	Cooking	Carbon on both surfaces; roughly smoothed both surfaces while wet; iron deposit on exterior near lip
RF, U, 6–7	n/a	D: 21	5.5	Serving?/ Cooking?	Roughly finished and grass vugs on both surfaces; carbon on all surfaces may be post-use
B, 6.5–8.5	n/a	D: 23 H: est. 7	7.5	Serving	Roughly made exterior; smoothed interior with grass vugs.
B, R, 3.5	n/a	D: 8 H: est. 3	5.5	Serving	Exterior rough with grass vugs; interior smoothed, with grass vugs
E, F, 10	n/a	D: 26	6.5–7.5	Serving	Chipped along exterior lip; grass vugs on exterior

TABLE 9.4. (cont'd.) Descriptive Data for Reconstructed Vessel Form

Project Location	Exc. Unit	Depth (cmbd)[a]	Catalog Number[b]	Ceramic Type[c]	Form and Size Class	Rim Form
	108	40–50	02827.01	MSGB	Bowl/Cup, small	Direct, Inverted
Millrace Northeast Exterior	206	80–90	10647.01	MSGB	Bowl or Comal	Direct
		120–140	15594.02/.11 & similar 15594.06 & .12	MSGB	Jar? WM Bowl? large	Direct, Inverted
			15594.05 & .07	SCB	Jar, WM	Recurved
			15594.09	MSGB	Plate	Direct, Everted
			15594.14	MSGB or WT	Bowl/Plate/ Scoop?	Direct
Reservoir Interior	137	80–90	05259.01	MSGB	Jar? MW Bowl?, medium	Direct, Inverted
			05259.04/.05	MSGB	Bowl	Direct, Inverted
		110–120	06172.01	WT? or SCB?	Jar	Direct, Inverted
	118	83–90	02743.01	MSGB	Bowl/Plate/Tray?	Direct
		130–136	03220.01 (Feature 8)	SBMB	Tray? Shallow Bowl?	Everted, tapered
			03220.02 (Feature 8) & non-feature 04432.01 similar	MSGB	Bowl, large	Direct
	273	116–130	15902.01	MSGB	Bowl, shallow	Direct, Slightly everted
	282	100–110	14595.01	WT?	Plate/Soup Bowl?	Direct, Everted
			14595.02	SCB	Bowl?, medium	Direct
		130–140	14748.01	SCB	Bowl, large or Jar, wide mouth	Recurved
			14748.02	SCB	Jar, wide mouth	Recurved
Mourning Area	329–331/ 331–332	124–161/ 165–179	30434/ 30425/ 32484/ 30567	MSGB Wheel?	Bowl, medium	Direct Undulating
	329–331 311	124–161 50–60	30383/ 30421 & 30446 & 30032.01/02	MSGB Wheel	Bowl, large	Direct Undulating

TABLE 9.4. (cont'd.) Descriptive Data for Reconstructed Vessel Form

Lip Form, Thickness (mm)	Base Form, Thickness (mm)	Dimensions (cm)[d]	Wall Thickness (mm)	Function	Comments
R, 5.5	n/a	D: 7	7.0	Serving	Undulating exterior and seed vugs on both surfaces
F, 5	n/a	D: 12	5.5	Cooking	Direction of rim is unclear, but heavy carbon/ soot on exterior
F, 7.5–8	n/a	D: 36	9.5	Serving?	None
R, 7	n/a	D: 20	12.0	Storage/ Transport	Shape reminiscent of water storage ollas
IB, 6	n/a	D: 12	6.5	Serving	None
R, narrow collar 1 cm wide on exterior, U, 4.5	n/a	D: 18 H: est. 5–7	4.5	Serving	Small, thin-walled, shallow bowl with red-washed interior and splatter on exterior
R, E, 5.5–7	n/a	D: 16	8.5	Cooking	Carbon on exterior surface
RF, 4	n/a	D: 22	7.5–8.5	Cooking?	Some carbon on exterior
R collar, 13 × 16	n/a	D: 8	6.0	Storage/ Transport	Rim profile shows rim folded over to exterior to form round ring around neck similar to that seen on Spanish storage jars and soapstone vessels in historical photograph (Figure 9.3).
BE, 12	n/a	D: 8? H: est. 3–4	6.5.0	Serving	Rim direction is unclear; bevel is polished from use which would favor it being a plate
RF, 4.5	n/a	D: 20	7.5–8.0	Serving?	Slow wheel; rim added as additional coil; made of local clay but well smoothed on both surfaces
B, RF, 3.5	n/a	D: 22	6.5–7.0	Cooking	Carbon on exterior
B, 7	n/a	D: 8	9.0	Serving?	Scratches on both surfaces; only exterior is oxidized
R with flattened area on interior, 4	n/a	D: 20	9.0	Serving	Fine sedimentary clay
R, 7	n/a	D: >20	7.0	Serving	Coil juncture in paste
RF, 8	n/a	D: 22 N: ?	9.0	Serving	Carbon streak, wiping marks for PA
RF, 8	n/a	D: 16 N: 3 Min: 13 @ 1.5	11.0	Storage/ Transport/ Water Jar?	None
Rounded 4.5	Likely rounded	D: 17	9.0–10.0 midwall; 14.0 toward base	Serving	Conjoins between Subfeatures 2 & 4. Silty brown paste; wiping marks both surfaces, multidirectional; some attempt to smooth interior (raising self-slip?) but exterior has many grass and nonplastic vugs and generally uneven surface; carbon deposits suggest post-breakage differential exposure to carbon; old chip in rim of 30567
Rounded 4.5–5.0	Likely rounded	D: 27	8.0 midwall	Cooking	3 rim fragments of same bowl with silty brown paste; exterior obscured by soot; interior carbon on roughly smoothed surface; 2 sections have been used as scraping tool with exterior chips or ground spaces.

TABLE 9.4. (cont'd.) Descriptive Data for Reconstructed Vessel Form

Project Location	Exc. Unit	Depth (cmbd)[a]	Catalog Number[b]	Ceramic Type[c]	Form and Size Class	Rim Form
	329–331	124–161	30386	MSGB Wheel?	Jar/Bowl, wide mouth	Slightly recurved
	329–331	124–161	30388	MSGB Wheel?	Jar/Bowl, wide mouth	Slightly recurved
	329–331	124–161	30411 & 30399/30412	MSGB	Jar, wide mouth	Recurved
	329–331	167	31645	MSGB oxy Wheel	Jar, wide mouth	Direct, Tapered, Undulating
	329–331	167	31749	MSGB oxy Wheel	Jar, wide mouth, Slightly undulating	Slightly recurved
	329–331	167	31641	MSGB oxy Wheel	Bowl, medium	Slightly recurved
	329–331	167	31746	MSGB oxy	Bowl,large	Direct
	332	125–190	30569/ 32523/ 32530.01 & .02	MSGB Wheel	Bowl, medium	Tapered, Undulating
	331–332	165–179	32127.01–06 & 07	MSGB Wheel?	Bowl, large	Tapered, Undulating
	331–332	165–179	32505	SCB?/ CDI? red-on-brown	Jar, wide mouth	Recurved
	331–332	165–179	32506	MSGB oxy? SCB?	Bowl?, large	Direct, Slightly tapered, Undulating
	331–332	165–179	31621 & 31631	MSGB Wheel?	Bowl, large	Direct, Everted
	311	80–90 71–77 60–70 50–60	30074.02/ 30074.03/ 30085/ 30086.01/ 30086.02 & 30032	MSGB Wheel	Bowl, very large	Direct, Tapered, Undulating
	311	60–70	30041.01	SCB?/CDI?	Jar, Wide mouth	Direct, Slightly recurved

TABLE 9.4. (cont'd.) Descriptive Data for Reconstructed Vessel Form

Lip Form, Thickness (mm)	Base Form, Thickness (mm)	Dimensions (cm)[d]	Wall Thickness (mm)	Function	Comments
Beveled, fine lip 3.5		D: 17	7.0	Serving?	Silty gray paste, smoothed both surfaces, vugs from dragged nonplastics; oxidized interior; very faint carbon exterior—possibly from original firing; carbon core
Beveled, fine lip 3.0		D: 14	9.0	Serving?	Very similar to 30386 despite slight variation in lip
Beveled 4.0	Rounded 15 cm	D: 32 est.	6.5	Serving	Similar to 30386; larger dimensions and more acute recurve though may be a function of small size of 30386 & 30388.
Beveled on interior	n/a	D: 17	8.0 bevel 3.0–.07 lip	Storage?/ Cooking	MSGB oxidized with polishing marks on uneven exterior, surface; interior has wiping bands, visible nonplastics up to 3.0 mm; grass vugs?
Rounded 3.5–4.5	n/a	D: 21 rim D: 19 mouth	11.0 shoulder, 7.5 midwall	Storage?/ Transport?	MSGB oxidized; smoothed horizontal bands in multidirections, leaving uneven exterior; interior roughly smoothed dragging nonplastics, vugs, and bits of clay.
Beveled on interior	n/a	D: 18 est. Max D: 25 at 3.5 cm below rim	8.0 midwall, 6.0 below max dia	Cooking	MSGB oxidized; smoothed/polished exterior but uneven near rim and with grass? vugs, "polished" beneath carbon and soot that extend from max diameter and below; interior roughly smoothed; most of lip chipped
Flat	n/a	D: 25 cm	7.0	Cooking	MSGB oxidized; soot and carbon on exterior; roughly smoothed interior with dragged nonplastics, vugs; carbon core
Beveled on interior 9.0–13.0	Rounded?	D: 13 (asymmetrical) H: 15 est.	15.0 midwall, 8.0 toward base	Serving	MSGB silty gray, roughly smoothed exterior w/ horizontal wiping; large wiping indentations in = Wheel thrown? Fine mica visible both surfaces. Soot staining postdeposition on exterior interior and exterior; eroded toward base
Beveled on interior 7.0–8.0	Rounded?	D: 25	9.0–10.0 midwall	Cooking	MSGB roughly smooth both surf; soot exterior; postdeposition carbon stain interior
Beveled 6	n/a	D: 20 at rim D: 16 at mouth	12.0 shoulder, 14.0 midwall	Cooking?	Heavy walled, smoothed exterior; paddle and anvil on inter shoulder; red paint on exterior obscured in part by carbon and soot area; soot on interior appears old
Rounded Flat 6	n/a	D: 34	6.0	Cooking?	Oxidized clay; roughly smoothed, nonplastic pops and vugs; faint carbon exterior
Rounded Flat 7.5	n/a	D: 25	7.0	Cooking	Polish on exterior, faint horizontal wiping marks both surfaces; carbon both surfaces; carbon core
Beveled 4–5	n/a	D: 35–37 H: 15 est.	9.0 midwall	Serving?/ Cooking? Large volume	Silty gray paste, wheel forming marks, multidirectional on exterior wider indentations on interior; some carbon may be use related; patches of soot postdeposition and post-breakage (see impact scar on 30032).
Beveled on interior 5	n/a	D: 16 at rim D: 14 at mouth	10.0 shoulder	Cooking?	Originally highly oxidized giving red appearance; surface covered by carbon from use; smoothed exterior, roughly smoothed interior. Rim may have been used as a scraping tool – lip remains in 1 of 20 cm of the rim lip, and the remaining has multiple chips, primarily on exterior, but several on interior. Paste contains fine rounded granitic grains and an occasional larger non-granitic lithic inclusion that was not identified.

TABLE 9.4. (cont'd.) Descriptive Data for Reconstructed Vessel Form

Project Location	Exc. Unit	Depth (cmbd)[a]	Catalog Number[b]	Ceramic Type[c]	Form and Size Class	Rim Form
	311	60–70 70–80 80–90	30041.02/ 30060/ 30074 30060 & 30041.03	MSGB Hand modeled	Bowl, small	Direct, Tapered, Undulating
	311	70–80	30060.02	MSGB Wheel	Bowl, large	Direct, Tapered
	311	60–70	30041.03	MSGB	Bowl, Low medium	Direct, Very slightly tapered
	311	60–70	30041.04/05	MSGB	Bowl, large	Tapered, Undulating
	311	80–90	30074.01	MSGB	Jar, wide mouth	Direct, Slightly recurved
	MTR 13499	None	42540	MSGB Hand modeled?	Bowl, small	Direct, Slightly tapered
	Sec 13141	28.0-28.5	42450	MSGB oxy	Bowl, medium	Direct, Slightly tapered
	Sec 13141	32–33	42422	MSGB? SCB?	Jar, wide mouth	Slightly recurved
	MTR 13499	26–57	42394.01 & 42394.02	MSGB Wheel	Jar, wide mouth	Slightly Recurved, Undulating
	MTR 13499	26–57	A42394.03	MSGB Wheel	Jar/Bowl, wide mouth	Direct, Slightly everted
	MTR 13455	None	42700.01	MSGB oxy Hand Modeled	Jar, Miniature	Direct, Slightly undulating
	EU 11534	9-50	40982.01	MSGB Wheel	Jar, wide mouth	Slightly recurved
	EU 11534	9-50	40982.02	MSGB	Jar/Bowl, medium	Direct, Slightly everted?
Native American House (Strat I)	13317	I	42892	MSGB Wheel	Jar/Bowl?, medium wide mouth	Direct, Tapered
(Strat III)	13319	III	42954	MSGB Wheel oxidized	Cup/Small Bowl?	Direct
	13320	III	43047	MSGB Hand Modeled?	Cup	Direct, Slightly tapered

TABLE 9.4. (cont'd.) Descriptive Data for Reconstructed Vessel Form

Lip Form, Thickness (mm)	Base Form, Thickness (mm)	Dimensions (cm) [d]	Wall Thickness (mm)	Function	Comments
Rounded, almost beveled on interior 6.5–8.5	Flattened 10–16 cm near base	D: 10	12.0 midwall, 10.0 near base	?	MSGB hand-modeled bowl; roughly smoothed exterior, even rougher interior; carbon deposits post-breakage and deposition, both surfaces
Beveled on interior 3.0–4.0 lip 9.0–10.0 bevel	n/a	D: 25	9.0	Cooking	Faint wide horizontal bands both surfaces, leaves exterior bumpy; carbon both surfaces; brown residue on interior near rim
Beveled 3.5	n/a	D: 13	8.0–9.0 midwall, 11.5 near base	Serving	Silty gray brown with many parallel narrow wiping marks in multidirections, both surfaces
Beveled on interior 7.0–8.0 Lip 3.0–4.0	n/a	D: 25	n/a	Cooking	3 rims (2 conjoin) from bowl very similar to Vessel 15 from Sub 4
Rounded 4–6	n/a	D: 13 at rim D: 12 at mouth	8.0	Cooking	Silty gray clay, smoothed exterior but parallel scratch marks random directions; interior scraping and scratch marks at neck/shoulder, then possibly paddle and anvil.
Rounded 6.0	n/a	D: 9	6.0	Serving	Small carbon stain on exterior post-breakage; smoothed with nonplastics pops
Rounded Flat with faint line inscribed in lip parallel to surfaces 6.5	n/a	D: 17	6.0	Serving	Oxidized; faint wiping marks both surfaces and grass vugs
Rounded 6.5	n/a	D: 17	9.0	Cooking	Traditional olla shape; faint carbon exterior surface; roughly smoothed
Beveled 4.0	n/a	D: 25	10.0	Cooking	Faint exterior carbon to lip; wiping marks and grass vugs both surfaces; interior oxidized
Flat 5.5	n/a	D: 35	9.0	Cooking	Faint carbon on exterior; interior oxidized; both surfaces roughly smoothed with vugs
Rounded 3.5–4.5	Flattened	D: 6.5–7.0 (slightly elliptical) at rim D: 8.6–8.8 max dia at 5.0–5.5 below rim N: 1.6 at 1.8 below rim	5.0 (est.)	Ceremonial	MSGB silty gray brown, hand-modeled olla; both surfaces uneven and bumpy; occasional nonplastics and grass vugs; occasional fingernail incisions on exterior remnant from manufacture; Height 8–8.5 cm;
Beveled on interior 9.0	n/a	D: 20?	8.0	Cooking	Faint carbon both surfaces; deep grass and nonplastics vugs both surfaces
Rounded 4.0	n/a	D: 20	6.0	Serving	Silty gray brown, no carbon on surfaces, but carbon core
Flat 4.5	n/a	D: 20	7.0	Cooking	Carbon on both sides; horizontal wiping marks on exterior
Rounded 5.5–6.5	n/a	D: 9	6.0	Serving	Exterior surface rough and bumpy with faint horizontal wiping marks; interior flat, smooth, with tiny grass vugs; oxidized appearance
Rounded 3.5–4.0	n/a	D: 8	9.0	Serving	Silty gray uneven surfaces with carbon core.

TABLE 9.4. (cont'd.) Descriptive Data for Reconstructed Vessel Form

Project Location	Exc. Unit	Depth (cmbd)[a]	Catalog Number[b]	Ceramic Type[c]	Form and Size Class	Rim Form
	13321	III	43418	MSGB	Bowl, medium	Direct, Slightly tapered
	13322	III	43184	MSGB	Jar, wide mouth	Direct; Body wall tapered
	13322	III	43093	MSGB	Jar? Medium, wide mouth	Recurved?
(Strat VIII)	13320	VIII	43117	MSGB Wheel	Bowl, medium	Direct
	13320	VIII	43015	MSGB Wheel	Bowl, medium	Direct, Slightly tapered
	13321	VIII	43345	MSGB Wheel	Bowl, medium	Direct
	13321	VIII	43247	MSGB Wheel	Bowl, medium	Direct, Slightly tapered
	13321	VIII	43243.01 (~43243.02, small)	MSGB	Jar?, wide mouth	Recurved
	13321	VIII	43251.01 (~43132 Strat I)	MSGB Wheel	Jar/ Bowl?, medium wide mouth	Direct, Tapered
	13322	VIII	43124	MSGB	Jar?, wide mouth	Slightly everted
	13322	VIII	43134/43294	MSGB	Bowl, medium, Possibly low bowl	Everted
	13322	VIII	43251.02	MSGB Hand modeled	Cup/Bowl, small	Direct, Outflaring, Undulating
	13322	VIII	43251.03	MSGB	Bowl, medium, Possibly low bowl	Direct, Outflaring
	13322	VIII	43150	MSGB	Jar, large, very wide mouth	Direct, Slightly tapered
	13322	VIII	43149	MSGB	Jar/Bowl? Medium wide mouth	Direct, Slightly everted
	13322	VIII	43126	MSGB	Bowl? medium	Direct, Undulating
	13322	VIII	43043	MSGB	Jar/Bowl? wide mouth	Direct, Undulating
	13322	VIII	43251.04	MSGB	Bowl, medium	Direct,Slightly everted, Undulating

TABLE 9.4. (cont'd.) Descriptive Data for Reconstructed Vessel Form

Lip Form, Thickness (mm)	Base Form, Thickness (mm)	Dimensions (cm)[d]	Wall Thickness (mm)	Function	Comments
Flat with incised line in middle of lip, parallel to sides 4.5	n/a	D: 15	7.5	Cooking	Carbon both surfaces; horizontal wiping marks on exterior and interior
Flat with incised line in middle of lip, parallel to sides 4.5	n/a	D: 20	7.0	Cooking	Carbon and patches of soot on exterior only; interior smoothed, with visible nonplastics
Flat 6.0–6.5	n/a	D: 25	?	Cooking	Carbon on exterior surface; interior surface smoothed
Flat 6.5	n/a	D: 20	7.5	Cooking?	Carbon on exterior; smoothed interior
Flat with thin protruding ridge (2 mm tall) 5.0	n/a	D: 20	7.5	Serving	Silty brown uneven exterior; interior smoothed but undulating; carbon core
Flat 6.0–6.5	n/a	D: 20	8.0	Cooking?/ Serving?	Carbon on exterior; deep, multidirectional horizontal wiping marks on exterior with several nonplastic vugs; silty brown interior with wiping marks and grass vugs
Flat 3.5	n/a	D: 20	6.5	Serving?	Uneven exterior with a few faint wiping marks; interior silty brown color and wiping indentations, a few grass vugs
Beveled on interior 9.0	n/a	D: 20	4.0	Cooking	Carbon and soot on exterior with deep wiping marks; faint carbon on rim interior
Flat 6.5–7.0	n/a	D: 25	9.0	Cooking	Soot on exterior obscures surface; silty brown interior with wiping marks
Beveled on interior 6.5 Flat lip 4.5	n/a	D: 20	7.5	Cooking	Carbon on exterior; silty brown interior with faint wiping marks
Beveled on interior 8.5 with rounded lip 4.0	n/a	D: 15	4.0	Cooking?	Exterior surface of sherd from VIII carbon and several deep wiping marks; conjoining sherd from no designation, has smoother carbon exterior; faint carbon on interior
Flat, slightly undulating 5.5–6.5	n/a	D: 8	4.5	Cooking?	Soot on both surfaces (either from cooking or being near flame); hand-modeled; uneven surfaces and undulating rim
Flat 7.5	n/a	D: 18	7.5	Heating?	Silty brown exterior, uneven surface; carbon on interior; hand-modeled
Flat with an interior bevel—almost an interior lid lip 7.5–11.0	n/a	D: 30	11.0	?	Unusual shape yet clay and finishing are similar to all other vessels in Feature 13254 (wiping marks and vugs on exterior, uneven faint wiping marks on interior; carbon core
Beveled on interior 9.0–11.0 With rounded lip 4.5	n/a	D: 20	9.0	Cooking?	Carbon on exterior and faint wiping marks; interior silty brown
Flat with line incised in lip parallel to sides 5.0	n/a	D: 12 est.	7.5	Serving?	Silty brown on both surfaces, with roughly smoothed exterior and faint wiping marks on interior
Flat with line incised in lip parallel to sides 4.5	n/a	D: 25	7.5	Serving?	Faint carbon and wiping marks on exterior; silty brown interior
Rounded 5.5	n/a	D: 15 est.	5.5	Serving	Oxidized brown uneven exterior; interior roughly smoothed with vugs and wiping marks

TABLE 9.4. (cont'd.) Descriptive Data for Reconstructed Vessel Form

Project Location	Exc. Unit	Depth (cmbd)[a]	Catalog Number[b]	Ceramic Type[c]	Form and Size Class	Rim Form
	13322	VIII	43378 & 43377 & 43238/ 43251 & poss 43243.01	MSGB	Bowl, medium	Direct, Slightly everted
Water Conveyance & Storage	MSU 12320	None	42137	MSGB Wheel Oxy	Bowl, medium	Direct
	MSU 12320	None	42139	MSGB wheel	Bowl, very large	Direct, Everted, Undulating
	MSU 12320	None	42445	MSGB Wheel Oxy	Bowl, medium	Direct, Slightly everted
	MSU 12320	None	42448	MSGB	Bowl, large	Direct, Very slightly everted
	MSU 12320	None	42390	MSGB Wheel	Jar/Bowl, wide mouth	Slightly recurved
	MSU 11023	92–130	42416.01 & .02	MSGB Wheel	Jar/Bowl, wide mouth	Slightly everted
	HSU 13464	None	42442	MSGB Wheel?	Bowl, large	Direct
	HSU 13464	None	42443	MSGB Wheel?	Bowl, large	Direct, Everted
	317	90–100	30294	SCB?	Jar/Bowl, medium-wide mouth	Recurved

One miniature jar was found in the monitoring sample from the mourning area and two kiln stilts; data recovery included four candlestick holders and one miniature bowl/plate and one miniature handled jar (Figure 9.8).

Many of the vessel rims were typed as "undulating" because the rim was not evenly finished and tended to dip sinuously. This trait has been observed by the author on vessels manufactured in the southern California desert, and less so on SCBW vessels, though this may be a result of the prevalence of direct rims on the former, and recurved rims on the latter, as undulations are less obvious on recurved rims.

Four, possibly five, of the vessels in the Native American house had a distinctive incised lip form not found elsewhere, suggesting possibly a single potter or a trait that was prevalent at that time. The line is inscribed parallel to the walls in the middle of what otherwise would be a flattened lip. The mourning area also contained two wide mouth jars typed as SCBW?/CDIBW?—these were likely brought to the site for use in the ceremonial area.

Over 90% of the ceramics consisted of vessels made from local clays and typed as MSGB: 34% showed evidence of manufacture or finishing with a wheel (MSGB-Wheel); 5% were hand-modeled; and 53% had the silty gray texture and semismoothed surface typed as MSGB. Clearly the preponderance of ceramics used at the mission was manufactured locally.

Vessel forms and attributes introduced by the Spanish and made with the local clays included plates, trays (possibly comals?), handled vessels, footrings on vessel bases, hand-modeled candlesticks, and kiln stilts.

Nonlocal Sherds

As early as 1776, Mission San Gabriel was a way station on the historic trade routes between the Southwest and the Pacific Coast. Spanish missionaries recounted specific incidences of having encountered native trading parties: Fa. Francisco Garcés met groups of Mohave in March and April 1776 coming and going to Mission San Gabriel in their quest for coastal shell beads (Coues 1900); Fa. Jacobo Sedelmayr met Mojave traders when

Table 9.4. (cont'd.) Descriptive Data for Reconstructed Vessel Form

Lip Form, Thickness (mm)	Base Form, Thickness (mm)	Dimensions (cm)[d]	Wall Thickness (mm)	Function	Comments
Beveled on interior 8.0–9.0	n/a	D: 15	4.0–6.0	Cooking	Multiple sherds likely from same vessel: carbon on exterior and deep wiping marks; interior silty brown with faint wiping marks
Rounded flat 7.0–7.5	n/a	D: 14	9.0	Serving	Wheel forming marks visible both surfaces (exterior uneven); paste very fine with crushed quartzitic grains; occasional mica visible on surfaces
Rounded 4.0	n/a	D: 35	5.5	Serving	Silty brown color with uneven bumpy exterior, faint mica and nonplastics visible both surfaces
Rounded 5.0	n/a	D: 20	9.0	Serving	Oxidized throughout, large nonplastics visible; nonplastic drags and pops on exterior; interior roughly surfaced
Rounded flat 3.0	n/a	D: 4	6.0	?	Exterior eroded; interior roughly smoothed
Beveled on interior 4 lip 8 bevel	n/a	D: 15	8.0	Cooking	Silty gray brown, wheel ridges on exterior; nonplastic pops and horizontal drags on interior. Faint carbon both surfaces
Beveled w rounded flat Lip 4	n/a	D: 30	12.0	Cooking	Silty gray brown; deep wheel ridges on interior; grass vugs on exterior; all surfaces reduced (carbon?)
Rounded flat 5.5	n/a	D: 24	7.5	Cooking?	Carbon on both surfaces, roughly smoothed both surfaces
Beveled 5.0	n/a	D: 25	6.0	Serving	Interior surface reduced (not carbon deposit from use)
Beveled on interior 3 lip 8 bevel	n/a	D: 12	9.0	Unknown	Smoothed surfaces

[a] EUs 105, 108, 118, 121,137, 149, and 206 reference Datum 3; EUs 273 and 282 reference Datum 12
[b] / = conjoined sherds; & = same vessel
[c] MSGB = Mission San Gabriel Brown (local silty clay; hand-modeled pinch pot or coil-scrape/slow wheel);
TB = Tizon Brown (residual clay; paddle-and-anvil); WT (wheel thrown; unknown origin; fine intermediate clay; fine parallel rills);
SCB = Southern California Brownware
[d] D = Diameter at Rim; N = Neck Height; Min = Minimum diameter @ x cm below rim; Max = Maximum diameter @ x cm below rim;
B = Base diameter; H = Height

Figure 9.8. Miniature plate/tray at left and miniature handled jar at right.

FIGURE 9.9. Decorated body sherds from jars manufactured in the Coachella Valley, Hedges Buff at left and Ocotillo Buff at right.

he visited Big Tujunga village north of San Gabriel in the San Fernando Valley and along a northern route to the Chumash region (Sedelmayr 1939).

Nonlocal sherds in the Mission San Gabriel ceramic samples include buffware imported from the Colorado Desert east of the mission and several southwestern Puebloan sherds. Undecorated Colorado Buff and Parker Buff types predominated the LCBW component of the monitoring sample; both types were manufactured along the Colorado River, one toward the southern end of the river, and one to the north near Parker. Two partial wide mouth jars found in the mourning area were typed as "SCBW/CDIBW?" and were likely made in the Coachella Valley, midway between the mission and the Colorado River. The data recovery sample included one decorated jar sherd each of Hedges and Ocotillo buff types; both types were manufactured in the Salton Basin/Coachella Valley (Figure 9.9).

One Puebloan sherd was recovered in each ceramic sample. A small, nondiagnostic, black-on-white sherd was collected in the data recovery sample and a larger, black-on-white sherd from a jar neck was found on the plastered surface near the Garden Wall in the water conveyance and storage area. It was tentatively identified as a Cibola White ware dating to the middle PIII period (AD 1100–1275), or possibly a nineteenth/early twentieth-century Kiapkwa Polychrome, a Zuni-Acoma historic style that mimicked earlier forms and designs (Figure 9.10; Griset 2018). Nonlocal sherds found throughout southern California are usually small single sherds; they were not reworked into other objects such as disks or die and appear to be curated curios.

Decoration in the San Gabriel-made ceramics was limited and consisted of intentionally inscribed lines on vessel lips, and red-washed exteriors or red-washed on both surfaces. Painted designs were restricted to two LCB sherds imported from the Coachella Valley and two Puebloan sherds. Comparatively few SCBW, CDIBW, or LCBW vessels were brought to/used at the mission.

Conclusions about Native American Ceramics at Mission San Gabriel

The conclusions drawn from the combined data recovery and monitoring ceramics are that the historic brownwares produced at Mission San Gabriel were made by a variety of techniques, dominated by wheel finished (possibly some wheel thrown) and hand-modeled vessels, all made from the silty gray local clays. These are historic methods, rather than the traditional coil/paddle-and-anvil prehistoric manufacturing regimen used in SCBW, CDIBW, and LCBW.

The preponderance of MSGB vessel forms is simi-

FIGURE 9.10. Black-on-white Puebloan jar neck sherd (exterior surface), found on plastered surface near the garden wall in the water conveyance and storage area.

lar to the vessels made prehistorically by the ceramic-producing peoples of southern California—bowls and jars in small, medium, large sizes, and occasionally very large—with a few new forms included handled and flat-bottomed vessels. The comal may have also been included as a new cooking form. A small number of hand-modeled forms included three miniature vessels, small bowls or cups, and four candlestick holders. The manufacturing techniques may have been imported, but the brownwares were seemingly made for native consumption, and presumably by native peoples trained at the mission.

A variety of MSGB likely made at the mission has been termed here MSGB-oxidized. These vessels retain the distinctive wheel-thrown ripples on interior and exterior surfaces. The paste is very fine and lacks the organics often seen in the core or vugs on the surfaces of MSGB wheel- or hand-modeled vessels. This conclusion was fostered, in part, by the discovery of the clay layer in the "ceramic workshop"; it is very fine in texture and lacks organic inclusions and appears to be much better prepared than the clay used for the other two varieties of MSGB.

Whether the same people made all three varieties of MSGB, whether they were made contemporaneously but for different uses, or for the same end user, are unknown at present.

Other Traditional Culinary Containers

Fragments of three soapstone vessels were recovered during the SGT data recovery. They demonstrate the continued use of traditional Tongva soapstone vessels as part of the culinary assemblage, and their adaptation to new forms and uses. The three fragments were recovered from three loci around the granary and represent at least two vessel forms—a bowl and a comal—neither is similar to the restricted neck soapstone vessels seen in Figure 9.2. The vessel fragments have direct rims with simple rounded lip.

All three soapstone specimens were submitted for residue analysis (Puseman et al. 2012). Specimen 6785 is a bowl with an estimated 30 cm diameter rim, wall thickness of 18 mm, and a direct tapered lip of 14 mm thickness. The rim fragment had a thick residue that FTIR analysis identified as cooked meat, bones, and fat, and cooked cattail roots. Specimen 11588 is a flat-bottomed tray or comal fragment with an estimated 32 cm diameter at the direct rounded rim, a wall thickness of 20 mm, lip thickness of 15.3 mm, and an estimated interior depth of 6–7 cm. The interior surface had burned residues identified as bay anchovy and trout. Specimen 15458 is an unknown vessel form with a wall thickness of 14.2 mm (like the bowl), with carbon residues on the exterior surface. It was subjected to starch and phytolith analyses;

no starches were found, but phytoliths of corn and other grasses were identified.

The results indicate that stone vessels served a much greater diversity of uses than is typically reported in the literature, that they were adapted to new crops, and that the same would no doubt be true of ceramic vessels, if they were also subjected to residue analyses.

Comparison with Other Historic Period Brownwares

Unfortunately, most of the ceramics analyzed in the combined Mission San Gabriel ceramic sample are from units representing trash deposits without stratigraphic context. Depositional context is not necessarily a good indication of which vessels, manufactured with which techniques, occurred at the beginning or end of ceramic production at the Mission, nor how those different vessel forms may have co-occurred in daily use. At best, it can be concluded that they were deposited in the same trash deposits and were likely used contemporaneously.

There is no difference in the type of vessel made by each method. Traditional vessel shapes were retained in the MSGB assemblage, and new shapes (plates/soup bowls, comals) were added as well, and made by hand and by wheel.

Sixty-three percent of the culinary vessels are bowls, generally with direct rims with rounded or rounded flat lips. Some of the larger bowls may well be cooking pots, as evidenced by the range of carbon present on body sherds in each unit. Although small bowls are occasionally found in prehistoric vessel assemblages, the more prevalent forms are cooking pots and storage jars. Jars constitute only 21% of the Mission San Gabriel sample; 16% were trays—a form not common in prehistoric samples.

Kealhofer (1991:371) observed that "The one form common to all the mission sites with brown wares is the flat-bottomed bowl, even though its production varies from hand-modeled to wheel-made. Possibly it served for meal rations." This was not the case at Mission San Gabriel—the only confirmed flat bottomed vessels at Mission San Gabriel were wheel-thrown, few in number, and typed as plates or soup bowls, especially when accompanied by foot rings. However, nearly half of the bowls cluster at a 11–14 cm diameter (and there are distinctively wheel-thrown examples, as well as hand-modeled MSGB versions). These may be the individual ration bowls mentioned by Ginn (2009) for northern missions.

Kealhofer (1991) at the Los Angeles Plaza site, May (1976) at Mission San Buenaventura, and Frierman (1982) at the Ontiveros adobe (about 19.3 km [12 mi] south of Mission San Gabriel) identify another vessel form—a brazier—used to burn fuel to warm a room or to cook small meals indoors. Kealhofer's identification is based on the presence of carbon deposits on vessel interiors; May's braziers have flat bottoms, diameters of 16–40 cm, and are 6.5–9.0 cm high; Frierman's braziers from a post-1813 adobe were described as large bowls 22–30 cm in diameter with rounded bottoms but no indication as to how these differed from large 30 cm diameter bowls identified as cooking pots. Braziers are a Spanish introduction; many prehistoric vessel assemblages have sherds with carbon residues on the interior surfaces—likely burnt residues from cooking or ceremonial activities (such as burning feathers in a pot)—so the presence of charcoal on a sherd interior is not sufficient to identify a sherd as a brazier. Perhaps the thick bases with "shiny black" interiors interpreted here as comals may derive from braziers. Discrimination of comals and braziers at San Gabriel remains a question to be solved.

San Gabriel is like other missions in its diversity of pottery-making techniques, and resembles the summation provided by Hoover and Costello (1985:32) for Mission San Antonio de Padua midway along the central coast of California: "There are vessels which have molded bases and coiled sides, molded bases and wheel-made sides, wheel-made bodies with applied ring bases, hand-modeled vessels, and coiled vessels with and without paddle and anvil finishing."

There, too, local natives did not traditionally make pottery, while later groups brought to Mission San Antonio from the lower San Joaquin Valley may have made coil-and-scrape pottery prehistorically. It is equally likely that the late ceramic tradition in the southern San Joaquin may be remnant from learning pottery at the missions (see Bailey, this volume); unfortunately, the ceramic samples in native village sites are small in number and size, and not well dated.

San Gabriel ceramics add the use of basket trays to form pots and our proposition that coiled vessels may have been scraped as well as shaped using a paddle and anvil. Similar diversity in clays, manufacturing techniques, and vessel forms were documented by Ginn (2009) and Peelo (2011) for missions in northern California, where pottery-making also had to be taught to the neophytes (Table 9.5)

Marshall reported on an excavation at the Ortega-Vigare adobe, roughly 183 m (200 yd) south of the Mission San Gabriel garden:

> The same clays (and perhaps the same ovens) seem to have been used in making pottery as were used in the manufacture of roofing tiles. In

TABLE 9.5. Pottery Traditions Documented for Northern California Missions

Site	Time Frame & Location of Recovery	Paste	Forming	Finishing[a]	Firing	Vessel Forms
Mission San Antonio de Padua	>1809 Dormitories	One local clay with granite/rhyolite sands 2 types of processing	Wheel 40%[a]		Open fire	Bowls Jars Platos
			Hand-modeled 26% Hand-modeled on slow wheel 27% Pinched 5% Slab built 4%		Open fire	Bowls Jars
			Coiled < 1%		Open fire	Unidentifiable
Mission San Carlos		One local clay with crushed granite 2 types of processing	Hand-modeled Coil/Paddle/Anvil Pinched	Smoothed Burnished	Open fire	Bowls Comales
Mission San Juan Bautista		One local clay with crushed granite	Coil/Paddle/Anvil Hand-modeled	Smoothed Burnished	Open fire	Bowls
Mission Santa Clara		Two local clays with sands	Wheel	Stamped Glazed	Open fire and/or kiln	Bowls—deep Jars—large
		2 types of processing	Hand-modeled Coiled/Paddle/Anvil	Scraped Smoothed Burnished	Open fire	Bowls—shallow Jars—small
Presidio San Francisco		One local clay with sands	Hand-modeled Pinched		Open fire	Bowls
		2 types of processing	Wheel	Slipped Glazed	Open fire	Bowls
				Unfinished	Open fire	Jars

Note: Data compiled from Ginn 2009 and from Peelo 2011

[a] Ginn considered paddle and anvil to be a finishing technique so does not list it as a forming technique

> fact, given the black underfired core common to both the Tizon Ware and the roofing and drain tile of the Mission, some thinner sherds of the tile could well be mistaken for the pottery. (Marshall 1982:26)

Although the ceramics from the current investigations of Mission San Gabriel do not commonly have a carbon streak, the ceramics from the data recovery and construction monitoring suggest that the mission residents employed an expedient approach to ceramic manufacturing, using locally available clays and multiple techniques taught to neophytes by Mexican settlers and soldiers, or by neophytes with natal traditions modified by access to new techniques.

ACKNOWLEDGMENTS

We thank the Alameda Corridor—East Construction Authority for supporting the work that generated the San Gabriel Mission data discussed here.

10 Mineralogy of Locally Produced Ceramics from Mission Santa Clara de Asís

Sarah Peelo, Christina Spellman, Chester Liwosz, Linda Hylkema, and Stella D'Oro

Any other clay was thought not to 'like her,'
and pottery made from it would be likely to crack.
Some clays were so highly regarded that
women would travel many miles to obtain them.
— Gena Van Camp

The Indian *Ranchería* at Mission Santa Clara (CA-SCL-30H; est. 1777) was occupied by a diverse community of indigenous peoples between 1784 and the 1840s (Figure 10.1). Fragments of Mission Santa Clara Plain Wares have recently been recovered from the ruins of traditional style homes, adobe barracks, interior and exterior hearths, and refuse pits associated with the Indian *Ranchería* (Figures 10.2–10.4; Allen 2010b; Allen et al. 2010; Garlinghouse et al. 2018; Panich 2014, 2015a, 2015b, 2016; Panich et al. 2014; Panich et al. 2018; Peelo et al. 2018; Skowronek, Blackman, Bishop, and Koons 2005; Skowronek, Blackman, Bishop, and Rosas 2005). Research suggests that these wares were made locally at the Mission (Skowronek et al. 2009, 2014). Their production occupied the time of indigenous men and women, and their use as cooking, tableware, and storage vessels suggests that they were part of the daily lives of nearly every individual living in the *Ranchería.*

In this paper, we examine the mineralogy of a sample of these broken vessels. Using a suite of techniques, including refiring, binocular sorting, petrographic analysis, and electron microprobe analysis, we present data concerning the raw materials used to produce ceramics made at Mission Santa Clara. Our mineralogical analysis identified a distinctive, local suite of mineral and rock inclusions, suggesting indigenous potters at Mission Santa Clara de Asís used a single clay source, characterized by red to yellowish-red color when fired, and nonplastics consisting of lithic sands of granite, quartzite, rhyolite, basalt, and the mineral inclusions of those rocks. Electron microprobe analysis illustrates that the silt fraction of the ceramics was composed of many silt-sized alkali feldspars and quartz grains. By using a generally homogeneous clay source to make their ceramics, indigenous potters at Mission Santa Clara formed a shared community of practice, out of which a shared identity may have formed.

Practice theory (Bourdieu 1977; Giddens 1979) informs our approach, and centers material culture as a medium by which people construct identities through daily practices, as they produce and reproduce their cultural dispositions in light of new historic events. Archaeological patterns represent the collective production of material culture by a *community of practice* who share a certain way of being in the world (Bourdieu 1977; Ortner 1999; Wegner 1999). By being active participants in social communities, people may construct identities in relation to them.

We argue that as indigenous potters participated in a shared tradition of ceramic production, they may have been creating social identities, informed by their precolonial disposition, in relation to those practices. The acquisition of raw materials is a production step observed by fellow workers, and therefore is a social action; potters of a community may select a particular clay because it is what other potters in their community choose

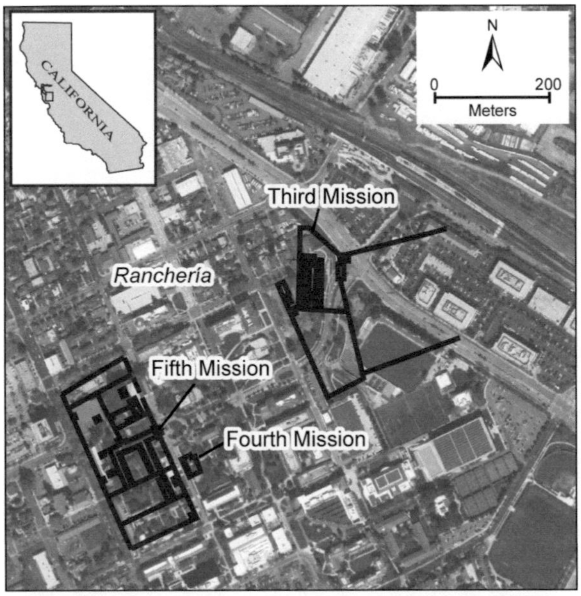

FIGURE 10.1. Mission Santa Clara de Asís (CA-SCL-30H).

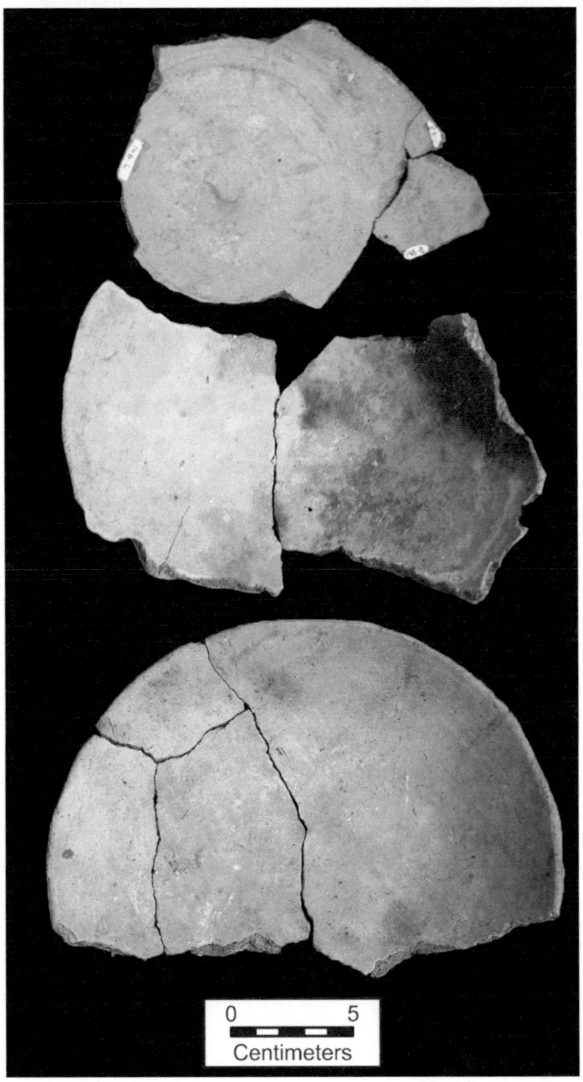

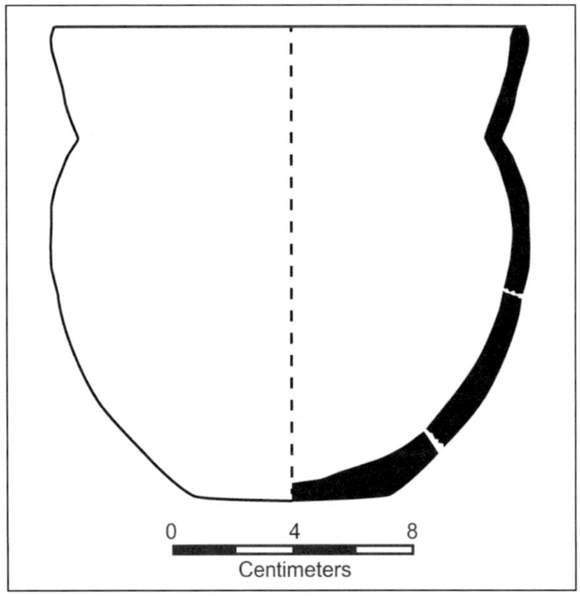

FIGURE 10.3. Feature 157 Santa Clara Plain Ware bowl, Paste Group 4. Drawing by Stella D'Oro.

FIGURE 10.4. Example of Santa Clara Plain Ware sherds recovered from Feature 503 within the Indian *Rancheria* at Mission Santa Clara de Asís, Paste Groups 2, 3, and 5.

FIGURE 10.2. Example of Santa Clara Plain Ware sherds recovered from Feature 57 and 57B within the Indian *Rancheria* at Mission Santa Clara de Asís, Paste Groups 4 and 6.

(Gosselain 2000). Importantly, this step is not visible to the consumer's eye on the finished product. While decoration as style has been argued as a marker of social identity (Wobst 1977), we believe visible production steps are not meaningful symbols of identity, but rather reflect superficial, situational, and temporary facets of identity that respond more readily to changing social, economic, or symbolic pressures (Gosselain 2000). Research suggests that production steps that do not leave visible traces on the finished product, at least to the naked eye, are more directly tied to social and cultural identities (Gosselain 2000; Hegmon et al. 2000; Pfaffenberger 1988). These local or regional identities are often negotiated through participation in steps that are observed by fellow workers (i.e., clay selection), but leave no visible traces on the finished product. As it is our goal to understand how social and cultural identities were reproduced through participation in ceramic communities of practice, we focus here on these "invisible" steps of the production sequence, those steps that Gosselain argues are more closely tied to identity-making. From a practice theory perspective, a shared social identity was created within the Indian *Ranchería* at Mission Santa Clara as potters made the same choice with regard to clay and temper selection.

The Indian *Ranchería* Community at Mission Santa Clara

In 1777, the first mission in Santa Clara was established, but relocated due to flooding and earthquakes. Ultimately, five separate mission churches would be built in Santa Clara, at three distinct locations. The Murguía Mission Complex (Third Mission), the Fourth Mission Church, the Fifth Mission Complex, and associated industrial resources such as an *acequía*, and the Indian *Ranchería*, are largely located within the boundaries of the present-day Santa Clara University (SCU) campus; all have been recommended eligible for inclusion in the National Register of Historic Places (CA-SCL-30H). The SCU University Operations Division, the SCU Cultural Resources Management Program and Albion Environmental, Inc. have teamed to execute an active archaeological program seeking to preserve or recover important data prior to construction activities. Through the execution of this program, Santa Clara University has mitigated impacts to archaeological resources related to the Indian *Ranchería*.

Movement of indigenous peoples to the Spanish missions was one of the many ways the colonial Spanish and Mexican governments and their supporters disrupted local native communities. Through this practice, Franciscan priests strategically disassociated Native communities from their homelands and cultural landscapes (Lightfoot 2005:65; Margolin 1989:33). Hylkema (1995:28) addresses the intent of the missionaries in bringing Native Americans into Mission Santa Clara:

> Spain's goal to colonize California depended entirely on the ability of the missionary priests to reorganize the Native populations into an agrarian work force. At the time of the Spanish explorations the indigenous people within the Ohlonean cultural sphere were organized into over fifty political units, or tribelets, with variations of language, custom and appearance... The large populations and their complexity of cultures were generally of little interest to the Spaniards who were intent upon breaking down traditional Indian ways to facilitate their reorganization (reducíón). Europeans of the 18th century cultivated a perception of moral superiority over non-Christian people, which of course served to justify the management of other cultures to attain their goals.

The historical record tells us this practice created mission populations composed of peoples from variable ethnolinguistic groups and very distant polities. At its peak, more than 1,400 Native Americans lived at Mission Santa Clara, and historic documents indicate a steady influx of Ohlone, northern Valley Yokuts, and Miwok populations from diverse villages within those ethnolinguistic territories. The Indian *Ranchería* at Mission Santa Clara is best viewed as a growing and changing amalgam of indigenous peoples drawn at first from the San Francisco Bay region, and later as far away as the San Joaquin Valley and the foothills of the Sierra Nevada. This highly variable population represented dozens of formerly autonomous tribelets of no more than a few hundred people, some closely related culturally and linguistically, and others from vastly different traditions. Not only did people at Mission Santa Clara speak different languages, they spoke variable dialects of the same language, had assorted cultural traditions, came from homeland groups near to and far from the mission, were of different ages, genders, social standings, and ultimately may have been baptized for different reasons.

The community, or perhaps communities within the Indian *Ranchería* at Mission Santa Clara, was forced to adjust to both the Spanish Colonial regime and to day-to-day relationships with indigenous people with whom they had previously little or no contact, or perhaps even formerly contentious relationships prior to the advent of the mission. After baptism, indigenous peoples found

TABLE 10.1. Technological Styles of Potting Traditions that Possibly Influenced Plainware Production

Technological style of:	Clay	Temper	Production Technique	Vessel Form	Finishing	Firing
Spanish Potters	Blended Clays	Quartz, Feldspar, Muscovite, Biotite, Calcite, Grog	Wheel Thrown	Bowls, Soup Plates, Plates, Jars, Ollas	Lead or Tin Glaze with Underpaint	Kiln—Oxidizing Atmosphere
Mestizo Potters	Blended Clays	Quartz, Feldspar, Muscovite, Biotite, Calcite, Grog	Wheel Thrown, Hand-modeling Techniques, Molds	Bowls, Soup Plates, Plates, Jars, Porringers	Lead or Tin Glaze, Smoothing, Scraping	Kiln—Oxidizing Atmosphere
Mexican Indian Potters	Local Clays	Large angular sand grains, Vegetable materials	Rim Coil, Hand-modeling Techniques, Molds, Coiled	Round bottomed bowls	Paddle and Anvil, Rubbed, Polished, Smoothing	Open Fire Pit Fire
Yokuts Potters	Local Clays	None	Molded Base, Coiled	Large, flat bottomed bowls	None, Scraping, Smoothing, Burnishing	Open Fire, Pit Fire
Southern California and Baja California Indigenous Potters	Local Clays	Natural inclusions in residual clay; granitic sands/grog for sedimentary clay	Molded Base, Coiled	Round bottomed bowls and jars	Paddle and Anvil	Open Fire, Pit Fire
California Basket Makers	N/A	N/A	N/A	Restricted rim, round bottomed bowls and jars	N/A	N/A

Sources: (Barnes 1980; Barnes and May 1972; Bates 1982, 1993; Bates and Lee 1990; Bettinger 1986; Bordaz 1964; Bowen 1976; Brott 1963; Cline 1979; Curtis 1962; Davis 1928, 1967; Daywalt 1949; Di Peso et al. 1953; Drover 1975; Eerkens 2001; Eerkens et al. 1998; Elasser 1960, 1978; Gayton 1929; Gerald 1951; Goggin 1970; Griset 1986; Hendry 1992; Jackson 1990; Joesink-Mandeville et al. 1986; Johnson 1990; Jornet et al. 1985; Kaplan 1994; Koerper and Flint 1994; Kroeber and Harner 1954; Lister and Lister 1982; Love and Resnik 1983; Mack 1990; May 1978, 1980; Muller and Hopkins 1974; Ortiz and Ludwig 1995; Polanich 1979, 1994; Van Camp 1979; Wallace 1990; Yamane 1997).

themselves forging new communities with others who spoke different Indian languages, claimed various tribal territories, and affiliated themselves with dissimilar lineage lines, all the while, interacting with a colonial presence that sought to transform them into "productive citizens" of the colony (Senkewicz 2002:23).

Alta California Plain Wares

In the communities of Spanish California, varied indigenous populations were required to engage with one another in a number of daily practices often foreign to them, including harvesting and processing grain, carpentry, and ceramic production. "Missionware" is the term commonly used to refer to low-fired earthenwares produced by indigenous and colonial peoples of California from AD 1769 to 1834 (Deetz 1991 [1963]; Farnsworth 1987; Hoover 1989). Here, we refer to these ceramics produced under these unique colonial conditions as Alta California Plain Wares, rather than "Missionwares," because communities throughout California missions, presidios, and pueblos produced this pottery (Peelo 2014). We suggest that refined terminology should be used to identify these wares by the site in which they were produced, meaning, for example, Mission Santa Clara Plain Wares (see Skowronek et al. 2014:178–217). However, by using a single term as a catch-all for the pottery made within a single mission, or even more broadly throughout Spanish Alta California, we do not mean to imply that plainwares are a homogeneous artifact type. Doing so would simplify the dynamic, complex social processes underlying the synergism of the plural communities that created these ceramic vessels (Lightfoot et al. 1998).

Numerous technological styles may have influenced ceramic production in the California Missions (Table 10.1). All actors participating in California colonial life understood cultural rules concerning how vessels, be they pots or baskets, were to be stylistically constructed at each step of the production sequence. Precolonial native peoples living on the California coast possessed nonceramic traditions for producing woven vessels (Bates 1982, 1993; Bates and Lee 1990; Elsasser 1960, 1978; Kroeber 1973; Moser 1986; Ortiz and Ludwig 1995; Polanich 1979, 1994; Rogers 1929; Shanks and Shanks 2006; Yamane 1997). In addition, Yokuts and indigenous peoples of Baja and southern California removed to the coastal missions may have brought their own precolonial ceramic traditions with them (Bean and Shipek 1978; Bean and Smith 1978; Bettinger 1986; Blackburn 1962; Drover 1975; Eerkins 2001; Eerkens et al. 1998; Gayton 1929; Jackson 1990; Johnson 1990; Koerper and Flint 1994; Kroeber and Harner 1955; Love and Resnick 1983; Mack 1990; May 1978; Rogers 1936; Sparkman 1908; Van Camp 1979).

In the 1790s, the president of the California missions, Father Lasuén, arranged for artisans and craftsmen from Mexico to travel to the different missions of California and teach the neophytes, or Christianized Indians, their skills (Engelhardt 1924:121; Guest 1973:302, 306, 336; Johnson 1985:54; Langelier and Rosen 1992:87; Schuetz-Miller 1994:91; Skowronek et al. 2006; Voss 2008:222; Webb 1952:126). "Master Potter and Tile Maker," Mariano Tapia, from Puebla, Mexico, taught ceramic production in the Monterey area between 1795 and 1796 (Schuetz-Miller 1994:99).[1] Native Californians from other mission communities were sent to Monterey to learn from Mariano Tapia (Guest 1973:302, 306, 336). In addition to assigned artisans, many soldiers of Alta California had training in ceramic production and their skills were conscripted by Franciscan priests. For example, a soldier and potter at the San Francisco Presidio, José Antonio Romero, was assigned to take the place of the deceased Mariano Tapia in 1797 (Schuetz-Miller 1994:91). In addition, a soldier named Casero, at the missionaries' direction, set up "portable manufacturing elements" for the production of earthenwares at Mission Santa Clara de Asís and Santa Cruz (Langelier and Rosen 1992:87), and the soldier Lorezo may have instructed neophytes in the making of pottery at Mission Santa Clara de Asís, Santa Cruz, and San Francisco (Engelhardt 1924:121).

Many of the colonial artisans, like many of the settlers in this frontier, were mestizo, mulatto, or Mexican Indian, and brought their own unique, culturally constructed understandings of ceramic production (Bordaz 1964; Bowen 1976; Daywalt 1949; DiPeso et al. 1953; Gerald 1951; Hendry 1992; Joesink-Mandeville 1986; Kaplan 1994; Muller and Hopkins 1974).

Methodology

Studies of Alta California Plain Ware technological style elucidate the ways in which ceramics were produced—wheel-throwing, coiling, slab-building, pinching, and molding clay over a basket (Costello 1985, 2007, 2014; Ginn 2009; May 1985; Peelo 2011; Skowronek, Blackman, Bishop, and Koons 2005; Skowronek, Blackman, Bishop, and Rosas 2005; Williams 1983). Using these methods, vessels were shaped into soup plates, ollas, and ceramic vessels resembling baskets (Costello 2014; Ginn 2009). Yet, by subjecting ceramics to fine-grained analytical methods, we can explore fabrication techniques beyond the scale of macroscopic observation.

In this study, we employ a number of techniques for investigating the microscopic qualities of Santa Clara Plain Ware raw materials. We examine ceramic paste using binocular sorting, refiring, petrographic analysis, electron microscopy, and instrumental neutron activation analysis (INAA).

Binocular Sorting

Pottery is constructed of clay minerals, fine crystals of other minerals such as feldspar, mica, and quartz, fragments of rock, and carbonaceous matter (Rice 1987: 31–53; Skowronek et al. 2014:138). A binocular sorting analysis of ceramics from an archaeological site allows for the recognition and standardization of general paste groups. Using low-powered, reflected light microscopy, one can observe visual characteristics of ceramic paste, or fabric, including inclusion size and angularity, and the amount and degree of sorting (either fine or coarse). Understanding the steps of the production sequence of a vessel via an examination of inclusion size, angularity, and degree of sorting enhances our understanding of ceramic production and the choices made by a potter. For example, the presence of large inclusions may indicate a choice of temper added to the clay that is advantageous to the potter, such as improved workability (Rye 1981:31). In addition, the varying attribute combinations observed under a binocular microscope can be used to determine the paste group category associated with a particular technological style or practice.

In our study, we used this technique to sort sherds into categories. Along with describing the color of the inclusions present, we made observations concerning the angularity of the inclusions, the quality of their sorting, and the percent quantity (Rye 1981:52).

In addition to visual examination of paste elements, further seriation of fabric sources can be achieved through elemental analysis of the chemical composition of ceramic pastes.

Refiring

One technique for investigating the source of clay represented in a given sample is the refiring of sherds to specific temperature levels (Rice 1987:343; Shepard 1968: 156). Broad color differences, or similarities, can inform our understanding of a ceramic assemblage and can indicate the amounts of chemical elements and minerals, such as iron, present in the clay used to produce the vessel. Refiring earthenware sherds at temperatures ranging from ~700–1,100°C allows one to burn out all carbonaceous matter while not overfiring and warping the sample (Rye 1981; Shepard 1968). For comparability, pastes must be fired to the same temperature, and fully oxidized (Shepard 1968:154–155). Refired pastes in the 2.5YR range and redder indicate high iron composition in the clay.

For the refire test, small chips were removed from the sherds and refired in an electric ceramic kiln to 1,000°C, ensuring complete oxidation. The visual color of refire samples was checked against the Munsell standard prior to and following refiring.

Petrographic Analysis

Petrography has a long history in archaeological application (Habicht-Mauche 1993; Linne 1934; Nordensklold 2009[1893]; Shepard 1968). This analysis allows one to identify and describe the rocks and minerals present in pottery to determine source and other technological aspects of ceramics. When thin sections of ceramic artifacts are viewed through a polarizing light microscope, the optical properties, such as pleiochroism or extinction angle, of various minerals contained within the clay allows for their identification. Petrographic analysis provides an inventory of the minerals present whereas chemical elements can be identified by complementary analytical techniques such as Instrumental Neutron Activation Analysis (INAA; described below). Petrographic analysis assumes that the mineralogical inclusions observed vary by geological source of the clay and temper.

We identified rocks and minerals both qualitatively and quantitatively. Qualitative observations indicate the types of inclusions present, while quantitative observations utilize the point-count technique to identify how much of a particular mineral or rock is present within a sample, and describes the size and shape of each grain (Rice 1987:379). We adopted a 1 mm counting interval and identified 100 points, excluding voids, per sample (Stoltman 1989). Clay minerals were identified as matrix; mineral grains smaller than 0.0625 mm were classified as silt; vacant spaces were labeled voids; and sand or grit grains (inclusions larger than 0.0625 mm) were cataloged by their angularity, sphericity, size class,[2] and mineral or lithic type. We conducted these qualitative and point-count methods using an Olympus (Model BH-2) polarizing microscope with a mechanical point-counting stage in the Ceramic Materials Research Laboratory in the Department of Anthropology, at the University of California, Santa Cruz.

Electron Microscopy

Electron microprobe analysis complemented the petrographic analysis to characterize the mineralogy of the silt fraction (grains smaller than 0.0625 mm) of the thin sections made for Feature 57 and 57b using this technique. Mineralogical identification of the silt fraction is not available to the ceramic petrographer; such grains are simply too small to confidently identify based on their mineralogical properties. However, electron microprobe analysis, which is a qualitative and quantitative method of nondestructive elemental analysis of micron-sized inclusions at the surface of materials, does have the ability to characterize such small inclusions. The technique works by bombarding a small section of a sample with a focused electron beam and analyzing the wavelengths of emitted X-rays produced by the bombardment (Birks 1971; Freestone 1982). The relative intensities of the X-rays produced at each wavelength specify the relative amount of each chemical element in the sample. Mineral types can thus be interpreted from the elemental compositions calculated, for instance, alkali feldspar inclusions are very high in potassium (K).

We conducted qualitative electron microprobe analysis using a CAMECA SX100 electron microprobe in the Department of Geology at the University of California, Davis. We collected X-ray map images of a 750 × 750 pixel region, at a pixel size of 3μ, of each ceramic thin section. Before analysis, thin sections were coated with a 250Å layer of carbon. X-ray maps were analyzed using 15kV filament voltage and 200nA beam current at a dwell time of 5 milliseconds. The microprobe was programed to characterize amounts of specific elements in mineral inclusions—Ca, Na, Si, K, and Al^3—thus helping to identify quartz (high in Si), alkali feldspar (high in K), and plagioclase feldspar grains (high in Na). These minerals were selected for this study because they were present in abundance in all samples. X-ray maps were analyzed using ImageJ software, which allowed quantification and analysis of the shape and size of quartz, plagioclase, and alkali feldspar minerals in the silt fraction.

Instrumental Neutron Activation Analysis (INAA)

One significant, collaborative study of architectural and plainware ceramics in Alta California (n = 1,540 sherds) used INAA to identify trace and major elements to examine the chemical characteristics of specific ceramic pastes (Skowronek et al. 2009, 2014:181). Their study included samples from four Presidial Districts: San Diego, Santa Barbara, Monterey, and San Francisco (Skowronek et al. 2014:186–212). INAA results identified distinct compositional profiles within each district and, with just one exception, within specific sites, suggesting that ceramics were "made from local resources proximate to each mission" (Skowronek et al. 2014:186).

In addition, some sites contained multiple profiles, suggesting that more than one clay source was used within specific missions. For example, Missions San Luis

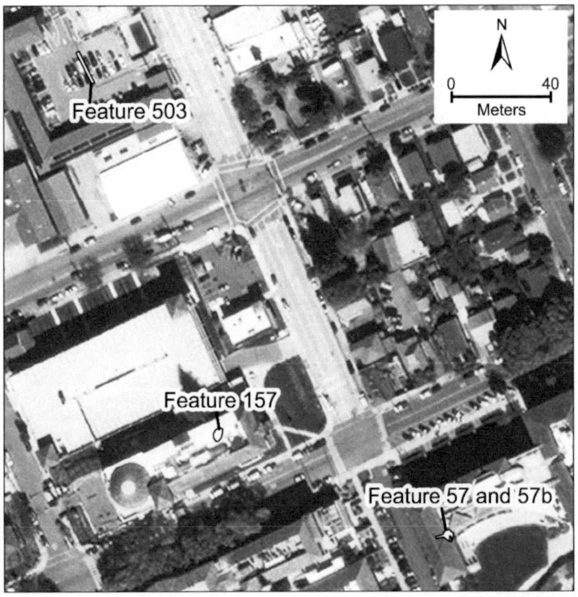

FIGURE 10.5. Locations of Features 57, 57B, 157, and 503 within the Indian *Ranchería* at Mission Santa Clara de Asís.

FIGURE 10.6. Features 57 and 57B, discovered in 2004.

Obispo and Santa Clara, as well as the San Francisco Presidio and Mission, each exhibited two distinct chemical groups, suggesting internal variation (Skowronek et al. 2014:203–206). This study strongly indicates that Alta California Plain Wares were variable chemically and mineralogically.

CERAMIC SAMPLE

For this study, we analyzed a total of 219 ceramic sherds recovered from four archaeological features found within the Indian *Ranchería* at Mission Santa Clara de Asís (Figure 10.5; Table 10.2). All of these ceramics were subject to refire and binocular sorting analyses; a subsample was selected for petrographic and electron microprobe analysis.

Feature 57

Feature 57 is a Native American housepit, dating to post AD 1800 (Mean Ceramic Date (MCD) AD 1790), and is likely associated with Yokuts-speaking native inhabitants at Mission Santa Clara de Asís (Allen 2010a, 2010b; Allen et al. 2010:234, 515). The feature was circular in plan view, 3 m (9.8 ft) in diameter, and had a shallow basin in profile, with sloping walls, a flat floor, and an entryway extending westward (Figure 10.6). A slightly raised berm extended around the eastern half of the pit. This may have continued around the west, but may have been truncated by the backhoe during excavation.

Burned vegetal material covered the floor of the housepit. This material contained varying amounts of *Arctostaphylos*, *Asteraceae*, *Quercus*, and *Salicaceae* (Cummings 2008). Beneath this layer, a hard-packed clay lined the floor and the entryway. It is probable that the entryway was not covered, but the depression and hard-packed floor were due to regular entrance and egress. Two hearths were excavated; one with intact ash fill was located in the center of the housepit, and a small secondary hearth was identified near the exit of the entryway. A posthole was situated just south of the centrally placed hearth. A second posthole, on the opposite side of the primary hearth, was truncated and expanded by the construction of Feature 57B, a large mission-era

TABLE 10.2. Ceramic Sample Counts

	Refire Analysis	Binocular Sorting	Qualitative Petrography	Quantitative Petrography	Electron Microscopy
Feature 57	37	37	5	5	5
Feature 57B	17	17	5	5	5
Feature 157	118	118	8	0	0
Feature 503	47	47	0	0	0
Total	219	219	18	10	10

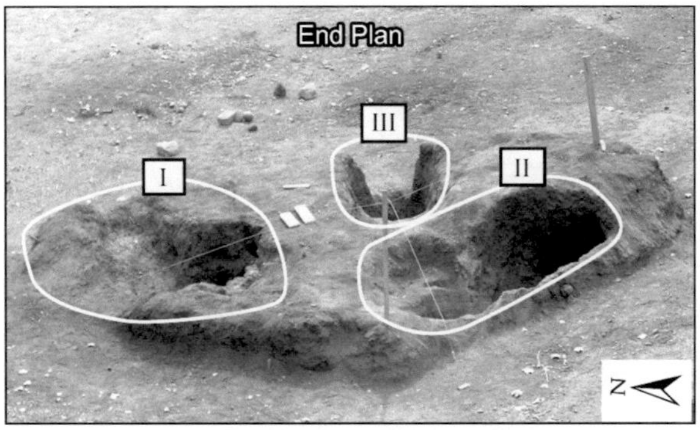

FIGURE 10.7. Feature 157, discovered in 2015. I, II, and III refer to the three pits discussed in the text.

pit that cut into the housepit subsequent to its burning and abandonment.

A total of 37 Mission Santa Clara Plain Ware sherds were recovered from Feature 57, all of which were subjected to refire analysis and binocular sorting. A sample of five sherds were selected for qualitative and quantitative petrographic analysis, and electron microscopy. All five sherds represented Paste Group 4, the dominant paste group, as our goal here was to understand variability within this dominant group.

Feature 57B

Feature 57, discussed above, was burned in place and abandoned. After abandonment, the area was reused for the excavation of two deep pits (Features 57B and 57C), likely primarily used for storage and secondarily used for refuse (Allen et al. 2010:269, 517).

Plainware sherds were found in Feature 57B (MCD 1789). The feature was oval in plan view and measured 0.9 m × 1.7 m (3 ft by 5.5 ft; see Figure 10.6). In profile, Feature 57B extended 1.2 m (4 ft) below the surface, had a flat floor, and was cone-shaped. It was filled with at least four distinct Mission Period strata, and contained a total of 17 sherds. All 17 sherds were analyzed through refire analysis and binocular sorting, and a sample of five, all from Paste Group 4, were selected for qualitative and quantitative petrographic analysis and electron microscopy.

Feature 157

Feature 157, located northwest of Features 57 and 57B, dates to post AD 1810 (MCD AD 1817). The feature measured 5 m × 3 m (16.4 ft × 9.8 ft) and was a communal refuse feature characterized by a large midden layer atop three distinct refuse pits (Pits I–III in Figure 10.7; Peelo et al. 2022). Within this feature we identified 36 unique cultural fill layers or surfaces. One pit (Pit I), had a shallow, sloping shelf on the east end, a deeper pit on the west end, and two distinct clay or adobe "bowls" within the deeper end of the pit. Contents of this pit included three cultural fill layers on the shallower east end, and four fill layers in the deeper west end. In addition to the aforementioned "bowls" and fill events, the deep end of Pit I also included evidence of adobe melt.

Pit II had a shallow step on the northern end and a deep pit on the southern end. Distinct to this pit was a very dense layer of mussel shell. Noteworthy deposits within this pit feature included an ash lens on the shallow north end, obsidian, and beads of bone, shell, and glass.

The third pit (Pit III), had a shallow shelf on the eastern side descending into a deeper pit on the west end. Unique to this pit was a distinct deposit of lime and evidence of burning in the form of oxidized soils along the interior of the pit.

Covering all three of these individual pits was a disturbed midden layer with a mix of American and Mission Period artifacts. A sample of material excavated from this feature recovered 118 Mission Santa Clara Plain Ware sherds.[4] All 118 sherds were analyzed through refire analysis and binocular sorting, and a sample of eight, representative of distinct paste groups, were selected for qualitative petrographic analysis.

Feature 503

Feature 503 is the northernmost mission-era archaeological features excavated to date in the *Ranchería* (Figure 10.8; Garlinghouse et al. 2018). The feature was a communal refuse pit created after AD 1790 (MCD 1794), and consisted of a very dense accumulation of Mission Period refuse, primarily cattle and bird bone, but also numerous artifacts, including local and nonlocal ceramics, *tejas* (roof tiles), *ladrillos* (floor tiles), glass, adobe, metal, shell and glass beads, and Native American stone and bone tools and ornaments. The bulk of the deposit was distributed for a length of approximately 3.4 m (11 ft) N-S within a utility trench; E-W dimensions of the feature extended beyond the trench walls and are thus unknown at this time. Material was found to a maximum depth of 1.8 m (6 ft), though the deposit was not uniform over its entire length. Soils were relatively homogenous, loosely compacted and loamy, dark brown in color, and contained very few gravels. These characteristics suggest soil matrix and bone were deposited in a "single episode" of deposition, possibly as the result of a deliberate instance of dumping.

A sample of material excavated from this feature recovered 47 Mission Santa Clara Plain Ware sherds[5]. All 47 sherds were analyzed through refire analysis and binocular sorting, but, due to budgetary constraints, were

a. Feature 503, Context 5012 in progress
b. Feature 503, Context 5012 in progress
c. Feature 503, Context 5012 in progress
d. North wall profile

NOTE: Trench is 61 centimeters wide.

FIGURE 10.8. Feature 503, discovered in 2012.

not analyzed through petrography or electron microprobe (Table 10.3).

As discussed above, these paste groups were distinguished based on the color of the inclusions visible at low magnification, and variabilities in shape and size. The vast majority of sherds (64.98%) fall within Paste Groups 3 and 4 (Table 10.4). These sherds all exhibited subangular white, black, and red inclusions. Compared to Paste Group 4, inclusions within Group 3 were better sorted which suggests variable paste processing techniques. Paste Groups 5 and 6 were also prominently represented (18.89%), and represented in each feature. These paste groups are defined by the presence of subangular white inclusions, and are either fairly well sorted (Paste Group 5) or poorly sorted (Paste Group 6). Paste Groups 1 and 2 were identified in the samples from Features 157 and 503, and are defined by the presence of subangular yellow inclusions. Paste Groups 7, 8, and 9, sparingly present in the assemblage (8.75%), are characterized by either angular inclusions (Paste Group 7), no discernable inclusions (Paste Group 8), or very small white inclusions (Paste Group 9), and are only represented within Feature 157.

Refire Color

As discussed above and presented in Table 10.1, all 219 sherds, from all four features were subjected to refire analysis. All sherds refired to similar, but slightly variable, Munsell colors (2.5YR 4/8 red; 2.5YR 5/8 red; 2.5YR 6/8 light red; 5YR 5/8 yellowish-red; 5YR 6/8 reddish-yellow).

Petrographic Analysis

We conducted petrographic analysis of 18 ceramic sherds, from Features 57 (n = 5), 57B (n = 5), and 157 (n = 8). Features 57 and 57B were studied both qualitatively and quantitatively, while Feature 157 was only studied qualitatively. Feature 503 was not studied through petrographic analysis; however, as discussed above, Feature 503 paste groups were also identified among the assemblages recovered from Feature 57, 57B, and 157.

Samples were selected for thin-sectioning such that they allowed us to understand variability within dominant paste groups, as well as observe possible differences between paste groups. From Features 57 and 57B, we selected ten samples from Paste Group 4 to study petrographically (five from each feature), as this paste group composed over 80% of the assemblage from each feature. From Feature 157, we selected eight samples, representative of all paste groups, except for Paste Group 8. Unfortunately, the slide made of Paste Group 8 was rendered unusable.

Based on our study, we suggest that Mission Santa Clara plainwares are all geologically similar to each other and are characteristic of the Cenozoic sediments of this region (Figure 10.9; Table 10.5; Brown et al. 1972:54). Data from Features 57 and 57B are quantified in Table 10.5, indicating that this dominant paste group (Paste Group 4) is largely characterized by inclusions of granite, rhyolite, quartzite, basalt, intermediate volcanics, and/or the mineral constituents of these rocks, including quartz, basaltic hornblende, hornblende, augite, and plagioclase feldspar. Clay pellets were also observed.

While not quantified, the thin sections observed from Feature 157 led to similar interpretations. Paste Groups 1 and 2 contained clay pellets, rhyolite, quartzite, intermediate volcanics, and the minerals derived from those rocks: quartz, plagioclase feldspar, augite, and biotite. Paste Groups 3, 4, and 7 dominantly contained granite and quartzite rocks, but rhyolite, basalt, and intermediate volcanics were also present. Minerals present within these paste groups included quartz and plagioclase feldspar. Paste Groups 5, 6, and 9 were also similar petrographically, exhibiting quartzite, weathered/decomposed granite and intermediate volcanics, and the mineral inclusions of rocks, such as quartz, plagioclase feldspar, biotite, and augite.

The presence of poorly sorted, subangular and subrounded inclusions suggest that a lithic sand may have been added to the clay by indigenous potters at Mission Santa Clara. While the paste groups identified through binocular sorting suggest variability among pastes used to produce plainwares, the petrographic analysis indicates that paste differences are primarily due to differences in size sorting and inclusion angularity, created through clay and temper *processing*, rather than source.

Electron Microscopy

Electron microprobe analysis illustrates the compositional qualities of the silt fractions of pottery at this mission (Figure 10.10): 99.2% of the points counted for the Mission Santa Clara Plain Ware samples were silt (smaller than 0.0625 mm). Also, electron microprobe analysis suggests that the silt fraction was consistently characterized by small percentages of alkali feldspars and higher percentages of quartz grains.

Discussion and Conclusions

Mission Santa Clara Plain Ware shares a common local clay source. The sampled sherds all refired to red/reddish-yellow/yellowish-red colors, sort into various paste groups differentiated primarily by inclusion sorting and size related to processing rather than source, are tempered with lithic sands composed of granite, rhyolite, basalt, and quartzite, and have high silt fractions characterized by small percentages of alkali feldspars and higher percentages of quartz grains. These data suggest that the potting community at Mission Santa Clara all used local clay, and tempered that clay with lithic sand characteristic of local geology.

While not evident in the data from this study, previous INAA examination of plainwares from Mission Santa Clara suggests that, at the clay chemical level, there are two statistically distinct groups (Skowronek et al. 2014:203). The discrepancy between the two studies may be due to the sample, but also illustrates the difference in scale of the different techniques, with one analyzing clay mineralogy and the other clay chemistry (Skowronek

Table 10.3. Binocular Paste Group Descriptions

	Paste Group 1	Paste Group 2	Paste Group 3	Paste Group 4
Inclusion Type 1	White (Quartz, Quartzite, or Granite?)	White (Quartz, Quartzite, or Granite?)	White (Quartz, Quartzite, or Granite?)	White (Quartz, Quartzite, or Granite?)
Powers' Scale of Roundness	Subangular, High Sphericity	Subangular, High Sphericity	Subangular, High Sphericity	Subangular, High Sphericity
Size (mm)	0.5–3.0	0.5–3.0	0.5–1.0	0.5–2.0
Percentage Inclusion	20%	20%	10%	10%
Sorting	Very Poor	Very Poor	Fair	Poor
Inclusion Type 2	Yellow (Rhyolite? Feldspar?)	Yellow (Rhyolite? Feldspar?)	Grey/Black (Basalt?)	Black (Basalt?)
Powers' Scale of Roundness	Subangular, Low Sphericity	Subangular to Subrounded, Low Sphericity	Subrounded, High Sphericity	Subangular, High Sphericity
Size (mm)	0.5–1.0	0.5–3.0	0.5–1.0	0.5–1.0
Percentage Inclusion	5%	5%	5%	5%
Sorting	Fair	Very Poor	Fair	Fair
Inclusion Type 3	Red (Clay Pellet?)	—	Red (Sherd?)	Red (Sherd?)
Powers' Scale of Roundness	Subangular, High Sphericity	—	Subangular, High Sphericity	Subangular, High Sphericity
Size (mm)	0.5–3.0	—	0.5–1.0	0.5–3.0
Percentage Inclusion	5%	—	5%	5%
Sorting	Very Poor	—	Fair	Very Poor

Table 10.4. Binocular Paste Group Distribution by Feature, (%)

	Feature 57 (n = 37)	Feature 57b (n = 17)	Feature 157 (n = 118)	Feature 503 (n = 47)	Total
Paste Group 1	0	0	5.085	4.255	3.687
Paste Group 2	0	0	1.695	12.766	3.687
Paste Group 3	11.429	0	45.763	51.064	37.788
Paste Group 4	85.714	82.353	10.169	6.383	27.189
Paste Group 5	0	0	11.864	25.532	11.982
Paste Group 6	2.857	17.647	9.322	0	6.912
Paste Group 7	0	0	11.017	0	5.991
Paste Group 8	0	0	2.542	0	1.382
Paste Group 9	0	0	2.542	0	1.382
Total	100	100	100	100	100

et al. 2014:149). The INAA results may suggest that, while geologically similar, a potting community at the mission may have used a slightly different recipe than one that followed common practice (Skowronek et al. 2014:149).

This examination of steps of the production sequence not visible on the finished vessel but would have been observed by fellow potters suggests that, as evidenced by the paste minerology, there was a single community of practice. While it is true that the choices of raw material selection are constrained by availability of suitable ceramic characteristics, it is important to also consider the social aspects of technology. We argue that in addition to economically influenced interpretations, elucidations about the construction of social identity can also be made from this demonstrated pattern of shared behavior. It is in the processes, in the actions, that culture is made. By participating in communities of practice, for whatever reason, people may have consciously or unconsciously constructed an identity in relation to that

TABLE 10.3. (cont'd.) Binocular Paste Group Descriptions

Paste Group 5	Paste Group 6	Paste Group 7	Paste Group 8	Paste Group 9
White (Quartz, Quartzite, or Granite?)	White (Quartz, Quartzite, or Granite?)	White (Quartz, Quartzite, or Granite?)	No Discernible Inclusions	White (Quartz, Quartzite, or Granite?)
Subangular, High Sphericity	Subangular, High Sphericity	Angular	—	Subangular, High Sphericity
0.5–2.0	0.5–2.0	0.5–1.0	—	0.5–1.0
10%	10%	5%	—	20%
Fair	Poor	Poor	—	Fair–Good
—	—	Red (Sherd?)	Wood-like texture	—
—	—	Angular, Low Sphericity	—	—
—	—	0.5–1.0	—	—
—	—	5%	—	—
—	—	Very Poor	—	—
—	—	Black (Basalt?)	Black Voids	—
—	—	Angular, High Sphericity	—	—
—	—	0.5–2.0	0.5–1.0	—
—	—	5%	5%	—
—	—	Fair	—	—

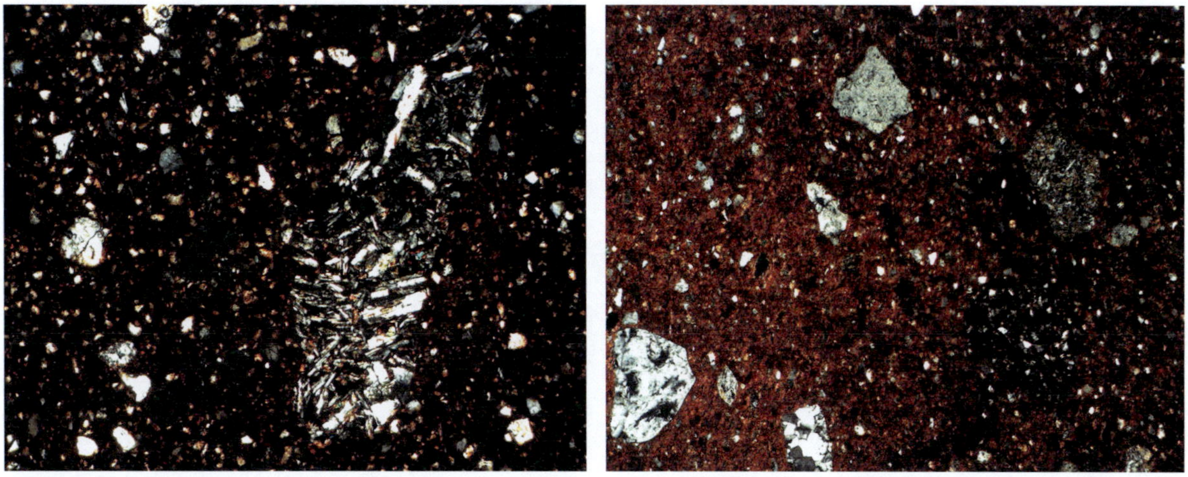

FIGURE 10.9. Photomicrographs of Mission Santa Clara Paste Group; 4 petrographic thin sections at x4 Cross Polar showing sand and lithic inclusions; from Feature 57.

community. As diverse indigenous peoples collected clay and temper from a local source, they were participating in the Santa Clara potting community, and likely formed a shared sense of belonging and identity—a Clareño identity—with its other members. This identity was thus mission-centered.

Through the research presented here, it is our goal to contribute to studies on colonial encounters, and to specifically develop ways to move our discipline out of projects that emphasize a colonized/colonizer dichotomy, and instead focus on studies that stress the complex day-to-day realities of colonial moments. To do this, we focus on the level of the community and apply a practice theory approach, which addresses how identities are dynamically and situationally produced through regular participation in different communities of practice. We

TABLE 10.5. Petrographic Point Count Analysis (n, out of 100 points counted)

	Point Type				Mineral Inclusions					Rock Inclusions					
	Matrix	Nonplastics	Voids	Quartz	Basaltic Hornblende	Hornblende	Augite	Biotite	Plagioclase Feldspar	Granite	Rhyolite	Quartzite	Basalt	Lithic	Clay Pellets
FEATURE 57															
Cat #164-17 (PG 4)	58	39	3	33	—	*a	*	*	4	1	*	—	—	—	—
Cat #133-57 (PG 4)	62	35	3	30	—	—	*	*	*	1	*	—	*	2	*
Cat #148-8 and 148-6 (PG 4)	56	34	10	31	1	1	—	—	*	—	1	—	—	—	—
Cat #133-150 and 133-32 (PG 4)	54	44	2	30	1	—	*	*	*	—	—	—	*	*	—
Cat #165-9 (PG 4)	53	42	5	26	—	—	—	—	2	—	*	—	*	—	—
FEATURE 57b															
Cat #135-46 (PG 4)	35	60	5	49	—	2	*	*	*	1	2	1	1	—	—
Cat #135-48 (PG 4)	42	55	3	38	—	*	3	*	2	*	*	—	1	1	*
Cat #149-59 (PG 4)	60	38	2	27	1	*	*	*	*	—	—	—	*	—	—
Cat #148-58 (PG 4)	31	63	6	36	4	*	*	*	1	*	*	*	*	*	—
Cat #141-5 (PG 4)	40	59	1	35	—	2	—	*	*	—	*	*	*	—	—

a * = present but not quantitatively sampled

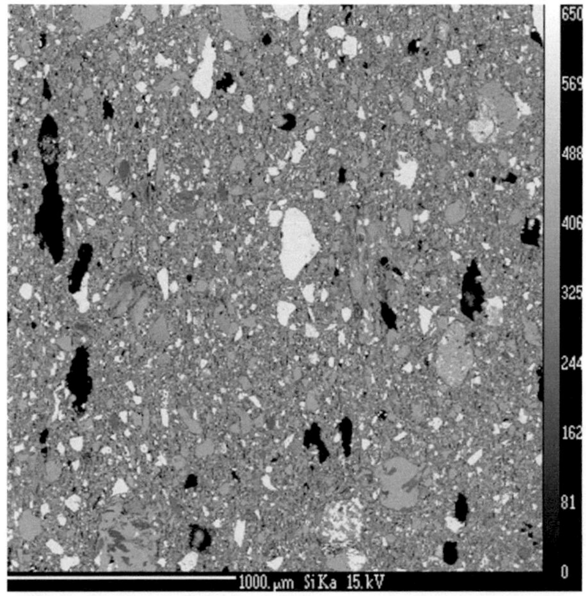

FIGURE 10.10. X-ray map of Mission Santa Clara Plain Ware, Feature 57B, Paste Group 4; Si-white grains represent quartz.

argue that the social process of community and identity-making can be accessed archaeologically through techno-material studies, which emphasize that the actions involved in producing objects are the "things" to be studied. We have applied these theoretical and methodological perspectives to a study of indigenous identity formation among the Spanish mission communities of California, where pluralistic groups of indigenous peoples forged an identity tied to the mission community in which they lived.

Prior to Spanish colonization, local indigenous peoples of the central coast missions had never produced ceramic culinary vessels. Nevertheless, these new, colonial practices provide insight into indigenous traditions being reproduced in this new space. As potters encountered novel cultural practices, it may have produced conditions under which they were able to modify their social identities in response. However, it is important to emphasize the ways colonial identities among these nascent potting communities were also reproductions of preexisting social and cultural rules. The mission-centered colonial identity that may have emerged among these potting communities at their respective missions was likely influenced by a local indigenous disposition structuring identity around place.

Prior to Spanish intrusion, California indigenous peoples formed cultural identities around village coalitions, which had strong connections to place (Kroeber 1932). These communities are described as autonomous, self-governing, and independent land-owning units, whose boundaries are marked by features about the landscape (Kroeber 1962:33, 37, 49). Through their "extraordinary localism" pattern of mobility, whereby people did not travel more than 16–24 km (10–15 mi) from their community of villages, California Indians marked cultural differences between people of different territories (Heizer and Elsasser 1980:203), and formed a sense of cohesion and belonging among members of their own multivillage group (Kroeber 1962:29). United by a territorial bond, people who lived in a particular village coalition formed a collective identity, or a shared sense of belonging to a particular homeland and people (Jones 1997:1).

Local community identities, at least among potting communities, were not left behind or forgotten, nor were they statically maintained, as diverse peoples left their tribal homelands to live together in this pluralistic mission community. Native cultural identities may have been reproduced as identities structured around place, in this case, around Mission Santa Clara, as its multiethnic population tried to make sense of their new surroundings.

Notes

1. Schuetz-Miller used many archival sources in her research of builders in Hispanic California, including baptismal registers, census reports, and account books. She found information about Mariano Tapia in the *Ramo de Californias* (49:241–242, 246, 367; 6A:unnumbered) located in the *Archivo General de la Nación, Mexico City* (1994:99, 207–208).
2. Silt = <0.0625 mm; Fine = 0.0625–0.25 mm; Medium = 0.25–0.5 mm; Coarse = 0.5–1.0 mm; Very Coarse = 1.0–2.0 mm; Gravel = >2.0 mm
3. Standards used for each element include: Na-Albite; Ba-Barite; Ca-Wollastonite; Si-Orthoclase; Al-Orthoclase.
4. For Feature 157, we 1/16" wet-screened 100% of the soils recovered. We then microsorted an assay sample (1–2 bags) from all contexts. In addition, because of the materials recovered through the assay process, we selected a more statistically representative sample from Phase II, Context 5718 (15%) and Contexts 5723 and 5739 (30%). The remaining unsorted materials are located in the Archaeology Lab at Santa Clara University and are available for future research.
5. For Feature 503, we 1/16" wet-screened 100% of the soils recovered. We then microsorted 50% from Context 5012. The remaining unsorted materials are located in the Archaeology Lab at Santa Clara University and are available for future research.

11 Directions Forward for Ceramic Studies in the Far Southwest

Don Laylander

Aboriginal ceramics are a conspicuous and important element in the archaeological landscapes of late prehistoric southern California, western Arizona, southern Nevada, northern Baja California, and western Sonora. However, it can be argued that a full exploitation of the research value of the region's relatively simple and usually undecorated ceramics has been poorly served by some of the conventions in analysis, interpretation, and reporting that have been applied to them. Alternative approaches advocated here include a classification system based on attributes rather than types, an interpretive system based on formulating and testing falsifiable hypotheses, and a reporting system based on creative use of the Web.

Against Typology

The most widely used approach to ceramic analysis in the Far Southwest has been to assign archaeologically recovered specimens to named wares, such as Lower Colorado Buff Ware, Tizon Brown Ware, and Owens Valley Brown Ware, and types, such as Tumco Buff, Salton Buff, San Diego Brown, and Hakum Brown.

Several systematic definitions and descriptions of groups of ceramic types have been offered (e.g., Colton 1939; Euler and Dobyns 1958; May 1978; Pippin 1986; Schaefer 1994b; Schroeder 1958; Van Camp 1979; Waters 1982a).[1] More limited studies have proposed new individual types or wares in order to address particular cases of localized ceramic variability (e.g., Bowen 1976; Evans 1969; Hildebrand et al. 2002; Meighan 1959; Schaefer 1993, 1995; Schaefer et al. 1987; Seymour 1997). It may be worthwhile to consider whether this approach has been productive, whether it is likely to be so in the future, and whether an alternative analytical strategy might be more fruitful.

In some fields of study, typology as an analytical approach offers important advantages. Types are commonly defined as polythetic categories that economically subsume a complex array of individual attributes into more manageable units. Type assignments are usually made on the basis of intuitively recognized similarities rather than through the application of a rigorous key. This permits the analyst to classify specimens much more rapidly than would be possible through a more rigorous step-by-step analysis. Types are often defined by similarity to a type specimen or a type population, making it possible subsequently to discover additional attributes of the type that were not recognized when it was originally defined. More dubiously, types also offer to the analyst the psychological satisfaction of giving an esoteric name to a phenomenon and thus enjoying the mystique of expertise.

An example of a field in which the typological approach is highly successful is in distinguishing biological species, at least when the species are considered only synchronically. Such species are true natural categories, discovered rather than arbitrarily defined. Because of the way biological evolution operates, intermediate cases tend to be comparatively rare. For most purposes, intuitively recognizing the similarities and differences between, for instance, foxes, wolves, coyotes, and dogs is more efficient than using rigorously keyed attribute definitions. As science has advanced, new attributes have been discovered, such as DNA signatures, which are strongly correlated with the previously observed attributes.

Another example of fruitful typology is the use of stratigraphic type sections for constructing a relative chronology in sedimentary geology. Paleontological assemblages usually intergrade through time rather than abruptly altering, and this tends to make period boundaries somewhat arbitrary. However, because evolution is generally cumulative and irreversible, these intergrading assemblages can still be seriated into true natural sequences. Small evolutionary changes in the assemblages have permitted geologists to make finer distinctions in relative chronology than the ones that have been possible or practicable in absolute chronology through the use of radiometric methods. New attributes of the type sections, for instance in their microfossils, can also subsequently be discovered and used to confirm type assignments.

On the other hand, some phenomena are not well suited to the typological approach. If a type distinction is relatively simple, perhaps based on a single attribute, then the use of a type name has no real advantage over the use of a more straightforward description. If sets of attributes do not fall into strong natural clusters, type definitions are likely to be both arbitrary and interpretively sterile or misleading. If type definitions are polythetic, if they are intuitive rather than rigorous, and if the defining attributes intergrade and are not strongly correlated with each other, type assignments are likely to be poorly replicable. As in the parable of the Blind Men and the Elephant, different analysts will often perceive or focus upon different aspects of the "type," and as a result they will arrive at highly inconsistent identifications.

It is arguable that prehistoric ceramic typology in the Far Southwest suffers from all of the above-mentioned problems. As a consequence, it is also arguable that its identifications, for the most part, have been and are likely to continue to be relatively arbitrary, poorly replicable, and interpretively sterile.

Some ceramic ware and type distinctions seem to have been based, either explicitly or implicitly, on a single attribute. For instance, the distinction between Tizon Brown Ware and Colorado Buff Ware has often been made on the basis of color alone.[2] If so, adding the label "Tizon" or "Lower Colorado" to the ware designation does not enhance its usefulness. The defining contrast between Owens Valley Brown Ware and Tizon Brown Ware may also be reducible to a single attribute: shaping either by coil-and-scrape or by paddle-and-anvil. Gena R. Van Camp (1979:66) argued that a ware ought in principle to be defined by a single attribute. Tiburón Plain and Historic Seri types are distinguished by the presence or absence of organic temper (Bowen 1976). In practice, if not in theory, the types defined by Ronald V. May (1978) and Michael R. Waters (1982b), as they are applied to undecorated body sherds, appear to be reducible to contrasts in paste inclusions.

A minor terminological anomaly is also produced by defining separate "types" on the basis of an attribute that may be present on some but not all parts of a single ceramic vessel. Thus, for instance, different potsherds from the same vessel might variously be typed as Colorado Buff and Colorado Red-on-buff in Waters's (1982b) system, or as Kumeyaay Buff Plain, Kumeyaay Buff Incised, Kumeyaay Buff Painted, Kumeyaay Buff Stuccoed, Kumeyaay Buff Appliquéd, and so on in Van Camp's (1979) system.

It may certainly be conceded that multiple ceramic attributes are frequently linked with each other, or at least that they are statistically correlated. It is also evident that the distributions of at least some attributes in space and time are nonrandom and therefore interpretively interesting. However, this does not mean that any strong, natural polythetic categories based on these patterned distributions have been discovered, or even that they are necessarily likely to exist. In the majority of cases, particular ceramic attributes are relatively simple phenomena that could easily vary independently of one another and that could have been picked up, discarded, or reinvented in a variety of different geographical, chronological, or cultural contexts.

Under the cover of a ware/type name, attribute patterns may be assumed rather than actually observed. An analyst who reports a specimen as being "Tizon Brown Ware" may be saying that this specimen was specifically seen to have been made from a residual rather than a sedimentary clay, or that it had been shaped by the paddle-and-anvil method rather than by coil-and-scrape. Usually the subsequent reader has no way to know if these observations were actually made, or if they were even possible, on the specimen in question. In most cases, a reported Tizon Brown Ware specimen is more likely a brown sherd that was recovered in a region where the other attributes of "Tizon" could merely be assumed to be present.

Ware/type names also tend to carry with them potentially unreliable or misleading interpretive baggage. Buff-colored pottery is observed to be more common than brown-colored pottery at most Colorado Desert sites, while the reverse is true at most sites in montane and coastal southern California. Sand-tempered sherds have perhaps been found more frequently than elsewhere at sites associated with the maximum shoreline of prehistoric Lake Cahuilla in the Salton Basin. These are empirically testable statistical patterns. But if a buff-colored, sand-tempered sherd *is* Salton Buff, then almost by definition, the sherd must have been manufactured in the Salton Basin between circa AD 950 and 1500 (Waters 1982a:564). In southern California, a brownware sherd containing a substantial amount of hornblende *is* Salton Brown; therefore, it must have been produced from sedimentary clay in the western Colorado Desert (Gallucci 2001; Hildebrand et al. 2002). Maybe these inferences are correct...but then again, maybe they are not.

How replicable are ceramic-type assignments in this region? That is to say, how consistently would different archaeologists independently assign a specimen to the same type? Clearly, analysts using even vaguely defined typologies can be expected to produce results that are more consistent than merely random assignments. It is also clear that perfect replication should not be expected; some discrepancies based on individual judgment are likely to occur even with very simple, well-defined attribute classifications. The issue is whether the replicability of a given classification is high enough to make the system a scientifically useful tool. There apparently have been few tests of replicability in this field. Karen Gallucci (2001:35–38) reported one test of the distinction between Tizon Brown Ware and Salton Brown Ware. Despite the fact that three experienced analysts conducted the experiment in laboratory settings, there was remarkably poor agreement in their specimen assignments. An unconfirmed, impressionistic judgment is that a blind test of replicability for distinctions between, for instance, Black Mesa Buff and Tumco Buff, or even between Tumco Buff and Colorado Buff, would show similarly poor consistency. If replicability is low, it is reasonable to ask whether the use of such categories is generating meaningful scientific data, or whether it is merely serving to fit observations into a priori interpretative categories based on the contexts in which the sherds were found.

In summary, an argument can be made that the analysis and interpretation of ceramic variability in the Far Southwest have not been well served by the ware/type system. Some of the ostensibly typological classifications are, in practice, single-attribute classifications, and they would be more expediently treated as simple attribute descriptions rather than as types. Other typological classifications are based on intuitive, polythetic types that do not appear to represent strong, natural clusters of attributes and that are probably poorly replicable. If these criticisms are valid, the typological approach to these ceramics is not yielding, and probably is not likely to yield, very effective analytical results.

An Attribute-Based Alternative

An alternative to the use of typologies in analyzing ceramic variability is to employ a descriptive, attribute-based approach. Previous discussions of the region's ceramics have considered a substantial range of attributes. For pottery vessels, these have included:

- color—core, exterior surface, interior surface; after controlled refiring; defined impressionistically or by Munsell codes
- surface modifications—polishing or burnishing, wiping, slipping, painting, incising, punctation, impression, appliqué, stucco, blackening, scumming
- post-firing modifications and use effects—hole drilling, edge grinding, surface residues, scratches
- method of shaping—paddle-and-anvil, coil-and-scrape, modeling, molding over basket or vessel base
- identity of paste inclusions—minerals, rocks, shells, sherds, organic materials; identified by naked eye, hand lens, reflected-light microscope, petrographic microscope, X-ray diffraction
- paste composition—frequency, size, shape, sorting of clay and nonplastics
- paste texture—fine, grainy, vugs
- chemical composition—identified through X-ray fluorescence (e.g., Griset 1996), inductively coupled plasma spectroscopy (e.g., Plymale-Schneeberger 1993), neutron activation analysis (e.g., Hildebrand et al. 2002; Koerper et al. 1978)
- firing conditions—oxidizing or reducing, carbon streak, firing temperature
- hardness—Mohs scale; hard or crumbly fracture
- vessel shape—bowl, jar, scoop, miniature
- vessel dimensions—rim diameter, wall thickness, curvature on body sherds (Hagstrum and Hildebrand 1990), neck size
- rim orientation—direct or recurved; horizontal, vertical or intermediate; inward or outward; undulating
- lip shape—rounded, flat, semiflattened; thickened or tapered; reinforced rim band
- base form—rounded, flat, pointed

Additional attributes have been used to characterize nonvessel forms, such as pipes, rattles, figurines, anvils, and disks (e.g., Fenenga et al. 2015; Hedges 1973; McCarthy 2014; True 1966).

Some attribute definitions may have a typological character; that is, they may be polythetic and/or intuitive. Examples might include the way differences in sets of mineral inclusions or in chemical composition are distinguished, or the recognition of differences in patterns of decoration. Nonetheless, these attribute definitions are likely to be closer to primary observations, more rigorous, and therefore more replicable than the vague polythetic type/ware definitions.

Obviously, the use of a ware/type classification is not likely to be routinely replaced by a "complete" description of all potential attributes on a studied specimen. In most cases, the analyst would choose to make a small number of attribute observations on the basis of their probable interpretive significance, as well as their high replicability and low cost. Through time, a professional consensus might emerge concerning which attributes merit being recorded as a part of standardized analyses. Attributes showing strong patterning in their chronological, geographical, or functional contexts would be favored. Attributes would be likely to be less frequently used if their recording is poorly replicable, if it is costly in time or equipment, or if it is destructive to the specimens. Attributes found to be strongly correlated with other attributes might be generally ignored as providing only redundant information.

This attribute-based approach would be more transparent than a typological analysis. It would be more open to critical assessment and refinement. It would permit the correlations among different attributes and between attributes and chronological, geographical, ethnic, and functional contexts to be tested rather than merely being assumed. It would reduce (although it would not eliminate) the problem of replicability.

Don't Just Fit—Test

Ceramic analyses in this region, whether they have been based on types or on attributes, have been used primarily to fit specimens into established categories, to assign sites or components of sites to established time periods, to link them with specific ethnic groups, or to confirm patterns of trade and travel. These uses may be legitimate and productive, but only to the extent to which the categories and correlations in question are solidly based. Some of the problems existing with regional ceramic typologies have already been suggested above.

The most widely used ceramic-period chronology—Malcolm J. Rogers's (1945a) Yuman I, II, and III sequence, renamed Patayan I, II, and III by Waters (1982a)—is problematic. Although initially Rogers could only work with tenuous links to an absolute chronology based on the infrequent associations between Yuman sherds and intrusive sherds from better-dated Southwestern pottery types, he made brilliant use of the episode of Lake Cahuilla supposedly dating between about AD 1000 and 1500 to break the late prehistoric period into three phases. According to this model, Yuman/Patayan ceramics were produced primarily on the lower Colorado River during the Yuman/Patayan I phase (ca. AD 600–1000). They subsequently spread westward into the Salton Basin when Lake Cahuilla was present during the Yuman/Patayan II phase (ca. AD 1000–1500) and were finally extended to montane and coastal southern California and Baja California during the Yuman/Patayan III phase (ca. AD 1500–1800), after the lake's stand had ended. A chronological sequence of buffware types and attributes could be inferred from the geographical distributions of those types and attributes.

Unfortunately for this scenario, radiocarbon dating has subsequently established the earlier occurrence of ceramics in the Salton Basin and at points farther west (e.g., Griset 1996). Radiocarbon dating has also shown that Lake Cahuilla was only intermittently present between AD 1000 and 1500 and that additional lake stands occurred both prior to AD 1000 and after 1500 (Laylander 1997; Love and Dahdul 2003; Schaefer and Laylander 2007; Waters 1983; Wilke 1978). This has seriously undermined the foundation of the Yuman/Patayan sequence and the associated chronological patterns proposed by Rogers and Waters for ceramic types and attributes.

Pottery types and traits have also long been used to identify the presence of specific ethnolinguistic groups in the archaeological record. In the Mojave Desert, for instance, the occurrence of Lower Colorado Buff Ware has been interpreted as evidence for the presence of River Yumans, and more specifically the Mohave, while Tizon Brown Ware has been associated with Takic speakers, and Owens Valley Brown and Paiute Brown have been associated with Numic speakers. Discussing Paiute-Shoshone pottery in the Great Basin, David D. Madsen noted:

> The use of the term Paiute-Shoshone implies that ceramic types found in archaeological settings were in fact produced by ethnographically definable populations, and it should be made clear that in many cases this is an assumption. However, the pottery types are virtually identical with those known to have been produced ethnographically, and it seems much better to assume that such pottery types are indeed Paiute-Shoshone rather than that they originate with some other, as yet undefined, prehistoric population. [Madsen 1986:209]

A third option is also available: not to make either of those two assumptions, except insofar as evidence to support one or the other is discovered. In many cases, the presumed ethnic associations may be correct, but there has usually been little independent evidence either to confirm or refute them. In southern California, south of the Mojave Desert, it seems clear that ceramic variability rather freely cuts across the major linguistic discontinuity that existed between Yuman-speaking Kumeyaay and Uto-Aztecan-speaking Cahuilla and Luiseño. Observed ceramic differences, at least in this latter region, seem to be better correlated with differences in physiographic settings or in the available clay sources than with ethnic identities. Van Camp (1979) attempted to sidestep this problem by projecting the linguistic boundaries of the ethnohistoric period back into prehistory and assigning ceramic specimens to "types" on the basis of their archaeological occurrence within such ethnic territories, defining a new system of types such as Kumeyaay Brown Plain, Northern Diegueño Brown Plain, Luiseño Brown Plain, Cahuilla Brown Plain, and so on. This seems to be an extreme example of fitting evidence into preconceived, unfalsifiable, and sterile interpretive categories (see True 1980). Variability in some ceramic attributes may well be correlated with ethnolinguistic boundaries or identities, but the correlations need to be discovered and verified, rather than merely assumed or defined.

An alternative to fitting ceramic data into such epistemologically dubious typological, chronological, or ethnic categories is to use the data to formulate and test falsifiable hypotheses. Existing syntheses such as the ones by Rogers, May, Van Camp, and Waters can be viewed as sets of hypotheses. However, as they were formulated and as they have subsequently been used, these syntheses have had more the character of definitive pronouncements, to be accepted on faith, based on their proponents' expertise and experience, rather than taking the form of propositions being weighed against explicitly presented evidence.

Falsifiability is a key. A favored hypothesis should be positioned, either explicitly or implicitly, beside plausible contrary, competing hypotheses. Scientific evidence becomes effective not when it conforms to a favored hypothesis, but when it contradicts or renders less tenable one or more alternative hypotheses.

A hypothesis concerning the ceramics of the Far Southwest is likely to take the form of a proposition that a particular attribute occurs exclusively, or with a statistically significant bias, in a particular chronological, geographical, ethnic, or functional context. An alternative hypothesis might be that no significant association exists. Archaeological studies should serve to provide ongoing, empirical tests of these propositions, rather than merely to fit specimens into preexisting interpretive pigeonholes.

Taking Small Steps toward a Sounder Conventional Wisdom

Another subject worthy of reconsideration concerns the ways in which the results of regional studies are being shared among ceramics analysts and with other archaeologists. The main channels for sharing data and ideas have included formal publications (books and journal articles), theses and dissertations, unpublished cultural resource management or academic reports, conference presentations, and informal, person-to-person communication. The availability of the Worldwide Web offers opportunities for important changes in the ways this information is managed and diffused. These potential changes are not unrelated to the shifts proposed above, toward attribute-based analyses and toward hypothesis testing.

The most important advantages that the Web brings to the task of information sharing are its low distribution costs and its potential for relatively effortless and rapid revision. Publications, theses, dissertations, and unpublished reports tend to be limited in their availability, in large part because of the costs involved in reproducing and distributing copies of them. The effectiveness of communication among ceramicists through conferences or in personal meetings is limited by travel costs and scheduling constraints, as well as by the perishable form in which the information is conveyed. Through the use of the Web, information can be reproduced and widely distributed at a minimal cost.

At least as important is the Web's potential for hosting a system of ongoing, incremental revision and updating of information. Comparatively few publications ever appear in second editions, even when they contain clear-cut mistakes or superseded findings. Moreover, a small advance in the identification of patterning within ceramic data, such as the occurrence of an attribute in a context that would have seemed too early, too late, or too geographically remote for its occurrence according to the prevailing Conventional Wisdom, might be identified within an unpublished report or in a conversation between analysts, but it might not be considered important enough to merit separate publication. As a consequence, most analysts and archaeologists inevitably continue to rely upon the Conventional Wisdom enshrined in publications that may be years or even decades out-of-date. The Web offers a potentially effective mechanism for capturing, distributing, and building upon the ongoing incremental advances that fall below the threshold for infrequent formal publications or even conference papers.

There may be many ways in which the Web could be used to advance the study of prehistoric ceramics in the Far Southwest. One possibility concerns improving replicability for visual observations of attributes that lack rigorous verbal descriptions. For instance, the mineral inclusions within sherds are commonly described as "abundant" or "moderate," as "well sorted" or "poorly sorted," as "rounded" or "angular," and as "frequently" protruding through vessel walls; texture is "fine" or "coarse"; rim lips are "rounded" or "flat"; and so on. Digital photographs of these phenomena posted on the Web, including both archetypal examples and borderline cases, could go far toward refining and standardizing the use of such categories by different analysts.

Digital format makes it practicable to analyze and distribute large sets of data involving multiple variables in ways that are either impossible or dauntingly cumbersome for data presented in other formats. The Web makes it practicable to share digital data. With complex sets of data on ceramic attributes and contexts available through the Web, it would be substantially easier for other analysts to test and to confirm or refute the original investigator's conclusions and to look for additional patterns.

A more ambitious structure could use the Web to formulate, test, and refine hypotheses about the chronological, geographical, ethnic, and functional distributions of ceramic attributes. Hypotheses representing an initial Conventional Wisdom concerning these distributions could be extracted from the standard published discussions. For instance, they might include as hypotheses:

- that direct (rather than recurved) rims on buffware jars were produced exclusively prior to AD 1000 (Waters 1982a);
- that reinforced rim bands were produced exclusively after AD 1500 (Waters 1982a);
- that basket molding of ceramic vessels was common prior to AD 1000 but rare afterward (Waters 1982a);
- that pottery tempered with beach sand was produced exclusively in the Salton Basin (Waters 1982b).

This list could go on, and additional hypotheses could be drawn from more recent studies. For example:

- that calcite-tempered buffware was produced primarily or exclusively in the Las Vegas Valley (Seymour 1997);
- that hornblende is common in brownware that was manufactured in the mountains of western southern California but is rare in brownware produced in the Salton Basin (Hildebrand et al. 2002).
- that, for brownware in southeastern San Diego County, symmetrical (rounded or flat) lip forms are significantly more common on vessels made from residual (mountain) clays than on vessels made from sedimentary (desert) clays (Cook 1986); and
- that remains of larger ceramic vessels in this region occur proportionately more frequently in short-term archaeological accumulations than in longer-term accumulations with similar functional and cultural contexts (Burton 2009, following Orton et al. 1993:Figure 16.1).

After the statement of each hypothesis, the nature of the evidence in support of it might be summarized. Then, perhaps in greater detail, the objections to the hypothesis, any contrary evidence, and alternative hypotheses might be presented. An important advantage of this system is that it would not have to be "published" (that is, posted on the Web) at once, fully formed and definitive. Instead, it could be developed and presented incrementally, and through the work of many hands. Proposals for adding new Conventional Wisdom hypotheses and for reversing, deleting, or refining previous ones, as well as for offering new arguments and evidence pro and con, might be collectively refereed by a panel of volunteers managing the Web page and communicating among themselves by email.

Conclusions

Three main arguments have been advanced here concerning studies of aboriginal ceramics in the Far Southwest: that they should be focused on attributes rather than on types or wares; that they should test competing hypotheses rather than merely file data away in interpretive pigeonholes; and that the Web should be used to diffuse collective, incremental advances in evidence and interpretation.

Are the proposed changes likely to happen? That is not clear. There is undeniably a comforting economy and a mystique in labeling a sherd "Salton Buff" that is not matched by using a more transparent, descriptive label, such as "sand-tempered, buff-colored." A hypothesis-testing format has the drawback of exposing only too clearly the insecure, tentative nature of our understanding of the archaeological record and of regional prehistory. Incremental additions and refinements contributed to a collective, Web-based synthesis of information and interpretation would require efforts not likely to be very well rewarded at present, either financially or in professional status or prestige, as compared with work that is done through other media. And yet... despite these obstacles, if the arguments advanced here are correct, attribute-based analysis, hypothesis testing, and Web reporting stand out as promising, and perhaps even indispensable, steps forward for ceramic studies in the region.

Acknowledgments

Thanks to Margie Burton for helpful comments and corrections on a draft of this paper.

Notes

1. The distinction between "wares" and "types" as commonly applied in this region has been merely hierarchical: a ware may potentially subsume several different types. The "series," an intermediate level of classification between the ware and the type, and the "variant," below the type, have also been suggested (e.g., May 1978; Schroeder 1958). The "style" has been suggested as a taxon standing parallel to a type but based specifically on design attributes (Van Camp 1979:67). Some analysts have suggested that a more fundamental distinction ought to be observed between wares and types: that a type should have a specific culture-historical (i.e., chronological and geographical) identity, whereas a ware should be merely a broad descriptive category (cf. Lyneis 1988c). In any event, the ways in which wares, series, types, styles, and variants have been defined and identified have all generally been typological in character.
2. Not all analysts have used color as the key in this distinction. Although Margaret Lyneis (1988c:149) seemed to accept color as the key attribute that distinguished Lower Colorado Buff Ware from Tizon Brown Ware, she noted that "there is probably more overlap than exclusiveness in the color ranges of the two wares." Suzanne Griset (2013) proposed a Southern California Intermediate Ware to address this problem. Some other analysts would argue that color is not a defining (i.e., a necessary or sufficient) attribute in distinguishing between Tizon Brown Ware and Lower Colorado Buff Ware (Jerry Schaefer, personal communication 2007).

References

Abbott, David R.

2000 *Ceramics and Community Organization Among the Hohokam.* University of Arizona Press, Tucson.

2008 The Process, Location, and History of Hohokam Buff Ware Production: Some Experimental and Analytical Results. *Journal of Archaeological Science* 35(2): 388–397.

2009 Extensive and Long-Term Specialization: Hohokam Ceramic Production in the Phoenix Basin, Arizona. *American Antiquity* 74(3):531–557.

Adams, Jenny L., and Mary F. Ownby

2018 The Manufacture and Burial of Hohokam Disk Beads in the Tucson Basin. *American Antiquity* 83(3): 536–551.

Ahlstrom, Richard V. N.

2008 Ceramic Period Chronology of the Central and Eastern Papaguería. In *Fragile Patterns: The Archaeology of the Western Papaguería*, edited by Jeffrey H. Altschul and Adrianne G. Rankin, pp. 471–492. SRI Press, Tucson.

Ahlstrom, Richard V. N., and Heidi Roberts

2002 Interpreting Formative Period Settlement in the Western Papaqueria. In *Culture and Environment in the American Southwest: Essays in Honor of Robert C. Euler*, edited by David A. Philips, Jr. and John A. Ware, pp. 113–146. SWCA Environmental Consultants, Phoenix.

Aitkens, Melvin J.

1985 *Thermoluminescence Dating.* Academic Press, London

1989 Luminescence Dating: A Guide for Non-Specialists. *Archaeometry* 31:147–159.

Allen, Rebecca

1995 An Archaeological Study of Neophyte Cultural Adaptation and Modification at Mission Santa Cruz, California, PhD dissertation, Department of American Civilization, University of Pennsylvania, Philadelphia.

2010a Alta California Missions and the Pre-1849 Transformation of Coastal Lands. *Historical Archaeology* 44(3):69–80.

2010b Rethinking Mission Land Use and the Archaeological Record in California: An Example from Santa Clara. *Historical Archaeology* 44(2):72–96.

Allen, Rebecca, R. Scott Baxter, Linda Hylkema, Clinton Blount, and Stella D'Oro

2010 Uncovering and Interpreting History and Archaeology at Mission Santa Clara: Report on Archaeological Data Recovery at the Leavey School Business, Murguía Parking Lot, and Jesuit Community Residence Project Areas. Report submitted to Santa Clara University by Past Forward, Inc., Santa Clara University Archaeology Research Lab, and Albion Environmental, Inc.

Allison, James R.

1990 Anasazi Subsistence in the St. George Basin, Southwestern Utah. Master's Thesis, Department of Anthropology, Brigham Young University, Provo.

2000 Craft Specialization and Exchange in Small-Scale Societies: A Virgin Anasazi Case Study. PhD dissertation, Department of Anthropology, Arizona State University.

Amsden, Charles Avery

1938 *An Analysis of Hohokam Pottery Design.* Medallion Papers XXII. Southwest Museum Gila Pueblo, Globe, Arizona.

Anderson, Sharlyn

2011 An Evaluation of the Performance Characteristics of Olivine Temper in Pueblo II Virgin River Puebloan Ceramics. Master's thesis, Department of Anthropology, University of Nevada, Las Vegas.

Andrews, Sherri, and Jerry Shaefer

2010 An Archaeological Survey of Target 95, Range 2512, NAF El Centro, East Mesa, Imperial County, California. ASM Affiliates, Inc., Carlsbad.

Apple, Rebecca McCorkle

2005 Pathways to the Past. *Proceedings of the Society for California Archaeology* 18:106–112.

Arkush, Brooke S.

1993 Yokuts Trade Networks and Native Culture Change in Central and Eastern California. *Ethnohistory* 40(4): 619–640.

Arnold, Dean E.

1985 *Ceramic Theory and Cultural Process.* Cambridge University Press, Cambridge.

Arnold, Jeanne E.

1992 Complex Hunter-Gatherer-Fishers of Prehistoric California: Chiefs, Specialists, and Maritime Adaptations of the Channel Islands. *American Antiquity* 57(1):60–84.

2001a The Chumash in World and Regional Perspectives. In *Origins of a Pacific Coast Chiefdom: The Chumash of the Channel Islands*, Edited by Jeanne E. Arnold, pp. 1–19. University of Utah Press, Salt Lake City.

2001b The Channel Islands Project: History, Objectives, and Methods. In *Origins of a Pacific Coast Chiefdom: The*

Chumash of the Channel Islands, edited by Jeanne E. Arnold, pp. 21–52. University of Utah Press, Salt Lake City.

2007 Credit Where Credit is Due: The History of the Chumash Oceangoing Plank Canoe. *American Antiquity* 72(2):196–209.

Arnold, Jeanne E., and Julienne Bernard

2005 Negotiating the Coasts: Status and the Evolution of Boat Technology in California. *World Archaeology* 37:109–131.

Arnold, Jeanne E., and Anthony P. Graesch

2004 The Later Evolution of the Island Chumash. In *Foundations of Chumash Complexity*, edited by Jeanne E. Arnold, pp. 1–16. Perspectives in California Archaeology, Volume 7. Cotsen Institute of Archaeology, University of California, Los Angeles.

Bailey, Catherine Elizabeth

2009 Scoping the Source of Chumash Pottery: A Petrographic Analysis of Brown Ware Sherds from Colonial Period Chumash Sites. Master's Thesis, Department of Anthropology, University of California, Los Angeles.

Baker, C. L., and Mary Maniery

2010 Historic Roads and Trails Historic Context Study, Naval Air Weapons Station China Lake, Kern, Inyo and San Bernardino Counties, California. Prepared by PAR Environmental Services for Naval Facilities Engineering Command, Southwest, San Diego. Report on file at Naval Air Weapons Station, China Lake.

Baldwin, Gordon C.

1950 The Pottery of the Southern Paiute. *American Antiquity* 16(1):50–56.

Banerjee, D., A. S. Murray, L. Bøtter-Jensen, and A. Lang

2001 Equivalent Dose Estimation using a Single Aliquot of Polymineral Fine Grains. *Radiation Measurements* 33(1):73–94.

Barnes, Mark

1980 Mexican Lead Glazed Earthenware. In *Spanish Colonial Frontier Research*, edited by Henry Dobyns. Center for Anthropological Studies, Albuquerque.

Barnes, Mark, and Ronald V. May

1972 Mexican Majolica in Northern New Spain. *Pacific Coast Archaeological Society Quarterly*, Occasional Paper No. 2.

Basgall, Mark E., and Matthew. C. Hall

1992 Fort Irwin Archaeology: Emerging Perspectives on Mojave Desert Prehistory. *Society for California Archaeology Newsletter* 26(5):1–7.

Bates, Craig

1982 *Yosemite Miwok/Paiute Basketry: A Study of Culture Change*. California Indian Library Collections, Berkeley.

1993 *Coiled Basketry of the Sierra Miwok: A Study of Regional Variation*. California Indian Library Collections, Berkeley.

Bates, Craig, and Martha J. Lee

1990 *Tradition and Innovation: A Basket History of the Indians of the Yosemite/Mono Lake Area*. Yosemite Association, Yosemite National Park, California.

Baxter, M. J.

1994 *Exploratory Multivariate Analysis in Archaeology*. Edinburgh University Press, Edinburgh.

Bean, Lowell John, and Florence Shipek

1978 Luiseño. In *California*, edited by R. F. Heizer, pp. 550–563. Handbook of North American Indians, vol. 8, edited by William C. Sturtevant. Smithsonian Institution Press, Washington, DC.

Bean, Lowell John, and Charles R. Smith

1978 Gabrielino. In *California*, edited by Robert F. Heizer, pp. 538–549. Handbook of North American Indians, vol. 8, edited by William C. Sturtevant. Smithsonian Institution, Washington, DC.

Beck, Margaret E.

2006 Lowland Patayan-Hohokam Interaction: A View from Southwestern Arizona. In *Beginnings: Proceedings of the 2005 Three Corners Conference*, edited by Mark C. Slaughter, Gregory R. Seymour, and Laureen M. Perry, pp. 33–50. The Nevada Archaeological Association, Las Vegas.

2008 Ceramic Use in the Western Papguería. In *Fragile Patterns: The Archaeology of the Western Papaguería*, edited by Jeffrey H. Altschul and Adrianne G. Rankin, pp. 491–505. SRI Press, Tucson.

Beck, Margaret E., and Hector Neff

2007 Hohokam and Patayan Interaction in Southwestern Arizona: Evidence from Ceramic Compositional Analysis. *Journal of Archaeological Science* 34(2): 289–300.

Beckwith, Kim E.

1988 Intrusive Wares and Types. In *The 1982–1984 Excavations at Las Colinas: Material Culture*, edited by David R. Abbott, Kim E. Beckwith, Patricia Crown, R. Thomas Euler, David A. Gregory, K. Ronald London, Marilyn B. Saul, Larry A. Schwalbe, and Mary Bernard-Shaw, pp. 199–256. Archaeological Series 162, Volume 4. Arizona State Museum, Tucson.

Beeler, Madison S., and Kathryn A. Klar

1977 Interior Chumash. *Journal of California Anthropology* 4(2):287–305.

Benson, Arlene

1997 *The Noontide Sun: The Field Journals of the Reverend Stephen Bowers, Pioneer California Archaeologist*. Ballena Press, Menlo Park, California.

Bernard, Julienne

2008 An Archaeological Study of Resistance, Persistence, and Culture Change in the San Emigdio Canyon, Kern County, California. PhD dissertation. Department of Anthropology, University of California, Los Angeles.

Betenson, Britt J.

2005 Pottery and Mobility: A Functional Analysis of Intermountain Brownware. Master's thesis, Department of Anthropology, University of Nevada, Las Vegas.

Bettinger, Robert L.

1986 Intersite Comparison of Great Basin Brown Ware

Assemblages. In *Pottery of the Great Basin and Adjacent Areas*, edited by Suzanne Griset, pp. 97–106. Anthropological Papers, No. 111. University of Utah, Salt Lake City.

1989 *The Archaeology of Pinyon House, Two Eagles, and Crater Midden: Three Residential Sites in Owens Valley, Inyo County, California*. Anthropological Papers, No. 67. American Museum of Natural History, New York.

Bierman, Agnes, and Albert Mohr

1947–1949 Field notes on file at Naval Air Weapons Station, China Lake, California.

Birks, L. S.

1971 Electron Probe Microanalysis. In *Chemical Analysis*. Second ed., vol. 17. Wiley-Interscience, New York.

Blackburn, Thomas C.

1962 Ethnohistoric Descriptions of Gabrielino Material Culture. *Annual Reports of the Archaeological Survey* 5:1–50. University of California, Berkeley.

Bolton, Herbert Eugene

1930 *Anza's California Expeditions*, Vols. I–IV. University of California Press, Berkeley.

1948 *Kino's Historical Memoir of Pimería Alta*. University of California Press, Berkeley. (Originally published in 1918).

Bordaz, Jacques

1964 Pre-Columbian Ceramic Kilns at Penitas: A Post-classic Site in Coastal Nayarit, Mexico. PhD dissertation, Department of Anthropology, Columbia University, New York.

Bourdieu, Pierre

1977 *Outline of a Theory of Practice*. Cambridge University Press, Cambridge.

Bowen, Thomas

1976 *Seri Prehistory: The Archaeology of the Central Coast of Sonora, Mexico*. Anthropological Papers 27. University of Arizona Press, Tucson.

Boxt, Matthew A., and Brian Dillon

2013 Prehistoric Pottery of Coastal Los Angeles County. *Pacific Coast Archaeological Society Quarterly* 47(3–4):45–87.

Braun, David

1983 Pots as Tools. In *Archaeological Hammers and Theories*, edited by A. Keene and J. Moore, pp. 107–134. Academic Press, New York.

Bronitsky, Gordon, and Richard Hamer

1986 Experiments in Ceramic Technology: The Effects of Various Tempering Materials on Impact and Thermal-Shock Resistance. *American Antiquity* 51(1):89–101.

Brott, Clark

1963 Pottery and Yuman History. *Omniart* 2(4).

Brown, Vinson, David Allan, and James Stark

1972 *Rocks and Minerals of California*. Naturegraph Publishers, Healdsburg, California.

Burton, Margie

2009 Using Pottery Collections with Limited Provenience to Explore Pre-contact Ceramic Traditions: An Example from the Anza-Borrego Desert. *Proceedings of the Society for California Archaeology* 21:215–225.

Byrne, Stephen

2011 Prehistoric Trails of the Picacho Basin in the Colorado Desert, Imperial County, California. *Proceedings of the Society for California Archaeology*, Volume 25.

Cachora, Lorey

1994 The Spirit Life of Yuman-Speaking Peoples: Lower Colorado River between Arizona and California. In *Recent Research along the Lower Colorado River*, edited by Joseph A. Ezzo, pp. 13–14. Technical Series No. 51. Statistical Research, Inc., Tucson, Arizona.

Caughey, John Walton, editor

1952 *The Indians of Southern California in 1852: The B. D. Wilson Report and a Selection of Contemporary Comment*. Huntington Library, San Marino, California.

Chapman, John

2000 *Fragmentation in the Prehistory of South Eastern Europe*. Routledge, London.

Chapman, John, and Bisserka Gaydarska

2007 *Parts and Wholes, Fragmentation in Prehistoric Context*. Oxbow Books, Oxford.

Charters, S., R. P. Evershed, L. J. Goad, A. Leyden, P. W. Blinkhorn, and V. Denham

1993 Quantification and Distribution of Lipid in Archaeological Ceramics: Implications for Sampling Potsherds for Organic Residue Analysis and the Classification of Vessel Use. *Archaeometry* 35(2):211–223.

Cleland, James H.

2005 The Sacred and the Mundane: Cultural Landscape Concepts and Archaeological Interpretation in the Colorado Desert. *Proceedings of the Society for California Archaeology* 18:130–135.

Cleland, James H., and Rebecca McCorkle Apple

2003 *A View across the Cultural Landscape of the Lower Colorado Desert: Cultural Resource Investigations for the North Baja Pipeline Project*. EDAW, San Diego.

Clewlow, C. William., Jr., and Helen F. Wells

1980 *Test Excavations at Bird Springs, Clark County, Nevada (26Ck1)*. Prepared by Ancient Enterprises, Inc., for the Las Vegas District Office, Bureau of Land Management, Las Vegas.

Cline, Lora L.

1979 *The Kumeyaay: Reflections on a Lost Culture*. Occasional Paper Number 5. Imperial Valley College Museum Society, El Centro, California.

Colton, Harold S.

1939 *An Archaeological Survey of Northwestern Arizona, Including the Description of Fifteen New Pottery Types*. Bulletin No. 16. Museum of Northern Arizona, Flagstaff.

1952 *Pottery Types of the Arizona Strip and Adjacent Areas in Utah and Nevada*. Ceramic Series No. 1. Museum of Northern Arizona, Flagstaff.

Compton, John S.

1991 Origin and Diagenesis of Clay Mineral in the Monterey Formation, Santa Maria Basin Area, California. *Clay and Clay Minerals* 39(5):449–466.

Cook, John R.
1986 If Tizon Could Talk. *Casual Papers* 2(2):85–97. Cultural Resource Management Center, San Diego State University.

Costello, Julia G.
1985 Ceramics and Other Ceramic Artifacts. In *Excavations at Mission San Antonio, 1976–1978*, edited by Robert Hoover and Julia Costello, pp. 20–56. vol. 26. Institute of Archaeology, University of California, Los Angeles.
1989 Santa Ines Mission Excavations, 1986–1988. *California Historical Archaeology*, No. 1. Coyote Press, Salinas, California.
1990 Variability and Economic Change in the California Missions: An Historical and Archaeological Study. PhD dissertation, Department of Anthropology, University of California, Santa Barbara.
2007 *Mission Pottery: A Typology and Drawings of Locally Made Earthenwares from Mission San Antonio de Padua, California*. Manuscript on file, Ceramics Research Lab, Department of Anthropology, University of California Santa Cruz, Santa Cruz, CA.
2014 A Typology of Mission Pottery: Drawings and Descriptions of Low-Fired Earthenwares from Mission San Antonio de Padua, California. In *Ceramic Production in Early Hispanic California*, edited by R. K. Skowronek, M. J. Blackman, and R. L. Bishop, pp. 69–92. University Press of Florida, Gainesville.

Coues, Elliott, trans.
1900 *On the Trail of a Spanish Pioneer: The Diary and Itinerary of Francisco Garcés (missionary priest) in His Travels through Sonora, Arizona, and California, 1775–1775; Translated from an Official Contemporaneous Copy of the Original Spanish Manuscript, and Edited with Copious Critical Notes*. Francis P. Harper, New York.

Cummings, Linda S.
2008 *Pollen, Phytolith, and Macrofloral Analysis of Sample from Feature 57 at the SCU Leavey Site, Santa Clara County*. Technical Report 07-72. PaleoResearch Institute, Golden, Colorado.

Curtis, Freddie
1962 The Utility Pottery Industry of Bailen, Southern Spain. *American Anthropologist* 64(3):486–503.

Dalley, Gardiner F., and Douglas A. McFadden
1988 *The Little Man Archaeological Sites Excavations on the Virgin River near Hurricane, Utah*. Cultural Resource Series No. 23. Utah State Office, Bureau of Land Management, U.S. Department of the Interior, Salt Lake City.

Davis, Edward H.
1928 Modern Pottery Vessels from San Diego County. *Indian Notes and Monographs* 5:93–96.
1935 Indian Basketry and Ollas. Manuscript on file, Bureau of Indian Affairs, Record Group 75, Mission Indian Agency, Central Classified Files, Box No. 64, File Unit 053, Indian History: Arts and Industries. National Archives Center, Los Angeles National Archives Branch. Published in 1967, *Pacific Coast Archaeological Society Quarterly* 3(1):59–66.
1967 Diegueño Basketry and Pottery. *Pacific Coast Archaeological Society Quarterly* 3(1):59–66.

Davis, James T.
1961 *Trade Routes and Economic Exchange among the Indians of California*. Archaeological Survey Report No. 54. University of California, Berkeley.

Daywalt, William E.
1949 *A Critical Survey of Contemporary Mexican Indian Pottery*. University of California, Los Angeles.

Deetz, James
1963 *Final Summary Report of Investigations at La Purisima Mission State Historical Monument*. State of California Department of Natural Resources, Division of Beaches and Parks, Sacramento.
1991 [1963] Archaeological Investigations at La Purisima Mission. In *The Archaeology of Alta California*, edited by Julia G. Costello and Leo R. Barker. Spanish Borderlands Sourcebooks, edited by David Hurst Thomas, vol. 15. Garland Publishing, Inc. New York.

Devereux, George
1961 *Mohave Ethnopsychiatry and Suicide: The Psychiatric Knowledge and the Psychic Disturbances of an Indian Tribe*. Bulletin 175:1–586. Bureau of American Ethnology, Smithsonian Institution, Washington, D.C.

Dibblee, Thomas W., Jr.
1986 Geologic Map of the Santa Barbara Quadrangle, Santa Barbara County, California. Dibblee Foundation Map Series. Santa Barbara Museum of Natural History, Santa Barbara.
1988 Geologic Map of the Ventura and Pitas Point Quadrangles, Ventura County, California. Dibblee Foundation Map Series. Santa Barbara Museum of Natural History, Santa Barbara.

Dietler, John, Heather Gibson, and James M. Potter, editors
2015 *Abundant Harvests: The Archaeology of Industry and Agriculture at San Gabriel Mission*. SWCA Anthropological Research Paper Number 11. SWCA Environmental Consultants, Pasadena.

Dietler, John, Alyssa Newcomb, Aaron Elzinga, Mandi Martinez, and Heather Gibson
2018 *More than a Mission: From Toviscanga to San Gabriel; Archaeological Monitoring for the San Gabriel Trench Project*. SWCA Environmental Consultants, Pasadena.

DiPeso, Charles, Arthur Woodward, Rex E. Gerald, and M. Virginia Gerald
1953 *The Sobaipuri Indians of the Upper San Pedro River Valley, Southeastern Arizona*. Publication No. 6. The Amerind Foundation, Dragoon, Arizona.

Doyel, David E.
2008 Edge Work: The Late Prehistory of the Gila Bend Frontier. In *Fragile Patterns: The Archaeology of the Western Papaguería*, edited by Jeffrey H. Altschul and Adrianne G. Rankin, pp 233–252. SRI Press, Tucson, Arizona.

Drover, Christopher E.
1975 Early Ceramics from Southern California. *Journal of California Anthropology* 2(1):101–107.

Duke, Daron, and Sarah K. Rice
2016 *Mormon Mesa Top (26CK9933): A 4,000-Acre Earth Oven Archaeological Site at the Virgin-Muddy River Divide, Clark County, Nevada*. Report submitted to the Bureau of Reclamation, Lower Colorado Regional Office. Far Western Anthropological Group, Henderson, Nevada.

Dunnell, Robert C., and James K. Feathers
1994 Thermoluminescence Dating of Surficial Archaeological Material. In *Dating in Exposed and Surface Contexts*, edited by Charlotte Beck, pp. 115–139. University of New Mexico Press, Albuquerque.

Earle, David D.
2003 *Ethnohistorical and Ethnographic Overview and Cultural Affiliation Study of the Fort Irwin Region and the Central Mojave Desert*. Report prepared by Earle and Associates for TRC Solutions, Inc., Salt Lake City. Report on file at Naval Air Weapons Station, China Lake, California.
2005 The Mojave River and the Central Mojave Desert: Native Settlement, Travel and Exchange in the Eighteenth and Nineteenth Centuries. *Journal of California and Great Basin Anthropology* 25(1):1–38.

Eerkens, Jelmer W.
2001 The Origins of Pottery among Late Prehistoric Hunter-Gatherers in California and the Western Great Basin. PhD dissertation, Department of Anthropology, University of California, Santa Barbara.
2002 The Preservation and Identification of Piñon Resins by GC-MS in Pottery from the Western Great Basin. *Archaeometry* 44(1):95–105.
2003 Towards a Chronology of Brownware Pottery in the Western Great Basin: A Case Study from Owens Valley. *North American Archaeologist* 24(1):1–27.
2005 GC-MS Analysis and Fatty Acid Ratios of Archaeological Potsherds from the Western Great Basin of North America. *Archaeometry* 47(1):83–102.

Eerkens, Jelmer W., Hector Neff, and Michael Glascock
1998 A New Look at Intermountain Brownware: Neutron Activation Analysis of Western Great Basin Ceramics. *Proceedings of the Great Basin Anthropological Conference,* Bend, Oregon.
1999 Early Pottery from Sunga'va and Implications for the Development of Ceramic Technology in Owens Valley, California. *Journal of California and Great Basin Anthropology* 20(2):275–285.

Eerkens, Jelmer W., and Carl L. Lipo
2013 Luminescence Dating of Pottery from Owens Valley and Death Valley. *Pacific Coast Archaeological Society Quarterly* 47(1&2):101–114.
2014 A Tale of Two Technologies: Prehistoric Diffusion of Pottery Innovations among Hunter-Gatherers. *Journal of Anthropological Archaeology* 35(1):23–31.

Elsasser, Albert B.
1960 The Archaeology of the Sierra Nevada in California and Nevada. *Anthropological Survey Report* 51:1–93. University of California, Berkeley.
1978 Basketry. In *California*, edited by R. F. Heizer, pp. 626–641, vol. 8. Handbook of North American Indians, edited by William C. Sturtevant. Smithsonian Institution, Washington, DC.

Engelhardt, Zephyrim, O. F. M.
1924 *San Francisco or Mission Dolores*. Franciscan Herald Press, Chicago.

Euler, Robert C.
1964 Southern Paiute Archaeology. *American Antiquity* 29(3):379–381.

Euler, Robert C., and Henry F. Dobyns
1958 Tizon Brown Ware: A Descriptive Revision. In *Pottery Types of the Southwest: Wares 14, 15, 16, 17, and 18, Revised Descriptions*, edited by Harold S. Colton, Ware 15. Ceramic Series No. 3D. Museum of Northern Arizona, Flagstaff.

Evans, William S., Jr.
1969 California Indian Pottery: A Native Contribution to the Culture of the Ranchos. *Pacific Coast Archaeological Society Quarterly* 5(3):71–81.

Evershed, R. P.
1993 Biomolecular Archaeology and Lipids. *World Archaeology* 25(1):74–93.
2008 Organic Residue Analysis in Archaeology: The Archaeological Biomarker Revolution. *Archaeometry* 50(6):895–924.

Ezell, Paul H.
1955 The Archaeological Delineation of a Cultural Boundary in Papagueria. *American Antiquity* 20(4): 367–374.

Farnsworth, Paul
1987 The Economics of Acculturation in the California Missions: A Historical and Archaeological Study of Mission Nuestra Señora de La Soledad. PhD Dissertation, Department of Anthropology, University of California, Los Angeles.

Feathers, James K.
1989 Effects of Temper on Strength of Ceramics: Response to Bronitsky and Hamer. *American Antiquity* 54(4): 579–588.
2000 Date List 7: Luminescence Dates for Prehistoric and Protohistoric Pottery from the American Southwest. *Ancient TL* 18(2):51–61.
2003 Use of Luminescence Dating in Archaeology. *Measurement Science and Technology* 14:1493–1509.
2006 Explaining Shell-Tempered Pottery in Prehistoric Eastern North America. *Journal of Archaeological Method and Theory* 13(2):89–113.
2016 Luminescence Dating of Ceramics from Sites in Eastern Imperial County near Yuma, Arizona. In *Prehistoric Lithic Procurement, Pottery Scatters, and Historic Mechanics Yards in the Colorado Desert, Imperial County, California: Archaeological Data Recovery for the All-American Canal Lining Project*, by Jerry Schaefer, Mark Becker, and Arlene Garcia-Herbst, Appendix B. ASM Affiliates, Inc., Carlsbad.

Feathers, James K., and David Rhode

1998 Luminescence Dating of Protohistoric Pottery from the Great Basin. *Geoarchaeology* 13(3):287–308.

Felton, Larry

2006 Mexican-Republic Era San Diego: An Archaeological Perspective. Paper presented at the Society for Historical Archaeology Annual Conference, Sacramento.

Fenenga, Gerrit L., Barbara Erwin, and William Erwin

2015 A Prehistoric Ceramic Rattle from the Southwestern Shoreline of Ancient Lake Cahuilla, Imperial County, California. *Pacific Coast Archaeological Society Quarterly* 51(1):1–20.

Ferguson, Timothy J.

2014 Keeping in Touch: Exchange as an Adaptive Strategy in Southern Nevada. Master's thesis, Department of Anthropology, University of Nevada, Las Vegas.

2016 Behavioral Ecology and Optimality: Seeking Alternative Views. *Journal of Archaeological Science* 5: 632–639.

Fish, Paul R.

1989 The Hohokam: 1,000 Years of Prehistory in the Sonoran Desert. In *Dynamics of Southwest Prehistory*, edited by Linda S. Cordell and George J. Gumerman, pp. 19–64. Smithsonian Institution Press, Washington, DC.

Forde, C. Darryl

1931 Ethnography of the Yuma Indians. *Publications in American Archaeology and Ethnology* 28(4):83–278. University of California, Berkeley.

Foster, Michael S., editor

1994 *The Pueblo Grande Project, Vol. 4: Material Culture.* Publications in Archaeology No. 20. Soil Systems, Inc., Phoenix. Available at: http://core.tdar.org/document/4549.

Freestone, Ian C.

1982 Applications and Potential of Electron Probe Micro-Analysis in Technological and Provenance Investigations of Ancient Ceramics. *Archaeometry* 24:99–116.

Friel, Breton D.

2005 Late Prehistoric Pottery: Toward a Ceramic Tradition in the Southeastern Great Basin. *Utah Archaeology* 18:33–48.

Frierman, Jay D.

1982 Southern California Brown Ware: Indian Made Pottery in the Pastoral Period. In *The Ontiveros Adobe: Early Rancho Life in Alta California*, edited by Jay D. Frierman, pp. 21–34. Greenwood and Associates, Pacific Palisades.

Furst, Jill L.

2001 *Mojave Pottery, Mojave People: The Dillingham Collection of Mojave Ceramics.* School of American Research Press, Santa Fe.

Gallucci, Karen

2001 From the Desert to the Mountains: Salton Brownware Pottery in the Mountains of San Diego. Master's thesis, Department of Anthropology, San Diego State University.

Gardner, Jill. K.

2007 The Potential Impact of the Medieval Climatic Anomaly on Human Populations in the Western Mojave Desert. *Archives of Great Basin Prehistory* 7. Coyote Press, Salinas, California.

Garlinghouse, Tom, Sarah Peelo, Clinton Blount, Stella D'Oro, Ryan Brady, John Ellison, and Linda Hylkema

2018 *Archaeological Data Recovery for the St. Clare Residence Hall Storm Drain System, Santa Clara University.* Albion Environmental, Santa Cruz, California.

Gayton, Anna H.

1929 Yokuts and Western Mono Pottery-Making. *Publications in American Archaeology and Ethnography* 24(3):239–255. University of California Press, Berkeley.

Gerald, Rex

1951 *A Description of a Historic Papago Redware and its Comparison with Other Late Redwares.* Arizona State Museum, Tucson.

Giambastiani, Mark A., Jill K. Gardner, T. M. Lechner, and S. Andrews

2009 An Archaeological Survey of 2,125 acres Between Robbers Mountain and Seep Spring, Naval Air Weapons Station, China Lake, San Bernardino County, California. Prepared by ASM Affiliates for Epsilon Systems Solutions, Inc. Report on file at Naval Air Weapons Station, China Lake.

Giddens, Anthony

1979 *Central Problems in Social Theory: Action, Structure, and Contradiction in Social Analysis.* University of California Press, Berkeley and Los Angeles.

Gifford, E. W., and E. Schenck

1926 Archaeology of the Southern San Joaquin Valley. *Publications in American Ethnology* XXIII:1–122. University of California, Berkeley.

Ginn, Sarah

2009 Creating Community in Spanish California: An Investigation of California Plainwares. PhD dissertation, Department of Anthropology, University of California, Santa Cruz.

Glascock, Michael D.

2002 Introduction: Geochemical Evidence for Long-Distance Exchange. In *Geochemical Evidence for Long-Distance Exchange*, edited by M. D. Glascock, pp. 1–11. Bergin and Garvey, Westport.

Glassow, Michael A., Lynn H. Gamble, Jennifer E. Perry, and Glenn S. Russell

2007 Prehistory of the Northern California Bight and the Adjacent Transverse Ranges. In *California Prehistory: Colonization, Culture, and Complexity*, edited by Terry L. Jones and Kathryn A. Klar, pp. 191–214. AltaMira Press, Lanham, Maryland.

Goggin, John M.

1970 The Spanish Olive Jar, An Introductory Study. *Papers in Caribbean Anthropology*, Volume 6. Department of Anthropology, Yale University Press.

Golla, Victor

2011 *California Indian Languages*. University of California Press, Oakland.

Gosselain, Olivier P.

2000 Materializing Identities: An Africanist Perspective. *Journal of Archaeological Method and Theory* 7: 187–217.

Greenwood, Roberta S., Jay D. Frierman, and John M. Foster

1983 *The Bandini-Cota Adobe, Prado Dam, Riverside County, California: Test Excavation*. Greenwood and Associates, Pacific Palisades, California.

Griset, Suzanne

1990 Historic Transformations of Tizon Brown Ware in Southern California. In *Anthropological Papers* Number 23, edited by Joanne M. Mack, pp. 179–200. Nevada State Museum, Carson City.

1996 Southern California Brownware. PhD dissertation, Department of Anthropology, University of California, Davis.

2006 Ceramic Artifacts from Lovejoy Springs. Report prepared for Applied Earthworks, Inc., Fresno, California.

2012 *Water Jar from CA-RIV-10127*. Report prepared for Applied Earthworks, Inc., Hemet. SWCA Environmental Consultants, Tucson.

2013 Ceramics from Lovejoy Springs, A Western Mojave Desert Waterhole. *Pacific Coast Archaeological Society Quarterly* 47 (3&4):1–23.

2015 Native American Ceramics. In *Abundant Harvests: The Archaeology of Industry and Agriculture at San Gabriel Mission*, edited by John Dietler, Heather Gibson, and James M. Potter, pp. 337–360. SWCA Anthropological Research Paper Number 11. SWCA, Inc., Pasadena.

2017 *Results of the Anza Borrego Desert State Park (ABDSP) Whole Vessel Documentation Project, Funded by the Begole Archaeological Research Fund, 2011 and 2012*. Report submitted to Anza-Borrego Desert State Park, Borrego Springs, California.

2018 *Native American Ceramics*. Report prepared for SWCA Pasadena.

Griset, Suzanne (editor)

1986 *Pottery of the Great Basin and Adjacent Areas*. Anthropological Papers No. 111. University of Utah Press, Salt Lake City.

Guest, Francis F.

1973 *Fermin Francisco de Lasuén (1736–1803)*. Academy of American Franciscan History, Washington, DC.

Habicht-Mauche, Judith

1993 *The Pottery from Arroyo Hondo Pueblo, New Mexico: Tribalization and Trade in the Northern Rio Grande*. Arroyo Hondo Archaeological Series 8. School of American Research Press, Santa Fe, New Mexico.

Hagstrum, Melissa B., and John A. Hildebrand

1990 The Two-Curvature Method for Reconstructing Ceramic Morphology. *American Antiquity* 55(2): 388–403.

Halpern, A. M.

1980 Sex Differences in Quechan Narrative. *Journal of California and Great Basin Anthropology* 2(1):51–59.

Harper, Christopher

2006 *A Room with a View: Data Recovery of an Early Historical Rockshelter Site Located in the Upper Moapa Valley, Clark County, Nevada*. Papers in Archaeology No. 5. HRA, Inc., Conservation Archaeology, Las Vegas.

Harrington, Mark

1927 A Primitive Pueblo City in Nevada. *American Anthropologist* 29(3):262–277.

Harrison, William M.

1965 Mikiw: A Coastal Chumash Village. In *Archaeological Survey, Annual Report* 1965:91–178. Department of Anthropology, University of California, Los Angeles.

Harry, Karen G.

2005 Ceramic Specialization and Agricultural Marginality: Do Ethnographic Models Explain the Development of Specialized Pottery Production in the Prehistoric American Southwest? *American Antiquity* 70(2): 295–319.

Harry, Karen G., and Jean (Nikki) Berkebile

2015 LAKE 12-038 (Roasting Pit Site). In *Final Report of the Shivwits Research Project 2012–2014 Field Season*, prepared by Karen G. Harry, pp. 46–62. Task Agreement No. J83R07100003, Cooperative Agreement No. H8R070600001. Report on file, Lake Mead National Recreation Area, Boulder City, Nevada.

Harry, Karen G., and Timothy Ferguson

2015 Pete's Pocket. In *Final Report of the Shivwits Research Project 2012–2014 Field Seasons*, prepared by Karen G. Harry, pp. 21–45. Task Agreement No. J83R07100003, Cooperative Agreement No. H8R070600001. Report on file, Lake Mead National Recreation Area, Boulder City, Nevada.

Harry, Karen G., Timothy J. Ferguson, James R. Allison, Brett T. McLaurin, Jeff Ferguson, and Margaret Lyneis.

2013 Examining the Production and Distribution of Shivwits Ware Pottery in the American Southwest. *American Antiquity* 78(2):385–396.

Haury, Emil W.

1931 Minute Beads from Prehistoric Pueblos. *American Anthropologist* n.s 33:80–87.

1937 Figurines and Miscellaneous Clay Objects. In *Excavations at Snaketown – I. Material Culture* by H. S. Gladwin, E. W. Haury, E. B. Sayles, and N. Gladwin. Medallion Papers No. 24. Gila Pueblo, Globe, Arizona.

Hayden, Irwin

1930 Mesa House. In *Archaeological Explorations in Southern Nevada: Report of the First Session's Expeditions, 1929*, pp. 26–92. Museum Papers No. 4. Southwest Museum, Los Angeles.

Heckman, Robert A., Barbara K. Montgomery, and Stephanie M. Whittlesey

2000 *Prehistoric Painted Pottery of Southeastern Arizona*, Technical Series 77. Statistical Research, Inc. Tucson.

Hedges, Ken
1973 Hakataya Figurines from Southern California. *Pacific Coast Archaeological Society Quarterly* 9(3):1–40.
Hegmon, Michelle, Margaret Ennes, and Mark C. Nelson
2000 Corrugated Pottery, Technological Style, and Population Movement in the Mimbres Region of the American Southwest. *Journal of Anthropological Research* 56:217–240.
Heizer, Robert F.
1941 The Direct Historical Approach in California Archaeology. *American Antiquity* 7(2):98–122.
1945 The Occurrence and Significance of Southwestern Grooved Axes in California. *American Antiquity* 11(3):187–193.
1968 The Indians of Los Angeles County: Hugo Reid's Letters of 1852. *Southwest Museum Papers 21.* Los Angeles.
Heizer, Robert. F., and R. K. Beardsley
1943 Fired Clay Human Figurines in Central and Northern California. *American Antiquity* 9(2):199–207.
Heizer, Robert F., and Albert Elsasser
1980 The Natural World of the California Indians. *California Natural History Guides* No. 46. University of California Press, Berkeley.
Hendry, Jean C.
1992 *Atzompa: A Pottery Producing Village of Southern Mexico in the Mid-1950's.* Vanderbilt University, Nashville, Tennessee.
Heron, Carl, and Richard P. Evershed
1993 The Analysis of Organic Residues and the Study of Pottery Use. *Archaeological Method and Theory* 5(1993):247–284.
Hildebrand, John
2003 Ceramics Excavated from the Lower Colorado River Region by the North Baja Pipeline Project. In *A View Across the Cultural Landscape of the Lower Colorado Desert: Cultural Resource Investigations for the North Baja Pipeline Project*, by James H. Cleland and Rebecca McCorkle Apple, pp. 245–260. EDAW, San Diego.
Hildebrand, John A., G. Timothy Gross, Jerry Schaefer, and Hector Neff
2002 Patayan Ceramic Variability: Using Trace Elements and Petrographic Analysis to Study Brown and Buff Wares in Southern California. In *Ceramic Production and Circulation in the Greater Southwest: Source Determination by INAA and Complementary Mineralogical Investigations*, edited by Donna M. Glowacki and Hector Neff, pp. 121–139. The Cotsen Institute of Archaeology, University of California, Los Angeles.
Hoover, Robert L.
1989 Spanish-Native Interaction and Acculturation in the Alta California Missions. In *Columbian Consequences: Archaeological and Historical Perspectives of the Spanish Borderlands West*, edited by David Hurst Thomas, pp. 395–406. vol. 1. Smithsonian Press, Washington, DC.
Hoover, Robert, and Julia Costello
1985 *Excavations at Mission San Antonio, 1976–1978.* Monograph XXVI. Institute of Archaeology, University of California, Los Angeles.
Horne, Stephen
1981 The Inland Chumash: Ethnography, Ethnohistory, and Archaeology. PhD dissertation, Department of Anthropology, University of California, Santa Barbara.
Hudson, Travis, and Thomas C. Blackburn
1987 *The Material Culture of the Chumash Interaction Sphere*, vol. V: *Manufacturing, Processes, Metrology, and Trade.* Ballena Press/Santa Barbara Museum of Natural History Cooperative Publication, Los Altos and Santa Barbara.
Hughes, Richard. E.
2010 Geochemical Research Laboratory Letter Report 2009-62. On file at Naval Air Weapons Station, China Lake.
Hunt, Alice
1960 *Archaeology of the Death Valley Salt Pan, California.* Anthropological Papers, No. 47. University of Utah, Salt Lake City.
Hylkema, Mark
1995 *Archaeological Investigations at Mission Santa Clara (CA-SCL-30) for the Re-Alignment of Route 82.* California Department of Transportation, District 4, Oakland.
Ingersoll, Raymond V., Thomas F. Fullard, Richard L. Ford, Joel P. Grimm, John D. Pickle, and Steven W. Sares
1984 The Effect of Grain Size on Detrital Modes; A Test of the Gazzi-Dickinson Point-Counting Method. *Journal of Sedimentary Research* 54(1):103–116.
Jackson, Thomas L.
1990 Prehistoric Ceramics of the Southwestern Sierra Nevada, California. In *Hunter-Gatherer Pottery from the Far West*, edited by Joanne Mack, pp. 159–169. Anthropological Papers Number 23. Nevada State Museum, Carson City.
Jennings, David
1976 Progress Report on Ker-307, Castaic. *San Luis Obispo Archaeological Society Artifact* 11:11–12.
Joesink-Mandeville, Leroy V.
1986 *Ceramics in Archaeological Cultures in Mexico.* Museum of Anthropology, University of Northern Colorado, Greely.
Johnson, Ann H.
1985 *Report of Phase III Research for Block 1, San Antonio Plaza, San Jose.* Report prepared for the Redevelopment Agency, City of San Jose, California. Theodoratus Cultural Research, Inc., Fair Oaks, California.
Johnson, Jerald J.
1990 Cosumnes Brownware: A Pottery Type Centered on the Lower Cosumnes and Adjacent Sacramento Rivers in Central California. In *Hunter-Gatherer Pottery from the Far West*, edited by Joanne M. Mack, pp. 145–158. Anthropological Papers No. 23. The Nevada State Museum, Carson City.

Johnson, John R.

1978 The Trail to Kashtiq. *Journal of California Anthropology* 5(2):188–198.

1984 Indian History in the Santa Barbara Back Country. *Los Padres Notes* 3:1–24.

1988 Chumash Social Organization: An Ethnohistoric Perspective. PhD dissertation, Department of Anthropology, University of California, Santa Barbara.

1989 The Chumash and the Missions. In *Columbian Consequences*, Volume 1, "Archaeological and Historical Perspectives on the Spanish Borderlands West" edited by David Hurst Thomas, pp. 365–375. Smithsonian Institution Press, Washington, DC.

2007 Ethnohistoric Descriptions of Chumash Warfare. In *North American Indigenous Warfare and Ritual Violence*, edited by Richard Chacon and Ruben Mendoza, pp.74–113. University of Arizona Press, Tucson.

Johnston, Bernice Eastman

1962 *California's Gabrielino Indians.* Frederick Webb Hodge Anniversary Publication Fund, Volume 8. Southwest Museum, Los Angeles.

Jones, Sian

1997 *The Archaeology of Ethnicity: Constructing Identities in the Past and Present.* Routledge Press, London.

Jornet, Albert, M. James Blackman, and Jacqueline Olin

1985 Thirteenth to Eighteenth Century Ceramics from the Paterno-Manises Area (Spain). In *Ancient Technology to Modern Science*, edited by William D. Kingery, pp. 235–255. Ceramics and Civilization, vol. 1. American Ceramic Society, Columbus, Ohio.

Kaplan, Flora

1994 *A Mexican Folk Pottery Tradition: Cognition and Style in Material Culture in the Valley of Puebla.* Southern Illinois University Press, Carbondale and Edwardsville.

Kealhofer, Lisa

1991 Cultural Interaction during the Spanish Colonial Period: The Plaza Church Site, Los Angeles. PhD dissertation, Department of Anthropology, University of Pennsylvania.

Kelly, Isabel T.

1976 *Paiute Indians II: Southern Paiute Ethnography.* Garland Publishing Inc., New York and London.

King, Chester

1976 Chumash Inter-Village Economic Exchange. In *Native Californians: A Theoretical Retrospective*, edited by Lowell John Bean and Thomas C. Blackburn, pp. 289–318. Ballena Press, Socorro, New Mexico.

Koerper, Henry C.

1996 A *Glycymeris* Shell Bracelet from Orange County, California. *Pacific Coast Archaeological Society Quarterly* 32(2&3):82–109.

Koerper, Henry C., and Nancy Desautels

2002 A *Glycymeris* Bracelet from CA-ORA-58. *Pacific Coast Archaeological Society Quarterly* 38(2&3): 99–104.

Koerper, Henry C., Christopher E. Drover, Arthur E. Flint, and Gary Hurd

1978 Gabrielino Tizon Brown Pottery. *Pacific Coast Archaeological Society Quarterly* 14(3):43–58.

Koerper, Henry C., and Arthur E. Flint

1994 Some Comments on "Cerritos Brown" Pottery. *Pacific Coast Archaeological Society Quarterly* 14(2):19–25.

Koerper, Henry C., and Ken Hedges

1996 Patayan Anthropomorphic Figurines from an Orange County Site. *Journal of California and Great Basin Anthropology* 18(2):204–220.

Kroeber, Alfred L.

1925 *Handbook of the Indians of California.* Bulletin 78. Bureau of American Ethnology, Smithsonian Institution, Government Printing Office, Washington, DC.

1932 The Patwin and their Neighbors. *Publications in American Archaeology and Ethnology* 49(4):253–423. University of California, Berkeley.

1962 Two Papers on the Aboriginal Ethnography of California. The Nature of Land Holding Grounds in Aboriginal California. *Archaeological Survey Reports* 56:21–58. University of California, Berkeley.

1973 *Basket Designs of the Mission Indians of California.* Ballena Press, Ramona, California.

Kroeber, Alfred L., and Michael J. Harner

1955 Mohave Pottery. *Anthropological Records* 16(1). University of California, Berkeley and Los Angeles.

Langelier, John P., and Daniel B. Rosen

1992 *El Presidio de San Francisco: A History under Spain and Mexico, 1776–1846.* Presidio of San Francisco, Golden Gate National Recreation Area, and National Park Service, San Francisco.

LaPierre, Kish

2012 Investigations of a Rock Feature Complex at the Mirror Point Site (CA-SBR-12134/H), Western Mojave Desert, San Bernardino County, California. Master's Thesis. Department of Anthropology, California State University, Bakersfield.

Larson, Daniel O., and Joel Michaelsen

1990 Impacts of Climatic Variabiity and Population Growth on Virgin Branch Anasazi Cultural Developments. *American Antiquity* 55(2):227–249.

Laylander, Don

1997 The Last Days of Lake Cahuilla: The Elmore Site. *Pacific Coast Archaeological Society Quarterly* 33(1–2):1–138.

2014 Redundancy, Avoidance, and Ideology in Prehistoric Southern California. *Proceedings of the Society for California Archaeology* 28:326–339.

Lightfoot, Kent

2005 *Indians, Missionaries, and Merchants: The Legacy of Colonial Encounters on the California Frontiers.* University of California Press, Berkeley.

Lightfoot Kent, Antoinette Martinez, and Anne Schiff

1998 Daily Practice and Material Culture in Pluralistic Social Settings: An Archaeological Study of Culture

Change and Persistence from Fort Ross, California. *American Antiquity* 63(2):199–222.

Linne, Sigvald
1934 *Archaeological Researches at Teotihuacan, Mexico.* Ethnographical Museum of Sweden, Stockholm.

Lister, Florence C., and Robert H. Lister
1982 *Sixteenth Century Majolica Pottery in the Valley of Mexico.* Anthropological Papers 39. Arizona State Museum, University of Arizona, Tucson.

London, Gloria
1981 Dung-Tempered clay. *Journal of Field Archaeology* 8(2):189–195.

Love, Bruce, and Mariam Dahdul
2003 Desert Chronologies and the Archaic Period in the Coachella Valley. *Pacific Coast Archaeological Society Quarterly* 38(2–3):65–86.

Love, Holly, and Rheta Resnik
1983 Mission-Made Pottery and Other Ceramics from Muwu, a Coastal Chumash Village. *Pacific Coast Archaeological Society Quarterly* 19(1):1–11.

Lyman, R. Lee, and Michael J. O'Brien
2001 The Direct Historical Approach, Analogical Reasoning, and Theory in Americanist Archaeology. *Journal of Archaeological Method and Theory* 8(4):303–342.

Lyneis, Margaret M.
1988a Appendix E: Ceramics Analysis. In *The Late Holocene Archaeology of Drinkwater Basin, Fort Irwin, San Bernardino County, California*, by Mark E. Basgall, Matthew C. Hall, and William R. Hildebrandt. Prepared for the U.S. Army Corps of Engineers, Los Angeles District, Los Angeles, by Far Western Anthropological Group, Davis, California.
1988b Appendix E: Ceramics Analysis. In *Archaeological Investigations in Tiefort Basin, Fort Irwin, San Bernardino County, California*, by Kelly R. McGuire, Matthew C. Hall, and Mark E. Basgall. Prepared for the U.S. Army Corps of Engineers, Los Angeles District, Los Angeles, by Far Western Anthropological Group, Davis, California.
1988c Tizon Brown Ware and the Problems Raised by Paddle-and-Anvil Pottery in the Mojave Desert. *Journal of California and Great Basin Anthropology* 10(2):146–155.
1989 Appendix E: Ceramics from the China Lake-Fort Irwin Joint Land Use Area, San Bernardino County, California. In *Survey and Test Evaluation of the China Lake-Fort Irwin Joint Land Use Area, San Bernardino County, California*, Volume II, by Paul D. Bouey and Patricia Mikkelsen. Far Western Anthropological Research Group, Inc., Davis.
1992 *The Main Ridge Community at Lost City: Virgin Anasazi Architecture, Ceramics, and Burials.* Anthropological Papers No. 117. University of Utah Press, Salt Lake City.
1994 East and onto the Plateaus? An Archaeological Examination of the Numic Expansion in Southern Nevada, Northern Arizona, and Southern Utah. In *Across the West: Human Population Movement and the Expansion of the Numa*, edited by David B. Madsen and David Rhode, pp. 141–149. University of Utah Press, Salt Lake City.
1995 The Virgin Anasazi, Far Western Puebloans. *Journal of World Prehistory* 9(2):199–241.
1996 Pueblo II–Pueblo III Change in Southwestern Utah, the Arizona Strip, and Southern Nevada. In *The Prehistoric Pueblo World, A.D. 1150–1350*, edited by Michael A. Adler, pp. 11–28. University of Arizona Press, Tucson.
2008a Ceramics. In *Persistent Place: Archaeological Investigations at the Larder and Scorpion Knoll Sites, Clark County Wetlands Park, Nevada*, edited by Richard V. N. Ahlstrom, pp. 169–172. Papers in Archaeology No. 7. HRA, Inc., Las Vegas.
2008b New and Revised Prehistoric Pueblo Pottery Wares and Types from North and West of the Colorado River: Gray Wares from the Western Area. *Pottery Southwest* 27(1):3–20.
2012 Appendix D: A Synopsis of the Yamashita Sites. In *A Prehistoric Context for Southern Nevada*, edited by Heidi Roberts and Richard V. N. Ahlstrom, pp. D1–D19. Archaeological Report No. 011-05. HRA Inc, Las Vegas.

Lyneis, Margaret M., and Kelly Hays-Gilpin
2008 Prehistoric Pueblo Pottery North and West of the Colorado River; Museum of Northern Arizona Ceramic Conference, November 9–10, 2007. *Pottery Southwest* 26(4):12–16.

Mabry, J. B.
1997 Rewriting Prehistory: Recent Discoveries at Cienega Phase Sites in the Santa Cruz Floodplain. *Newsletter* Vol. II, No. 3. Center for Desert Archaeology, Tucson.

Mack, Joanne
1990 Siskiyou Utility Ware: Hunter-Gatherer Pottery, It's Not Just for Cooking. In *Hunter-Gatherer Pottery from the Far West*, edited by Joanne M. Mack, pp. 123–130. Anthropological Papers No. 23. The Nevada State Museum, Carson City.

Madsen, David B.
1983 Prehistoric Ceramics. In *Great Basin*, edited by Warren L. D'Azevedo, pp. 206–215. Handbook of North American Indians, Vol. 12. Smithsonian Institution, Washington DC.

Malainey, Mary E.
1997 The Reconstruction and Testing of Subsistence and Settlement Strategies for the Plains, Parkland, and Southern Boreal Forest. PhD dissertation, Department of Anthropology, University of Manitoba.
2011 *A Consumer's Guide to Archaeological Science: Analytical Techniques.* Springer Science and Business Media, New York.

Malainey, Mary E., R. Przybylski, B. L. Sherri
1999 The Effects of Thermal and Oxidative Degradation on the Fatty Acid Composition of Food Plants and Animals of Western Canada: Implications of the

Identification of Archaeological Vessel Residues. *Journal of Archaeological Science* 26:95–103.

Margolin, Malcolm

1989 *Monterey in 1776: Life in a California Mission.* Heyday Books, Berkeley.

Marshall, Ralph P.

1982 An Archaeological Survey of the Ortega-Vigare Adobe, a Historical Site. *Pacific Coast Archaeological Society Quarterly* 18(1):1–61.

Martin, Steve L.

1999 Virgin Anasazi Diet as Demonstrated through the Analysis of Stable Carbon and Nitrogen Isotopes. *Kiva* 64(4):495–514.

Martin, Debra L., and Jennifer L. Thompson

2008 Skeletal Analysis of the Lost City Human Remains. Ms. on file, Department of Anthropology and Ethnic Studies, University of Nevada, Las Vegas.

May, Ronald V.

1976 An Analysis of Certain Ceramics from the San Buenaventura Mission. In *The Changing Faces of Main Street*, edited by Roberta S. Greenwood, pp. 211–225. Greenwood and Associates, Pacific Palisades, California.

1978 A Southern California Indigenous Ceramic Typology: A Contribution to Malcolm J. Rogers Research. *Journal* 2(2). Archaeological Survey Association of Southern California, Inc., La Verne.

1980 Ceramic Artifacts. In *An Investigation in the Southern Sierra*, edited by A. Garfinkel and K. R. McGuire, Appendix 2. Report prepared for BLM Bakersfield District, Bakersfield, by Far Western Anthropological Group, Davis, California.

1985 Spanish Period Ceramics from the San Antonio Plaza Project. In *Report of Phase III Research for Block 1, San Antonio Plaza, San Jose.* Report prepared for City of San Jose, California by Theodoratus Cultural Research, Inc., Fair Oaks, California.

McCarthy, Daniel F.

1993 Prehistoric Land-Use at McCoy Spring: An Arid-Land Oasis in Eastern Riverside County, California. Master's thesis, Department of Anthropology, University of California, Riverside.

2014 An Early Ceramic Pipe from the San Bernardino Mountains. *Pacific Coast Archaeological Society Quarterly* 49(3–4):47–55.

McCartney, Peter, and Margaret Glass

1990 Simulation Models and the Interpretation of Archaeological Diversity. *American Antiquity* 55(3):521–536.

McCawley, William

1996 *The First Angelinos: the Gabrielino Indians of Los Angeles.* Malki Museum Press/Ballena Press, Banning and Novato, California.

McFadden, Douglas

1996 Virgin Anasazi Settlement and Adaptation on the Grand Staircase. *Utah Archaeology* 9(1):1–34.

McLendon, Sally, and John R. Johnson (Editors)

1999 *Affiliation and Lineal Descent of Chumash Peoples in the Channel Islands and Santa Monica Mountains.* Report submitted to the Archaeology and Ethnography Program, National Park Service, Washington DC. Santa Barbara Museum of Natural History, Santa Barbara, and Hunter College, City University of New York.

Meighan, Clement W.

1959 Archaeological Resources of Borrego State Park. *Annual Report* 1958–1959:235–44. Archaeological Survey, Department of Anthropology & Sociology, University of California, Los Angeles.

Middleton, Andrew P., Ian C. Freestone, and Morven N. Leese

1985 Textural Analysis of Ceramic Thin Sections: Evaluation of Grain Sampling Procedures. *Archaeometry* 27(1):64–74.

Miksa, Elizabeth, and James M. Heidke

1995 Drawing a Line in the Sands: Models of Ceramic Temper Provenance. In *The Roosevelt Community Development Study, Volume 2: Ceramic Chronology, Technology, and Economics*, edited by James M. Heidke and Miriam T. Stark pp. 133–204. Anthropological Papers No. 14. Center for Desert Archaeology, Tucson.

Mitchell, Douglas R., editor

1989 *Archaeological Investigations at the Grand Canal Ruins: A Classic Period Site in Phoenix, Arizona*, vol. 1. Publications in Archaeology No. 12. Soil Systems, Inc., Phoenix.

Monastero, Andrew

2007 A Test of the Central Place Foraging Model at the Bierman Cave Site (CA-SBR-8), South Range, China Lake Naval Air Weapons Station, California. Master's thesis, Department of Anthropology, California State University, Bakersfield.

Morss, Noel

1954 Clay Figurines of the American Southwest. *Papers* XLIX(1). Peabody Museum of American Archaeology and Ethnology, Harvard University, Cambridge.

Moser, Christopher

1986 *Native American Basketry of Central California: Catalog for the Exhibition of "Native American Basketry of Central California" from the permanent collection of the Riverside Municipal Museum.* Riverside Museum Press, Riverside.

Muller, Florencia, and Barbara Hopkins

1974 *A Guide to Mexican Ceramics.* Minutiae Mexicana, Mexico.

Munson, Patrick J., Paul W. Parmalee, and Richard A. Yarnell

1971 Subsistence Ecology of Scovill, a Terminal Middle Woodland Village. *American Antiquity* 36(4):410–431.

Murray, A. S., and A. G. Wintle

2000 Luminescence Dating of Quartz using an Improved Single-Aliquot Regenerative-Dose Protocol. *Radiation Measurements* 32(1):57–73.

National Institute of Standards and Technology (NIST)

2002 *NIST/EPA/NIH Mass Spectral Library.* The National Institute of Standards and Technology, Gaithersburg.

Neff, Hector (editor)
1992 *Chemical Characterization of Ceramic Pastes in Archaeology*. Prehistory Press, Madison, Wisconsin.
Neff, Hector
1993 Theory, Sampling, and Analytical Techniques in the Archaeological Study of Prehistoric Ceramics. *American Antiquity* 58(1):23–44.
Nordensklold, Gustaf
2009 [1893] *The Cliff Dwellers of the Mesa Verde, Southwestern Colorado: Their Pottery and Implements.* Rio Grande Press, Glorieta, New Mexico.
Northern Arizona University
2001 Ceramic Manual. Available at: http://www2.nau.edu/~sw-ptry/
Northwest Economic Associates (NEA) and Chester King
2004 *Ethnographic Overview of the Angeles National Forest: Tataviam and San Gabriel Mountain Serrano Ethnohistory*. Prepared for U.S. Department of Agriculture, Southern California Province, Angeles National Forest, by Northwest Economic Associates, Vancouver, Washington and Topanga Anthropological Consultants, Topanga, California.
Olson, Kathryn
1980 Appendix 1, Ceramics. In *Test Excavations at Bird Springs, Clark County, Nevada (26Ck1)*, by C. William Clewlow, Jr., and Helen F. Wells. Prepared by Ancient Enterprises, Inc., for the Las Vegas District Office, Bureau of Land Management, Las Vegas.
Ortiz, Beverly, and David Ludwig
1995 *Pomo Basketweavers: A Tribute to Three Elders*. Creative Light Productions and University of California Extension Center for Media and Independent Learning, Berkeley.
Ortner, Sherry
1999 *The Fate of "Culture": Geertz and Beyond*. University of California Press, Berkeley.
Orton, Clive, Paul Tyers, and Alan Vince
1993 *Pottery in Archaeology*. Cambridge University Press, Cambridge.
Panich, Lee
2014 Native American Consumption of Shell and Glass Beads at Mission Santa Clara de Asis. *American Antiquity* 79(4):730–748.
2015a Mission Santa Clara in a Changing Urban Environment. *Boletin* 31(1):36–45. Journal of California Mission Studies Association, Santa Clara, California.
2015b "Sometimes They Bury the Deceased's Clothes and Trinkets": Indigenous Mortuary Practices at Mission Santa Clara de Asis. *Historical Archaeology* 49(4):110–129.
2016 Beyond the Colonial Curtain: Investigating Indigenous Use of Obsidian in Spanish California through the pXRF Analysis of Artifacts from Mission Santa Clara. *Journal of Archaeological Science* 5:521–530.
Panich, Lee, Helga Afaghani, and Nicole Mathwich
2014 Assessing the Diversity of Mission Populations through the Comparison of Native American Residences at Mission Santa Clara de Asis. *International Journal of Historical Archaeology* 18:467–488.
Panich, Lee, Sarah Peelo, and Linda Hylkema
2018 Archaeological Insights into the Persistence of Multiscalar Native Communities at Mission Santa Clara de Asís. In *The Forging of Communities in Colonial Alta California, 1769–1834*, edited by Kathleen L. Hull and John G. Douglass. Archaeology of Indigenous-Colonial Interactions in the Americas. The University of Arizona Press, Tucson.
Peck, Stuart L., and Gerald A. Smith
1957 The Archaeology of Seep Spring. *Association Quarterly* 4(4) *Scientific Series* No. 2. San Bernardino County Museum, Redlands.
Peelo, Sarah
2011 Pottery-Making in Spanish California: Creating Multi-Scalar Social Identity through Daily Practice. *American Antiquity* 76(4):642–666.
2014 The Mineralogy of California Plain Wares: Technology and Social Reproduction in the California Spanish Missions. In *Ceramic Production in Early Hispanic California: Craft, Economy, and Trade on the Frontier of New Spain*, edited by Russell K. Skowronek, M. John Blackman, and Ronald L. Bishop, pp. 152–169. University Press of Florida, Gainesville.
Peelo, Sarah, Clinton Blount, Tom Garlinghouse, Stella D'Oro, John Ellison, Ryan Phillip, Christina Spellman, Linda Hylkema, Mark Hylkema, Eric Wohlgemuth, and Cristie M. Boone
2022 The Indian Rancheria at Mission Santa Clara de Asis: Cultural Resources Mitigation for Parking Garage and Art and Art History Building. Santa Clara University.
Peelo, Sarah, Lee Panich, Christina Spellman, John Ellison, and Stella D'Oro
2018 Marriage and Death in the Neophyte Village at Mission Santa Clara: Preservation of Ancestral and Elite Communities. In *Forging Communities in Colonial Alta California, 1769–1835*, edited by Kathleen L. Hull and John G. Douglass, pp. 162–190. Archaeology of Indigenous-Colonial Interactions in the Americas Series. The University of Arizona Press, Tucson, Arizona.
Perissnotto, Giorgio (Editor)
1998 *Documenting Everyday Life in Early Spanish California: The Santa Barbara Presidio Memorias y Facturas*. Santa Barbara Trust for Historic Preservation, Santa Barbara.
Pfaffenberger, Bryan
1988 Fetished Objects and Humanized Nature: Towards an Anthropology of Technology. *Man* 23(2):236–252.
Phillips, George Harwood
2004 *"Bringing Them Under Subjection": California's Tejon Indian Reservation and Beyond, 1852–1864*. University of Nebraska Press, Lincoln.
Phillips, Philip, James A. Ford, and James B. Griffin
1951 *Archaeological Survey in the Lower Mississippi Valley, 1940–1947*. Papers No. 25. Peabody Museum

of Archaeology and Ethnology, Harvard University, Cambridge.

Pippin, Lonnie C.

1986 Intermountain Brown Ware: An Assessment. In *Pottery of the Great Basin and Adjacent Areas*, edited by Suzanne Griset, pp. 9–22. University of Utah Anthropological Papers No. 111. Salt Lake City.

Plymale-Schneeberger, Sandra

1993 Application of Quantifiable Methodologies in Ceramic Analysis: Petrographic and Geochemical Analysis of Ceramics from Riverside County, California. *Proceedings of the Society for California Archaeology* 6:257–276.

Polanich, Judith

1979 *California Indian Basketry: The Aesthetic Aspect*. Institute for Cultural Resources Monograph. California State University, Stanislaus.

1994 Mono Basketry: Migration and Change. PhD Dissertation, Department of Anthropology, University of California, Davis.

Prince, Eugene R.

1986 Shoshonean Pottery of the Western Great Basin. In *Pottery of the Great Basin and Adjacent Areas*, edited by Suzanne Griset, pp. 3–8. Anthropological Papers No. 111. University of Utah Press, Salt Lake City.

Puseman, Peter Kováčik, Chad Yost, Linda Scott Cummings, and Melissa K. Logan

2012 *Pollen, Phytolith, Macrofloral, Protein, and Organic Residue (FTIR) Analyses on Samples from the Mission San Gabriel Garden Complex, Site CA-LAN-184H, California*. Technical Report 12-020. PaleoResearch Institute, Golden, Colorado.

Quinn, Charles Russell, and Elena Quinn (editors)

1965 *Edward H. Davis and the Indians of Southwest United States and Northwest Mexico*. Self-published by Elena Quinn, Downey, California.

Quinn, Patrick, and Margie Burton

2008 Compositional Analysis of Prehistoric Ceramics from the Anza-Borrego Desert—Seeking Provenience and Technology. Manuscript on file, Begole Archaeological Research Center, Anza Borrego Desert State Park, Borrego Springs.

2009 Ceramic Petrography and the Reconstruction of Hunter-Gatherer Craft Technology in Late Prehistoric Southern California. In *Interpreting Silent Artefacts*, edited by Patrick S. Quinn, pp. 267–295. Archaeopress, Oxford.

Quinn, Patrick S., Margie M. Burton, David Broughton, and Sophie Van Heymbeeck

2013 Deciphering Compositional Patterning in Plainware Ceramics from Late Prehistoric Hunter-Gatherer Sites in the Peninsular Ranges, San Diego County, California. *American Antiquity* 78(4):779–789.

Reid, Kenneth C.

1984 Fire and Ice: New Evidence for the Production and Preservation of Late Archaic Fiber-Tempered Pottery in the Middle Latitude Lowlands. *American Antiquity* 49(1):55–76.

Rhode, David

1994 Direct Dating of Brown Ware Ceramics using Thermoluminescence and Its Relation to the Numic Spread. In *Across the West: Human Population Movement and the Expansion of the Numa*, edited by David B. Madsen and David Rhode, pp. 124–130. University of Utah Press, Salt Lake City.

Rice, Prudence M.

1987 *Pottery Analysis: A Sourcebook*. University of Chicago Press, Chicago and London.

Rick, Torben C.

2004 Social and Economic Dynamics on Late Holocene San Miguel Island, California. In *Foundations of Chumash Complexity*, edited by Jeanne E. Arnold, pp. 97–112. Cotsen Institute of Archaeology, University of California, Los Angeles.

Roberts, Heidi

1997 A Comparative Analysis of Human Skeletal Remains from Parowan, Fremont, Virgin Anasazi, and Kayenta Anasazi Sites. *Utah Archaeology* 10:31–44.

2012 Post-Puebloan Period (A.D. 1300–1776). In *A Prehistoric Context for Southern Nevada*, edited by Heidi Roberts and Richard V. N. Ahlstrom, pp. 165–207. Archaeological Report No. 11-05. HRA, Inc. Las Vegas.

Roberts, Heidi, and Richard V. N. Ahlstrom

2012 Gray, Buff, and Brown: Untangling Chronology, Trade, and Culture in the Las Vegas Valley, Southern Nevada. In *Meetings at the Margins: Prehistoric Cultural Interactions in the Intermountain West*, edited by David Rhode, pp. 211–228. University of Utah Press, Salt Lake City.

Robinson, David W.

2006 Landscape, Taskscape, and Indigenous Perception: The Rock-Art of SouthCentral California. PhD dissertation, Department of Archaeology, University of Cambridge.

Rogers, Malcolm J.

1928 A Question of Scumming. *Arizona Old and New* 1(2):5, 18, 20–21.

1929 Yuman Pottery Making. *American Anthropologist* 45(3):1–53.

1936 *Yuman Pottery Making*. San Diego Museum Papers No. 2. Ballena Press, 1973 reprint. [Griset 9]

1945a An Outline of Yuman Prehistory. *Southwestern Journal of Anthropology* 1(2):167–198.

1945b Final Yuman Pottery Types Nomenclature with Synonyms. Manuscript on file, San Diego Museum of Man.

Rouse, Irving B.

1939 *Prehistory in Haiti: A Study in Method*. Publications in Anthropology No. 21. Yale University, New Haven.

Ruby, Jay, and Thomas Blackburn

1964 Occurrence of Southwestern Pottery in Los Angeles County, California. *American Antiquity* 30(2): 209–210.

Russell, John C., Clyde M. Woods, and Jackson Underwood

2002 *An Assessment of the Imperial Sand Dunes as a Native American Cultural Landscape*. EDAW, San Diego.

Rye, Owen S.
1976 Keeping Your Temper Under Control: Materials and the Manufacture of Papuan Pottery. *Archaeology and Physical Anthropology in Oceania* 11(2):106–137.
1981 *Pottery Technology: Principles and Reconstruction.* Taraxacum, Washington.

Sakai, Sachiko
2014 Explaining Change in Production and Distribution of Olivine-Tempered Ceramics in the Arizona Strip and Adjacent Areas in the American Southwest. PhD Dissertation, Department of Anthropology, University of California, Santa Barbara.

Saldaña, Melanie
2010 New Obsidian Source Data from the South Range, China Lake Naval Air Weapons Station. Paper presented at the 32nd Great Basin Anthropological Conference, Layton, Utah, October 2010.
2012 Pothunter Spring: A Search for Meaning in Prehistoric Rock Shelter Complexes of the West-Central Mojave Desert. Paper presented at the 33rd Great Basin Anthropological Conference, Stateline, Nevada.

Sampson, C. Garth, and John C. Vogel
1996 Fibre Temper in Later Stone Age Ceramics from the Upper Karoo. *South African Archaeological Bulletin* 51(164):99–105.

Schaefer, Jerome
1993 Historic Native American Pottery from the Mining Town of Hedges/Tumco, California. In *The Results of Historical Research, Oral History, Inventory, and Limited Test Excavations Undertaken at the Hedges/Tumco Historic Townsite, Oro Cruz Operation, Southwestern Cargo Muchacho Mountains, Imperial County, California*, edited by Claudia B. Hemphill, pp. B.1–B.11. Burney and Associates, Boulder, Colorado.
1994a The Challenge of Archaeological Research in the Colorado Desert: Recent Approaches and Discoveries. *Journal of California and Great Basin Anthropology* 16(1):60–80.
1994b The Stuff of Creation: Recent Approaches to Ceramic Analysis in the Colorado Desert. In *Recent Research along the Colorado River*, edited by Joseph A. Ezzo, pp. 81–100. Technical Series No. 51. Statistical Research, Inc., Tucson.
1995 Ceramics. In *Archaeological, Ethnographic, and Ethnohistoric Investigations at Tahquitz Canyon, Palm Springs, California*, by Lowell John Bean, Jerry Schaefer, and Sylvia Brakke Vane, pp. IX.1–IX.73. Cultural Systems Research, Menlo Park, California.
1996 Ceramics Analysis Results. In *Archaeology on the North Shoreline of Ancient Lake Cahuilla: Final Results from Survey, Testing, and Mitigation-Monitoring*, by Bruce Love, pp. 51–67. CRM TECH, La Quinta, California. Prepared for U.S. Home Corporation.
2002 *Scratching the Surface of Ceramics in the Colorado Desert: Petrographic and Neutron Activation Analysis of Three Lower Colorado Buff Ware Pot Drops.* ASM Affiliates, Inc., San Diego.

Schaefer, Jerry, and Sherri Andrews
2005 *Class II and III Cultural Resources Inventory and Evaluation for the All-American Canal Lining Project, Imperial County, California.* ASM Affiliates, Inc., San Diego.

Schaefer, Jerry, Sherri Andrews, and Mark Becker
2013 *House Pits, Hearths, and Habitat: Archaeological Investigations at Two Fishing Camps on the Northeastern Shore of Ancient Lake Cahuilla, Riverside County, California.* Prepared for the Coachella Valley Water District, Coachella, California. ASM Affiliates, Inc., Carlsbad.

Schaefer, Jerry, Lowell J. Bean, and C. Michael Elling
1987 *Settlement and Subsistence at San Sebastian: A Desert Oasis on San Felipe Creek, Imperial County, California.* Brian F. Mooney Associates, San Diego.

Schaefer, Jerry, Mark Becker, and Arlene Garcia-Herbst
2016 *Prehistoric Lithic Procurement, Pottery Scatters, and Historic Mechanics Yards in the Colorado Desert, Imperial County, California; Archaeological Data Recovery for the All-American Canal Lining Project.* ASM Affiliates, Inc., Carlsbad.

Schaefer, Jerry, Ken Hedges, Diane Hamann, and Michael Steven Shackley
1993 *Hunter-Gatherer Settlement, Subsistence, and Symbolism at White Tanks, Yuma Proving Ground, Arizona*, vol. I Technical Report. Brian F. Mooney Associates, San Diego.

Schaefer, Jerry, and Don Laylander
2007 The Colorado Desert: Ancient Adaptations to Wetlands and Wastelands. In *California Prehistory: Colonization, Culture, and Complexity*, edited by Terry L. Jones and Kathryn A. Klar, pp. 247–258. AltaMira Press, Lanham, Maryland.
2014 A. G. Tassin's 1877 Manuscript Account of the Mohave Indians. *Journal of California and Great Basin Anthropology* 34(1):61–79.

Schiffer, Michael B.
1986 Radiocarbon Dating the "Old Wood" Problem: The Case of the Hohokam Chronology. *Journal of Archaeological Science* 13(1):13–30.

Schroeder, Albert H.
1955 *Archeology of Zion Park.* Anthropological Papers No. 22. Department of Anthropology, University of Utah, Salt Lake City.
1958 Lower Colorado Buff Ware: A Descriptive Revision. In *Pottery Types of the Southwest*, edited by Harold S. Colton. Ceramic Series No. 3D. Museum of Northern Arizona, Flagstaff.

Schroth, Adella B., and Mary E. Kearney
2007 Collections from the Mojave B Range/Randsburg Wash Portion of Naval Air Weapons Station China Lake, Previously Housed at the San Bernardino County Museum. *San Bernardino Museum Association Quarterly* 53(3).

Schuetz-Miller, Mardith K.

1994 *Building and Builders in Hispanic California, 1769–1850*. Southwest Mission Research Center and The Santa Barbara Trust for Historic Preservation, Tucson, Arizona and Santa Barbara, California.

Sedelmayr, Jacobo

1939 *"Relacion of 1746" No. 9*. Bulletin No. 123. Bureau of American Ethnology, Smithsonian Institution. Government Printing Office, Washington, DC.

Senkewicz, Robert

2002 The California Context. In *Telling the Santa Clara Story: Sesquicentennial Voices*, edited by Russell K. Skowronek, pp. 20–27. City of Santa Clara and Santa Clara University, Santa Clara, California.

Seymour, Gregory R.

1997 A Reevaluation of Lower Colorado Buff Ware Ceramics: Redefining the Patayan in Southern Nevada. Master's thesis, Department of Anthropology, University of Nevada, Las Vegas.

Seymour, Gregory R., and Laureen Perry

1998 *A Guide to the Ceramic Type Collection at the Harry Reid Center for Environmental Studies, University of Nevada, Las Vegas and the Bureau of Reclamation, Lower Colorado Region*. HRC Report No. 1-3-31. Report on file, Department of Anthropology, University of Nevada, Las Vegas.

Shackley, Michael Steven

1991 Tank Mountains Obsidian: A Newly Discovered Archaeological Obsidian Source in East-Central Yuma County, Arizona. *Kiva* 57(1):17–25.

Shanks, Ralph, and Lisa Woo Shanks

2006 *Indian Baskets of Central California: Art, Culture, and History*. Costaño Books in association with Miwok Archaeological Preserve of Marin, Novato, California.

Shaul, David Leedom, and John M. Andresen

1989 A Case for Yuman Participation in the Hohokam Regional System. *The Kiva* 54(2):105–126.

Shaul, David Leedom, and Jane H. Hill

1998 Tepimans, Yumans, and Other Hohokam. *American Antiquity* 63:375–396.

Shennan, Stephen

1997 *Quantifying Archaeology*. University of Iowa Press, Iowa City.

Shepard, Anna O.

1968 (1956) *Ceramics for the Archaeologist* (sixth printing). Publication 609. Carnegie Institution of Washington, Washington, DC.

Shutler, Richard Jr.

1961 *Lost City: Pueblo Grande de Nevada*. Anthropological Papers No. 5. Nevada State Museum, Carson City.

Skibo, James M.

1992 *Pottery Function: A Use-Alteration Perspective*. Springer Science and Business Media, New York.

2013 *Understanding Pottery Function*. Manuals in Archaeological Method, Theory and Technique. Springer Science and Business Media, New York.

Skibo, James M., Michael B. Schiffer, and K. C. Reid

1989 Organic-Tempered Pottery: An Experimental Study. *American Antiquity* 54(1):122–143.

Skowronek, Russell K., Ronald L. Bishop, M. James Blackman, Sarah Ginn, and M. Heras

2001 Chemical Characterization of Earthenwares on the Alta California Frontier. Paper presented at the Society for California Archaeology Annual Meeting, Modesto, March.

Skowronek, Russell K., M. James Blackman, and Ronald L. Bishop

2009 Locally-Made or Imported? Identifying Ceramic Composition Variation in the San Francisco Presidio Jurisdiction. *Historical Archaeology* 43(4):1–21.

2014 *Ceramic Production in Early Hispanic California: Craft, Economy, and Trade on the Frontier of New Spain*. University Press of Florida, Gainesville.

Skowronek, Russell K., M. James Blackman, Ronald L. Bishop, and Vanessa Koons

2005 *Santa Barbara Presidio (PMQ), Casa de la Guerra (PMR), and Mission Santa Barbara (PMS): Report on Neutron Activation Analysis of Earthenwares*. Department of Anthropology, National Museum of Natural History, Smithsonian Institution, Washington, DC.

Skowronek, Russell K., M. James Blackman, Ronald L. Bishop, and Carmen Rosas

2005 *Mission La Purisima Concepcion (PMO): Report on Neutron Activation Analysis of Earthenwares*. Department of Anthropology, National Museum of Natural History, Smithsonian Institution, Washington, D.C.

Skowronek, Russell K., M. James Blackman, Ronald L. Bishop, and Marisa Tsukiji

2005 *Mission Santa Ines (PMP): Report on Neutron Activation Analysis of Earthenwares*. Department of Anthropology, National Museum of Natural History, Smithsonian Institution, Washington, DC.

Skowronek, Russell K., M. James Blackman, Ronald L. Bishop, and Erin White

2005 *Mission San Buenaventura (MMI): Report on Neutron Activation Analysis of Earthenwares*. Department of Anthropology, National Museum of Natural History, Smithsonian Institution, Washington, DC.

Skowronek, Russell K., Elizabeth Thompson, and Veronica L. Johnson

2006 *Situating Mission Santa Clara de Asis: 1776–1851, Documentary and Material Evidence of Life in the Alta California Frontier*. Academy of American Franciscan History, Berkeley, California.

Slaughter, Mark C., Daron G. Duke, and Renee C. Kolvet

2005 Rock Shelter Roof Sticks in Southern Nevada. *Nevada Archaeologist* 20 and 21:85–88.

Smith, Erin M., and Mikael Fauvelle

2015 Regional Interactions between California and the Southwest: The Western Edge of the North American Continental System. *American Anthropologist* 117(4):710–721.

Sparkman, Phillip S.

1908 The Culture of the Luiseño Indians. *Publications in American Archaeology and Ethnology* 8(4):187–234. University of California, Berkeley.

Steinberg, Spencer M., Brenda Buck, Janice Mortan, James Dorman

2008 The Speciation of Iodine in the Salt Impacted Black Butte Soil Series along the Virgin River, Nevada, USA. *Applied Geochemistry* 23(2008):3589–3596.

Steward, Julian H.

1933 Ethnography of the Owens Valley Paiute. *Publications in American Archaeology and Ethnography* 33(3):233–350. University of California, Berkeley.

1938 *Basin-Plateau Aboriginal Sociopolitical Groups.* Bulletin No. 120. Bureau of American Ethnology, Washington, DC.

1942 The Direct Historical Approach to Archaeology. *American Antiquity* 7(4):337–343.

Stoltman, John B.

1989 A Quantitative Approach to the Petrographic Analysis of Ceramic Thin Sections. *American Antiquity* 54(1): 147–160.

Sutton, Mark Q.

1989 Late Prehistoric Interaction Spheres in the Mojave Desert. *North American Archaeologist* 10(2):95–121.

1996 The Current Status of Archaeological Research in the Mojave Desert. *Journal of California and Great Basin Anthropology* 18(2):221–257.

Sutton, Mark Q., Jill K. Gardner, Kenneth W. Gobalet, and Nancy Valente

2016 Archaeological Investigations at the Manifold Site (CA-KER-4220), Buena Vista Lake, Southern San Joaquin Valley, California. *Pacific Coast Archaeological Society Quarterly* 52(4):15–82.

Treganza, A. E.

1942 An Archaeological Reconnaissance of Northeastern Baja California and Southeastern California. *American Antiquity* 8(2):152–163.

True, Delbert Leroy

1966 Archaeological Differentiation of Shoshonean and Yuman Speaking Groups in Southern California. PhD dissertation, Department of Anthropology, University of California, Los Angeles.

1980 Review of Van Camp 1979. *Journal of California and Great Basin Anthropology* 2(1):148–150.

Tuohy, Donald

1990 Second Thoughts on Shoshoni Pots from Nevada and Elsewhere. In *Hunter-Gatherer Pottery from the Far West*, edited by Joanne Mack, pp. 84–105. Anthropological Papers, No. 23. Nevada State Museum, Carson City.

2000 Virgin Anasazi Figurines from Lost City, Nevada. In *Archaeological Passages, A Volume in Honor of Claude Nelson Warren*, edited by Joan S. Schneider, Robert M. Yohe II, and Jill K. Gardner, pp. 169–181. Publications in Archaeology No. 1. Western Center for Archaeology and Paleontology, Hemet, California.

Tuohy, Donald R., and Mary B. Strawn

1986 A Comparative Analysis of Thin Sections from Plain Brown Pottery Vessels found in the Desert West. In *Pottery of the Great Basin and Adjacent Areas*, edited by Suzanne Griset, pp. 85–96. Anthropological Papers No. 111. University of Utah, Salt Lake City.

Underwood, Jackson

2004 A Posited Patayan Travel Route Between Pilot Knob and Buttercup Pass. In *The Human Journey and Ancient Life in California's Deserts. Proceedings from the 2001 Millennium Conference*, edited by Mark W. Allen and Judyth Reed, pp. 239–243. Maturango Museum Publication No. 15. Ridgecrest, California.

2006 Discovering the Desert Kawaiisu. In *A Festschrift Honoring the Contributions of California Archaeologist Jay von Werlhof*, edited by R. L. Kaldenberg, pp. 170–192. Publication Number 20. Maturango Museum, Maturango Press, Ridgecrest, California.

U.S. Army Corps of Topographical Engineers

1871 *Map of Explorations and Surveys South of the Central Pacific Railroad.* Available at: http://digital.library.unlv.edu/u?/LV_Maps,622.

Vallejo, Guadalupe

1890 Ranch and Mission Days in Alta California. *Century Magazine* 41(2):183–192.

Van Camp, Gena S.

1979 *Kumeyaay Pottery: Paddle-and-Anvil Techniques of Southern California.* Anthropological Papers No. 15. Ballena Press, Socorro, New Mexico.

Vance, Meghann M.

2021 Sacaton Red-on-buff. Electronic document, https://swvirtualmuseum.nau.edu/wp/index.php/artifacts/pottery/hohokam-buff-ware/sacaton-red-on-buff/, accessed April 30, 2021.

Vivian, R. Gwinn

1965 An Archaeological Survey of the Lower Gila River, Arizona. *The Kiva* 30:95–146.

Vokes, Arthur W.

2001 The Stone and Clay Jewelry Assemblage. In *Tonto Creek Archaeological Project. Life and Death along Tonto Creek*, edited by J. J. Clark and P. D. Minturn, pp. 421–458. Anthropological Papers No. 24. Center for Desert Archaeology, Tucson.

Voss, Barbara

2008 *The Archaeology of Ethnogenesis: Race and Sexuality in Colonial San Francisco.* University of California Press, Berkeley.

Walker, Edwin Francis

1951 *Five Archaeological Sites in Los Angeles County, California.* Publications of the Frederick Webb Hodge Anniversary Publication Fund, Volume 6. Southwest Museum, Los Angeles.

Wallace, Henry D.

2001 Time Seriation and Typological Refinement of the Middle Gila Buffware Sequence: Snaketown through Soho Phases. In *The Grewe Archaeological Research Project*, vol. 2, Part 1. *Ceramic Studies*, edited by

David R. Abbott, pp. 177–262. Anthropological Papers No. 99-1. Northland Research, Tempe.

2004 Update to the Middle Gila Buff Ware Ceramic Sequence. In *Hohokam Farming on the Salt River Flood-plain: Refining Models and Analytical Methods*, edited by T. Kathleen Henderson, pp. 59–141. Anthropological Papers No. 43. Center for Desert Archaeology, Tucson.

Wallace, William J.

1962 Test Excavations at BW 9, a Late Prehistoric Site in Anza-Borrego Desert State Park. In *Archaeological Explorations in the Southern Section of Anza-Borrego Desert State Park, California*, Chapter III. Archaeological Report No. 5. Department of Parks and Recreation, Division of Beach and Parks, Interpretive Services Section, State of California, Sacramento.

1986 The Pottery of Mesquite Flat, Death Valley, California. In *Pottery of the Great Basin and Adjacent Areas*, edited by Suzanne Griset, pp.71–74. Anthropological Papers, No. 111. University of Utah Press, Salt Lake City.

1990 Another Look at Yokuts Pottery-Making. In *Hunter-Gatherer Pottery from the Far West*, edited by Joanne Mack. Anthropological Papers, vol. 23. Nevada State Museum, Carson City.

Walsh, Michael R.

1988 Mission Ware Ceramics from the Santa Barbara Presidio. Report submitted to Woodward-Clyde Consultants, Oakland, CA. On file at the Santa Barbara Trust for Historic Preservation, San Barbara.

Walsh, Michael R., and Clarus J. Backes, Jr.

2005a *Documentation and Evaluation of Prehistoric Resources at Seep Spring, China Lake Naval Air Weapons Station, California*. Report submitted to China Lake Naval Air Weapons Station Environmental Area, China Lake. Ancient Enterprises, Inc., Santa Monica.

2005b Disputed Lands: Marking Borders in the Northwestern Mojave Desert. Paper presented at the 39th Annual Meeting of the Society for California Archaeology, Sacramento.

Wasley, William W., and Alfred E. Johnson

1965 *Salvage Archaeology in Painted Rocks Reservoir, Western Arizona*. Anthropological Papers No. 9. University of Arizona, Tucson.

Waters, Michael R.

1982a The Lowland Patayan Ceramic Tradition. In *Hohokam and Patayan: Prehistory of Southwestern Arizona*, edited by Randall H. McGuire and Michael B. Schiffer, pp. 275–297. Academic Press, New York.

1982b The Lowland Patayan Ceramic Typology. In *Hohokam and Patayan: Prehistory of Southwestern Arizona*, edited by Randall H. McGuire and Michael B. Schiffer, pp. 537–570. Academic Press, New York.

1982c Ceramic Data from Lowland Patayan Sites. In *Hohokam and Patayan, Prehistory of Southwestern Arizona*, edited by Randall H. McGuire and Michael B. Schiffer, pp. 571–580. Academic Press, New York.

1982d Trail Shrines at Site SDM C-1. In *Hohokam and Patayan, Prehistory of Southwestern Arizona*, edited by Randall H. McGuire and Michael B. Schiffer, pp. 533–535.

1983 Late Holocene Lacustrine Chronology and Archaeology of Ancient Lake Cahuilla, California. *Quaternary Research* 19(3):373–387.

Watkins, Christopher and Glen Rice

2010 A Tale of Two Cemeteries: Hohokam-Patayan Co-residence at Gillespie Dam. Paper presented at the Biennial Three Corners Conference, University of Nevada, Las Vegas.

Webb, Edith Buckland

1952 *Indian Life at the Old Missions*. Warren F. Lewis, Los Angeles.

Wedel, Waldo

1941 *Archaeological Investigations at Buena Vista Lake, Kern County, California*. Bulletin 130. Bureau of American Ethnology, Smithsonian Institution, Government Printing Office, Washington, DC.

Wegner, Etienne

1999 *Communities of Practice: Learning, Meaning, and Identity*. Cambridge University Press, Cambridge, UK.

Wells, Helen

2014 A Separate Space: Female-associated Features at Seep Spring. Paper presented at the Great Basin Anthropological Conference, Boise, Idaho, October 16, 2014.

Wells, Helen F., and Clarus J. Backes, Jr.

2007 Robbers Mountain: Revisiting the Archaeology and Rock Art of Bierman Caves. *San Bernardino County Museum Association Quarterly* 53(4).

2010a Living on the Edge, Late Prehistoric Foragers on the South Range. *Pacific Coast Archaeological Society Quarterly* 43(1–2):113–134.

2010b The Same Thing, Only Different: Three Late Prehistoric Rock Shelter Complexes on the South Range, NAWS. Paper presented at the Society for California Annual Meeting, Riverside, March 2010.

Wells, Helen F., and C. William Clewlow, Jr.

1981 Radiocarbon Dates from the Bird Spring Site, Clark County, Nevada. *Journal of California and Great Basin Anthropology* 3(2):283–285.

Wells, Helen, Melanie Saldaña, and Victoria Stosel

2011 Investigations by California State University, Los Angeles, at the Lead Pipe Spring Site (CA-SBR-43/H), South Range, Naval Air Weapons Station, China Lake, San Bernardino County, California. Report on file, Command Archaeologist, Naval Air Weapons Station, China Lake. Ancient Enterprises, Santa Monica.

Wells, Helen, Victoria Stosel, and Clarus Backes

2008 Prehistoric Archaeology of the Lead Pipe Spring Area, China Lake Naval Air Weapons Station: Preliminary Investigations. Paper presented at the 31st Great Basin Anthropological Conference, Portland, Oregon, October 2008.

Wells, Susan J.
1991 *The Shivwits Plateau Survey: Archeology at Lake Mead National Recreation Area.* Western Archeological Conservation Center, Tucson.

Whitehead, Richard S.
1996 *Citadel on the Channel: The Royal Presidio of Santa Barbara, Its Founding and Construction, 1782–1798,* edited by Donald C. Cutter. Presidio Trust and the Arthur H. Clark Co., Santa Barbara.

Wilke, Philip J.
1978 *Late Prehistoric Human Ecology at Lake Cahuilla, Coachella Valley, California.* Contributions No. 38. Archaeological Research Facility, University of California Berkeley.

Wilkerson, Brenna
2016 The Proof is in the Pots: Residue Analysis of Virgin Branch Puebloan Ceramics. Master's thesis, Department of Anthropology, University of Nevada, Las Vegas.

Williams, Jack S.
1983 Early Nineteenth Century Plainware Pottery from Mission San Antonio de Padua, California. Manuscript on file, Ceramics Research Lab, Department of Anthropology, University of California, Santa Cruz.

Wobst, Martin H.
1977 Stylistic Behavior and Information Exchange. In *For the Director: Research Essays in Honor of James B. Griffin,* edited by Charles E. Cleland, pp. 317–342. Anthropological Papers No. 61. Museum of Anthropology, University of Michigan, Ann Arbor.

Yamane, Linda
1997 *Weaving a California Tradition: A Native American Basketmaker.* Lerner Publications Company, Minneapolis.

Zigmond, Maurice L.
1986 Kawaiisu. In *Great Basin,* edited by Warren L. d'Azevedo, pp. 398–411. Handbook of North American Indians, vol. 11, edited by William C. Sturtevant. Smithsonian Institution, Washington, DC.

Contributors

Catherine Bailey, MA
Masters Research conducted at Department of Anthropology
University of California, Los Angeles
cebailster@gmail.com

Stella D'Oro, MA
Albion Environmental, Inc.
1414 Soquel Avenue, Suite 205, Santa Cruz, CA 95062
SDoro@albionenvironmental.com

Jelmer W. Eerkens, PhD
Department of Anthropology Evolutionary Wing
University of California, Davis, CA 95616
jweerkens@ucdavis.edu

Jeffrey R. Ferguson
Missouri University Research Reactor
1513 Research Park Drive, Columbia, MO 65211
fergusonje@missouri.edu

Suzanne Griset, PhD
SWCA Environmental Consultants
343 W. Franklin St., Tucson, AZ 85701
sgriset@swca.com

Karen G. Harry, PhD
Department of Anthropology
Box 455003, University of Nevada, Las Vegas, NV 89154-5003
karen.harry@unlv.edu

Lynda Hylkema
Cultural Resources Manager
Santa Clara University, Santa Clara, CA
lhylema@scu.edu

Don Laylander, MA
ASM Affiliates, Inc. (emeritus)
2034 Corte Del Nogal, Carlsbad, CA 92011
dlaylander@cox.net

Carl P. Lipo, PhD
Binghamton University
P.O. Box 6000, Binghamton, NY 13902-6000
clipo@binghmton.edu

Chester Liwosz, PhD
Mesa Prieta Petroglyph Project
P.O. Box 407, Velarde, NM 87582
chester@mesaprietapetroglyphs.org

Sarah Peelo, PhD
Albion Environmental
1414 Soquel Avenue, Suite 205, Santa Cruz, CA 95062
SPeelo@albionenvironmental.com

Sachiko Sakai, PhD
Department of Anthropology and
Luminescence Dating Laboratory IIRMES
California State University
Long Beach, 1250 Bellflower Blvd., Long Beach, CA 90840
Sachiko.Sakai@csulb.edu

Jerry Schaefer, PhD
ASM Affiliates, Inc. (emeritus)
2034 Corte Del Nogal, Carlsbad, CA 92011
jerryandbubba@yahoo.com

Christina Spellman, BA
Albion Environmental, Inc.
1414 Soquel Avenue, Suite 205, Santa Cruz, CA 95062
CSpellman@albionenvironmental.com

Spencer M. Steinberg, PhD
Department of Chemistry and Biochemistry
University of Nevada, Las Vegas, NV 89154-5003
spencer.steinberg@unlv.edu

Helen F Wells, PhD
Department of Anthropology, California State University
Los Angeles, CA 90032
helenfwells@gmail.com

Brenna Wilkerson, MA
Advising Center, Colorado Mesa University
1100 North Ave., Grand Junction, CO
brennawilkerson1@gmail.com